Plant-Microbe Interactions

Volume 6

Edited by

Gary Stacey
University of Missouri, Columbia

Noel T. Keen
University of California, Riverside

APS PRESS
The American Phytopathological Society
St. Paul, Minnesota

This book has been reproduced directly from computer-generated copy submitted in final form to APS Press by the editors of the volume. No editing or proofreading has been done by the Press.

Library of Congress Control Number: 95-10088
International Standard Book Number: 0-89054-303-8

Printed in the United States of America on acid-free paper

The American Phytopathological Society
3340 Pilot Knob Road
St. Paul, Minnesota 55121-2097 U.S.A.

Series Editors

Advisory Board

In memoriam

Dr. Noel T. Keen, who served as co-editor of this series, passed away from leukemia on April 18, 2002. He will be greatly missed by all those who knew and worked with him. At the time of his death, he was serving as President of the American Phytopathological Society. Dr. Keen was world renowned for his accomplishments. This is reflected in the numerous positions of influence held, as well as honors and awards he received. These included election as a member of the National Academy of Sciences in 1997 as well as Fellow of APS, the American Academy of Microbiology and the American Association for the Advancement of Science. He was a recipient of the APS Ruth Allen Award, the top research award given by the society for individuals who have made an outstanding, innovative contribution to research in plant pathology. He received this award in 1995 together with Dr. Brian Staskawicz for their pioneering work on pathogen-derived host specificity. He was a University of California Presidential Chair and held the position of Distinguished Professor/William and Sue Johnson Endowed Chair in Molecular Plant Pathology. He received the Secretary's Honor Award for personal and professional excellence from the U.S. Department of Agriculture and the Award of Merit from CSREES, USDA in 1996. Again that year he was named Faculty Research Lecturer, the highest honor conferred by his fellow UC Riverside faculty. Throughout his career, he contributed more than 170 technical publications.

Noel received his BS and MS from Iowa State University, and PhD from the University of Wisconsin, and then took a faculty position at The University of California, Riverside in 1968 where he remained for his entire career. His image is part of a mural near the entrance to campus.

Noel's research interests were in the field of genetics, molecular biology and biochemistry of host-pathogen interactions. Early in his career, he worked on establishing factors involved in host specificities using *Phytophthora megasperma* var. *sojae* on soybean as a model pathosystem. This work initiated his interest in characterizing pathogen "elicitors" (a term that he coined) of active defense in plants, and the role of phytoalexins in defense processes. He also investigated the connection between host selective toxins such as victorin produced by *Helminthosporium victoriae* and elicitors of plant defense.

Noel's pioneering work in molecular plant pathology played an instrumental role in moving the field of plant-pathogen interactions forward. He championed the "elicitor-receptor" model in support of gene-for-gene interactions, thus providing a testable hypothesis that eventually led to the cloning of plant disease resistance genes. Together with Dr. Staskawicz using the soybean/*Pseudomonas syringae* pv. *glycinea* system, he was a part of the group that was first to clone and molecularly characterize an avirulence gene from a pathogen. His work in this area eventually led to the identification and characterization of syringolide glycolipid elicitors produced by *P. syringae* pathovars and the cognate resistance gene Rpg4 in soybeans.

In addition to his work with avirulence and resistance, Noel had an equal interest in virulence and pathogenicity mechanisms, focusing work on macerating and other degrading enzymes from various bacterial and fungal rot pathogens. He was the first to clone and sequence pectate lyases using the soft-rot pathogen, *Erwinia chrysanthemi*. In collaboration with the lab of Dr. Fran Jurnak at UC Riverside, he defined a new class of protein structure (the parallel beta helix) through the three-dimensional structure analysis of an *Erwinia* pectate lyase. He most recently was participating in the structural and functional analysis of the *E. chrysanthemi* genome.

Noel was a dedicated teacher both in the laboratory and classroom. Among his various course responsibilities, he taught a graduate course in Physiological Plant Pathology. His amazing knack for detail was evident in his course lectures, which incorporated the full spectrum of historical background, up-to-date literature and even unpublished research results. He was a strong proponent of associating names with research accomplishments and expected his students to accurately connect researchers with their accomplishments in the field. His method of course grading was ahead of its time and included journal article presentations and grant proposal writing, because he believed these exercises had longer lasting value for graduate students.

Noel had a terrifying reputation in Ph.D. qualifying exams for asking very basic questions designed to measure a student's ability to think under pressure, as well as determine if they had read the latest issues of Science and Nature. Such questions included, "Why do monkeys have tails?", "How do batteries work?" and, "What is the tallest mountain on Earth (his answer: Hawaii) and what is a mountain anyway?" He managed his laboratory in a loose, yet stern manner, with high expectations for all. He set a high work standard by example. Importantly, his benchwork showed creativity and consistent positive results, creating an excellent role model for his students. His near photographic memory aside, Noel was an assiduous note taker at the bench, nonverbally communicating its importance to lab members. Despite his tireless work habit, he was always open to interruptions by questions from anyone. This sometimes created a 'lazy' atmosphere in his lab, since it was much easier to ask him than to look up an answer to a simple question. In these cases, one might be subjected to disciplinary action from Noel, in which the offender would be accused of being a 'Bozo' and then be struck on the head with an imaginary mallet followed by the sound effects of a vibrating gong. Nonetheless, the question would be answered.

A product of Marshalltown, Iowa, Noel's Midwest upbringing certainly could be detected in his outwardly brash, 'cowboy' appearance, complete with a swagger in his walk. The only things missing were a hat, six-shooter and holster. In fact at a recent APS annual meeting, a "Keen for Sheriff" sign mysteriously appeared at the grand reception. Searching for Noel in a crowd was easy because his distinct strut combined with his tall, but not quite lanky physique was detectable from afar. Noel possessed little fear in his scientific approach. His general research philosophy was to "skim the cream and let others work out the details". However, Noel's idea of "skimming the cream" usually left little details for others to work out. He advocated presentation of models and hypotheses to the scientific community based on available evidence, thereby allowing them to be confirmed or disproved by others. To him (and at the expense of possibly being wrong -- although he was most often right), this approach provided the most rapid means to advance science.

Those who knew Noel well also experienced a more personable, caring and giving side. His style was to often acknowledge others, deferring credit and deflecting attention away from himself. For example, when asked about his likeness being added to the mural near campus he is quoted as saying, "I suppose they have to have someone to fill up the wall". And, when interviewed regarding the fundamental breakthrough describing the newly identified protein structure he ignored his role, commenting, "For Fran Jurnak's lab, it's a real coup because historically, the major protein structure types were elucidated in the early 1970s". When approached regarding his reaction to selection as Faculty Research Lecturer, he is quoted as saying, "I was surprised, since there is only one such award presented each year". This was a part of his personality that clearly became evident in not acknowledging his health condition to his colleagues until he could no longer effectively conduct his professional responsibilities. We know now that, although he was aware of his condition at the time he assumed the position of APS president, he took the demanding honor because, in his own words, "it was time to give back to his society". He had a passion to entertain; he often threw parties at his home that included offerings of oysters (despite a departmental experience of food poisoning during one such gathering) and large batches of chili. Such parties were preceded by a prep night, which was in essence, a pre-party that on one occasion ended in a food fight with Noel as a participant *in his own kitchen*. Other entertainment favorites that he routinely hosted included Halloween costume parties complete with ridiculous games in which all were required to participate.

In a recent conversation that recollected some memorable laboratory events, Noel laughed about the lasting mark his laboratory members left him some 15 years ago. (His laminar flow hood caught fire, resulting in a melted plastic grate and cracked side glass.) As he rounded the corner of the hallway and realized that thick black smoke was bellowing from his lab, his "Noel Keen" strut changed to a gallop down the hallway. He reached his lab only to be greeted by a group of his lab members holding a fire extinguisher. He asked them in a rather loud and excited voice, "What the (expletive deleted) is going on here?" In a remark that left him speechless and thus his lab personnel devoid of disciplinary action, one student replied, "That's the problem with you, Noel, you're always so suspicious!"

Noel will be forever remembered as a great man for his accomplishments and contributions to the scientific community. But for those that knew him well, he also will be remembered as a kind and giving, enigmatic and simple, yet complicated human being. One of his lasting legacies is that he could never pour a glass of beer from a pitcher without generating an excessive head of foam, making it difficult to drink in a timely manner. Most felt he just never accomplished the proper touch to pour from a pitcher. But in retrospect, he may have had an ulterior motive in leaving more beer in the pitcher for himself...despite the fact that, to the satisfaction of all, he was usually the one buying. For those of us privileged to partake of Noel's company it is uniformly appreciated that his head, whether poured from a pitcher or upon his shoulders, was most generous and admirable.

Donald Kobayashi and Scott Gold

It was a great honor and pleasure to have the opportunity to work with Noel on this book series. I miss him.

Gary Stacey

Preface to the Plant-Microbe Interactions Series

If one were to plot the number of research publications per year dealing with various aspects of plant-microbe interactions, it would be clear that information in this area is increasing exponentially. This work is of obvious importance since plant-microbe interactions, in the form of pathogenicity, beneficial symbioses, biocontrol, etc., greatly impact agriculture. The recent rapid increase in knowledge can be largely correlated with the application of modern molecular methods to the understanding of plant-microbe interactions. Indeed, researchers interested in how plants and microbes interact were among the first to apply such molecular methods to biology.

For example, one of the great scientific discoveries of the 20th century was the elucidation of interkingdom gene transfer through analysis of crown gall disease. In the years to come, we will see the full fruition of this work through its practical impact on agriculture. Likewise, the discovery of the lipo-chitin nodulation signals produced by rhizobia and their effect on the legume host serves as a model for host-symbiont interactions. These initial studies on *Agrobacterium* and *Rhizobium* led to the development of technologies that are widely applied not only to studies of plant-microbe interactions but in all areas of biology. Considering that plants and microbes have been interacting for eons on this planet can we have any doubt that similar amazing discoveries await the prepared investigator of these interactions?

Indeed, the recent discovery of the first plant disease resistance genes heralds the beginning of a new age of discovery. It seems that many avenues are open to uncover the signal pathways involved in plant resistance, the nature of bacterial and fungal virulence mechanisms, and the interplay of regulatory signals between plant and pathogen. We are in the developing era of genomics with several important plants/ pathogens/ symbionts now under active investigation. The knowledge of the DNA sequence of these organisms will clearly lead to new routes to investigate and manipulate for human benefit important plant-microbe interactions.

These investigations will add to the long list of contributions that the study of plant-microbe interactions has made to plant biology and biology in general. Indeed, the long debated role of auxin/cytokinin ratios in controlling plant morphogenesis received its strongest support from the study of the function of T-DNA genes of *Agrobacterium*. Likewise, recent studies have provided the first solid evidence that secondary plant metabolites are important defense agents, an idea that has been forcibly argued for many years. The ability of microorganisms to perturb the normal growth and development of plants has long been used as a method to study plant processes. This has led to the discovery of important plant growth regulators (e.g., gibberellens).

This book series has as its goal to chronicle the future research on plant-microbe interactions. Moreover, this series will hopefully prepare the new generations of scientists that will make these future breakthroughs. Without a doubt remarkable discoveries will be made. It is safe to predict that new plant growth regulators will be discovered. It will be a pleasure to see plant cell biology reach and then surpass the level of understanding that now exists for animal cells. The ability to easily manipulate the genetics of the plant and microbial genome will give investigators advantages not seen in many animal systems. Besides the excitement to be expected from such basic studies, practical applications of this work are now appearing and the pace of such advances will accelerate. It is the goal of this series to contribute to the advancement of the science of plant-microbe interactions.

Gary Stacey
Noel T. Keen

Preface to Plant-Microbe Interactions, Volume 6

This volume continues the exploration of interesting plant-microbe interactions, including nematode-plant interactions.

The first three chapters deal with the interesting phenomenon of microbial-induced gall formation on plants.

Chapter 1 by Wu and Hohn brings us up-to-date with the current understanding of the molecular mechanism of T-DNA transfer from *Agrobacterium tumefaciens* to plants and its subsequent integration into the plant genome. Although this is perhaps the best described plant-microbe association, there are clearly new frontiers that are being explored.

Chapter 2 by Manulis and Barash describes the transformation of *Erwinia herbicola* from a normal plant epiphyte into a gall-forming pathogen. As in many plant and animal pathogens, virulence factors, delivered to the plant via a type III secretion system, play an important role in *E. herbicola* pathogenicity.

Chapter 3 by Vereecke et al. describes the pathogen *Rhodococcus fascians,* which induces gall formation on plants. Modulation of phytohormone levels appears to be involved in gall formation. Recent molecular studies have yielded a great deal of information on the molecular basis of pathogenicity in this organism.

Chapter 4 by Cannon and Young describes the genomic architecture and evolution of nucleotide-binding-site- leucine-rich-repeat plant resistance genes. Clearly, one of the major accomplishments of the last decade is the elucidation of the important role that these proteins play in plant defense. The increasing amount of genomic sequence information now makes it possible to classify these genes and to deduce their evolutionary relationships.

Chapter 5 by Taylor presents an exhaustive review on the role of various transporters in plant-microbe interactions. Transporters have been grouped into specific classes based on their structure and mechanism. This review covers the roles of these transporters in bacteria and fungal pathogens, as well as their plant hosts.

Chapter 6 by Gold explores our current understanding of the important fungal pathogen *Ustilago maydis*. Since this fungus has well-developed genetic systems, it is serving as a model organism to investigate fungal-plant pathogenicity.

Chapter 7 by Chin-A-Woeng et al describes the use of *Pseudomonas* species as biocontrol agents to protect against plant pathogens. This work grew out of the observation that certain soils can "suppress" the virulence of plant pathogens. A wealth of information is now being developed on the mechanisms by which Pseudomonads can protect plants from pathogens.

Chapter 8 by Alfano and Guo specifically discusses the role of the type III protein secretion system in the pathogenicity of *Pseudomonas syringae.* As mentioned above, it is now clear that type III secretion systems are critically important to the pathogenicity of a variety of animal and plant pathogens. Research on plant-bacterial associations is adding significantly to our understanding of this important virulence determinant.

Chapter 9 by Schoelz et al discusses the plant response to infection by Cauliflower mosaic virus. Here again, we see commonality between the plant host response to viral, bacterial and fungal infection. The HR (hypersensitive) response is accompanied by localized cell death that shares similarity to apoptotic cell death first described in animal systems. The relative simplicity of the viral genome makes this an excellent system to dissect pathogen factors contributing to plant disease resistance and cell death.

Chapter 10 by Smant et al describes the current state of information on the interaction of plants with parasitic nematodes. These pathogens are among the most devastating and, therefore, are of great importance to agriculture. Application of modern molecular and genomic methods is allowing real progress toward understanding the mechanisms of pathogenicity.

Chapter 11 by Timmer and Bhatia describes a large number of plant diseases, which still have not been unequivocally associated with a specific pathogen. Many of these diseases are caused by graft-associated pathogens, while others may involve weak pathogens, which are opportunistic when conditions are favorable. Although most of these diseases are currently of limited concern, they do represent a possible reservoir of pathogens that could become major problems in the future.

The final chapter, Chapter 12, by Felle describes the role of ion fluxes in the initial response of legume roots to the lipo-chitooligosaccharide nodulation signals produced by symbiotic rhizobia. These Nod factors are essential for the ability of the rhizobia to invade the legume root and induce de novo organogenesis, resulting in the formation of a nodule, which they colonize. Given the high chemical specificity of these molecules and their activity at very low concentrations, they represent very potent phytomorphogens and there is considerable interest in their mode of action. One of the first observable plant responses to the Nod factor is ion flux and this chapter presents an excellent overview of current knowledge.

The editors gratefully acknowledge the assistance of Martin B. Dickman in the preparation of this volume.

Gary Stacey

Contributors

James R. Alfano
University of Nebraska
Lincoln, Nebraska

Jaap Bakker
Wageningen University
Wageningen, The Netherlands

Isaac Barash
ARO The Volcani Center
Bet Dagan, Israel

Alka Bhatia
University of Florida
Lake Alfred, FL

Guido V. Bloemberg
Leiden University
Leiden, The Netherlands

John Cawly
University of Missouri
Columbia, MO

Steven Cannon
University of Minnesota
St. Paul, MN

Thomas F. C. Chin-A-Woeng
Leiden University
Leiden, The Netherlands

Anthony B. Cole
University of Missouri
Columbia, MO

Hubert H. Felle
Justus-Liebig-Universität
Giessen, Germany

Koen Goethals
Ghent University
Gent, Belgium

Scott E. Gold
University of Georgia
Athens, GA

Aska Goverse
Wageningen University
Wageningen, The Netherlands

Ming Guo
University of Nebraska
Lincoln, Nebraska

Johannes Helder
Wageningen University
Wageningen, The Netherlands

Barbara Hohn
Freidrich Miescher Institute
for Biomedical Research
Basel, Switzerland

Marcelle Holsters
Ghent University
Gent, Belgium

Mondher Jaziri
Université Libre de Bruxelles
Brussels, Belgium

Loránt Király
University of Missouri
Columbia, MO

Ben J.J. Lugtenberg
Leiden University
Leiden, The Netherlands

Shulamit Manulis
ARO The Volcani Center
Bet Dagan, Israel

Karuppaiah Palanichelvam
University of Missouri
Columbia, MO

Ling Qin
Wageningen University
Wageningen, The Netherlands

James E. Schoelz
University of Missouri
Columbia, MO

Arjen Schots
Wageningen University
Wageningen, The Netherlands

Geert Smant
Wageningen University
Wageningen, The Netherlands

Janet L. Taylor
National Research Council Canada
Plant Biotechnology Institute
Saskatoon, Saskatchewan

Wim Temmerman
Ghent University
Gent, Belgium

L.W. Timmer
University of Florida
Lake Alfred, FL

Danny Vereecke
Ghent University
Gent, Belgium

You-Qiang Wu
Freidrich Miescher Institute
for Biomedical Research
Basel, Switzerland

Nevin Young
University of Minnesota
St. Paul, MN

Contents

Plant-Microbe Interactions

Volume 6

Cellular Transfer and Chromosomal Integration of T-DNA During *Agrobacterium tumefaciens* – Mediated Plant Transformation

You-Qiang Wu and Barbara Hohn

1. Introduction

The study of *Agrobacterium* mediated plant transformation is propelled by two parallel and often complementary research interests. On one hand, this unique process provides the scientist with fundamental insights into bacterial and plant biology. On the other hand, it is a powerful technological tool and as such facilitates transgenesis of many agronomically important plant species. Recently, several excellent reviews that summarize the complete *Agrobacterium* transfer biology or certain aspects thereof have appeared (8, 20,27,55,67). This review will focus on events that occur inside the plant cell, and only briefly comment on earlier steps leading to transfer of the DNA to the cytoplasm.

2. Steps leading to T-DNA transfer

The Ti (tumor inducing) plasmid is one of two plasmids that, together with two chromosomes, makes up the complete genome of *Agrobacterium tumefaciens* strain C58 (24, 61). The virulence region of this plasmid becomes transcriptionally activated when the bacterium receives chemical signals emanating from wounded plant cells. This process triggers the synthesis of the virulence proteins that excise the T-DNA (Transferred DNA), from the Ti plasmid, and facilitate T-DNA's export from the bacterial cell. Vir (virulence) proteins D1 and D2 liberate single-stranded T-DNA, by site- and strand specific cleavage at the border sequence that delineate and thereby define the T-DNA. As a consequence, VirD2, the catalytic subunit of the endonuclease, becomes covalently attached to the single-stranded (ss) T-DNA via a phosphodiester bond involving a tyrosine and the nucleotide at the 5' position from the nick site. The resulting DNA-protein complex is transported to plant cells (see below). The structure responsible for T-DNA export is a type IV secretion system that is also comprised of virulence proteins and consists of a translocation machine and a filamentous pilus. Gene products of the VirB operon as well as the VirD4 protein are components of these macromolecular transport complexes. Following transfer of the T-DNA-VirD2 complex into the plant nucleus T-DNA integrates into chromosomal DNA and T-DNA located genes, being eukaryotic in nature, become expressed. Some of the T-DNA encoded enzymes produce unique compounds called opines while other enzymes carry out synthesis of plant growth hormones. The opines can be used by the bacterium as an exclusive nutritional source, while the hormone driven mitogenic activity turns the genetic transformation into a neoplastic transformation event, ultimately causing tumors to develop at the crown of naturally infected plants. By deleting the genes responsible for tumor formation and replacing them with the gene(s) to be expressed in plants, *Agrobacterium's* unique property of interkingdom DNA transfer is used extensively for molecular crop design (Review references to this paragraph are listed in the Introduction).

3. Cellular uptake of T-DNA

The T-DNA-VirD2 complex is transported out of the bacterial cell and enters the plant cell to which the bacterium is attached. The crossing of the nonpolar membrane must be a special challenge for a charged DNA molecule. Whereas the bacterial membranes are traversed by the complex with the help of a specialized transfer apparatus, no obvious route is known through the hydrophobic plant cell membranes. Could VirE2 help by neutralizing the changes of DNA? After all, this protein binds tightly and cooperatively to single-stranded DNA (9, 10, 14, 23, 46) However, a complex consisting of T-DNA, VirD2 and Vir E2 (called T-complex or T-DNA complex) apparently does not form in the bacterium, but instead, the T-DNA-VirD2 complex and VirE2 travel to the plant cell separately. In a coinoculation T-DNA transfer experiment (42), a T-DNA deficient, VirE2 protein production proficient bacterium, can complement a T-DNA proficient, VirE2 protein deficient bacterium More recent experiments corroborated the independent transfer hypothesis through inhibition of transfer of specifically only one of the two components to be transferred (4, 21, 32, 49). In an especially clear analysis, plants were regenerated that constitutively expressed VirE2 protein. Inoculation of such plants with *Agrobacterium* lacking VirE2 led to efficient T-DNA transfer, proving that uncoated T-DNA could indeed reach the plant (13). Conversely, in an elegantly designed analysis T-DNA transfer independent mobilization of manipulated VirE2 could be detected (59). Transfer of both components requires the same transport engine and virulence pilus. Additional evidence for independent transfer stems from functional analysis of VirE1, a molecular chaperone of VirE2. It interacts with VirE2 at domains required for single-stranded DNA binding and cooperative interaction. This interaction prevents VirE2 from aggregating, enhances VirE2 stability and probably maintains VirE2 in an export-competent state (16, 50, 63). Further evidence revealed that the interaction between VirE1 and VirE2 is strong enough to inhibit VirE2 from binding ssDNA and interacting with VirE2 itself (16, 63). Therefore, these results imply that VirE2 cannot coat the complex of ss-T-DNA-VirD2 in *A. tumefaciens* cells due to the presence of VirE1.

However, why should VirE2 be moved to plant cells separately if its function is to coat and protect the T-DNA? Maybe the larger T-DNA complex would not be able to be transported by the transfer machinery; maybe VirE2 protein does have another function - the size of the 63kD VirE2 protein by far exceeds those of other single-stranded DNA binding proteins. Earlier cell fractionation experiments indeed demonstrated partial localization of VirE2 in inner and outer membranes of virulence-induced agrobacterial cells (9), a partition not easily reconcilable with DNA binding activity. Reevaluation of VirE2 activities led to the detection of a membrane channel that consisted of VirE2 protein molecules, was voltage gated and specific for passage of single-stranded nucleic acids through artificial membranes (18). Transposed to agrobacterial biology, this new finding may mean that by sending pore forming protein molecules into plants cells attached to bacterial cells, the eukaryotic partner becomes competent to receive single-stranded DNA (Fig. 1A).

Although the relevance of these findings needs to be demonstrated in the context of *Agrobacterium* biology, a number of intriguing questions seem permitted: why does T-DNA not get wrapped into a VirE2 coat inside the bacterium? In line with bacterial conjugation, whose evolutionary descendant T-DNA transfer to plants most likely is, single-stranded T-DNA may exit the bacterium as it is produced; alternatively, or in addition, VirE1, VirE2's chaperone may keep VirE2 both from interacting with T-DNA (see above) and with membranes. Another exciting question concerns the regulation of channel opening; a VirE2 channel in the plant membrane should be gated to avoid toxic effects - could VirD2, the T-DNA pilot, have this effect? As shown below, the T-DNA-VirD2 complex needs to be coated by VirE2 protein units in order to be imported into the nuclear compartment and in order to gain protection from nucleolytic attack. For this complex to form, free VirE2 protein molecules must be available for the T-DNA-VirD2 complex entering the plant cell. Are the pore-forming VirE2 subunits released from the plant cell membrane or are additional molecules recruited from the large store inside induced bacteria, and, if so, how? A highly pertinent question relates to the several distinct roles the VirE2 protein may fulfill and their respective structural bases: in one form of its life VirE2 binds to VirE1 which keeps it from aggregating, inserting into membranes and complexing to DNA (16, 50, 63). In another form it may pass through the virulence region encoded transfer machine. To form a membrane pore VirE2 may have to expose lipophilic residues to the outside and hydrophilic ones to the inner part of the channel. In order to bind to ssDNA, yet another conformation must probably be taken up while for nuclear import VirE2 bound to T-DNA may interact with host proteins.

Virulence proteins VirD2 and VirE2 have been shown to be exported from bacteria also in a pathway independent from the transporter machinery (7). The role this transport route plays in virulence is unclear; in addition, it may constitute only a minor pathway.

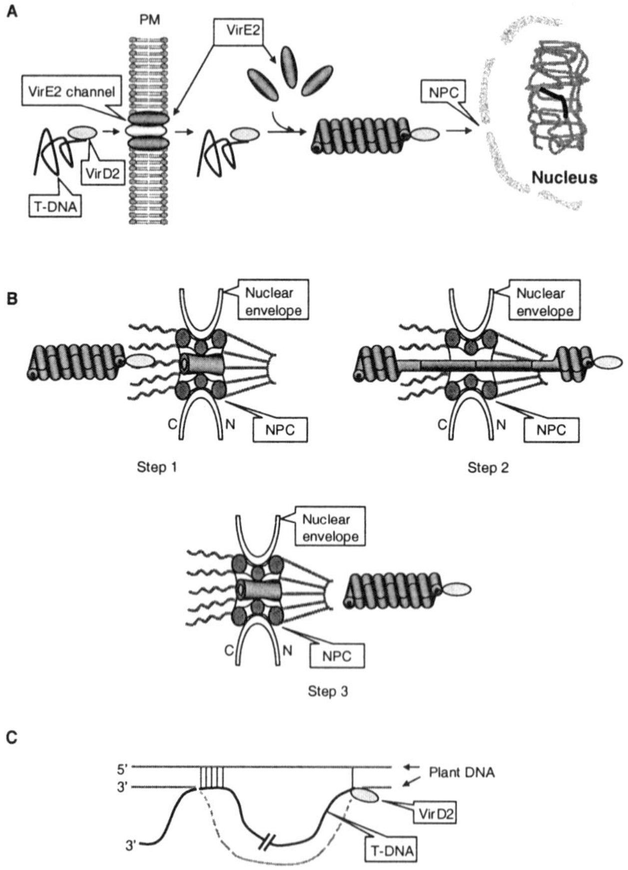

Fig. 1 The transfer and integration of T-DNA (see text for details)

4. Nuclear import of T-DNA

Once inside a plant cell, by whatever mechanism, the next goal for T-DNA on its way to transform a plant cell and subvert its metabolism is to access the nucleus. Classical import gates are nuclear pore complexes (NPCs) that permit, under conditions specified below, access for proteins to the nucleoplasm (28, 35, 58). Travel of the T-DNA complex through the cytoplasm, to NPCs, may be guided by cytoskeletal infra-architecture. Indeed, agents specifically perturbing it drastically change the efficiency with which T-DNA genes express in an integration independent transient assay (M. Duckely, personal communication; S. Gelvin, personal communication). The involvement of import promoting factors such as importins/karyopherins scanning the cytoplasmic compartment for substrates may also contribute to recruitment of T-DNA complexes to the nuclear pore. The biologically relevant advantage that the T-DNA complex may have over biolistically supplied transforming DNA is that the former has been evolved to efficiently pirate the plant cell's autonomy: the T-DNA comes along, equipped with its own signal sequence that permits access to the nuclear pore; VirD2, the T-DNA's pilot protein, contains nuclear targeting sequences (NLSs), that are important, if not essential, for nuclear entry of the T-DNA (12,36, 45, 47, 53). The second requirement for nuclear entry is the presence of VirE2 coating the T-DNA.

The large size of VirD2-T-DNA coated by VirE2 protein [12.6 nm in diameter (11), exceeds the diameter of diffusion through the nuclear pore (9 nm) (19). However, the nuclear pore can open up to 23 nm during active nuclear import (19). Therefore the T-DNA complex may be actively imported. A combination of *in vitro* import experiments with isolated nuclei (65) and microinjection experiments (68) showed that the VirD2 protein mediates nuclear import through its C-terminal NLS. Also VirE2 possesses two NLSs shown to mediate plant cell nuclear localization of VirE2 fused to a reporter protein (13). In microinjection experiments VirE2 bound to DNA was able to mediate nuclear import of 800 nucleotide long ssDNA without the presence of the VirD2 protein (68). In contrast, *in vitro* import experiments conducted with purified plant nuclei, showed that import of short ssDNA was dependent on VirD2 alone. This import was mediated by the NLS of VirD2. Import of long ssDNA additionally required the octopine VirE2 protein. Free VirE2 was imported in nuclei, but VirE2 bound to ssDNA was not (65). This observation led to the suggestion that the NLSs of VirE2 were not exposed once VirE2 is bound to ssDNA; the role of VirE2 for nuclear import therefore may be limited to shape the T-DNA complex in a stretched structure that would be accepted by the NPCs for translocation into the nucleus. This hypothesis was further supported by the substitution of the VirE2 function by another bacterial ssDNA binding protein, RecA, devoid of NLS motifs (65).

This analysis led to a model, depicted in Fig. 1B, according to which nuclear import of the T-DNA complex can be divided into several steps: 1.) The T-DNA complex, consisting of ss-T-DNA and VirD2, matures by the acquisition of VirE2 subunits, from whatever source, to form the T-complex consisting of ss-T-DNA, covalently attached VirD2 and cooperatively bound VirE2. This complex, according to a model based on extensive electron microscopical data, can form a super twisted structure resembling a telephone cord (11). The first step of nuclear import of a T-complex may involve karyopherin α dependent recognition of NLS sequences residing on VirD2; this step may allow positioning of the T-DNA complex at the NPC gate and, in case of very short ss nucleic acids, may allow nuclear entrance (65). Longer DNA molecules apparently require the additional presence of VirE2 for nuclear import. This requirement may be based on a purely structural influence; the binding of VirE2 to the DNA may change the conformational properties of the T-DNA complex to match import requirements (65). Alternatively, or in addition, it may allow to recruit proteins binding to the complex which themselves attract importins factors (52); in contrast to VirD2 which has been shown to bind the importin karyophorin α, VirE2 lacked these capacities to bind at least to a known importin (3). Instead, a plant protein found to interact with VirE2, VIP1, was proposed to mediate interaction of VirE2 protein subunits with nuclear import mediating proteins (56). Although interaction of this host component to VirE2 bound to T-DNA was not demonstrated, the binding of VirE2 to VIP1 may, in one or another form, mediate nuclear import of T-DNA. This interpretation is in contrast to *in vitro* nuclear import studies showing that VirE2's nuclear import capacities that allow entry of the VirE2 plant nuclei are hidden once VirE2 protein is bound to ssDNA (65).

In the second step of the nuclear import pathway (Fig. 1B step 2) the telephone wire-like structure of the T-DNA complex, as imposed by the binding of VirE2 to the ssDNA-VirD2 complex, is proposed to be locally extended to form a long, thin filament fitting through the NPC. VIP1 and/or other cellular components may aid in this process. As the T-DNA complex moves through the nuclear pore complex, the original superstructure is resumed in the nuclear part of the translocating complex (Fig. 1B step 3). The reformation of this super-form may contribute to the energy required to move a large complex such as the T-DNA complex through the nuclear pore.

Import of macromolecules through NPCs is a highly conserved process. Yet it came somewhat as a surprise that such a sophisticated complex could also be imported into nuclei of *Drosophila* cells and *Xenopus* oocytes (in this experiment nuclear import depended on the activity of VirE2 only) (26), and mammalian cells (demonstrated by *in vitro* nuclear import of VirD2 and VirE2 containing complexes) (64).

These experiments, as well as the ones demonstrating *Agrobacterium* mediated transformation of various fungal cells (see below) point to a functional conservation among various eukaryotic organisms in using very specific DNA - protein complexes as substrates for nuclear import. Furthermore, they possibly pave the way to the development of *Agrobacterium* -- mediated transformation on other non - plant eukaryotes.

5. Integration of T-DNA

The final step of genetic transformation consists in stable integration of the T-DNA, leading to heritable change. Integration of T-DNA is not target-specific. In the plants analyzed, T-DNA insertion was found to be equally distributed over the chromosomes and no preference for integration into any particular part of the tagged genes could be detected, except that A/T rich regions were preferred (1). An analysis of 9000 independent transformation events in the genome of *Arabidopsis thaliana* confirmed the earlier conclusion, showing an average of about 6 insertions in 100 kb (A. Lecharny and V. Brunaud, personal communication). In addition, integration events were decreasing, in parallel to the gene density, towards the centromeres. However, at this point it is not clear whether the underrepresentation of heterochromatic integration events is due to supression of integration into heterochromatic regions or downregulation of expression of integrated sequences, a process required for selection of transformants. Within the individual genes, the highest insertion frequencies were close to the ATG codon (A. Lecharny and V. Brunaud, personal communication). These characteristics of course are the basis for the wide use of *Agrobacterium* as an unspecific and reliable gene tagging device (1).

Analysis of integration specificity with respect to T-DNA sequences revealed that the general mechanism of illegitimate recombination (or nonhomologous end joining) is mostly used, but that *Agrobacterium* specific peculiarities also exist (22, 33, 34); the use of small homologies at the junctions of T-DNA to plant DNA, sometimes combined with small sequence rearrangements at the target sites are hallmarks of illegitimate integration. Also the use of "filler" sequences at the junctions is a frequent characteristic of nonhomologous end joining. Integration is accompanied by small deletions of usually below 100 bp of the target DNA. Of special importance, since T-DNA specific, is the junction between the "right" (5') end of the T-DNA and plant DNA; in many of the reported cases the very nucleotide to which VirD2 is attached is found linked to plant DNA, with decreasing numbers of cases carrying a T-DNA deletion of one, two or more bases (22, 34). In light of this observation it was suggested that VirD2 remained DNA - bound and that it played a direct, e.g. enzymatic, or indirect, e.g. structural role in integration. This characteristics clearly distinguishes integration of T-DNA from general illegitimate recombination. In contrast, small deletions to various extents from the 3' end of the T-DNA are almost the rule. Also circularization of T-DNA, as analyzed following inoculation of plants with *Agrobacterium* carrying a viral T-DNA, exhibited the above mentioned characteristics (2).

The involvement of VirD2 in right border junction has been tested by genetic and biochemical approaches. A particular mutation in the *vir*D2 gene yielded a low number of transformants with truncations at the right border, but the efficiency of integration was not changed (51, 52, 54). Another DNA relaxase, the MobA protein of the plasmid RSF1010 could replace VirD2 in integration of bacterial into chromosomal DNA (5). This established roles for VirD2 and MobA integration. However, *in vitro* experiments excluded an enzymatic contribution of VirD2; integration into model target DNA of synthetic T-DNA-VirD2 complexes required a DNA ligase proper (62, 66, Y-Q Wu, unpublished). As ligases, both the bacteriophage T4 enzyme or *Arabidopsis* DNA ligase I could be used. Taken together, these experiments allow the conclusion that plant DNA ligase(s) must be involved to accomplish T-DNA integration.

Another virulence protein involved in T-DNA integration is VirE2. Transformation of plants using a bacterial strain deleted of it's *vir*E2 gene was four orders of magnitude less efficient; only severely truncated versions of the T-DNA could be recovered (44). Reduced efficiency of T-DNA transfer may be due to lack of one of several VirE2 functions (44), but the truncation of T-DNA points to a direct, protective role of the VirE2 proteins coating the T-DNA. It is not known whether a single- or double-stranded version of T-DNA integrates; VirE2, by binding to single-stranded DNA, may inhibit the major part of the T-DNA from annealing to complementary stretches on chromosomal DNA and thus may indirectly promote integration of only complete (or almost complete) units.

Any model of T-DNA integration must acknowledge the structural and functional specificities of the interacting partners: one partner consists of the complete T-DNA complex, including covalently linked VirD2 protein and VirE2 covering the entire length of the single-stranded DNA. The other partner is chromatin, probably containing nicks or breaks in the DNA. What is not known is whether T-DNA integrates in a single-stranded or double-stranded version (see above). What is known is that a high proportion of ssDNA becomes double-stranded and hence transcriptionally active, leading to transient phenotypic change of recipient tissue. This transient expression system is frequently used in analysis of the T-DNA transfer process. Most of these free double-stranded molecules probably get degraded as only a small fraction of cells that express these units become stably transformed. The left and right extremities of the T-DNA anneal, via microhomologies and VirD2 aided processes to probably nicked chromosomal DNA (Fig. 1C). Interestingly, sequence complementarity of only one bp, adjacent to the nucleotide to which VirD2 is bound, is frequently detected (54); however, the importance of this interaction is not understood. Another puzzling fact is the close proximity on chromosomal DNA of the entry points of the two T-DNA extremities; no factor is known that may enforce a preintegration coherence between the T-DNA termini. Information is also lacking concerning the temporal sequence of the repair reactions at the two T-DNA extremities. The order of these processes may depend on relative speed and efficiency of the two T-DNA ends in recruiting plants factors, finding microhomologies and/or localizing a nick in the plant DNA.

Since the virulence proteins carried along with T-DNA have only limited activities, the main functional and structural features required for integration must be contributed by the host. Genetic screens and direct analyses of DNA-repair mutants in model organisms are expected to yield information. Two radiation sensitive *Arabidopsis* mutants were tested for T-DNA integration proficiency, but results were found to be dependent on experimental detail (40, 48). An extensive screen of ecotypes of *Arabidopsis thaliana* yielded one radiation sensitive and T-DNA transformation deficient isolate; this hints to a link between DNA repair and T-DNA integration (39). A more directed approach consisted in a screen of a population of T-DNA tagged *Arabidopsis* mutants impaired in transformation (41). Several of the tagged genes are predicted to function in early steps of bacterium-plant interaction, whereas the mutant *rat5* is deficient in a particular histone H2A (38). It is unclear how H2A affects T-DNA integration. The mutant phenotype depended on the tissue analyzed; it was only observed in a tumor assay in roots and not in the female gametophytes, the targets for transformation in the germline transformation procedure (37). Histone H2A may be considered as influencing chromatin structure and function at prospective targeting sites. An interesting parallel exists to functions proposed for histone H2A of *Saccharomyces cerevisiae*; phosphorylation is this nucleosomal subunit seems to be required for efficient DNA double-stranded break repair by non-homologous end joining (17). However, further experimentation is required to test such a model and its possible application to T-DNA integration in plants. A further complication is connected to the fact that there are 13 H2A-like sequences in the genome of *Arabidopsis thaliana* (http://chromdb.biosci.arizona.edu).

Another approach to the identification of host functions makes use of the yeast *Saccharomyces cerevisiae* which can be transformed by *Agrobacterium* (6, 43). If T-DNA carries homologies to yeast DNA, integration occurs by homologous recombination. Since in the absence of DNA homology integration occurs by an illegitimate pathway, thus mimicking the plant pathway, mutational analysis of T-DNA integration into yeast chromosomes could be undertaken (57). Proteins Ku70, Rad50, Mre11, Xrs2, Lig4 and Sir4, which are involved in non-homologous end joining in yeast, were shown to be required for T-DNA integration into the yeast genome. In contrast, the proteins Rad51 and Rad52 belonging to the homologous recombination pathway were non essential for yeast transformation with *Agrobacterium* carrying a T-DNA that lacks homologies to yeast DNA (57). Plant orthologs of these proteins are therefore expected to play important roles in T-DNA integration in plant cells.

In addition to enzymatic activities, structural requirements on the part of the target locus will have to be met. It may be suggested that the expressional status of the plant locus aimed at by a particular T-DNA will influence the choice; indeed, gene-poor centromeric regions seem to be avoided by T-DNA (see above). Histone-modifying enzymes such as acetylases, deacetylases and methylases may, in conjunction with DNA methylation, lead to attraction or rejection of T-DNA. Chromatin remodeling factors may free or block chromosomal DNA from nucleosomes, thereby enhancing or reducing the chances for integration of a T-DNA at a particular locus.

6. Host range of *Agrobacterium* mediated T-DNA transfer

Generally, the determination of the host range depends on the definition of the host range. The original definition was based on the phenotype of a crown gall tumor, which obviously is the result of all steps of T-DNA transfer, integration, expression and phenotypic conversion of the effected plant cell. Now that more and more stages of this sophisticated pathogenic attack become apparent, the host range may be defined more specifically. For instance, new criteria for host range could be established with the use of selectable markers that render the assays independent of the formation of tumors. The successful use of yeast cells as recipients for T-DNA transfer not only established the notion of a rather promiscuous horizontal distribution of genetic information but also led to the establishment of *Saccharomyces cerevisiae* as an excellent model host for studies of T-DNA transfer characteristics of fundamental importance (see above).

Of special importance is the finding that T-DNA transfer occurs not only to cells of dicotyledonous plants, but also to those of the monocotyledonous families of agronomically important plants. Examples include the first demonstration of T-DNA transfer to maize (25), the first demonstration of stable transformation of the monocotyledonous, important crop plant rice with *Agrobacterium* (28) and the first demonstration of stable transformation of maize with *Agrobacterium* (29). These accomplishments constitute hallmarks in molecular crop-design.

Stable integration of T-DNA can be demonstrated in organisms as distantly related to plants as *Saccharomyces cerevisiae* or *Aspergillus awamori* (6, 15, 43). Also, the demonstration of *Agrobacterium* mediated T-DNA transfer to animal cells represents evidence of trans-kingdom DNA transfer (31). Although the conditions of the propagation of agrobacterial cells used for the experiments quoted above did not exactly match those known to be required for high efficiency of *Agrobacterium tumefaciens* mediated T-DNA transfer, precise integration of T-DNA integration in at least one transformant could be demonstrated (31). Nevertheless, the unique properties of precise integration of foreign DNA sequences may be of potential use for animal cell transformation. This may be a special case of the more general, but possible inefficient case of conjugation between bacterial and mammalian cells (60).

7. Conclusions and future challenge

Intensive research has been invested in analyzing the steps of agrobacterial conquest of plant cells, but a number of exciting tasks are still ahead of us. On the way to resolve these important issues, general knowledge on plant (and animal) cell biology will be improved, because small entities such as viruses or a virus-like T-DNA particle will serve as explorers of eukaryotic biology.

More specifically, imminent questions include those asking for

a) the plant factors allowing entry of bacterial T-DNA; is there a signal, and if so, which one, to allow entry of bacterial DNA into the plant cell? Does attachment of a bacterial cell to a plant cell by itself constitute such a signal? This is an important question, as receipt of a signal from a wounded plant is sufficient to trigger expression of virulence proteins, but actual transfer of genetic information may depend on a specific plant license.

b) the cellular entry permission. Do bacterial proteins, as suggested (18), render plant cells susceptible to T-DNA transfer? If so, how do different conformational states of the VirE2 protein allow the different functions attributed to this protein? What regulates the permeability of the postulated channel?

c) the regulation of nuclear entry of the T-DNA complex; is the plant cytoskeleton involved in escorting the T-DNA complex to the nuclear pore? What is the energy requirement for the passage of the T-DNA-VirD2-VirE2 super complex through the nuclear pore?

d) the selectivity T-DNA complexes exhibit for their target sites. Is there an influence of the nuclear architecture on the choices T-DNA complexes make for integration? Is there a mechanism for recruitment of T-DNA to sites in the chromosome that need repair? Is there a special selection of euchromatic segments to attract astray DNA units, and if so, how is this attraction accomplished? Does acetylation/methylation of histones, as well as methylation of DNA play a role in the selection of a "suitable" target for the T-DNA? These questions are important with respect to a general understanding of T-DNA transfer, a general understanding of chromatin-infrastructure and localized activity as well as with respect to applied research on chromosome-locus dependent expression of transgenes.

Whatever the question, research on the biology of *Agrobacterium tumefaciens* mediated transformation of plants (or other organisms) remains a challenge.

Acknowledgements

We acknowledge the critical comments from our colleague Pawel Pelczar. We thank Stanton Gelvin, Myriam Duckely, Véronique Brunaud and Alain Lecharny for unpublished information. We acknowledge financial help from the Novartis Research Foundation and the National Science Foundation, USA.

References

1. Azpiroz-Leehan R, Feldmann KA (1997) T-DNA insertion mutagenesis in *Arabidopsis*: going back and forth. Trends Genet. 13:152-6
2. Bakkeren G, Koukolikova-Nicola Z, Grimsley N, Hohn B (1989) Recovery of *Agrobacterium tumefaciens* T-DNA molecules from whole plants early after transfer. Cell 57:847-57
3. Ballas N, Citovsky V (1997) Nuclear localization signal binding protein from *Arabidopsis* mediates nuclear import of *Agrobacterium* VirD2 protein. Proc. Natl. Acad. Sci. U S A 94:10723-8
4. Binns, A N, Beaupre CE, Dale EM (1995) Inhibition of VirB-mediated transfer of diverse substrates from *Agrobacterium tumefaciens* by the IncQ plasmid RSF1010. J. Bacteriol. 177:4890-9
5. Bravo-Angel, A M, Gloeckler V, Hohn B, Tinland B (1999) Bacterial conjugation protein MobA mediates integration of complex DNA structures into plant cells. J. Bacteriol. 181:5758-65
6. Bundock P, den Dulk-Ras A, Beijersbergen A, Hooykaas PJ (1995) Trans-kingdom T-DNA transfer from *Agrobacterium*

tumefaciens to *Saccharomyces cerevisiae.* EMBO J. 14:3206-14

7. Chen L, Li CM, Nester EW (2000) Transferred DNA (T-DNA)-associated proteins of *Agrobacterium tumefaciens* are exported independently of *virB*. Proc. Natl. Acad. Sci. U S A 97:7545-50
8. Christie, P J (2001) Type IV secretion: intercellular transfer of macromolecules by systems ancestrally related to conjugation machines. Mol. Microbiol. 40:294-305
9. Christie P J, Ward JE, Winans SC, Nester EW (1988) The *Agrobacterium tumefaciens virE2* gene product is a single-stranded DNA binding protein that associates with T-DNA. J. Bacteriol. 170:2659-67
10. Citovsky V, De Vos G, Zambryski P (1988) Single-stranded DNA binding protein encoded by the *virE* locus of *Agrobacterium tumefaciens.* Science 240:501-504
11. Citovsky V, Guralnick B, Simon MN, Wall JS (1997) The molecular structure of *Agrobacterium* VirE2-single stranded DNA complexes involved in nuclear import. J. Mol. Biol. 271:718-27
12. Citovsky V, Warnick D, Zambryski P (1994) Nuclear import of *Agrobacterium* VirD2 and VirE2 proteins in maize and tobacco. Proc. Natl. Acad. Sci. U S A 91:3210-4
13. Citovsky V, Zupan J, Warnick D, Zambryski P (1992) Nuclear localization of *Agrobacterium* VirE2 protein in plant cells. Science 256:1802-5
14. Das A (1988) *Agrobacterium tumefaciens virE* operon encodes a single-stranded DNA- binding protein. Proc. Natl. Acad. Sci. U S A 85:2909-13
15. de Groot MJ, Bundock P, Hooykaas PJ, Beijersbergen AG (1998) *Agrobacterium tumefaciens*-mediated transformation of filamentous fungi. Nat. Biotechnol. 16:839-42
16. Deng W, Chen L, Peng WT, Liang X, Sekiguchi S, Gordon MP, Comai L, Nester EW (1999) VirE1 is a specific molecular chaperone for the exported single- stranded-DNA-binding protein VirE2 in *Agrobacterium*. Mol. Microbiol. 31:1795-807
17. Downs JA, Lowndes NF, Jackson SP (2000) A role for *Saccharomyces cerevisiae* histone H2A in DNA repair. Nature 408:1001-4
18. Dumas F, Duckely M, Pelczar P, Van Gelder P, Hohn B (2001) An *Agrobacterium* VirE2 channel for transferred-DNA transport into plant cells. Proc. Natl. Acad. Sci. U S A 98:485-90
19. Forbes DJ (1992) Structure and function of the nuclear pore

complex. Annu. Rev. Cell. Biol. 8:495-527
20. Gelvin SB (2000) *Agrobacterium* and plant genes involved in T-DNA transfer and integration. Annu. Rev. Plant Physiol. Plant Mol. Biol. 51:223-256
21. Gelvin SB (1998) *Agrobacterium* VirE2 proteins can form a complex with T strands in the plant cytoplasm. J. Bacteriol. 180:4300-2
22. Gheysen G, Villarroel R, Van Montagu M (1991) Illegitimate recombination in plants: a model for T-DNA integration. Genes Dev. 5:287-97
23. Gietl C, Koukolikova-Nicola Z, Hohn B (1987) Mobilization of T-DNA from *Agrobacterium* to plant cells involves a protein that binds single-stranded DNA. Proc. Natl. Acad. Sci. U S A 84:9006-10
24. Goodner B, Hinkle G, Gattung S, Miller N, Blanchard M, Qurollo B, Goldman BS, Cao Y, Askenazi M, Halling C, Mullin L, Houmiel K, Gordon J, Vaudin M, Iartchouk O, Epp A, Liu F, Wollam C, Allinger M, Doughty D, Scott C, Lappas C, Markelz B, Flanagan C, Crowell C, Gurson J, Lomo C, Sear C, Strub G, Cielo C, Slater S (2001) Genome sequence of the plant pathogen and biotechnology agent *Agrobacterium tumefaciens* C58. Science 294:2323-2328
25. Grimsley N, Hohn T, Davies JW, Hohn B (1987) *Agrobacterium*-mediated delivery of infectious maize streak virus into maize plants. Nature 325:177-179
26. Guralnick B, Thomsen G, Citovsky V (1996) Transport of DNA into the nuclei of *Xenopus* oocytes by a modified VirE2 protein of *Agrobacterium.* Plant Cell 8:363-73
27. Hansen G, Chilton MD (1999) Lessons in gene transfer to plants by a gifted microbe. Curr. Top. Microbiol. Immunol. 240:21-57
28. Hiei Y, Ohta S, Komari T, Kumashiro T (1994) Efficient transformation of rice (*Oryza sativa* L) mediated by *Agrobacterium* and sequence analysis of the boundaries of the T-DNA. Plant J. 6:271-82
29. Ishida Y, Saito H, Ohta S, Hiei Y, Komari T, Kumashiro T (1996) High efficiency transformation of maize (*Zea mays* L) mediated by *Agrobacterium tumefaciens.* Nat. Biotchnol. 14: 745-50
30. Komeili A, O'Shea EK (2001) New perspectives on nuclear transport. Annu. Rev. Genet. 35:341-364
31. Kunik T, Tzfira T, Kapulnik Y, Gafni Y, Dingwall C, Citovsky V (2001) Genetic transformation of HeLa cells by *Agrobacterium.* Proc. Natl. Acad. Sci. U S A 98:1871-6
32. Lee LY, Gelvin SB, Kado CI (1999) pSa causes oncogenic

suppression of *Agrobacterium* by inhibiting VirE2 protein export. J. Bacteriol. 181:186-96

33. Matsumoto S, Ito Y, Hosoi T, Takahashi Y, Machida Y (1990) Integration of *Agrobacterium* T-DNA into a tobacco chromosome: possible involvement of DNA homology between T-DNA and plant DNA. Mol. Gen. Genet. 224:309-16
34. Mayerhofer R, Koncz-Kalman Z, Nawrath C, Bakkeren G, Crameri A, Angelis K, Redei GP, Schell J, Hohn B, Koncz C (1991) T-DNA integration: a mode of illegitimate recombination in plants. EMBO J. 10:697-704
35. Merkle T (2001) Nuclear import and export of proteins in plants: a tool for the regulation of signalling. Planta 213:499-517
36. Mysore KS, Bassuner B, Deng X-B, Darbinian NS, Motchoulski A, Ream W, Gelvin SN (1998) Role of the *Agrobacterium tumefaciens* VirD2 protein in T-DNA transfer and integration. Mol. Plant-Microbe Int. 7: 668-683
37. Mysore KS, Kumar CT, Gelvin SN (2000) *Arabidopsis* ecotypes and mutants that are recalcitrant to *Agrobacterium* root transformation are susceptible to germ-line transformation. Plant J. 21:9-16
38. Mysore KS, Nam J, Gelvin SB (2000) An *Arabidopsis* histone H2A mutant is deficient in *Agrobacterium* T-DNA integration. Proc. Natl. Acad. Sci. U S A 97: 948-53
39. Nam J, Matthysse AG, Gelvin SB (1997) Differences in susceptibility of *Arabidopsis* ecotypes to crown gall disease may result from a deficiency in T-DNA integration. Plant Cell 9:317-33
40. Nam J, Mysore KS, Gelvin SB (1998) *Agrobacterium tumefaciens* transformation of the radiation hypersensitive *Arabidopsis thaliana* mutants *uvh1* and *rad5*. Mol. Plant Microbe Interact. 11:1136-41
41. Nam J, Mysore KS, Zheng C, Knue MK, Matthysse AG, Gelvin SB (1999) Identification of T-DNA tagged *Arabidopsis* mutants that are resistant to transformation by *Agrobacterium*. Mol. Gen. Genet. 261:429-38
42. Otten L, De Greve H, Leemans J, Hain R, Hooykaas P, Schell J (1984) Restoration of virulence of Vir region mutants of *Agrobacterium tumefaciens* strain B6S3 by coinjection with normal and mutant *Agrobacterium* strains. Mol. Gen. Genet. 195:159-163
43. Piers LK, Heath JD, Liang X, Stephens KM, Nester EW (1996) *Agrobacterium tumefaciens*-mediated transformation of yeast. Proc. Natl. Acad. Sci. 93: 1613-1618
44. Rossi L, Hohn B, Tinland B (1996) Integration of complete

transferred DNA units is dependent on the activity of virulence E2 protein of *Agrobacterium tumefaciens.* Proc. Natl. Acad. Sci. U S A 93:126-30

45. Rossi L, Hohn B, Tinland B (1993) The VirD2 protein of *Agrobacterium tumefaciens* carries nuclear localization signals important for transfer of T-DNA to plant. Mol. Gen. Genet. 239:345-53
46. Sen P, Pazour GJ, Anderson D, Das A (1989) Cooperative binding of *Agrobacterium tumefaciens* VirE2 protein to single-stranded DNA. J. Bacteriol. 171:2573-80
47. Shurvinton CE, Hodges L, Ream W (1992) A nuclear localization signal and the C-terminal omega sequence in the *Agrobacterium tumefaciens* VirD2 endonuclease are important for tumor formation. Proc. Natl. Acad. Sci. U S A 89:11837-41
48. Sonti RV, Chiurazzi M, Wong D, Davies CS, Harlow GR, Mount DW, Signer ER (1995) *Arabidopsis* mutants deficient in T-DNA integration. Proc. Natl. Acad. Sci. U S A 92:11786-90
49. Stahl LE, Jacobs A, Binns AN (1998) The conjugal intermediate of plasmid RSF1010 inhibits *Agrobacterium tumefaciens* virulence and VirB-dependent export of VirE2. J. Bacteriol. 180:3933-9
50. Sundberg CD, Ream W (1999) The *Agrobacterium tumefaciens* chaperone-like protein, VirE1, interacts with VirE2 at domains required for single-stranded DNA binding and cooperative interaction. J. Bacteriol. 181:6850-5
51. Tinland B (1996) The integration of T-DNA into plant genomes. Trends Plant Sci. 1:178-184
52. Tinland B, Hohn B (1995) Recombination between prokaryotic and eukaryotic DNA: integration of *Agrobacterium tumefaciens* T-DNA into the plant genome. Genet. Eng. 17:209-29
53. Tinland B, Koukolikova-Nicola Z, Hall MN, Hohn B (1992) The T-DNA-linked VirD2 protein contains two distinct functional nuclear localization signals. Proc. Natl. Acad. Sci. U S A 89:7442-6
54. Tinland B, Schoumacher F, Gloeckler V, Bravo-Angel AM, Hohn B (1995) The *Agrobacterium tumefaciens* virulence D2 protein is responsible for precise integration of T-DNA into the plant genome. EMBO J. 14:3585-95
55. Tzfira T, Rhee Y, Chen MH, Kunik T, Citovsky V (2000) Nucleic acid transport in plant-microbe interactions: the molecules that walk through the walls. Annu. Rev. Microbiol. 54:187-219

56. Tzfira T, Vaidya M, Citovsky V (2001) VIP1, an *Arabidopsis* protein that interacts with *Agrobacterium* VirE2, is involved in VirE2 nuclear import and *Agrobacterium* infectivity. EMBO J. 20:3596-607
57. van Attikum H, Bundock P, Hooykaas PJJ (2001) Non-homologous end-joining proteins are required for *Agrobacterium* T-DNA integration. EMBO J. 20:6550-6558
58. Vasu SK, Forbes DJ (2001) Nuclear pores and nuclear assembly. Curr. Opin. Cell Biol. 13:363-75
59. Vergunst AC, Schrammeijer B, den Dulk-Ras A, de Vlaam CM, Regensburg-Tuink TJ, Hooykaas PJ (2000) VirB/D4-dependent protein translocation from *Agrobacterium* into plant cells. Science 290:979-82
60. Waters VL (2001) Conjugation between bacterial and mammalian cells. Nat. Genet. 29:375-6
61. Wood DW, Setubal JC, Kaul R, Monks DE, Kitajima JP, Okura VK, Zhou Y, Chen L, Wood GE, Almeida Jr NF, Woo L, Chen Y, Paulsen IT, Eisen JA, Karp PD, Bovee Sr D, Chapman P, Clendenning J, Deatherage G, Gillet W, Grant C, Kutyavin T, Levy R, Li M-J, McClelland E, Palmieri A, Raymond C, Rouse G, Saenphimmachak C, Wu Z, Romero P, Gordon D, Zhang S, Yoo H, Tao Y, Biddle P, Jung M, Krespan W, Perry M, Gordon-Kamm B, Liao L, Kim S, Hendrick C, Zhao Z-Y, Dolan M, Chumley F, Tingey SV, Tomb J-F, Gordon MP, Olson MV, Nester EW (2001) The Genome of the natural genetic engineer *Agrobacterium tumefaciens* C58. Science 294:2317-2323
62. Wu YQ, Hohn B, Ziemienowic A (2001) Characterization of an ATP-dependent type I DNA ligase from *Arabidopsis thaliana.* Plant Mol. Biol. 46:161-70
63. Zhao Z, Sagulenko E, Ding Z, Christie PJ (2001) Activities of *virE1* and the VirE1 secretion chaperone in export of the multifunctional VirE2 effector via an *Agrobacterium* type IV secretion pathway. J. Bacteriol 183:3855-65
64. Ziemienowicz A, Gorlich D, Lanka E, Hohn B, Rossi L (1999) Import of DNA into mammalian nuclei by proteins originating from a plant pathogenic bacterium. Proc. Natl. Acad. Sci. U S A 96:3729-33
65. Ziemienowicz A, Merkle T, Schoumacher F, Hohn B, Rossi L (2001) Import of *Agrobacterium* T-DNA into plant nuclei two distinct functions of VirD2 and VirE2 proteins. Plant Cell 13:369-84
66. Ziemienowicz A, Tinland B, Bryant J, Gloeckler V, Hohn B (2000) Plant enzymes but not *Agrobacterium* VirD2 mediate T-DNA ligation in vitro. Mol. Cell. Biol. 20:6317-22

67. Zupan J, Muth TR, Draper O, Zambryski P (2000) The transfer of DNA from *Agrobacterium tumefaciens* into plants: a feast of fundamental insights. Plant J. 23:11-28

68. Zupan JR, Citovsky V, Zambryski P (1996) *Agrobacterium* VirE2 protein mediates nuclear uptake of single-stranded DNA in plant cells. Proc. Natl. Acad. Sci. U S A 93:2392-7

Molecular Basis for Transformation of an Epiphyte into a Gall-Forming Pathogen as Exemplified by *Erwinia herbicola* pv. *gypsophilae*

Shulamit Manulis and Isaac Barash

The Diverse Habitats and Hosts of *Erwinia herbicola*

Erwinia herbicola (*Pantoea agglomerans*) is widespread in nature as an epiphyte on many different plants (108). In addition to its prevalence on plant surfaces, it has been characterized as an endophyte in various plants (60) and has been isolated from seeds, water and humans (e.g., wounds, blood, urine, internal organs) as well as from animals (40). *E. herbicola* is also known to produce antibiotics (see, e.g.,120) which could facilitate its survival in various ecological niches. The adaptation of *E. herbicola* to widely diverse microenvironments suggests that this species maintains high genetic plasticity. *E. herbicola* seems to be readily accessible to horizontal gene transfer driven by plasmids and other mobile elements, a trait that may explain its flexibility in adapting to different life styles. Indeed, as will be further described, many different bacteria, that presumably encountered *E. herbicola* in its various habitats, have left their fingerprints on its genome and, presumably, were instrumental in its conversion into a plant pathogen.

The transformation of *E. herbicola* into a tumorigenic bacterium appears to constitute a major evolutionary path in this species. The bacterium has been reported to cause crown and root galls on gypsophila (*Gypsophila paniculata* L.) (20), beet (*Beta vulgaris* L.) (16), wisteria (*Wisteria sinensis* L.) (94), Douglas-fir (*Pseudotsuga menziesii* L.) (28) and cranberry (*Vaccinium macrocarpon* Aiton) (121). Galls produced by *E. herbicola* are generally similar in their appearance to crown galls incited by *Agrobacterium tumefaciens*. The wide host range of *A. tumefaciens* has probably caused field workers to attribute any gall symptom in a variety of plants to this bacterium, without isolating the causal agent. Therefore, it might be anticipated that additional plant species will be revealed to be hosts for gall formation by *E. herbicola*. In contrast to *A. tumefaciens*, pathogenic strains of *E. herbicola* exhibit a restricted host range and may, therefore, be divided into pathovars similar to those of *Pseudomonas* or *Xanthomonas* spp. An additional major difference between *E. herbicola* and *A. tumefaciens* is the mechanism of pathogenesis. Gall formation by *E.*

Figure 1. Pathogenicity of *Erwinia herbicola* pvs. *gypsophilae* and *betae* on gypsophila cuttings. *Ehg*824-1 - gypsophila pathovar; *Ehb*4188 - beet pathovar.

herbicola does not involve transformation of DNA into host cells as in *Agrobacterium* (19) but, as will be further described, pathogenicity of *E. herbicola* relies on the translocation of type III virulence effectors into host cells and to a lesser extent by hormone production by the bacterium. Although gall formation appears to be a predominant symptom of pathogenic *E. herbicola*, other symptoms, such as stalk and leaf necrosis of onion have also been reported (49).

E. herbicola pv. *gypsophilae* (*Ehg*), the main subject of this review, is the most destructive pathogen of gypsophila and acts as a limiting factor in its propagation(20, 122). Gypsophila is an ornamental plant used for commercial cutflower production (104). *Ehg* induces gall formation at wound sites mainly in the crown region of the stem, and is most prevalent during the development of rooted cuttings in nurseries. Gall formation weakens the plant, and causes defoliation and ultimately death of the whole plant (122). Neither resistant clones nor effective chemical control are available, and the only control measure is the production of pathogen-free cuttings through culture indexing (79). In contrast to *Ehg*, whose pathogenicity appears to be restricted to gypsophila, the beet pathovar, *E. herbicola* pv. *betae* (*Ehb*) incites galls on both beet and gypsophila (16). Galls produced by *Ehb* on gypsophila are morphologically distinct from those produced by *Ehg* (Fig. 1). Tumors on table beets results in an economic loss because infected beets cannot be mechanically processed (16). The incidence of the disease on beet differs greatly from year to year.

The Pathogenicity Plasmid of *Erwinia herbicola* pv. *gypsophilae*

Strains of *E. herbicola* isolated from gypsophila appear to fall into several serotypic groups (78, 79, 81). These groups contain pathogenic as well as nonpathogenic strains, which indicates that there is no association between serotypes and pathogenicity. All strains tested contained one to four plasmids with approximate sizes that ranged from 100-MDa to less than 10-MDa (79). Southern analysis with a 7.5-kb *Eco*RI DNA fragment harboring the IAA and cytokinin biosynthetic genes, demonstrated that hybridization occurred only with plasmid DNA from pathogenic strains but not with that from nonpathogenic ones (79). These results suggest that all the tested pathogenic strains harbor a pathogenicity-associated plasmid that has been designated as pPATH. The pPATH plasmids of different strains may differ in size but share similar genes or DNA sequences. In the present review the pPATH plasmid of strain *Ehg*824-1 will be referred to as $pPATH_{Ehg}$. The use of transposon mutagenesis of a cosmid library constructed from plasmid DNA of *Ehg*824-1 has enabled many virulence genes to be isolated and characterized on the $pPATH_{Ehg}$ plasmid. A similar pathogenicity plasmid has also been identified in various strains of the beet pathovars. The pathogenicity plasmid of strain *Ehb*4188 will be referred to as $pPATH_{Ehb}$. Attempts to cure $pPATH_{Ehg}$ or mobilize it into a nonpathogenic strain have been unsuccessful but the possibility that under *in vivo* conditions mobilization of the pPATH into nonpathogenic strains is driven by a conjugation factor analogous to the Ti of *Agrobacterium* (98) cannot be ruled out.

The $pPATH_{Ehg}$ plasmid from strain *Ehg*824-1 has been extensively investigated (Fig. 2). The plasmid's size is approximately 150-kb and it appears to accommodate a putative pathogenicity island of less than 60-kb. The various virulence genes that have so far been characterized on $pPATH_{Ehg}$ can be divided into three groups according to their function in pathogenicity: a) Hrp gene cluster (86, 91), b) Hrp-dependent virulence genes encoding type III effectors proteins (31, 86, 116) and c) Hrp-independent virulence genes encoding enzymes for IAA and cytokinin biosynthesis (18, 37, 67, 68). In addition to virulence genes, $pPATH_{Ehg}$

harbors numerous copies of IS elements representing five different families (45, 69).

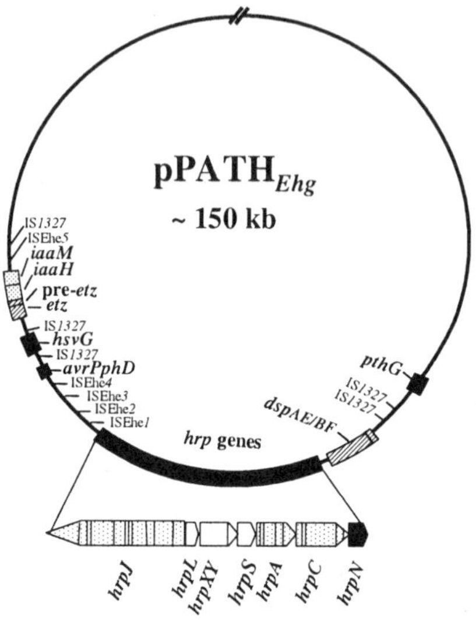

Figure 2. Schematic map of the pathogenicity plasmid of *Erwinia herbicola* pv. *gypsophilae*. The various genes and IS elements shown in the figure are described in the text.

The *hrp* Genes of *Ehg* and Their Regulation

The presence of *hrp* (**HR** and **p**athogenicity) genes is essential for pathogenicity of most Gram-negative phytopathogenic bacteria. Mutations in *hrp* genes abolish the pathogenicity of the bacteria in susceptible host plants and their ability to elicit the hypersensitive response in resistant host or nonhost plants (11). Genetic and biochemical studies have demonstrated that *hrp* genes encode components of a type III secretion pathway, regulatory proteins that allow the bacteria to sense the host environment, and harpins, a class of proteinaceous elicitors of the hypersensitive response (HR) in nonhost plants (70). The *hrp* genes are organized in large clusters of 22 to 40-kb, and contain six to eight complementation groups (11, 70). The nucleotide sequences of *hrp* gene clusters revealed high similarities between pathogens belonging to different genera (11). Those genes with broad conservation among many type III systems have been renamed *hrc* (HR and conserved) genes (9). The *hrp* clusters of *E. amylovora* and *P. syringae* are closely related yet distinct from the *hrp* genes of *X. campestris* and *R. solanacearum*, which are similar to one another and form a second lineage (11, 62). In Gram-negative pathogenic bacteria of animals and plants, the type III secretion pathway enables the bacteria to inject virulence determinants directly into cells of their eukaryotic hosts (51). For plant pathogens, the plant cell wall represents an extra challenge for such injection. A pilus structure (Hrp pilus) that is associated with translocation via the type III machinery appears to overcome this barrier (reviewed in 100). It has been recently demonstrated that type III secretion occurs only at the site of Hrp pilus assembly, and that the Hrp pilus guides the transfer of effector proteins outside the bacterial cell (54). A non-homologous injection system, e.g., a type IV secretion pathway, is present in *A. tumefaciens*, and its function is associated with the appearance of a pilus structure that is morphologically similar to that of the type III system (100).

It is noteworthy that until the discovery of *hrp* genes on pPATH$_{Ehg}$ (91), all the *hrp* gene clusters were found on the chromosome (128) with the exception of those of *R. solanacearum*, which harbors the *hrp* cluster on a megaplasmid (13). Furthermore, there seem to be no *hrp* gene equivalents present in any tumorigenic bacteria, including *A. tumefaciens* (62). The *hrp* gene cluster on pPATH$_{Ehg}$ was mapped on two overlapping cosmids by saturation mutagenesis with Tn*3*-Spice and mini-Tn*10* (86). To delineate the complete *hrp* gene cluster of *Ehg*, the region containing the Hrp^{-} mutants was sequenced (86), and the results indicate that the *hrp* genes of *Ehg* are remarkably similar to and collinear with those of *Erwinia amylovora* and *Pantoea stewartii.* With few exceptions, the percentage identities of *Ehg* nucleotides and of the deduced proteins of the various *hrp* operons, with those of *E. amylovora* and *P. stewartii* ranged from 60 to 90%. The *hrp* cluster of *Ehg* appeared to contain genes for all the required Hrp functions, namely protein secretion via the type III system (i.e., *hrpJ*, *hrpA*, and *hrpC* operons), regulation (i.e., *hrpL*, *hrpXY*, and *hrpS* operons), and HR elicitation on nonhost plants (i.e., *hrpN*) (86). The nine broadly conserved genes designated *hrc* (9) were also present.

The only major difference between the *hrp* cluster of *Ehg* and that of *E. amylovora* is located in the space between *hrpN* and the type III virulence effector *dspAE/BF,* in the right terminus of the cluster (Fig. 2) (86). In *Ehg*, this region was 1-kb as compared with 4-kb in *E. amylovora*, in which four ORFs are arranged in two operons (58). One

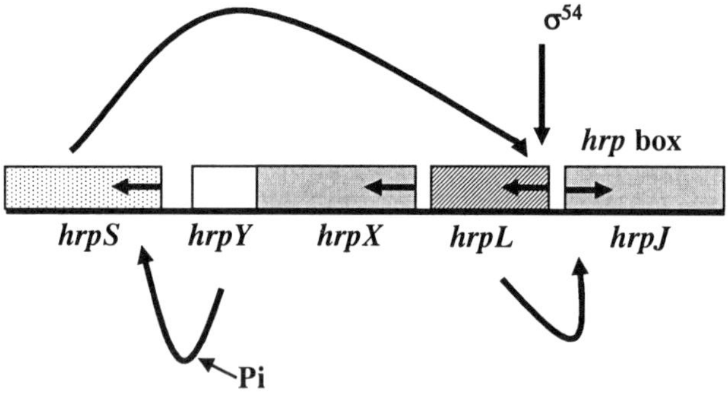

Figure 3. A proposed model for *hrp* regulation in *Ehg*.

of the ORFs in *E. amylovora* is *hrpW* whose deduced protein resembles harpin in its high glycine content but which also has homology to pectate lyase. Although HrpW appears to be distributed widely among several *Erwinia* species, only a remnant of this gene (50-bp) has been detected in *Ehg* (Mor *et al.*, unpublished results). The role of harpin in pathogenicity and HR elicitation on nonhosts has been assessed with marker-exchanged mutants obtained by transposition with pTn*3*-Spice (86). *Ehg* mutants deficient in harpin production retained pathogenicity and barely caused reduction in the HR response in tobacco. Despite having some physical and chemical properties in common, e.g., heat stability, glycine richness, and acidity, the harpins from different genera seem to be quite distinct from each other with regard to their amino acid compositions (70). The percentage identities of the amino acids of HrpN_{Ehg} with those of the harpins of *P. stewartii*, *E. amylovora*, *E. chrysanthemi* and *E. carotovora* were 69, 60, 52, and 48%, respectively (86).

Sequence analysis of the *hrp/hrc* regulatory region in *Ehg* has revealed four open reading frames, in order, *hrpL, hrpX, hrpY* and *hrpS* (Fig. 3), all transcribed in the same direction (86). These ORFs, which show high similarity (70-75% identity) and co-linearity with the regulatory genes of *E. amylovora* and *P. stewartii*, correspond to three complementation groups, with *hrpX* and *hrpY* together in one operon. The *hrpL* gene encodes an alternate sigma factor that recognizes conserved promoter sequences called "*hrp* boxes"(132) and directs the transcription of other *hrp* genes and type III virulence effectors. The *hrpXY* operon shows high homology to a putative two-component signal transduction system, with HrpX as a cytoplasmic sensor-kinase and HrpY as a response regulator (125). HrpS shows homology to a σ^{54}-dependent transcriptional activator of the NtrC family (87), but lacks the receiver domain so it does not have to be phosphorylated.

Several lines of evidence support the proposed model for *hrp* gene regulation in *Ehg* (Fig. 3). a) Mutations in each of the regulatory genes, and complementation tests indicate that *hrpY, hrpS,* and *hrpL* are mandatory for pathogenicity, whereas a nonpolar mutation in *hrpX* does not affect pathogenicity (92, 93). Plasmids expressing *hrpY, hrpS* and *hrpL* from a constitutive *lac* promoter were tested for complementation of these mutations. Nonpathogenic *hrpY, hrpS* and *hrpL* mutants could be complemented by *lacp-hrpL*. Mutants in *hrpY* and *hrpS* but not in *hrpL* were complemented by *lacp-hrpS*. Finally, *lacp-hrpY* could complement *hrpY* mutation but not *hrpS* or *hrpL* mutants. b) The effects of over expressing the regulatory genes (with the *lac* promoter *in trans*), on the transcriptional activity of these genes and of other *hrp* genes, namely *hrpJ* and *hrpN*, were measured in culture with the ice nucleation reporter gene *inaZ* (92). Thus, *lacp-hrpS* stimulated (by two to three orders of magnitude) the transcription of *hrpS, hrpL,* and *hrpN*; *lacp-hrpL* stimulated only *hrpJ* and *hrpN*, whereas no stimulation of any *hrp* gene was observed with *lacp-hrpY* or *lacp-hrpX*. c) The effects of mutations in the *hrp* regulatory genes on transcriptional activity of *hrp* genes *in planta* were investigated. Mutations in *hrpY, hrpS* and *hrpL* but not in *hrpX* significantly (by two orders of magnitude) reduced the transcriptional activity of the downstream regulatory genes as well as those of *hrpJ* and *hrpN* (93). Similar results were obtained when the transcriptional activities of isolated promoters of these genes were fused upstream to the *inaZ* reporter and introduced *in trans* to the mutants (92). d) The transcription of *hrpS* and *hrpL* is induced *in planta* as compared with growth in rich or minimal A media. In contrast, the transcription of *hrpY* is constitutive and was similar in different environments (92). e) Conversion of the aspartate (D57) of HrpY into either glutamate or alanine by site directed mutagenesis eliminated the transcriptional induction of *hrpS,* suggesting that HrpY is active in its phosphorylated form.

The proposed model (Fig. 3) suggests that the HrpX sensor that is hypothesized to phosphorylate the HrpY response regulator and converts it to an active form is non-functional in *Ehg*. HrpY, in its phosphorylated form, directly or indirectly activates *hrpS*, HrpS activates *hrpL*, and HrpL in turn enables the RNA polymerase to recognize *hrp* boxes. This basic model is generally consistent with the proposed model for *P. stewartii* (85) but differs from that for *E. amylovora* (125). In *E. amylovora*, a mutation in *hrpX* resulted in attenuated virulence whereas no significant effect on virulence could be detected in *Ehg*. Moreover, in the proposed model for *E. amylovora*, HrpS and HrpY simultaneously activate *hrpL*, and transcription of *hrpS* is not affected by *hrpXY* (125). In contrast, phosphorylated HrpY induces transcription of *hrpS* in *Ehg*. Since transcription of *hrpY* appears to be constitutive, its phosphorylation seems to be the crucial step in triggering the regulatory cascade of *Ehg*. It might be postulated that an alternate kinase activates HrpY in response to yet unknown plant signal(s).

Hrp-Dependent Virulence Genes

As indicated earlier, Gram negative phytopathogenic bacteria employ specialized type III secretion systems to deliver an arsenal of virulence proteins directly into host cells. Although the type III secretion pathway (Hrp pathway) shows remarkable conservation among Gram negative mammalian and plant bacterial pathogens (38), the secreted type III effectors vary widely (22, 59). The proteins that are secreted, either to the milieu or delivered into host cells are known as Hops (**H**rp-dependent **o**uter **p**roteins) (3). These variable arsenals of secreted effectors (i.e., Hops) include **avir**ulence (Avr) proteins and **d**isease **s**pecific **p**roteins (Dsps). Avirulence (*avr*) genes determine the inability of a given bacterial strain to infect a plant carrying the corresponding resistant (R) gene by eliciting HR (57). Avirulence genes have been extensively studied and numerous bacterial *avr* genes in pathovars of *P. syringae* and *Xanthomonas* spp. have been described (65). In contrast to the "negative acting" Avr proteins that induce resistance (HR), Dsps are regarded in this review as "positive acting" determinants that induce susceptibility. A Dsp mutant is recognized by its loss of virulence but retention of HR elicitation on nonhost plants. It is most likely that phytopathogenic bacteria, like their mammalian counterparts (see, e.g., 17), produce a wide variety of Dsps that suppress host defenses, cause the release of nutrients for the benefit of the pathogen and determine host specificity at the species or even the genus level. However, the information on Dsp proteins is very scanty, as compared with that on Avrs. The following *dsp* genes have been characterized in *Ehg* and *Ehb*.

hsvG (**h**ost **s**pecific **v**irulence gene for **g**ypsophila) determines the ability of *Ehg* and *Ehb* to incite galls on gypsophila (116). *hsvG* has been isolated and sequenced from both plasmids, pPATH$_{Ehg}$ and pPATH$_{Ehb}$. A slight difference between the sequences of the gene in the two pathovars was detected, but most of the sequence alterations in the deduced proteins were found in the C-terminal region. Mutation in *hsvG* eliminated the ability of *Ehg* and *Ehb* to cause galls on gypsophila, but allowed the retention of full pathogenicity of *Ehb* on beet (Table 1) and HR induction in tobacco. DNA sequence analysis of *hsvG* revealed an ORF of 2-kb with a potential ribosome binding site and a putative "*hrp* box" upstream to the starting codon (116). The ORF had no significant sequence homology to known genes although a partial homology has recently been observed with *psvA,* a plasmid-borne virulence gene from *Pseudomonas syringae* pv. *eriobotryae*, which is pathogenic on loquat trees (55). The predicted protein has a molecular mass of about 72 kDa. HsvG is predominately hydrophilic and lacks transmembrane domains and a signal peptide. A truncated *hsvG* gene was still partially able to complement an *hsvG* mutant, indicating that the C-terminus (30% of the protein) is not essential (116).

Table 1: Effects of mutations in *hsvG* and *pthG* on pathogenicity of *Erwinia herbicola* pvs. *gypsophilae* and *betae* on gypsophila and table beet

Bacterial strain/ mutant	**Relevant characteristics**	**Pathogenicity[a] on Gypsophila**	**Beet**
*Ehg*824-1	Gypsophila pathovar wild type	+	- (HR)
*Ehb*4188	Beet pathovar wild type	+	+
*Ehg*824-1Mx14	*hsvG*	-	- (HR)
*Ehb*4188Mx14	*hsvG*	-	+
*Ehb*4188/S2.8	*pthG in trans*	+	- (HR)
*Ehg*824-1MxE27	*pthG*	±	+

[a](+) gall formation; (-) no gall formation, (+-) reduced gall size; (HR) hypersensitive response.

By employing the ice nucleation reporter gene *inaZ*, it was found that the transcriptional activity of *hsvG* in *Ehg* cells grown in gypsophila stems (i.e., apoplast) was significantly induced (by three orders of magnitude) within 24 hr (115). A similar induction rate was also detected in carnation or bean stems, indicating that the observed induction is nonhost-specific. On the other hand the *hsvG-inaZ* activity on bean leaf surfaces was much lower than that on bean stems suggesting that maximal induction is triggered by the apoplast environment (115). Over-expression of HrpL or HrpS significantly stimulated the transcriptional activity of *hsvG* in minimal A media to the level of induction *in planta*. Mutations in either *hrpL* or *hrpS* caused substantial reduction in *hsvG-inaZ* activity in bacteria grown in LB or minimal media and *in planta*. In Western blots, HsvG could be detected in cell sonicates, but not in culture supernatant, following overexpression of HrpL or HrpS (115). All the foregoing data clearly demonstrate that transcription of *hsvG* is under the control of the *hrp* regulon.

A heterologous system was employed to demonstrate type-III-mediated secretion and translocation of HsvG. By using the calmodulin-dependent adenylate cyclase (CyaA) reporter system (130, 131), it was shown that HsvG can be translocated into human HeLa cells via the type III secretion system of an enteropathogenic *E. coli* (EPEC) strain (117). Fusions of HsvG-CyaA containing 271, 39, 11 and 3 amino acids of the N-terminus of HsvG were introduced into a wild-type EPEC and, as controls, into mutants deficient in secretion (*escV*) and translocation (*espB*). Significant secretion was detected in EPEC/HsvG-CyaA and the *espB* mutant but not in the *escV* mutant. Translocation into HeLa cells was detected with the wild-type EPEC but not with the two mutants. Both secretion and translocation were observed when the N-terminus of HsvG contained at least 39 codons (114). Several reports have demonstrated reciprocal secretion of type III effectors by plant and animal pathogens, (4, 48, 101), but reciprocal translocation has not been previously reported. Although a signal peptide is not required for recognition of substrates by the type III system, the sequence of the N-termini of virulence effectors determines their secretion and translocation specificity (51). Thus, secretion signals in some Yops (***Y****ersinia* **o**uter **p**roteins) of *Yersinia pseudotuberculosis* are confined to N-terminal 15-17 codons, whereas translocation signals are located in the 50-100 codons (103, 107). Recently, the signals required for secretion and translocation of AvrBs2 from *X. campestris* pv. *vesicatoria* have been analyzed (89). By using the C-terminus of *Pseudomonas syringae* AvrRpt as a host-specific reporter on *Arabidopsis thaliana* RPS2, it was demonstrated that the first 28 codons of AvrBs2 were sufficient for its secretion, whereas 58 codons were required for its translocation. In the case of HsvG it appears that the signals for secretion and translocation by the EPEC type III system are co-localized, but more precise analysis must be performed to substantiate this observation. The fact that the secretion of the HsvG-CyaA hybrid protein by the type III pathway of EPEC does not require the expression of a specific *Ehg* chaperone suggests that its recognition might be mediated through its mRNA sequence (5). However, the roles of the mRNA secretion signal and the translocation signal in directing substrate proteins to the type III secretion system remain ambiguous (1, 71).

The characteristics of HsvG clearly identify this protein as a Hop that belongs to the Dsp class of proteins. Its features are reminiscent of the *avr* genes that have been linked to the activities of the *hrp* gene cluster (65) and have been shown, albeit indirectly, to deliver Avr proteins into the host plant cell through the type III secretion system (see, e.g., 42, 118). The similar characteristics observed for Dsp (HsvG) and Avr proteins can be explained in the light of their common origin. It may be postulated that Avr proteins are Dsp proteins, which have been recognized as incompatible rather than compatible virulence determinants by the defense gene surveillance system of the host (59). This hypothesis is supported by the presence of a few bifunctional *avr* genes that play a role in virulence on hosts that lack the corresponding R genes (see, e.g., 74, 99). It should, however, be pointed out that deletion of *avr* genes may not result in a loss of pathogenicity (12), which could suggest that they have no major role in intrinsic pathogenicity.

pthG (**path**ogenicity gene on **g**ypsophila). *pthG* was isolated by mobilizing a cosmid library of *Ehg* DNA into *Ehb* and screening the transconjugants for pathogenicity on beet (31). This gene was found to be functional only in *Ehg* and to reside on $pPATH_{Ehg}$ (Fig. 2), although homologous sequences were detected on $pPATH_{Ehb}$ (31). The *pthG* ORF is 1.5-kb with a putative "*hrp* box" in its promoter region. It encodes a polar 56 kDa protein that lacks an N-terminal signal peptide and contains a putative short *trans*-membrane helix (TMH) in its C terminus (31). The ORF had no significant sequence homology to known genes, although homology was recently observed between the N-terminus of PthG and a protein from a pathogenicity island of *Ralstonia solanacearum* (64). In *Ehg*, PthG acts as a virulence factor in gypsophila and as an elicitor of HR in beet. Mobilizing *pthG* into the beet pathovar *in trans* caused it to elicit an HR response in beet, and thereby prevented gall formation. The *Ehb* transconjugants retained full pathogenicity on gypsophila (Table 1). Most interestingly, marker exchange of a *pthG* mutation into *Ehg* caused the gypsophila pathovar to extend its host range and induce galls on beet while substantially reducing gall formation on gypsophila (Table 1). Mobilization of the mutated *pthG* into *Ehb in trans* did not prevent gall formation by the beet pathovar. Neither the *Ehg* mutant nor the *Ehb* transconjugants lost their ability to induce HR on tobacco plants. PthG is plant-induced and *hrp*-regulated (32). Its HR phenotype on beets is dependent on a functional type III secretion system and metabolically active plant and bacterial cells (30). In contrast to *avr* genes, the HR induction by PthG in beet is not cultivar-specific and is expressed by several different varieties of *Beta vulgaris* (30).

Injection of purified PthG protein into beet leaves did not elicit a HR, which suggests that this effector acts within the host cell rather than through the cell membrane. This hypothesis was confirmed by biolistically cobombarding beet leaves with plasmids expressing the beta-glucuronidase (GUS) gene and *pthG.* A significant reduction in GUS expression within 48 hr was indicative of cell death caused by PthG (30). Similarly to the case of HsvG, it was demonstrated that the type III secretion system of EPEC could recognize PthG for both secretion into the medium and translocation into HeLa cells. The MATCHMAKER LexA Two-Hybrid System (Clontech) was used to identify binding proteins for PthG in a cDNA library of gypsophila. Preliminary results suggest interactions of PthG with proteins homologous to serine/ threonine-specific kinase-like proteins from *Arabidopsis thaliana* (accessions NP 190906 and NP 200394) (30). It is noteworthy that the first R gene to be cloned was *Pto*, which encodes a kinase (83).

DspAE/BF is an operon isolated from the pPATH$_{Ehg}$ (86). It was first discovered in *E. amylovora* and was shown to be homologous to *avrE* of *P. syringae* (8, 39). The *dspAE* and *dspBF* ORFs were 5.5 and 0.38-kb respectively, encoding predicted proteins of 201.2 and 13.7-kDa respectively (86). A potential "*hrp* box" promotor was identified upstream of the operon. The percentage identities of the amino acid of DspAE with those of *E. amylovora* and *P. stewartii* subsp. *stewartii* were 61 and 75%, respectively, whereas DspBF exhibited 65.3% identity with both bacteria (86). Mutations in *dspAE* abolished pathogenicity of *Ehg* on gypsophila but not HR elicitation on tobacco. The transcription of *dspAE* is *hrp*-regulated and the secretion of DspAE protein is dependent on a functional type III system (86). DspBF is assumed to be a specific chaperon of DspAE that is required for type III secretion.

AvrPphD$_{Ehg}$ has been isolated from the flanking region of the *hrp* gene cluster in pPATH$_{Ehg}$ (45). It is located within the cluster of IS elements characterized in this DNA region (Fig. 2). *avrPphD* was originally isolated from *Pseudomonas syringae* pv. *phaseolicola* and is widely distributed among various pathovars of *P. syringae* (6). In *Ehg*, *avrPphD* contains an ORF of 2121 bp as compared to 2130 bp in *P. syringae* pv. *phaseolicola*. The two genes exhibit 91.9% similarity in base pairs and 81% similarity in amino acids. In addition, the G+C content of the gene in *Ehg* is 52.6% as compared to 55% of *P. syringae* pv. *phaseolicola* (6). Insertional mutagenesis of *avrPphD*$_{Ehg}$ with a Km resistance cassette, reduced the gall size in gypsophila cuttings by approximately 85% (45). This gene has also been detected in pPATH$_{Ehb}$ of the beet pathovar and the two ORFs share 95% homology.

Host Specificity of *Ehg* and *Ehb*

Two concepts, which are not necessarily mutually exclusive, have been proposed to determine host specificity at plant species level in Gram-negative phytopathogenic bacteria. The first is based on *avr* genes that restrict host range by eliciting the HR response in plants that carry the corresponding R genes (25, 65). This view gained some support from the demonstration that single cloned *avr* genes from a pathogen of one host species can cause an otherwise virulent pathogen of another host species to become avirulent on its own host (24, 61, 126, 127). Thus, the possibility has been suggested, that heterologous *avr* genes not only limit the bacterial host range within the host plant species but that many are also genetically dominant determinants in limiting the host range of phytopathogenic bacteria on multiple plant species (25, 57). An alternative view of host range determination, based on positive-functioning *hsv* (**h**ost-**s**pecific **v**irulence) genes has been proposed (36). This notion was inferred from the primary function of positive-acting, host specific *nod* genes of *Rhizobium* (72) and from the argument that the role of *avr* genes in nonhost incompatibility is generally gratuitous, so that they may not be suitable to evolve as primary determinants of host specificity (35, 123). The fact that avirulence is superimposed on the basic capacity of a bacterium to become a pathogen and that host specificity determined by *avr* genes is generally restricted to the cultivar level rather than to the species or genus level further support this view. However, evidence supporting the role of positive-acting virulence genes in host range determination of plant pathogenic bacteria has been very limited (75, 102, 110, 123) and, with the exception of *pthA* from *Xanthomonas citri* (111), none of these putative *hsv* genes have been isolated and characterized. Similar to *hsvG*, *pthA* of *X. citri* is a positive-acting Hrp-dependent gene that determines host specificity at the plant species level (110). However, there are major differences between the two genes. Expression of *pthA* in citrus cells was sufficient to elicit the entire set of symptoms of Asiatic citrus canker (29). In contrast to *pthA*, *hsvG* seems to act in concert with other Dsp virulence effectors, such as PthG and DspAE (31, 86) to elicit gall formation in gypsophila. Moreover, *pthA* belongs to the *avrBs3* gene family and confers cultivar-specific avirulence when introduced into other *Xanthomonas* pathovars (111). No similar pleiotropic action has yet been detected with *hsvG*.

It is noteworthy that in *Rhizobium* and, to a lesser extent, *Agrobacterium*, host specificity is mediated by plant signals that activate regulatory genes implicated in virulence. In the case of *Rhizobium*, specific flavonoids exuded by the host roots and interacting with NodD represent the first level of host-specific recognition (72). In *Agrobacterium* the VirA/VirG two-component system controls the sensing and perception of plant signal molecules and the expression of *vir* genes (113): VirA proteins from different *Agrobacterium* strains seem to prefer different phenolic compounds. The differential affinity of the VirA/VirG to plant signals produced by various hosts may influence host specificity (27). A similar phenomenon has not been observed in *Ehg* or any other phytopathogenic bacteria. In Gram-negative plant pathogenic bacteria, the *hrp* genes are analogous to the *nod* genes of *Rhizobium* or *vir* genes of *Agrobacterium*. As pointed out above, induction of *hsvG* transcription is *hrp*-regulated but nonhost-specific. These results are consistent with other reports, which indicate that inducing media for transcriptional activation of *avr* and *hrp* genes from different bacteria have similar compositions (2, 119). Thus, although a functional *hrp* gene cluster is mandatory for *hsvG* expression, the possibility that host specificity of *Ehg* or any other plant pathogenic bacteria is governed by regulation of the *hrp*/type III system can be ruled out. Another potential mechanism for host specificity could be based on the translocation of virulence effectors into host cells. It has recently been demonstrated that the Hrp pilus, which is composed of pilin proteins, is required for type III secretion and the translocation of Hrp and Avr proteins in *P. syringae* pv. *tomato* and *Erwinia amylovora*, as well as other phytopathogenic bacteria (54, 100, 124). However, the possibility that Hrp pilus may play a role in host specificity of phytopathogenic bacteria could be excluded (100).

Since neither the *hrp* regulon nor the translocation of the virulence effector is involved in host-specificity, we postulate that the general model proposed for R gene-mediated recognition of Avr proteins (see, e.g., 26, 63) is also applicable to host-specific virulence effectors. Thus the host specificity of *Ehg* must be determined by specific interaction of the HsvG protein with intracellular plant target(s) of gypsophila. Our working model for HsvG therefore assumes its injection into the gypsophila cell via the type III system, where it may be directly or indirectly recognized by either a host-specific protein or DNA sequences. The former interaction may trigger a signal transduction pathway that culminates in the activation or suppression of host genes that are necessary for the transformation of the plant into a susceptible host, and the consequent elicitation of symptoms. The recognition process between type III effectors and R genes inside the host cell is complex and is most likely not a simple receptor-ligand interaction (90). Although no recognizable domains, such as nuclear localization sequences, (NLSs) or transcriptional activators (63, 135), could be identified in the HsvG protein, the possibility that it might enter the nucleus or act directly on the DNA cannot be entirely excluded. It can also be speculated that disease development is initiated by several host-specific virulence genes and nonhost-specific *dsp* genes, acting in concert, rather than by a single host-specific gene (such as *pthA*) that was sufficient to cause Asiatic citrus canker (111) or an *avr* gene that was sufficient to elicit HR on a host cultivar containing the corresponding R gene. In relation to the latter example, it is noteworthy that the repeat domain of the *avrBs3* family of *Xanthomonas campestris* determines host specificity of avirulence/virulence, albeit at the cultivar but not the species level (12). We further speculate that nonhost-specific virulence genes, such as *dspAE*, are superimposed on the host-specific virulence genes, although both are required for full disease expression. The extremely small number of characterized *hrp*-dependent *hsv* genes, as compared with a few nonhost-specific *dsp* genes and numerous *avr* genes, may reflect the difficulties involved in their detection. Identification of *hsv* genes requires a pathogen with simultaneous pathogenicity on two different hosts, and screening of mutants for a loss of pathogenicity on only one host.

The differential host range of *Ehg* and *Ehb* (Table 1) can be examined in the light of two alternative hypotheses: (i) that host specificity is determined exclusively by positive-acting host-specific virulence *(hsv)* genes, in which case *Ehg* should carry only *hsvG* whereas *Ehb* should carry both *hsvG* and a presumed equivalent *hsv* gene that determines host specificity on beet namely, "*hsvB*" (*hsv* gene on **b**eet); and (ii) that host specificity is determined by interaction between positive-acting and negative-acting genes. In this case both pathovars should carry both *hsvG* and "*hsvB*", whereas *Ehg* also carrying a gene encoding an HR elicitor of beet that precludes the expression of "*hsvB*" and pathogenicity. Our findings support the second hypothesis and suggests that "*hsvB*" might be present in both pathovars, since the marker-exchange mutant of *Ehg* in *pthG* became pathogenic on beet (Table 1). Thus, the presence of PthG protein in *Ehg* is the only factor that prevents this pathovar from eliciting galls in beet.

On the basis of the present findings, we propose that *Ehg* and *Ehb* originated from a common ancestor that exhibited pathogenicity on both beet and gypsophila. Recognition of one of the virulence genes (i.e., *pthG*) by the beet defense gene surveillance system caused a hypersensitive response that prevented pathogenicity on beet and resulted in the evolution of the current gypsophila pathovar. The beet pathovar may have evolved from the gypsophila pathovar by evading the beet defense response. The latter assumption is supported by the presence of a modified and partially deleted *pthG* gene in *Ehb* (31). Alternative gene(s) presumably replaced the role of *pthG* in pathogenicity of *Ehb* on gypsophila. Thus, although both pathovars elicit galls on gypsophila they may not necessarily carry identical genes for pathogenicity on this host. This supposition is supported by the differing morphologies of galls induced by the two pathovars on gypsophila (16).

Hrp-Independent Pathogenicity Genes

The contribution of the phytohormones indole-3-acetic acid (IAA) and cytokinins in gall formation by *Ehg* was investigated by characterizing the genes encoding their biosynthetic pathways and evaluating their roles in pathogenicity by mutational analysis.

IAA BIOSYNTHESIS AND REGULATION

Pathogenic and nonpathogenic strains of *E. herbicola* produce similar amounts of IAA in culture (79), in contrast to *P. syringae* pv. *savastanoi*, in which the accumulation of IAA in culture was correlated with virulence on oleander (105). This finding prompted us to investigate the biochemical routes for IAA production in *Ehg*. Two major pathways for IAA biosynthesis from tryptophan were characterized (82): (i) the indole-3-acetamide (IAM) route, namely, L-tryptophan → IAM → IAA and (ii) the indole-3-pyruvate (IPyA) route namely, L-tryptophan → IPyA → indole-3-acetaldehyde → IAA. However, in contrast to the IPyA pathway, which was present in pathogenic as well as nonpathogenic strains, the IAM pathway was detected exclusively in pathogenic strains and was located on the $pPATH_{Ehg}$ (Fig. 2). The two genes of the IAM pathway, tryptophan-2-monooxygenase (*iaaM*) and IAM hydrolase (*iaaH*) constitute an operon (18, 37). Sequence analysis and expression of the genes in minicell-producing *E. coli* indicated that *iaaM* and *iaaH* encode proteins of 62 and 49 kDa, respectively. Both genes show moderate to high homology with IAA synthesis genes of *A. tumefaciens* and *P. syringae* pv. *savastanoi* (37). The gene encoding IPyA decarboxylase (*ipdC*), the key enzyme of the IPyA pathway, was isolated and characterized in a nonpathogenic strain of *E. herbicola* (14).

The regulation of the IAA biosynthetic pathways was studied by using the *inaZ* ice nucleation reporter gene (73). The apparent transcriptional activity of *iaaM-inaZ* fusion increased slightly in cells of *Ehg* grown on bean (non-host) and gypsophila leaves, compared with that in culture, whereas very high levels of induction were observed in cells injected into gypsophila stems (80). In contrast, a moderate increase in the level of *ipdC* transcription was observed in both bean and gypsophila leaves as well as in gypsophila stems, compared with the level in culture. In addition, the level of transcription of *iaaM* gene within stems was apparently much higher than that of *ipdC* in cells of *Ehg* in any habitat (80). These results suggest that the IAM pathway is primarily adapted to function in the plant apoplast, in contrast to the regulation of the IPyA pathway, which exhibits a considerably lower induction by the plant and does not show preferential adaptation to any plant microenvironment.

CYTOKININ BIOSYNTHESIS AND REGULATION

Production of cytokinins in culture was detected only in pathogenic strains of *E. herbicola*. Zeatin, zeatin riboside, *iso*-pentenyladenine, and two immunoreactive zeatin-type compounds were the predominant cytokinins identified in the supernatant (66). An operon conferring cytokinin production has been shown to reside on $pPATH_{Ehg}$, in a cluster with the genes that specify IAA biosynthesis (Fig. 2). This operon consists of two genes: the first ORF (pre-*etz*) is of unknown function (encodes for 169 aa) whereas the second one (*etz*) encodes isopentenyl transferase (237 aa)(67). Northern hybridization performed with the wild-type strain grown in LB broth revealed two transcripts, of which an *etz*-specific transcript (0.8-kb) was predominant (44). Upstream DNA fragments of either pre-*etz* or *etz* fused to the ice nucleation reporter gene *inaZ* increased the transcriptional activity of the transconjugants by 4.5 orders of magnitude, as compared with promoter-less *inaZ,* confirming the presence of two promoters (44). Interestingly, sequence analysis of the operon revealed two putative promoters (44): an IHF-like promoter (41) upstream to pre-*etz* and a CAP/CRP-like promoter (112) upstream to *etz.*

Transcription from both promoters was similarly induced when the transconjugants were introduced into stem cuttings of gypsophila or bean, or were applied on the leaf surfaces of these plants (44). These results suggest that the cytokinin biosynthetic genes are plant-induced but, in contrast to the IAM pathway, no particular adaptation to the plant apoplast could be detected.

THE ROLES OF IAA AND CYTOKININS IN GALL FORMATION AND EPIPHYTIC FITNESS OF *Ehg*

Insertional mutations in *iaaM* and *iaaH* caused a reduction in gall size but did not affect production of IAA in culture (18). A major finding of our study was the demonstration of differential contribution of the IAM and IPyA pathways to both pathogenicity and epiphytic fitness (80). While inactivation of the IAM pathway reduced gall formation by approximately 40%, little effect was observed when IPyA was inactivated (Table 2). In contrast, the epiphytic bacterial population was about 14 times smaller than that of the wild-type strain when the IPyA pathway was disrupted, whereas no change in epiphytic fitness was observed when the IAM pathway was disrupted (80). These results are in accordance with the calculation that the apparent level of transcription of *iaaM* in cells on leaves is, at most, only about 3% of that in cells in stems (80). In contrast, the transcription of *ipdC* is similar in *Ehg*, both within and on plants, suggesting that IAA from the IPyA pathway is more abundant on leaves than that from the IAM pathway. The positive effect of the IPyA route on epiphytic fitness has been reported previously (15). Although the IAM pathway has been occasionally detected in higher plants (see, e.g., 56), it is generally considered to be a microbial IAA biosynthetic route (97). It has been postulated that the IPyA pathway, which is commonly distributed in higher plants, is under stringent regulation in *Ehg* to control the IAA supply (82). By utilizing the IAM pathway, which can be up regulated in the site of infection, the pathogen can accumulate the large amounts of IAA necessary for gall development. The presence of the IAM pathway in other gall-forming bacteria (134) supports its important role in the pathogenicity of these bacteria.

A marker-exchanged mutant of *etz*, which did not produce cytokinins, exhibited a reduction in gall size on gypsophila cuttings (Table 2) (67). Insertional mutation or a frameshift (non-polar) mutation in pre-*etz* resulted in a sharp decrease in the level of cytokinin production and a reduction in virulence, but to a lesser extent than that of the *etz* mutation. It is noteworthy that the finding that *etz* was preceded by pre-*etz,* which affects its expression, is unique and has not been reported for any other cytokinin biosynthetic genes. The prevalence of the two ORFs in *Ehb* (67) also suggests that this locus evolved prior to host specialization by the gypsophila and beet pathovars. Cytokinin overproduction, obtained by

Table 2. Effects of inactivation of the pathways for IAA and cytokinin biosynthesis on the pathogenicity and epiphytic fitness of *Erwinia herbicola* pv. *Gypsophilae*

Strain/mutant	Genotype	Pathogenicity (gall size)[a]	Epiphytic Fitness[c]
*Ehg*824-1	Wild type	100 a[b]	+
*Ehg*824-1MX119	*ipdC*	84 a	-
*Ehg*824-1MX54	*iaaH*	63 b	+
*Ehg*824-1MX16	*iaaH, ipdC*	59 b	-
*Ehg*824-1MX37	*etz*	53 b	+
*Ehg*824-1MX211	*iaaM, iaaH, etz*	53 b	+
*Ehg*824-1MX132	*iaaM, iaaH, etz, ipdC*	49 b	-

[a] Pathogenicity was determined on gypsophila cuttings by measuring gall size (79). Results are presented as percentages of the size measured on a wild type strain.

[b] Means followed by the same letter do not differ significantly from one another according to Duncan's new multiple range test.

[c] Epiphytic fitness was determined on bean leaves as described in (80). (+) indicates no effect; (-) represents a significant reduction.

introducing the *etz* gene on a multicopy plasmid (67), resulted in larger galls and emergence of shoots, as described for the *tms* locus of *A. tumefaciens* (88). Disruption of cytokinin biosynthesis has no effect on epiphytic fitness (Table 2)(80). Furthermore, a mutant having simultaneous disruptions of IAA by the two IAA pathways and by cytokinin production (*etz, iaaM, iaaH, ipdC*) caused slightly less galling than mutants deficient in cytokinin and in IAA production via the IAM pathway (Table 2). The latter mutant exhibited the same effect on epiphytic fitness as the *ipdC* mutant (80).

The finding that simultaneous inactivation of the two IAA pathways and cytokinin biosynthesis caused substantial reduction in gall size but did not eliminate gall initiation is supported by the observation that mutations in *hrp* genes encoding for the type III system or for regulatory proteins completely eliminated gall formation (86, 91). Since the transcription of the phytohormones genes is not *hrp*-regulated (44, and unpublished results) it may be concluded that gall initiation by *Ehg* or *Ehb* apparently occurs via translocation of type III effectors into the host cells.

In contrast to *Ehg*, IAA and cytokinin biosynthetic genes in cooperation with other oncogenes on the T-DNA are responsible for gall initiation and development by *Agrobacterium* (7). The latter phenomenon might occur because the intracellular expression of the phytohormone genes results in higher levels of endogenous auxin and cytokinin together with the possible effect of the other oncogenes on either the metabolism of plant hormones or the response of plant cells to those hormones (7). Although both IAA and cytokinin contribute significantly to gall development by *P. syringae* pv. *savastanoi* (23, 134), their contribution to gall initiation is not conclusively proved. Since this pathogen appears to possess *hrp* cluster (Nizan *et al.*, unpublished), it would be of interest to determine whether gall formation is *hrp*-dependent. The latter study, together with a rigid mutation analysis of the pathways involved in IAA and cytokinin biosynthesis might resolve this question.

The Presence of IS Elements and a Pathogenicity Island on the pPATH$_{Ehg}$

Several IS elements of different families have been identified on pPATH$_{Ehg}$. IS*1327,* which belongs to the IS*6* family, was the first IS of this family to be characterized in phytopathogenic bacteria (69). Southern blot analysis of plasmid DNA of *Ehg* and *Ehb* revealed the presence of six copies of this insertion element in the gypsophila pathovar and four copies in the beet pathovar. In *Ehg*824-1 the six copies of IS*1327* element were located exclusively on pPATH$_{Ehg}$ (69, and unpublished results). An additional four IS elements, designated as ISEhe*1, 2*, *3* and *4*, have been located on the flanking regions of the *hrpJ* operon (Fig. 2) (45). Two copies of another IS element (ISEhe*5*) have been identified in the upstream region of the IAA operon. Homology of amino acids and conserved domains indicates that ISEhe*1* (accession no. AF32676) belongs to the IS*630* family, ISEhe*2* (accession no. AF327444) to the IS*5* family, ISEhe*3* (accession no. AF327445) and ISEhe*4* (accession no. AF324174) to two different groups of the IS*3* family, and ISEhe*5* (accession no. AF327446) to the IS*1* family (45). With the exception of ISEhe*4*, one to three copies of all the above IS elements were exclusively identified in pathogenic strains of *Ehg* and *Ehb*, which suggests that they might be associated with the plasmid evolution of pPATH. In contrast, ISEhe*4* was present in pathogenic as well as nonpathogenic strains and might not necessarily be involved in the formation of a pathogenicity plasmid.

The apparent specificity of IS*1327* and ISEhe*1*, *2*, *3* and *5* to the pPATH could have resulted from their inability to transpose to other plasmids or to the chromosomal DNA. Alternatively, these IS elements may have been actively distributed on pPATH prior to its acquisition by *E. herbicola*, in which they then became inactive. At present we do not have evidence to support current transposition of these IS elements, although copies of IS*1327* have been transcribed and the size of the transcripts can accommodate the putative transposase (69). Detailed research would be required to determine whether the observed polymorphism between the gypsophila and beet pathovars, which is manifested in fragment size in the case of IS*1327* and in copy number in the cases of IS*1327* and the other IS elements, could result from active transposition, or rearrangements of plasmids, after divergence of the pathovars. Nevertheless, the hypothesis of a common origin of pPATH in the two pathovars is supported by the presence of these IS elements on the pPATH in both pathovars, as well as by the apparent conservation of the *hrp*-gene cluster and *dspAE/BF* (Mor *et al*., unpublished), of the phytohormone gene cluster (67) and of the virulence genes *hsvG* (116) and $avrPphD_{Ehg}$. Analyses of the homology and organization of the various genes in the T-DNA, including *iaaM*, *iaaH* and *ipt*, suggested that they may have a common origin with those of other bacteria, e.g., *P. syringae* pv. *savastanoi*, by horizontal gene transfer by means of IS elements. The IAA biosynthetic genes of *P. syringae* pv. *savastano*i have been found to undergo insertions and deletions involving IS*51*, IS*52*,and IS*53* (106, 133). Thus, IS elements could mediate genomic rearrangements that would lead to the evolution of new plasmids that affect bacterial pathogenicity.

Studies of the mechanisms of bacterial pathogenesis have demonstrated associations between ISs and many pathogenic and virulence functions. Such an association has been observed in animal pathogens, e.g., *Bacillus* (77), *Yersinia* (33, 43), *Escherichia* (50) and *Vibrio* (109); plant pathogens, e.g., *Agrobacterium* (95) and *Pseudomonas* (133); and symbionts, e.g., *Rhizobium* (34). The phenomenon in which several different IS elements are clustered in "islands" within plasmid genomes has also been often observed (76) and may serve to promote plasmid integration, excision and other rearrangements.

During recent years the concept of pathogenicity islands (PAIs) has emerged to describe genomic regions of pathogens, which carry virulence genes together with loci whose presence strongly indicates horizontal gene transfer between different species or even genera (47). According to Hacker et al. (46) the major criteria for defining a PAI include: (i) carriage of (often many) virulence genes; (ii) presence in genomes of pathogenic organisms but not in genomes of nonpathogenic organisms of the same or closely related species; (iii) G+C content that differs from that of the DNA of host bacteria; (iv) occupation of large genomic regions; (v) presence of (often cryptic) 'mobility' genes (IS elements, integrases, transposases, origins of plasmid replication); (vi) association with tRNA genes and/or IS elements at their boundaries; (vii) representation of compact, distinct genetic units, often flanked by direct repeats; and (viii) instability. The original definition of the PAIs included chromosomal location (46). However, the increasing availability of sequence data for virulence plasmids supports the view that parts of virulence plasmids can also be considered as PAIs (47). Thus, plasmid-borne PAIs in animal and plant pathogenic bacteria have already been described (52, 53, 96 129).

Current data on the location and nature of the virulence genes and mobile elements present on pPATH$_{Ehg}$ satisfy the major criteria for a PAI and unequivocally support its presence on this plasmid. Our hypothesis that additional genetic loci associated with virulence remain to be discovered prevents delimitation of the PAI on pPATH$_{Ehg}$. However, it should be noted that all the virulence genes that have so far been characterized on pPATH$_{Ehg}$ reside on three consecutive overlapping cosmids (i.e., pLA244, pLA352 and pLA150) that occupy approximately 55-kb of the plasmid. The pPATH$_{Ehg}$-borne PAI (Fig. 2) contains the *hrp/hrc* gene cluster, a cluster of IAA and cytokinin biosynthetic genes, genes encoding type III virulence effectors (i.e., *hsvG, pthG, dspAE/BF, avrPphD*$_{Ehg}$) and a cluster of IS elements as well as scattered ones. In addition, remnants of known genes from *Yersinia pestis, Xylella fastidiosa, Actinobacillus pleuropneumoniae* and *E. coli* were detected on the same cosmid (45). Additional support for the foreign nature of the genes that constitute the PAI derives from their G+C contents. The characteristic G+C content of *E. herbicola* (*P. agglomerans*) was found to range from 55.1 to 56.8-mol% (40, 84). Comparison of these values with the G+C contents of the virulence-associated loci on the pPATH$_{Ehg}$ clearly demonstrates a significant deviation from the species-distinctive values (Table 3). The presence of a type III secretion system on the pPATH$_{Ehg}$ (as a constituent of the *hrp* gene cluster (86) reinforces the identification of a PAI on this plasmid. Type III secretion systems have been shown to act as an essential component in many PAIs of Gram-negative animal and plant pathogenic bacteria (reviewed by Galan and Collmer, 38 and Hueck, 51). Thus, the presence of a PAI on the pPATH$_{Ehg}$ appears to be well established.

Concluding Remarks

The pathogenicity island characterized on the plasmid pPATH$_{Ehg}$ strongly suggests that *Ehg* is a recently evolved pathogen, and provides a unique model for understanding the "switch" from an epiphyte into a biotrophic pathogen. It is quite plausible that traits that confer pathogenicity on gypsophila have been acquired by horizontal transfer of gene clusters through one or several steps rather than by slow adaptive evolution. The pathogenicity traits are superimposed on others that confer epiphytic fitness; a situation which causes *Ehg* to be well adapted for living both on plant surfaces and within the apoplast of its host. Although we have made substantial progress in our current study, we are still at the

Table 3: The G+C content of genes and IS elements present on the $pPATH_{Ehg}$

Gene/IS element	G+C content (%)[a]	Function
iaaM	50.3	IAA biosynthesis
iaaH	52.8	IAA biosynthesis
pre-*etz*	34.8	Cytokinin biosynthesis
etz	41.3	Cytokinin biosynthesis
hsvG	65.4	Pathogenicity and host-specificity
pthG	51.6	Pathogenicity and HR elicitation
dspEF	49.9	Pathogenicity
avrPphD	52.6	Pathogenicity
hrpL	47.7	Hrp regulation
hrpS	52.9	Hrp regulation
hrpXY	49.1	Hrp regulation
hrpN	53.0	Harpin
hrpJ	52.0	Type III secretion system
hrcC	50.4	Type III secretion system
hrpG	44.8	Type III secretion system
hrpF	48.0	Type III secretion system
hrpB+hrcG	47.8	Type III secretion system
ISEh*1*	49.2	IS element (IS*630* family)
ISEh2	51.2	IS element (IS*5* family)
ISEh*3*	47.7	IS element (IS*3* family)
ISEh*4*	53.9	IS element (IS*3* family)
ISEh*5*	43.9	IS element (IS*1* family)
IS*1327*	50.4	IS element (IS6 family)

[a] The characteristic G+C content of *E. herbicola* (*P. agglomerans*) is 55.1-56.8-mol% (40).

beginning stages of understanding the molecular mechanisms for host specificity and virulence of *Ehg* and many open questions remain to be addressed. For example, a) What is the complete inventory of virulence type III effectors delivered into plant cells by *Ehg* that is necessary to transform this epiphyte into a pathogen? b) Are the genes encoding for these effectors located mainly on $pPATH_{Ehg}$, or have many been mobilized into the chromosome? c) How these effectors interact with intracellular plant components to convert it into a susceptible host and induced symptom production? d) What is the share of *hrp*-independent virulence genes in pathogenicity of *Ehg*?

A significant outcome of our studies is the isolation and characterization of *hsvG* as a primary determinant of host specificity on gypsophila in both *Ehg* and *Ehb*. We hypothesize that *hsv* genes may operate as primary factors in host specificity of other Gram-negative plant pathogenic bacteria. Characterization of such additional genes is necessary for proving this hypothesis and understanding the nature of host specificity at the species or genus level. An immediate challenge is the isolation of the presumed *hsvB* gene that determines host specificity on beet and is expected to be present in both the beet and the gypsophila pathovars (31). However, as found with other plant-associated bacteria, determination of host specificity is a complex phenomenon, in which several factors might be involved (27, 72). Thus, for example, host specificity of *Ehg* on gypsophila is determined by interplay between positive-acting (HsvG) and negative-acting (PthG) effectors, although the latter is superimposed on the former. The finding that PthG is the only HR elicitor that prevents *Ehg* from infecting beet and thus expands its host range is unique. It should be further investigated in order to determine whether PthG interacts with a species-specific intracellular component as opposed to Avr proteins that interact with a corresponding cultivar-specific R gene product.

An interesting finding is the differential role of the two IAA biosynthetic pathways in pathogenicity and epiphytic fitness. Although epiphytic *E. herbicola* contains a chromosomal IAA pathway (IPyA), an additional pathway (IAM) on a plasmid was acquired during its conversion into a pathogen. This pathway allows an excessive production of IAA in the apoplast by presumably avoiding any restrictive regulation by the plant.

The findings that *hrp* mutants completely abolished gall formation (91) and that simultaneous inactivation of all the pathways for IAA and cytokinin biosynthesis reduced the size of galls but did not eliminate their development (80) clearly indicate that type III effectors are involved with gall initiation by *Ehg*. The latter observation could suggest that growth regulators synthesized by the plant in response to elicitation are responsible for initiation of the hyperplasia and hypertrophy involved in gall initiation. Elucidation of the chemical nature of these factors could lead to the discovery of a new class of growth regulators regulated by the host plant. Alternatively, the introduced type III effectors may alter the sensitivity of the plant cells to endogenous regulators.

The pathogenicity of *Ehg* and *Ehb* depends on the presence of similar but not identical plasmids (i.e., $pPATH_{Ehg}$ and $pPATH_{Ehb}$). We speculate that the two pathovars have diverged from a common ancestor by adopting different paths during their interaction with the host plants (31). Thus, it would be interesting to compare the virulence effectors of the two pathovars and to find out to what extent similar functions in virulence might be performed by different genes. Furthermore, molecular analyses of pathogenicity determinants in pathovars that are virulent on cranberry, wisteria and Douglas fir will facilitate the evaluation of their evolutionary divergence.

Acknowledgments

Our work was supported by research grants from BARD, the US-Israel Binational Agricultural Research and Development Fund (US-2063-91C, US-2505-94, US-2816-96), and by the DFG program for Trilateral Cooperation between Palestine, Israel and Germany (EI 1440/11-1).

References

1. Aldridge P, Hughes K T (2001) How and when are substrates selected for type III secretion? Trends in Microbiology 9:209-214.
2. Alfano J R, Collmer A (1996) Bacterial pathogens in plants: life up against the wall. Plant Cell 8:1683-1698.
3. Alfano J R, Collmer A (1997) The type III (Hrp) secretion pathway of plant pathogenic bacteria: trafficking harpins, Avr proteins, and death. J. Bacteriol. 179:5655-5662.
4. Anderson D M, Fouts D E, Collmer A, Schneewind O (1999) Reciprocal secretion of proteins by the bacterial type III machines of plant and animal pathogens suggests universal recognition of mRNA targeting signals. Proc. Natl. Acad. Sci. USA 96:12839-12843.
5. Anderson D M, Schneewind O (1997) A mRNA signal for the type III secretion of Yop proteins by *Yesinia enterocolitica.* Science 278:1140-1143.
6. Arnold D L, Gibbon M J, Jackson R W, Wood JR, Brown J, Mansfield J W, Taylor J D, Vivian A (2001) Molecular characterization of *avrPphD*, a widely-distributed gene from *Pseudomonas syringae* pv. *phaseolicola* involved in non-host recognition by pea (*Pisum sativum*). Pysiol. Mol. Plant Pathol. 58:55-62.
7. Binns AN, Costantino P (1998) The *Agrobacterium* oncogenes. In: The *Rhizobiaceae*, molecular biology of model plant-associated bacteria. H. P. Spaink, A. Kondorosi, and P. J. J. Hooykaas (ed.), Kluwer Academic Publisher, Dordrecht / Boston / London.
8. Bogdanove A, Bauer D W, Beer S V (1998) *Erwinia amylovora* secretes DspE, a pathogenicity factor, and functional AvrE homolog through the Hrp (type III secretion) pathway. J. Bacteriol. 180:2244-2247.
9. Bogdanove A J, Beer S V, Bonas U, Boucher C A, Collmer A, Coplin D L, Cornelis G R, Hunang H C, Hutcheson S W, Panopoulos N J, Van-Gijsegem F (1996a) Unified nomenclature

for broadly conserved hrp genes of phytopathogenic bacteria. Mol. Microbiol. 20:681-683.

10. Bogdanove A J, Wei Z M, Zhao L, Beer S V (1996) *Erwinia amylovora* secretes harpin via a type III pathway and contains a homolog of *yop*N of *Yersinia*. J. Bacteriol. 178:1720-1730.
11. Bonas U (1994) *hrp* genes of phytopathogenic bacteria. Curr. Top. Microbiol. Immunol. 192:79-98.
12. Bonas U, Van den Ackerveken G (1999) Gene-for-gene interactions: bacterial avirulence proteins specify plant disease resistance. Curr. Op. Microbiol. 2:94-98.
13. Boucher C A, Van Gijsegem F, Barberis P A, Arlat M, Zischek M (1987) *Pseudomonas solanacearum* gene controlling both pathogenicity and hypersensitivity on tobacco are clustered. J. Bacteriol. 169:5626-5632.
14. Brandl M T, Lindow SE (1996) Cloning and characterization of a locus encoding an indolepyruvate decarboxylase involved in indole-3-acetic acid synthesis in *Erwinia herbicola*. Appl. Environ. Microbiol. 62:4121-4128.
15. Brandl MT, Lindow SE (1997) Environmental signals modulate the expression of an indole-3-acetic acid biosynthetic gene in *Erwinia herbicola*. Mol. Plant-Microbe Interact. 10:499-505.
16. Burr TJ, Katz BH, Abawi GS, Crosier DC (1991) Comparison of tumorigenic strains of *Erwinia herbicola* isolated from table beet with *E. h. gypsophilae*. Plant Dis. 75:855-858.
17. Cheng, LW, Schneewind O (2000) Type III machines of gram-negative bacteria: delivering the goods. Trends in Microbiology 8:214-220.
18. Clark E, Manulis S, Ophir Y, Barash I, Gafni Y (1993) Cloning and characterization of *iaaM* and *iaaH* from *Erwinia herbicola* pathovar *gypsophilae*. Phytopathology 83:234-240.
19. Clark E, Vigodsky-Haas H, Gafni Y (1989) Characteristics in tissue culture of hyperplasias induced by *Erwinia herbicola* pathovar gypsophilae. Physiol. Mol. Plant Pathol. 35:383-390.
20. Cooksey DA (1986) Galls of *Gypsophila paniculata* caused by *Erwinia herbicola*. Plant Dis. 70:464-468.
21. Cornelis GR (1994) *Yersinia* pathogenicity factors. Curr. Top. Microbiol. Immunol. 192:243-263.
22. Cornelis GR (1998) The *Yersinia* death kiss. J. Bacteriol. 180:5495-5504.
23. Costacurta A, Vanderleyden J (1995) Synthesis of phytohormones by plant-associated bacteria. Crit. Rev. Microbiol. 21:1-18.
24. Dangl J (1992) The major histocompatibility complex a la carte: are there analogies to plant disease resistance genes on the menu? Plant J. 2:3-11.

25. Dangl JL (1994) The enigmatic avirulence genes of phytopathogenic bacteria. Curr. Top. Microbiol. Immunol.192:99-118.

26. Dangl JL, Jones JDG (2001) Plant pathogens and integrated defense response to infection. Nature 411:826-833.

27. Deng W, Nester EW (1998) Determinants of host specificity of *Agrobacterium* and their function. In: The *Rhizobiaceae*, molecular biology of model plant-associated bacteria. H. P. Spaink, A. Kondorosi, and P. J. J. Hooykaas (ed.). Kluwer Academic Publisher, Dordrecht / Boston / London.

28. DeYoung R M, Copeman R J, Hunt R S (1998) Two strains in the genus *Erwinia* cause galls on Douglas-fir in southwestern British Columbia. Can. J. Plant Pathol. 20:194-200.

29. Duan Y P, Castaneda A, Zhao G, Erdos G W, Gabriel DW (1999). Expression of a single host-specific bacterial pathogenicity gene in citrus cells elicits division, enlargement and cell death. Mol. Plant-Microbe Interact. 12:556-560.

30. Ezra D (2002) The dual function in virulence and host range restriction of *pthG*, a gene isolated from the $pPATH_{Ehg}$ plasmid of *Erwinia herbicola* pv. *gypsophilae*. Ph.D. Thesis, Tel-Aviv University.

31. Ezra D, Barash I, Valinsky L, Manulis S (2000) The dual function in virulence and host range restriction of a gene isolated from $pPATH_{Ehg}$ plasmid of *Erwinia herbicola* pv. *gypsophilae*. Mol. Plant-Microbe Interact. 13:693-698.

32. Ezra D, Manulis S, Barash I (2000) Expression of *pthG*, a virulence protein of *Erwinia herbicola* pv. *gypsophilae* is *hrp* regulated and dependent on a functional type III secretion system. Phytopathology 90:S22.

33. Filippov AA, Oleinikov PN, Drozdov AV, Protsenko OA (1990) The role of IS-elements of *Yersinia pestis* (Lehmann, Neumann) in the emergence of calcium-independent mutations. Genetika 26:1740-1748.

34. Freiberg C, Fellay R, Bairoch A, Broughton WJ, Rosenthal A, Perret X (1997) Molecular basis of symbiosis between *Rhizobium* and legumes. Nature 387:397-401.

35. Gabriel D, Rolf B (1990) Working models of specific recognition in plant-microbe interactions. Annu. Rev. Phytopathol. 28:365-391.

36. Gabriel DW (1989) Genetics of plant parasite populations and host-parasite specificity. Pages 343-379 vol. 3. In: Plant Microbe Interactions- Molecular and Genetic Perspectives. T. Kosuge, and E W. Nester, eds. McGraw-Hill Publishing Company, New York.

37. Gafni Y, Manulis S, Kunik T, Lichter A, Barash I, Ophir Y (1997) Characterization of the auxin synthesis genes of *Erwinia herbicoola* pv. *gypsophilae.* Israel J. Plant Sci. 45:279-284.
38. Galan JE, Collmer A (1999) Type III secretion machines: bacterial devices for protein delivery into host cells. Science 284:1322-1328.
39. Gaudriault S, Malandrin L, Paulin J-P, Barny M-A (1997) DspA, an essential pathogenicity factor of *Erwinia amylovora* showing homology with AvrE of *Pseudomonas syringae*, is secreted via the Hrp secretion pathway in a DspB-dependent way. Mol. Microbiol. 26:1057-1069.
40. Gavini F, Mergaret J, Beji A, Mielcarek C, Izard D, Kersters K, De Ley J (1989) Transfer of *Enterobacter agglomerans* (Beijerinck 1888) Ewing and Fife 1972 to *Pantoea* gen.nov. as *Pantoea agglomerans* comb. nov. and description of *Pantoea dispersa* sp. nov. Int. J. Syst. Bacteriol. 39:337-345.
41. Giladi H, Gottesman M, Oppenheim AB (1990) Integration host factor stimulates the phage lambda pL promoter. J. Mol. Biol. 213:109-121.
42. Gopalan S, Bauer DW, Alfano JR, Loniello AO, He SY, Collmer A (1996) Expression of the *Pseudomonas syringae* avirulence protein AvrB in plant cells alleviates its dependence on the hypersensitive response and pathogenicity (Hrp) secretion system in eliciting genotype-specific hypersensitive cell death. Plant Cell 8:1095-1105.
43. Groisman EA, Ochman H (1996) Pathogenicity islands: bacterial evolution in quantum leaps. Cell 87:791-794.
44. Guo M, Manulis S, Barash I, Lichter A (2001) The operon for cytokinin biosynthesis of *Erwinia herbicola* pv. *gypsophilae* contains two promoters and is plant induced. Can. J. Microbiol. 47:1126-1131.
45. Guo M, Manulis S, Mor H, Barash I (2002) The presence of diverse IS elements and an *avrPphD* homologue that acts as a virulence factor on the pathogenicity plasmid of *Erwinia herbicola* pv. *gypsophilae*. Mol. Plant-Microbe Interact.15 (in press).
46. Hacker J, Blum-Oehler G, Muhldorfer I, Tschape H (1997) Pathogenicity islands of virulent bacteria: structure, function and impact on microbial evolution. Mol. Microbiol. 23:1089-1097.
47. Hacker J, Kaper JB (1999) The concept of pathogenicity islands. In: Pathogenicity islands and other mobile virulence elements. J. B. Kaper and J. Hacker, eds. ASM Press, Washington, D C.
48. Ham JH, Bauer DW, Fouts DE, Collmer A (1998) A cloned *Erwinia chrysanthemi hrp* (type III protein secretion) system functions in *Escherichia coli* to deliver *Pseudomonas syringae*

Avr signals to plant cells and to secrete Avr proteins in culture. Proc. Natl. Acad. Sci., USA 95:10206-10211.
49. Hattingh MJ, Walters DF (1981) Stalk and leaf necrosis of onion caused by *Erwinia herbicola*. Plant Dis. 65:615-618.
50. Hu ST, Lee CH (1988) Characterization of the transposon carrying the STII gene of enterotoxigenic *Escherichia coli*. Mol. Gen. Genet. 214:490-495.
51. Hueck HC (1998) Type III protein secretion systems in bacterial pathogens of animals and plants. Microbiol. Mol. Biol. Rev. 62:379-433.
52. Iriarte M, Cornelis GR (1999) The 70-kilobase virulence plasmid of *Yersiniae*. Pages 91-126. In: Pathogenicity islands and other mobile virulence elements. J. B. Kaper and J. Hacker,eds. ASM Press, Washington, D. C.
53. Jackson J F, Athanassopoulos E, Tsiamis G, Mansfield JW, Sesma A, Arnold DL, Gibbon M J, Murillo J, Taylor JD, Vivian A (1999) Identification of a pathogenicity island, which contains genes for virulence and avirulence, on a large native plasmid in the bean pathogen *Pseudomonas syringae* pathovar *phaseolicola*. Proc. Natl. Acad. Sci. USA 96:10875-10880.
54. Jin Q, Hu W, Brown I, McGhee G, Hart P, Jones A L, He S Y (2001) Visualization of secreted Hrp and Avr proteins along the Hrp pilus during type III secretion in *Erwinia amylovora* and *Pseudomonas syringae*. Mol. Microbiol. 40:1129-1139.
55. Kamiunten H (1999) Isolation and characterization of virulence gene *psvA* on a plasmid of *Pseudomonas syringae* pv. *eriobotryae*. Ann. Phytopathol. Soc. Jpn. 65:501-509.
56. Kawaguchi M, Fujioka S, Sakurai A, Yamaki YTR, Syono K (1993) Presence of a pathway for the biosynthesis of auxin via the indole-3-acetamide in trifolia orange. Plant Cell Physiol. 34:121-128.
57. Keen NT (1990) Gene-for-gene complementarity in plant pathogen interactions. Ann. Rev. Genet. 24:447-463.
58. Kim J F, Beer SV (1998) HrpW of *Erwinia amylovora*, a new harpin that contains a domain homologous to pectate lyases of a distinct class. J. Bacteriol. 180:5203-5210.
59. Kjemtrup S, Nimchuk Z, Dangl JL (2000) Effector proteins of phytopathogenic bacteria: bifunctional signals in virulence and host recognition. Curr. Op. Microbiol. 3:73-78.
60. Kobayashi DY, Palumbo JD (2000) Bacterial endophytes and their effects on plants and uses in agriculture. In: Microbial endophytes. C. W. Bacon and J. F. White, eds. Marcel Decker, Inc., New Brunswick, New Jersey.
61. Kobayashi DY, Tamaki S J, Keen NT (1989) Cloned avirulence genes from the tomato pathogen *Pseudomonas syringae* pv.

tomato confer cultivar specificity on soybean. Proc. Natl. Acad. Sci. 86:157-161.

62. Laby R J, Beer SV (1992) Hybridization and functional complementation of the *hrp* gene cluster from *Erwinia amylovora* strain Ea321 with DNA of other bacteria. Mol. Plant-Microbe Interact. 5:412-419.
63. Lahaye T, Bonas U (2001) Molecular secretes of bacterial type III proteins. Trends Plant Sci. 6:479-485.
64. Lavie M, Eguiluz C, Cunnac S, Grimsley N, Boucher C (2001) A pathogenicity island of *Ralstonia solanacearum* encodes an avirulence gene related to the AvrBst/YopP protein family. Proc. 10th International Congress on Molec. Plant-Microbe Interact., July10-14, abstr. 682, Madison, WI.
65. Leach JE, White FF (1996) Bacterial avirulence genes. Annu. Rev. Phytopathol. 34:153-179.
66. Lichter A (1995) Cytokinin production by *Erwinia herbicola* pv. *gypsophilae*: characterization of the genes involved in cytokinin biosynthesis and their role in gall formation. Ph.D. thesis, Tel-Aviv University.
67. Lichter A, Barash I, Valinsky L, Manulis S (1995) The genes involved in cytokinin biosynthesis in *Erwinia herbicola* pv. *gypsophilae*: characterization and role in gall formation. J. Bacteriol. 177:4457-4465.
68. Lichter A, Manulis S, Sagee O, Gafni Y, Gray J, Meilan R, Morris R O, Barash I (1995) Production of cytokinins by *Erwinia herbicola* pv. *gypsophilae* and isolation of a locus conferring cytokinin biosynthesis. Mol. Plant- Microbe Interact. 8:114-121.
69. Lichter A, Manulis S, Valinsky L, Karniol B, Barash I (1996) IS*1327*, a new insertion-like element in the pathogenicity-associated plasmid of *Erwinia herbicola* pv. *gypsophilae* . Mol. Plant-Microbe Interact. 9:98-104.
70. Lindgren P B (1997) The role of *hrp* genes during plant-bacterial interactions. Annu Rev. Phytopathol. 35:129-152.
71. Lloyd S A, Norman M, Rosqvist R, Wolf-Watz H (2001) *Yersinia* YopE is targeted for type III secretion by N-terminal, not mRNA signals. Mol. Microbiol. 39:520-531.
72. Long SR (1996) *Rhizobium* symbiosis: nod factors in perspective. Plant Cell 8:1885-1898.
73. Loper J, Lindow SE (1996) Reporter gene systems useful in evaluating *in situ* gene expression by soil and plant-associated bacteria. Pages 482-492. In: Manual of Environmental Microbiology. C.J. Hurst, ed. American Society for Microbiology Press, Washington, D C.
74. Lorange JM, Shen H, Kobayashi D, Cooksey D, Keen NT (1994) *avrA* and *avrE* in *Pseudomonas syringae* pv. *tomato* PT23 play a

role in virulence on tomato plants. Mol. Plant-Microbe Interact. 7:208-215.

75. Ma QS, Chang M.-F, Tang J-L, Feng J-X,. Fan M-J, Han B, Liu T (1988) Identification of DNA sequences involved in host specificity in pathogenesis of *Pseudomonas solanacearum* strain T2005. Mol. Plant-Microbe Interact. 1:169-174 1:169-174.

76. Mahillon J, Chandler M (1998) Insertion Sequences. Microbiol. Mol. Biol. Rev. 62:725-774.

77. Mahillon J, Rezohazy R, Hallet B, Delcour J (1994) IS231and other *Bacillus thuringiensis* transposable elements: a review. Genetica 93:13-26.

78. Manulis S (1992) Evaluation of a DNA probe for detecting *Erwinia herbicol*a strains pathogenic on *Gypsophila paniculata*. Plant Pathol. 41:342-347.

79. Manulis S, Gafni Y, Clark E, Zutra D, Ophir Y, Barash I (1991) Identification of a plasmid DNA probe for detection of *Erwinia herbicola* pathogenic on *Gypsophila paniculata*. Phytopathlogy 81:54-57.

80. Manulis S, Haviv-Chesner A, Brandl MT, Lindow SE, Barash I (1998) Differential involvement of indole-3-acetic acid biosynthetic pathways in pathogenicity and epiphytic fitness of *Erwinia herbicola* pv. *gypsophilae*. Mol. Plant-Microbe Interact 11:634-642.

81. Manulis S, Kogan N, Valinsky L, Dror O, Kleitman F (1998) Detection of *Erwinia herbicola* pv. *gypsophilae* in gypsophila plants by PCR. Eur. J. Plant Pathol. 104:85-91.

82. Manulis S, Valinsky L, Gafni Y, Hershenhorn J (1991) Indole-3-acetic acid biosynthetic pathways in *Erwinia herbicola* in relation to pathogenicity on *Gypsophila paniculata*. Physiol. Mol. Plant Pathol. 39:161-171.

83. Martin GB, Brommonschenkel SH, Chunwongse J, Frary A, Canal M W, Spivey R, Wu T, Earle ED, Tanksley SD (1993) Map-based cloning of a protein kinase gene conferring disease resistance in tomato. Science 262:1432-1436.

84. Mergaret J, Verdonck L, Kersters K, Swings J, Boeufgras JM, De Ley J (1984) Numerical taxonomy of *Erwinia* species using API systems. J. Gen. Microbiol. 130:1893-1910.

85. Merighi M, Majerczak DR, Coplin DL (2000) The *hrp* genes of *Pantoea stewartii* are regulated by a complex system that senses environmental signals. Proc. 10th Int. Conf. Plant Path. Bacteria. Charlottetown, PEI.

86. Mor H, Manulis S, Zuc M, Nizan R, Coplin DL, Barash I (2001) Genetic organization of the *hrp* gene cluster and dspAE/BF operon in *Erwinia herbicola* pv. *gypsophilae*. Mol. Plant-Microbe Interact. 14:431-436.

87. Morret E, Segovia L (1993) The s54 bacterial enhancer-binding protein family: Mechanisms of action and phylogenetic relationship of their functional domains. J. Bacteriol. 175:6067-6074.
88. Morris RO (1986) Genes specifying auxin and cytokinin biosynthesis in phytopathogens. Ann. Rev. Plant Physiol. 37:509-538.
89. Mudgett MB, Chesnokova O, Dahlbeck D, Clark ET, Rossier O, Bonas U, Staskawicz BJ (2000) Molecular signals required for type III secretion and translocation of *Xanthomonas campestris* AvrBs2 protein of pepper plants. Proc. Natl. Acad. Sci. USA 97:13324-13329.
90. Nimchuk Z, Rohmer L, Chang JH, Dangl JL (2001) Knowing the dancer from the dance: *R*-gene products and their interactions with other proteins from host and pathogen. Curr. Op. Plant Biol. 4:288-294.
91. Nizan R, Barash I, Valinsky L, Lichter A, Manulis S (1997) The presence of *hrp* genes on the pathogenicity- associated plasmid of the tumorigenic bacterium *Erwinia herbicola* pv. *gypsophilae*. Mol. Plant-Microbe Interact. 10:677-682.
92. Nizan-Koren R, Manulis S, Barash I (2001) The *hrp* regulatory cascade of *Erwinia herbicola* pv. *gypsophilae*. Proc. 10th International Congress on Molecular Plant-Microbe Interactions, July10-14, abstr. 664. Madison, WI.
93. Nizan-Koren R, Manulis S, Mor H, Iraki NM, Barash I (1999) Characterization of the *hrp* regulon in *Erwinia herbicola* pv. *gypsophilae*. Proc. 9th International Congress on Molecular Plant-Microbe Interactions. July 25-30, p170, Amsterdam.
94. Opgenorth DC, Hendson TM, Clark E (1994) First report of a bacterial gall of a *Wisteria sinensis* caused by *Erwinia herbicola* pv. *milletiae* in California. Plant Dis. 78:1217.
95. Otten L, Canaday J, G'rard J, Fournier CP, Crouzet P, Paulus F (1992) Evolution of *Agrobacteria* and their Ti plasmids-A review. Mol. Plant Microbe Interact. 5:279-287.
96. Parsot C, Sansonetti J (1999) The virulence plasmid of *Shigellae*: an archipelago of pathogenicity islands. Pages 151-165. In: Pathogenicity islands and other mobile virulence elements. J. Hacker and J. B. Kaper, ed. ASM Press, Washington, D. C.
97. Patten CL, Glick BR (1996) Bacterial biosynthesis of indole-3-acetic acid. Can. J. Microbiol. 42:207-220.
98. Piper KR, von Bodman SB, Farrand SK (1993) Conjugation factor of *Agrobacterium tumefaciens* regulates Ti plasmid transfer by autoinduction. Nature 362:448-450.

99. Ritter C, Dangl JL (1995) The *Pseudomonas syringae* pv. *maculicola avrRpm1* gene is required for virulence on *Arabidopsis*. Mol. Plant-Microbe Interact. 8:444-453.
100. Romantschuk M, Roine E, Taira S (2001) Hrp pilus-reaching through the plant cell wall. Eur. J. Plant Pathol.107:153-160.
101. Rossier O, Wengelnik K, Hahn K, Bonas U (1999) The X*anthomonas* Hrp type III system secretes proteins from plants and mammalian bacterial pathogens. Proc. Natl. Acad. Sci. USA 96:9368-9373.
102. Salch YP, Shaw PD (1988) Isolation and characterization of pathogenicity genes of *Pseudomonas syringae* pv. *tabaci*. J. Bacteriol. 170:2584-2591.
103. Schesser K, Frithz-Lindsten E, Wolf-Watz H (1996) Delineation and mutational analysis of the *Yersinia pseudotuberculosis* Yop E domains, which mediate translocation across bacterial and eukaryotic cellular membranes. J. Bacteriol. 178:7227-7233.
104. Shilo R (1985) *Gypsopila paniculata.* Pages 83-87. In: Handbook of Flowering. A. E. Halevy, ed. CRC Press, Boca Raton, FL.
105. Smidt M, Kosuge T (1978) The role of indole-3-acetic acid accumulation by a -methyltryptophan resistant mutants of *Pseudomonas savastanoi.* Physiol. Plant Pathol. 13:203-214.
106. Soby S, Kirkpatrick B, Kosuge T (1994) Characterization of high-frequency deletions in the-iaa-containing plasmid, pIAA2, of *Pseudomonas syringae* pv. *savastanoi*. Plasmid 31:21-30.
107. Sory M, Boland A, Lambermont I, Cornelis G R (1995) Identification of YopE and YopH domains required for secretion and internalization into cytosol of macrophages, using the *cyaA* gene fusion approach. Proc. Natl. Acad. Sci. USA 92:11998-12002.
108. Starr MP (1981) The genus *Erwinia,* Pages 1260-1271. In: The Prokaryotes. M. P. Star, H.G. Truper, A Balows, and H.G. Schlegel, ed. Springer-Verlag, Berlin.
109. Stroehr UH, Jedani KE, Dredge BK, Morona R, Brown MH, Karageorgos LE, Albert M, Manning PA (1995) Genetic rearrangements in the rfb regions of *Vibrio cholerae* O1 and O139. Proc. Natl. Acad. Sci. USA 92:10374-10378.
110. Swarup S, De Feyter R, Brlansky RH, Gabriel DW (1991) A pathogenicity locus from *Xanthomonas citri* enables strains from several pathovars of *X. campestris* to elicit canker like lesions on citrus. Phytopathology 81:802-809.
111. Swarup S, Yang Y, Kingsley MT, Gabriel DW (1992) A *Xanthomonas citri* pathogenicity gene, *pthA*, pleiotropically encodes gratuitous avirulence on nonhosts. Mol. Plant-Microbe Interact. 5:204-213.

112. Taniguchi T, O'Neill M, de Crombrugghe B (1979) Interaction site of *Escherichia coli* AMP receptor protein on DNA galactose operon promoters. Proc. Natl. Acad. Sci. U.S.A. 76:5090-5094.

113. Tzfira T, Citovsky V (2000) From host recognition to T-DNA integration: the function of bacterial and plant genes in the *Agrobacteium* -plant cell interaction. Molec. Plant Pathol. 1:201-212.

114. Valinsky L (2001) Isolation and characterization of *hsvG*, a pathogenicity gene from the pPATH of *Erwinia herbicola* pv. *gypsophilae*. Ph.D. Thesis, Tel-Aviv University, Tel-Aviv.

115. Valinsky L, Barash I, Chalupowicz L, Ezra D, Manulis S (2002) Regulation of *hsvG*, a host-specific virulence gene from *Erwinia herbicola* pv. *gypsophilae*. Physiol. and Mol. Plant Pathol. 60 (in press).

116. Valinsky L, Manulis S, Nizan R, Ezra D, Barash I (1998) A pathogenicity gene isolated from the pPATH of *Erwinia herbicola* pv. *gypsophilae* determines host specificity. Mol. Plant-Microbe Interact. 11:753-762.

117. Valinsky L, Nisan I, Tu X, Nisan G, Rosenshine I, Hanski E, Barash I, Manulis S (2002) A host-specific virulence protein of *Erwinia herbicola* pv. *gypsophilae* is translocated into human epithelial cells by the type III secretion system of enteropathogenic *Escherichia coli*. Mol. Plant Pathol. 3:97-101.

118. Van den Ackerveken GF, Marois E, Bonas U (1996) Recognition of the bacterial avirulence protein AvrBs3 occurs inside the host plant cell. Cell 87:1307-1316.

119. Van Gijsegem F (1997) *In planta* regulation of phytopathogenic bacteria virulence genes: relevance to plant-derived signals. Eur. J. Plant Pathol. 103:291-301.

120. Vanneste JL, Yu J, Beer SV (1992) Role of antibiotic production by *Erwinia herbicola* Eh252 in biological control of *Erwinia amylovora*. J. Bacteriol. 174:2785-2796.

121. Vasanthakumar A, McManus PC (2001) Etiology of cranberry stem gall. (Abstr), No. 228. 10th International Congress on Molecular Plant-Microbe Interactions, University of Wisconsin, Madison WI.

122. Volcani Z (1985) Bacterial diseases of plants in Israel. Agricultural Research Organization, The Volcani Center, Bet Dagan, Israel.

123. Waney VR, Kingsley MT, Gabriel DW (1991) *Xanthomonas campestris* pv. *translucens* genes determining host-specific virulence and general virulence on cereals identified by Tn5-*gusA* insertion mutagenesis. Mol. Plant-Microbe Interact. 4:623-627.

124. Wei W, Plovanich-Jones A, Deng W-L, Jin O-L, Huang H-C, He SY (2000) The gene coding for the Hrp pilus structural protein is

required for type III secretion of Hrp and Avr proteins in *Pseudomonas syringae* pv. *tomato*. Proc. Natl. Acad. Sci. 97:2247-2252.

125. Wei Z M, Kim JF, Beer SV (2000) Regulation of *hrp* genes and type III protein secretion in *Erwinia amylovora* by HrpX/HrpY, a novel two component system, and HrpS. Mol. Plant-Microbe Interact. 13:1251-1262.

126. Whalen MC, Innes R, Bent A, Staskawicz B (1991) Identification of *Pseudomonas syringae* pathogens of *Arabidopsis thaliana* and a bacterial gene determining avirulence on both *Arabidopsis* and soybean. Plant Cell 3:49-59.

127. Whalen MC, Stall RE, Staskawicz BJ (1988) Characterization of a gene from a tomato pathogen determining hypersensitive resistance in non-host species and genetic analysis of this resistance in bean. Proc. Natl. Acad. Sci. USA 85:6743-6747.

128. Willis DK, Rich JJ, Hrabak EM (1991) *hrp* gene of phytopathogenic bacteria. Mol. Plant-Microbe Interact. 4:132-138.

129. Winans SC, Kalogeraki V, Jafri S, Akakura R, Xia Q (1999) Diverse roles of *Agrobacterium* Ti plasmid-borne genes in the formation and colonization of plant tumors. Pages 289-307. In: Pathogenicity islands and other mobile virulence elements. J. B. Kaper and J. Hacker, ed. ASM Press, Washington, D. C.

130. Wolff C, Nisan I, Hanski E, Frankel G, Rosenshine I (1998) Protein translocation into host epithelial cells by infecting enteropathogenic *Escherichia coli.* Mol. Microbiol. 28:143-155.

131. Wolff J, Cook GH, Goldhammer AR, Berkowitz SA (1980) Calmodulin activates prokayotic adenylate cyclase. Proc Natl Acad Sci USA 77:3840-3844.

132. Xiao Y, Hutcheson S (1994) A single promoter sequence recognized by newly identified alternate sigma factor direct expression of pathogenicity and host range determinants in *Pseudomonas syringae.* J. Bacteriol. 176:3089-3091.

133. Yamada T, Lee PD, Kosuge T (1986) Insertion sequence elements of *Pseudomonas savastanoi*: nucleotide sequence homology with *Agrobacterium tumefaciens* transfer DNA. Proc. Natl. Acad. Sci. USA 83:8263.

134. Yamada Y (1993) The role of auxin in plant-disease development. Annu. Rev. Phytopathol. 31:253-273.

135. Zhu W, Yang B, Chittoor JM, Johnson LB, White FF (1998) AvrXA10 contains an acidic transcriptional activation domain in the functionally conserved C terminus. Mol. Plant-Microbe Interact. 11:824-832.

Toward an understanding of the *Rhodococcus fascians*-Plant Interaction

Danny Vereecke, Wim Temmerman, Mondher Jaziri, Marcelle Holsters, and Koen Goethals

Introduction

The phytopathogenic Actinomycete *Rhodococcus fascians* infects a wide range of plants provoking different symptoms, the most dramatic being the formation of leafy galls. These galls are dense centers of ongoing shoot meristem initiation accompanied by suppression of shoot outgrowth (45). Initially, leafy galls were thought to be a particular case of crown gall, induced by a specialized form of *Agrobacterium tumefaciens* (14). Subsequent work showed the responsible bacterium to be a Gram-positive Nocardioform, first determined as *Corynebacterium fascians* (32), but later reclassified in the genus *Rhodococcus* on the basis of biochemical and DNA sequence analysis (36, 46, 69, 91, 92, 96).

The genus *Rhodococcus* is classified in the family *Mycobacteriaceae* (18) and is closely related to *Mycobacterium*, a genus encompassing several species that are pathogenic to humans and animals. This taxonomic relationship is evoked also by some of the *R. fascians* genes that are recruited for pathogenesis and persistence strategy during infection. Within the genus, *R. fascians* is the only phytopathogen but animal pathogens and symbionts have been described. For an overview of the general characteristics of the genus *Rhodococcus*, we refer to Bell *et al.* (10).

Leafy gall formation results from the bacterial production of specific plant hormone-like signals. The strategy employed by *R. fascians* to generate galls is quite distinct in genetics, biochemistry, and physiology when compared to the plant hormone-producing and gall-forming pathogens *Pseudomonas savastanoi* and *Pantoa agglomerans*.

R. fascians has a broad host range and provokes different symptoms

The symptoms induced by *R. fascians* were described first on sweet peas (14, 61, 110), but, ever since, the host range of *R. fascians* has been shown to be extensive (6, 12, 37, 77). The susceptibility toward infection varies within the genus, species, and even cultivar of the host (62, 113), and dicots as well as monocots respond to *R. fascians*. Currently the host range includes 39 plant families and 68 genera (105, 113). In this broad host spectrum the bacterium resembles *Agrobacterium* and is unlike the gall-forming bacteria *P. savastanoi* and *P. agglomerans*, which have a restricted host range (16, 41, 42).

The type of morphological changes that are caused by *R. fascians* range from leaf deformation, witches' broom formation, and fasciation to the initiation of leafy galls. The symptoms can be affected by the plant species and age, the bacterial strain, and bacterial growth conditions (33, 37). Also the inoculation method markedly influences the symptoms and, although wounding is no absolute prerequisite, it augments both the degree and amount of symptoms (6, 62, 99, 113).

The weakest symptom is leaf deformation that consists of wrinkling of the lamina and swelling of the petioles and veins. In tobacco plants this deformation is the result of enlarged parenchyma cells and secondary growth of the vascular tissues (113). Often, patches of "green islands" on the leaf lamina are observed.

A witches' broom consists of a cluster of fleshy stems with misshapen leaves that develop on the crown of the host plant. In pea this symptom is accompanied by initial stimulation of epicotyl growth (100) followed by an arrest of the apex growth, resulting in dwarfed plants with reduced blossoming (6, 14, 61, 100). The hypertrophied shoots in witches' brooms contain regions with meristematic centers, enlarged cortical parenchyma cells, and multiple, centrally located vascular bundles (61, 99). Fasciations are the result of a coalescence of several of these hypertrophied shoots (99).

The most severe symptom is the leafy gall that results from the amplification of embryonic buds whose outgrowth is inhibited shortly after their formation. Gall formation is limited to the infection site and no secondary gall formation at non-infected sites are found. The galls are non-autonomous structures and the presence of bacteria is not only required for the multiplication of the inhibited shoots in the gall but also for their persistence (100, 113). The inhibition of shoot outgrowth can be interpreted as an extreme form of apical dominance whereby the different shoot primordia mutually exclude further development. When the bacteria are inhibited in isolated leafy galls by antibiotic treatment, a synchronous outgrowth of the shoots occurs. These shoots spontaneously develop roots and eventually grow to normal, fertile plants (99, 100, 113). Because of the broad host range, leafy gall formation followed by elimination of the bacteria has been proposed as a method for propagation and regeneration of plant species that are recalcitrant in classic regeneration procedures (56). The synchronous relief of the shoots from apical dominance by inhibition of the bacteria is currently used for the isolation of plant genes involved in apical dominance and shoot outgrowth (M. Jaziri, unpublished data).

First, shoot meristems and buds were reported to be the only affected sites of the plant (6, 62, 65, 99). Later, it was demonstrated that leafy galls can be produced also at the leaf margins and the veins and that *de novo* meristem formation can be provoked by *R. fascians* in tobacco petioles

(113). When tobacco is locally infected at the shoot axils, *R. fascians* induces *de novo* cell division and meristem formation in subepidermal cortical cells. This initiation of cell division in developed tissue is correlated with an induction of the promoter of the Nicta;*CYCB1;1* gene (a mitotic marker) and an enhanced transcription of the Nicta;*CYCD3;2* gene (involved in the regulation of the G1-to-S transition of the cell cycle) (27). Thus, *R. fascians* can trigger cells to re-enter the cell cycle in a controlled and patterned way that results in the formation of shoot meristems.

Also the root system of the host is affected by *R. fascians* infection with a thickening of the main root and the absence of secondary roots as a result (37, 61, 99, 110). When germinating seedlings are infected, root growth is completely inhibited and this is accompanied by a thickening of the hypocotyl and an arrest of the seedling growth (113). In *Arabidopsis thaliana* roots infected by *R. fascians* a marked decrease of the meristematic activity is accompanied by a lower number of roots and a shorter root length (113). At the same time, the infection initiates new lateral roots in the pericycle, but, shortly afterwards, growth of these newly formed roots is arrested. Thus, root meristems react similarly to *R. fascians* infection as shoot meristems; initially their formation is triggered, but subsequently their further outgrowth and activity are arrested.

Leafy galls are distinct from the surrounding plant tissues in their hormone, amino acid, and phenolic content (35, 112, 115). In tobacco galls the relative concentrations of different phenolics change markedly when compared with non-infected tissues; a relatively high concentration of the coumarin 7-methyl esculin is found while this compound is absent in the non-infected parts of the plant. However, there is no evidence that phenolics, which are characteristic for a defense response in tobacco, occur. Until now, no other apparent pathogen response, such as hypersensitive response or pathogenesis-related gene expression has been detected (unpublished data).

The galls that are active centres of meristem production do not develop necrotic lesions but remain green and active long after the mother plant has succumbed (113). Although the galls can be considered as a sink for the remainder of the plant, mild infection does not harm the plant to the extent that it deteriorates or shows a marked decrease in viability under greenhouse and gnotobiotic conditions. However, *R. fascians* infection can affect severely the commercial value of ornamentals by changes in morphology and reduced flower production.

R. fascians colonizes the surface and interior of the host

Earlier work suggested that *R. fascians* was mostly present on the exterior of the fasciations and leafy galls or that bacteria in the inner tissues were in a physiological state that did not permit their isolation (37, 63). The bacteria seldom invaded epidermal cells and a few underlying cell layers, causing death of the invaded cells and growing further intercellularly up to six cell layers deep (61). Lacey (63) showed also that gall filtrates induced leafy gall formation and suggested that the bacteria occurred in the plant tissues as L-forms that had lost their cell wall. Interestingly, the *Mycobacterium tuberculosis* infection cycle involves also the formation of L-forms (57), suggesting that part of the infection strategies of these related pathogens would be rather similar.

Re-evaluation of the etiology of *R. fascians* on tobacco and *Arabidopsis* shows that the bacteria preferentially colonize the leaf surface and to a much lesser extent the stem and the crown (22, 23). The bacteria spread by growth and hyphae formation and are embedded in a slimy material from unknown origin. Often they are present in cavities and at epidermal cell wall junctions, which might represent a way to avoid environmental stress on the leaf (9). Plant parts that are colonized by *R. fascians* do not always show symptoms, indicating that the production and/or activity of bacterial signals implicated in pathogenesis is restricted.

Stomatal cavities can be colonized but there is no evidence that these sites represent a specific entryway for the bacteria to the inner tissues. Instead, in leaf and stem tissues, bacteria enter through ingressions that result from a collapse of plant cells. These ingression or penetration sites are not accompanied with plant cell necrosis, although some plant cells in the vicinity of these sites show increased auto-fluorescence.

By using an adapted fluorescence *in situ* hybridization technique (FISH) (3, 4, 22) and confocal microscopy analysis, bacteria can be localized in the intercellular spaces of the inner tissues of infected leaves and leafy galls. The bacteria are found throughout the tissues but their incidence decreases in the deeper cell layers. In contrast to other phytopathogens, such as *Ralstonia solanacearum, A. tumefaciens, P. savastanoi*, and *P. agglomerans* (26, 38, 73, 111, 119), *R. fascians* has never been detected in vascular bundles. This observation is in agreement with the absence of secondary leafy gall formation upon inoculation at a particular site of the plant.

Interestingly, in infected leaves and leafy galls, bacteria can be surrounded by a plant cell wall without signs of decay or cell death of the invaded plant cells (21, 22), hinting at the presence of intracellular bacterial forms; this finding was confirmed in infected Bright Yellow-2 (BY-2) tobacco cell cultures, but the intracellular nature needs substantiation by electron microscopy.

Symptom development precedes the occurrence of endophytic forms, be it intercellular or intracellular. Therefore, penetration and colonization of plant tissues are phases in the infection cycle that follow the onset of leafy gall formation by signals provided by the population of *R. fascians* on the host surface.

The epiphytic behavior of the bacteria was confirmed by immunolocalization with an *R. fascians*-derived polyclonal antibody (23). However, this technique failed to detect endophytic forms shown by FISH suggesting that the endophytic bacteria have a changed cell wall structure or have lost their cell wall entirely, as is the case for L-forms.

Phytohormones and leafy gall formation

The nature of the bacterial signals that are responsible for gall formation has not been elucidated yet. Whatever the compounds involved, they are not diffused at a great distance (99, 120) and grafting of normal plants with symptomatic scions does not result in transmission of symptoms (120).

Several symptoms such as shoot initiation, wrinkled leaves, formation of dark green patches, delayed senescence, and root inhibition are characteristic of cytokinin effects. Addition of cytokinins can indeed mimic some of the symptoms (59, 87) and the bacterium produces several types of cytokinins that are secreted in the culture supernatant (5, 34, 50, 59, 97, 102). Although one report noted a positive correlation between the virulence of *R. fascians* strains and cytokinin secretion (81), Crespi *et al.* (24) found no differences in the cytokinin concentration in the supernatant of cultures of virulent and non-virulent strains. Also Eason *et al.* (34) detected only minor differences in the amounts of secreted cytokinins and could not correlate virulence with type and level of known biologically active cytokinins. Deducing a role for cytokinins in leafy gall formation is complicated further by the amounts secreted by *R. fascians*, which are up to 100-fold lower than those secreted by *A. tumefaciens* and *P. savastanoi* (2, 81, 94). Nevertheless, the latter phytopathogens do not induce leafy galls or initiate shoots at infection sites. The amounts of regular cytokinins that are secreted by *R. fascians* are thus too low to account for the abundant shoot proliferation, but several explanations have been proposed. In the plant, the bacteria continuously provide the cytokinins directly to target cells or the cytokinin production is greatly enhanced when the pathogen is in close proximity to its host (24, 34).

Alternatively, the bacterial cytokinins could play a secondary role and the cytokinin production by the plant might be stimulated upon infection (109). In all these cases elevated levels of cytokinins are expected in diseased tissues when compared with those of non-infected healthy plants or plants infected with a non-virulent strain. Although in an early report Balazs and Sziráki (7) had found more extractable cytokinin activity in *R. fascians*-infected *Pelargonium zonale* than in healthy plants, similar observations have not been made by others (27, 34, 113).

The nature of signal molecules produced by *R. fascians* and implicated in leafy gall formation is still unknown, but several lines of evidence point to the involvement of a cytokinin-like compound. Crespi *et al.* (24) demonstrated that the presence of an isopentenyl transferase (*ipt*) gene in *R. fascians* strain D188 is absolutely required for virulence. Isopentenyl transferases are key enzymes in cytokinin biosynthesis that catalyze the formation of isopentenyl adenine from 5'AMP and dimethylallyl pyrophosphate (17). The *ipt* genes have first been described in *A. tumefaciens* and *P. savastanoi* and later in *P. agglomerans* where they were shown to be involved in virulence (49, 66, 67, 93). In these bacteria, however, *ipt* genes are not absolutely indispensable for virulence but contribute to the type or degree of symptom development. In *Agrobacterium*, mutants of the *ipt* gene of the T-DNA still produce crown galls, be it with the formation of bundles of roots emerging from tumorous calli (1, 8, 15). In *P. savastanoi*, *ipt* mutants produce smaller galls with a changed anatomy (55) and in *P. agglomerans* galls of *ipt* knock-out mutants have a reduced size. Cytokinin overproduction significantly enlarge the galls produced by these pathogens (66, 67).

These data are in contrast with the absolute requirement of the *ipt* gene in leafy gall formation by *R. fascians* strain D188. This observation was further confirmed by the strict correlation of its presence with the virulence of different *R. fascians* isolates (105).

When the overall amino acid sequence of the *ipt*-derived protein of *R. fascians* is compared with that of the protein sequences of *P. savastanoi*, *P. agglomerans*, and different *Agrobacterium* species, the low overall sequence identity ranging from 20 to 26% (24, 106) is in contrast with the relatively high sequence identities that are found when the *ipt*-derived proteins of the latter bacteria are compared. The sequence identity with the *R. fascians* protein is mainly restricted to three regions, one of which corresponds to a protein domain involved in the binding of ATP. The *R. fascians* protein has a cytokinin biosynthetic activity when the classical substrates are used, but only with low efficiency (24). Furthermore, cytokinin activity in the supernatant of *R. fascians* D188 cultures as detected with classical cytokinin bioassays cannot be correlated with the *ipt* gene expression and an *ipt* mutant cannot be complemented by the exogenous application of isopentenyl adenine (106). Altogether, these data suggest that the function of the *R. fascians ipt* gene is distinct from mere production of classical cytokinins.

Plants with leafy galls show a marked increase in the level of the auxin indole-3-acetic acid (27, 113) that is secreted by *R. fascians* in the culture supernatant (M. Jaziri, unpublished data). This finding is in agreement with several symptoms provoked by *R. fascians*, such as cell swelling, secondary differentiation of vascular tissues, and lateral root initiation. Besides a possible direct role of auxin in leafy gall initiation, a function in the epiphytic survival of the bacterium can be considered also (13, 72).

In *P. savastanoi*, auxin is the major virulence factor in knot formation by stimulating cell division in the cambium and the proliferation of disorganized tissue (55). Also, the amount of auxin produced by distinct strains relates with their virulence on different hosts in the *Oleaceae* plant family (44, 54, 98, 104). In *P. agglomerans*, auxins are also involved in virulence but, as for cytokinins, they are not indispensable for gall formation (19, 66, 67). Instead, an *hrp* gene cluster was identified that is obligatory for gall formation (78, 83, 84), suggesting a role for a proteinaceous factor that is injected in the host cells by a type III delivery system (20, 39).

The eventual role of the host's phytohormones in symptom development is currently being assessed by infecting *A. thaliana* mutants defective in synthesis and/or perception of ethylene, cytokinin, auxin, gibberellin, and abscisic acid and by treating *R. fascians*-infected *Arabidopsis* plants with different hormones or hormone inhibitors.

Molecular genetics of *R. fascians* virulence

Reports on the possible involvement of plasmids in *R. fascians* virulence had been controversial (47, 64, 81). Thanks to tools for the molecular analysis of virulence genes of *R. fascians*, mainly elaborated by Desomer *et al.* (28-31), who constructed suitable vectors and developed transformation and insertion mutagenesis methods, the discussions ended with the finding of a large conjugative linear plasmid (pFiD188) that is essential for pathogenesis (24). The *R. fascians* strain D188 carries also a circular plasmid that is involved in cadmium resistance but does not play a role in pathogenesis (29). The observation of a linear plasmid as a major determinant of pathogenicity has been expanded to other *R. fascians* strains (105). Linear replicons have been described in the Actinomycetes *Streptomyces*, *Rhodococcus*, and *Mycobacterium*, where they are linked to diverse processes, such as antibiotic production, autotrophic growth, and degradation of complex compounds (51, 89). Linear plasmids described in *Borellia* have a characteristic hairpin telomere structure, whereas those of *Streptomyces* and *Nocardia* and the *R. fascians* pFiD188 carry termini that are covalently bound by proteins at the 5' end (51; unpublished data). Although the chromosome of *R. fascians* had been suggested to be linear as well (24), later data proved the genome to be circular (91).

After a random mutagenesis of *R. fascians* D188, different virulence mutants have been isolated that mapped on pFiD188 (24). Three types of mutants have been described: *fas* mutants that are non pathogenic, *att* mutants that show attenuated virulence, and a *hyp* mutant with a hypervirulent phenotype. Although important, the *fas* and *att* loci are not sufficient for pathogenicity because a strain cured for pFiD188 and carrying a cosmid spanning these loci is still non-virulent. This characteristic implies that other loci encoded by the linear plasmid are indispensable for leafy gall formation and, more recently, another pFiD188 locus has indeed been isolated that is necessary for full virulence (24, 70).

The *att* locus produces an autoregulatory compound involved in the regulation of virulence gene expression

Infection of plants with bacteria that are mutated in the *att* locus results in a range of phenotypes. Some plants remain unaffected, whereas most develop small or loose galls. Seedlings infected with *att* mutants are inhibited only partially, with an intermediary growth as a result (71).

The *att* mutants successfully colonize their hosts (23), but wounding, although not necessary for virulence of wild-type bacteria, is necessary for gall formation by *att* mutants on detached tobacco leaves (71).

Transcription of the *att* genes is induced by the amino acid histidine in combination with pyruvate or succinate. Although this would suggest that the natural inducer is histidine or a derivative, there is strong evidence that the inducer has a different structure. The *att* locus is involved in the synthesis of an autoregulatory inducer that is present in gall extracts and that also induces expression of the *fas* genes. The chemical structure of this inducer is still unknown (71).

By sequence analysis of the *att* locus, a regulatory gene *attR* was found, which is homologous to LysR-type regulatory genes, together with nine open reading frames (ORFs) homologous to arginine and ß-lactam biosynthetic genes (71). Induction of *att* gene expression requires the presence of *attR*. Depending on the induction condition, two different compounds that need an intact *att* locus are secreted by *R. fascians* in the supernatant. Both these compounds induce *att* gene expression and at least one of them is present in extracts of leafy galls, but not in extracts of galls induced by *att* mutant bacteria. The compounds are related chemically and possibly carry a ß-lactam ring but differ from histidine in several characteristics.

During infection of tobacco plants, expression of the *att* genes is not located in particular regions of the plant, it decreases gradually, and it is found only in bacteria that are situated on the plant surface (23). Thus, under specific conditions during the infection of the plant surface, the bacteria are confined, creating the settings that are necessary to build up a critical amount of *att*-derived inducers. This leads to a positive feedback loop, further enhancing the synthesis of the *att* inducers to levels that can sufficiently induce *fas* gene expression. Later during infection, this autoregulation may be interrupted and another regulatory system installed for the continuing expression of the *fas* genes.

The attenuated phenotype provoked by *att* mutants may be explained by a decrease in the synthesis of the *fas* product due to the lack of inducer. Such a function does not exclude the possibility that the *att* products serve other tasks in the galling process. Expression of the *att* genes is relatively high and co-infection of plants with *att* and *fas* mutant bacteria does not complement the *fas* phenotype, but results in typical *att* mutant symptoms. The *att*-derived inducers are secreted in the environment and are found to diffuse within the plant. Additional functions of the *att* products can be envisioned. To exert such functions the *att* compounds should be produced in the bacteria that express the *fas* genes or at least in such bacteria that are in close contact.

Symptom development requires the *fas* locus

EXPRESSION OF THE *FAS* LOCUS IS TIGHTLY CONTROLLED

The *fas* locus is genetically delimited as a 6-kb fragment carrying six ORFs oriented in the same transcriptional orientation (25). ORF4 corresponds to the *ipt* gene (24) and ORF1, ORF2, and ORF3 encode a cytochrome P450 (ORF1) and ancillary proteins (ORF2 and ORF3) that are involved presumably in the electron delivery for the cytochrome P450 activity. The product of ORF5 is significantly homologous to cytokinin oxidases of different plant species, whereas ORF6 codes for a protein, which is homologous to lysine decarboxylases that are involved in the synthesis of the polyamine cadaverine.

In culture, expression of the *fas* locus is tightly controlled and detectable only when specific conditions are met (107). A crucial factor is the presence of extracts of infected plants, tissues that contain the *att* inducers. Environmental signals, such as acidic pH, particular carbon sources, and a high cell density are favorable for *fas* induction, whereas inorganic phosphate, anaerobic and micro-aerobic conditions and most amino acids have a negative effect. Histidine in combination with succinate or other α-keto acids efficiently induce *fas* expression.

Transcription of the *fas* genes is constitutive and independent of the pH and the carbon or nitrogen source supplied, showing that under non-inducing conditions translation is repressed and that the *fas* gene expression is controlled mainly at the translational level (107). The post-transcriptional nature of the control mechanisms leading to *fas* expression is also evident from analysis of the non-virulent *fasR* deletion mutant. The regulatory gene *fasR* is located upstream of the *fas* locus, belongs to the AraC family of transcriptional regulators, and is essential for *fas* gene expression (107). Although *fasR* encodes a transcriptional regulator, it has only a minor effect on the transcription of the *fas* genes, whereas their translation depends completely on this gene, suggesting that *fasR* exerts its effect indirectly via a translational regulator that acts on *fas* gene translation. The identity of this translational regulator is unknown but a possible candidate may be encoded by the *hyp* locus. A mutant in this locus causes the development of larger leafy galls on decapitated plants, implying that *hyp* modulates the activity of the virulence signal(s) and/or represses the expression of virulence genes (24). Sequence analysis of the *hyp* locus revealed the presence of four ORFs oriented in the same direction (106). The deduced amino acid sequence of ORF3 is homologous to the "DEAD-box" family of RNA helicases that are involved in diverse cellular processes, including RNA splicing, ribosome assembly, translation initiation, and regulation of mRNA expression during development (103). The *hyp* locus may thus correspond to a regulatory locus implicated in the binding of RNA and/or the stability of secondary structures in the *fas* mRNA.

In this respect the finding of some inverted repeat sequences upstream from ORF1 and ORF4 of the *fas* locus is interesting. In the mRNA transcript these sequences can give rise to secondary structures that comprise the ribosome-binding site associated with the respective ORF (106). Hence, these secondary structures may constitute a target site for the action of RNA helicases and thereby be part of a regulatory mechanism governing translational control of *fas* expression. Possibly, the *hyp*-encoded protein(s) unwind or destroy a special structure that facilitates initiation of translation. Alternatively they may stabilize or form a specific stem-loop structure in the *fas* transcript, preventing efficient translation of the mRNA or they may affect the stability of the *fas* transcript. A second transcriptional regulator controlling *fas* expression must be present on the linear plasmid because *fas* transcription in an *R. fascians* strain that lacks pFiD188 is reduced by 50% when compared with the wild-type (107).

When translation of the *fas* locus is assayed *in planta*, it is induced both in bacteria located at the plant surface and the interior of the plant. The expression starts early during infection and persists for a long time, in contrast to expression of the *att* genes that gradually decreases during infection and is only detectable in bacteria at the plant surface (23). Although important for initial expression of the *fas* locus, the *att*-produced inducer(s) are not required for the continuous expression of the *fas* genes during later stages of infection. The *in planta* expression of the *fas* genes in *att* mutant bacteria is markedly delayed but occurs at normal levels when the bacteria have penetrated and colonized the plant tissues.

Overall, *fas* gene expression is under the control of a complex regulatory mechanism involving both transcriptional and translational regulators that integrate a variety of environmental signals. Part of this network is independent of the *att*-controlled regulation and becomes active when bacteria have penetrated the plant tissues. The bacteria seem to employ a subtle method to alter the developmental program of the plant by the controlled release of signal molecules.

THE *FAS* LOCUS IS INVOLVED IN CYTOKININ METABOLISM

Mutants in ORF1 and ORF4 are non-virulent whereas an insertion mutant of ORF5 is fully virulent on seedlings, but, when assayed on older plants, causes the development of leafy galls in which the shoot outgrowth is not inhibited (106). These observations suggest that the *fas*-encoded proteins are required to produce signal molecules that mediate both shoot initiation and growth inhibition and that ORF5 and/or ORF6 are important for the shoot inhibition process.

The ORF5-encoded protein is homologous to cytokinin oxidases of *A. thaliana* and *Zea mays* (53, 79). Cytokinin oxidases irreversibly inactivate cytokinins by catalyzing the cleavage of the N^6 side chain (118). The presence of a cytokinin oxidase gene downstream of *ipt*, involved in cytokinin production, raises the question as to why a bacterium would spend energy to produce cytokinin that is subsequently degraded. A possible explanation is that the cytokinin oxidase is activated only at a certain cytokinin threshold level. In such a model, it would act as a substrate inducible enzyme to maintain the cytokinins produced by the *ipt* gene product at a level suitable for stimulation of cell division, as proposed for cytokinin oxidase of habituated plant tissues (75). Alternatively, the cytokinin oxidase is involved in the biosynthesis of a specifically modified cytokinin. Cytokinin oxidases act via the formation of an unstable aldimine intermediate with an activated N^6-atom, which is hydrolyzed to yield adenine or adenosine and the aldehyde corresponding to the N^6-side chain of the cytokinin substrate (40). When another molecule is present and allowed to react with this N^6-atom, the reaction product would be a derivative carrying another side chain at the N^6-position. It is also possible that the side chain is not cleaved but that a tertiary amine is formed, resulting in a derivative carrying two side chains. In either case, the molecule may be more active than the initially produced cytokinin, allowing symptom formation of both young and older plants. This strategy would ensure the production of a functional cytokinin and, hence, the capacity of *R. fascians* to induce symptoms on at least some plants in case the complete *fas* product cannot be made.

The ORF6-deduced amino acid sequence shows significant homology to lysine decarboxylases (LDC) from several organisms, that from *Eikenalla corrodens* being the most homologous. LDCs catalyze the formation of the polyamine cadaverine from lysine and are required for full virulence in several animal pathogens (76, 88). Although the role of cadaverine in plant biology remains unclear, polyamines in general are known to play a role in initiation and control of cell division and to affect patterns of cell differentiation and morphogenesis.

Two ORFs located upstream of the *ipt* are extensively homologous to P450 cytochromes (ORF1) and the ancillary iron-sulfur redox proteins (ferredoxins; ORF2) found in biodegradative and biosynthesis pathways of actinomycetes (for reviews, see refs 85 and 101). A ferredoxin reductase, the third component of these oxido-reduction systems, could not be detected. Frequently, these reductases are not encoded within the P450/ferredoxin operon (86). However, the ORF2 product has an additional carboxyl-terminal domain that resembles the α-subunit of the pyruvate dehydrogenase component of the pyruvate dehydrogenase complex of several organisms. In Gram-positive and some Gram-negative bacteria and in eukaryotes as well, this enzyme, which catalyzes the oxidative decarboxylation of pyruvate that requires thiamine pyrophosphate (TPP) as a cofactor, is a heterotetrameric protein composed of two α- and two β-subunits (11, 82). Interestingly, ORF3 encodes a protein similar to the β-subunit of these enzymes. In particular, the regions involved in TPP binding and conserved among TPP-requiring enzymes are found in ORF2 and ORF3 (80). The fusion between a ferredoxin-like domain and a TPP-binding domain in the ORF2-encoded protein is reminiscent of the pyruvate:ferredoxin oxidoreductases, a class of enzymes responsible for the oxidation of pyruvate in several bacteria (60, 90). These enzymes can use the highly reducing power of pyruvate for reactions that need stronger reductants than NADH (58). The presence of such an enzyme in the *fas* locus may be functionally relevant to the action of the cytochrome P450 encoded by ORF1. In most bacterial cytochrome P450 systems the reducing power is generated by the oxidation of NAD(P)H through the action of a ferredoxin reductase. The electrons are subsequently delivered to the cytochrome P450 by a ferredoxin (85). The *fas*-encoded cytochrome P450 system could be unique in its ability to use pyruvate or another α-keto acid as electron donor. The high-energy electrons, generated by the oxidative decarboxylation of this molecule through the action of the ORF2- and ORF3-encoded proteins, could be delivered directly to the cytochrome P450 via the ferredoxin-like domain of the ORF2 product.

THE *FAS* PRODUCT EXERTS SPECIFIC EFFECTS ON PLANTS

Because several observations point to a clear involvement of cytokinins in *R. fascians*-induced symptoms and by considering the sequence data of the *fas* locus, a search for a specific *fas*-dependent cytokinin-like molecule was initiated. When extracts of induced D188 culture supernatant are applied to tobacco plants, symptoms reminiscent of *R. fascians* effects develop, including the reduction of internode length, leaf size and root development (106). These effects are not observed when extracts of non-induced or *fas* mutant cells are used. However, D188 extracts have only a very low cytokinin activity when assayed on etiolated seedlings of *Amaranthus caudatus* and a similar activity is detected with extracts from a pFiD188-cured strain. This observation indicates that cytokinin production is of chromosomal origin and that virulence of *R. fascians* is not due only to secretion of typical cytokinins. Indeed, several experiments have revealed that the *fas*-derived product acts differently when compared to standard cytokinins.

Addition of pre-induced D188 cells, or culture supernatant extracts thereof, to synchronized tobacco BY-2 cells results in a *fas*-dependent broadening of the mitotic index peak and a prolonged prophase. In contrast, cytokinins increase the proportion of cells entering mitosis. The *fas*-derived product overrides this effect, suggesting that this molecule acts differently on plant cells than cytokinins (108).

By analyzing culture supernatant extracts with thin-layer chromatography and high-pressure liquid chromatography techniques, a fraction containing a *fas*-dependent molecule has been isolated that similarly provokes the specific effect on BY-2 cells. This fraction induces the initiation of lateral roots and the development of green leaves when applied to developing *Arabidopsis thaliana* seedlings in the dark (106). A reduction of hypocotyl length is not observed. This morphogenic effect differs from that of the typical cytokinins that lead to reduced hypocotyls length and development of green tissues, but not to lateral root initiation.

Interestingly, when *Araceae* are treated with cytokinins in combination with imazalil, an imidazol-type fungicide, symptoms are observed that are very similar to the *R. fascians*-induced phenotypes (116). The shoot-inducing effect of cytokinin is also enhanced by other imidazole fungicides and by the triazole growth retardant paclobutrazol. The structural feature shared by these compounds is a heterocycle ring containing an sp^2-hybridized nitrogen with a lone electron pair. The target enzymes of molecules bearing these features are P450 cytochromes, such as methylhydroxylases, involved in biosynthesis of gibberellins, abscisic acid, cytokinins, and sterols (48, 95). In another study, (117) gibberellin has been shown to inhibit the abundant shoot proliferation in *Araceae* treated with imidazole fungicides and cytokinins. Werbrouck *et al.* (117) hypothesized that, by means of an unknown mechanism, the full shoot induction potential of exogenous cytokinins is reduced by endogenous gibberellins, a phenomenon previously observed in other plants (43). Addition of imazalil, or related compounds, removes this block by inhibiting gibberellin biosynthesis and, as a consequence, shoot proliferation is enhanced. Interestingly, the phenylurea-type cytokinin thidiazuron (TDZ) (Figure 1) induces structures that are very similar to leafy galls (106). The requirement of both an imidazol-like moiety and a cytokinin to elicit leafy gall-like

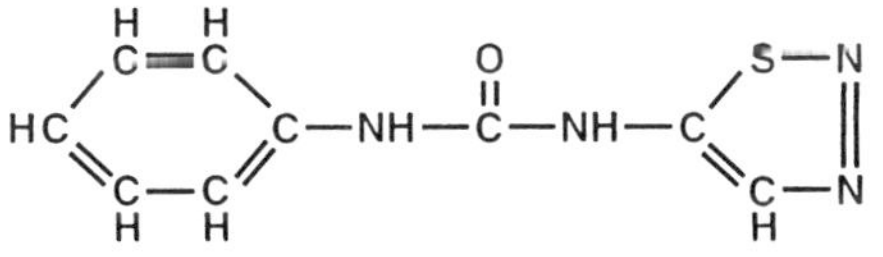

Figure 1. Chemical structure of thidiazuron.

phenotypes (116), is combined in TDZ, which has an intrinsic cytokinin activity and a sp^2-hybridized nitrogen. These results suggest that during the *R. fascians*-plant interaction compounds are produced possessing either one of these characteristics and that the combined presence of these molecules results in the abundant shoot proliferation. The *fas* product, essential for pathogenesis, is probably one of these compounds or may indeed combine both characteristics. Alternatively, the *fas* locus may produce more than one compound.

The chromosomal *vic* locus is necessary for bacterial survival in the plant

After an insertion mutagenesis round with an integrating promoter probe vector, an *R. fascians* mutant X798 has been isolated that exhibits reduced virulence. When compared with the wild-type D188, strain X798 inhibits only partially seedling development (114). Upon infection after decapitation, the leafy galls formed are either small and loosely organized or elongated (114). Isolation and sequencing of the wild-type locus indicated that the vector has integrated into a gene located on the chromosome encoding a malate synthase homologue. The locus has been designated *vic* for virulence in the chromosome and the interrupted gene *vicA*. Typically, malate synthase catalyzes the condensation of acetyl coenzyme A with glyoxylate to form malate. Together with isocitrate lyase, malate synthase constitutes the glyoxylate shunt of the tricarboxylic acid cycle. Upon growth on C_2-carbons as sole carbon source, the shunt circumvents the two CO_2-producing steps of the tricarboxylic acid cycle, thus allowing carbohydrate assimilation.

The role of VicA in the glyoxylate shunt is corroborated by different observations. On rich media, both the wild-type strain and the mutant X798 have comparable growth profiles. However, in contrast to the wild-type strain, mutant X798 cannot grow on acetate as sole carbon source, has lost its malate synthase activity completely, and accumulates glyoxyate during incubation on acetate; finally, glyoxylate represses growth on glycerol of strain X798, but not of strain D188.

Several indications point toward a function of the *vic* locus in the *in planta* growth of the pathogen. Expression of *vic*A is induced by acetate, a typical feature of shunt genes. However, also the presence of the C_3 carbon pyruvate and complex plant and leafy gall extracts can activate *vic*A expression. When the mutant bacteria are grown on leafy gall extracts as sole carbon source, glyoxylate accumulates and the cells do not enter stationary phase but die. Under these conditions strain X798 experiences a general metabolic defect as suggested by the inability to metabolize common amino acids. These defects are not observed when strain X798 is grown on plant extracts as sole carbon source. Finally, the continuous presence of bacteria is required for maintenance of the leafy gall structure (113). The phenotype of the *vic* mutant hints toward a reduced viability or fitness of the bacteria responsible for symptom persistence. Determination of the epiphytic and endophytic populations in infected plants showed that strain X798 is equally capable of colonizing its host as the wild-type strain. However, when colonization of symptomatic tissue is evaluated, the *vic* mutant is clearly less represented.

Based on these data, a model has been proposed for the driving force behind the interaction of *R. fascians* with its host and for the role of *vicA*. After epiphytic colonization of the plant, *R. fascians* enters the plant tissue through ingression sites (22). The virulence genes are activated, resulting in the formation of meristematic tissues and subsequently of shoots. The bacteria mainly inhabit the intercellular spaces, but sometimes invade the plant cells. As a consequence of the induction of symptomatic tissue, the metabolic state is altered in parts of the plant. Hence, the array of nutritional compounds available for *R. fascians* is changed and efficient use of these sources requires a dietary shift. During catabolism of the leafy gall nutrients, glyoxylate is formed that is detoxified by VicA. Because VicA is not present in strain X798, feeding inside the forming leafy gall will lead to an accumulation of glyoxylate accompanied with a growth arrest or death of the bacterial cells. Accordingly, the obligatory production of signal molecules for symptom maintenance is interrupted and aberrant phenotypes are formed. The phenotypic data together with the colonization results suggest that the population inhabiting the non-symptomatic parts of the plant are not involved in maintaining the leafy gall structure. In conclusion, the need for nutrients drives *R. fascians* to interact intimately with plants. Through the induction of hyperplasia and the consequent quantitative and/or qualitative changes in the plants metabolites, a nutrient pool inaccessible to others builds up and, hence, a specific niche is created where *R. fascians* has a selective advantage over other plant-associated bacteria. Such a strategy of metabolic habitat modification is probably used by many, if not all, hyperplasia-inducing bacteria.

Clearly, the presence of an intact glyoxylate cycle is a prerequisite for the survival of *R. fascians* in the plant and for sustained virulence. Interestingly, in the animal pathogens *M. tuberculosis* and *Candida albicans* a functional glyoxylate shunt is important for persistence and virulence. Expression of the isocitrate lyase-encoding gene (*icl*) of the Actinomycete *M. tuberculosis* is highly induced during intracellular infection of macrophages (52). By inactivating the *icl* gene in this organism, persistence and virulence are attenuated, without affecting bacterial growth during the acute phase of infection (74). The data show that the carbon metabolism of *M. tuberculosis* experiences a "C_2 shift" concomitant with the host's response to infection. In the fungus *C. albicans*, phagocytosis upregulates isocitrate lyase and malate synthase, and a functional *icl* gene is essential for full virulence (68). This probably reflects the glucose-deficient nature of the phagolysosome where *C. albicans* has to use fatty acids through the glyoxylate cycle to synthesize glucose.

Altogether, these data show that the glyoxylate cycle in bacteria and fungi is imperative for survival inside a macrophage. Our data indicate that also in the plant-pathogenic interaction of *R. fascians* with its host a similar requirement of the glyoxylate shunt exists. Interestingly, an 18-kb region containing the *vic* locus is syntenic with chromosomal regions of *Mycobacterium* species that encompass other "persistence" loci of these mammalian pathogens. *R. fascians* mainly colonizes the intercellular spaces of the plant tissues, but penetrates occasionally the plant cell. It remains to be determined whether the functional shunt is needed for survival of the intercellular and/or of the intracellular forms. Nevertheless, a shift to a C_2 diet and the concomitant use of the glyoxylate cycle seem to be a prerequisite for virulence and persistence in both animal and plant pathogens.

The infection cycle of *R. fascians*

An overview of the different steps of the infection process of *R. fascians* is presented in Figure 2. Initially, *R. fascians* colonizes epiphytically, spreads by growth and hyphae formation, and is imbedded in a slimy matter. The bacteria form large colonies on the leaf surface of the host, preferring cavities and cell wall junctions. At this point the expression of the *att* and *fas*, and possibly other, virulence genes is activated, which results in the production of an autoregulatory compound and a morphogenic cytokinin-like molecule, respectively. The secretion of these compounds provokes *de novo* cortical cell divisions and the activation of existing axillary meristems. The bacteria now progress into the plant tissues by entering natural openings such as stomata, but more importantly by creating ingression sites that render the deeper cell layers accessible. As the bacteria penetrate the plant tissues, their cell wall structure changes and the expression of the *att* genes is shut down. The meristems further develop into shoots giving body to the emerging leafy gall. Meanwhile, the surface but not the internal expression of the *fas* genes is arrested, ensuring that the signals essential for leafy gall development are continuously produced at the target sites. The colonization of the inner tissues goes on, permitting the persistence of the induced structure; besides the bacteria inhabiting the intercellular spaces, some will penetrate intracellularly. Altogether, leafy gall formation changes the nutrient landscape encountered by the bacteria on their exploration of the plant. Hence, at this stage of the infection, survival in these tissues requires a dietary shift involving the glyoxylate shunt and the *vic* locus. As a result of this metabolic habitat modification a niche is created for *R. fascians* that is inaccessible to others.

Future research

From the above, it is evident that several important questions remain to be answered. Of prior importance is the elucidation of the chemical structure of the compounds produced by the *fas* and the *att* loci.

For the *fas* molecule the current approach is to overexpress the *fas* genes by placing them under control of the *att* promoter, hence omitting the tight post-transcriptional control, combined with the identification of an easy and fast bioassay.

For the characterization of the two *att* molecules ^{14}C-labeled products are isolated by incubating the bacteria under defined induction conditions in batch cultures in the presence of ^{14}C-acetate. These products are used as markers in large-scale purifications of culture supernatants and leafy gall extracts. As a bioassay the capacity to induce the expression of fusions between *att* and *fas* with β-glucuronidase is tested.

Finally the intriguing analogy between the persistence strategies of *R. fascians* and several mammalian pathogens merits further efforts to determine whether virulence in general is conserved between *R. fascians* and *M. tuberculosis*. A first step to evaluate this hypothesis is to resolve whether the synteny observed for chromosomal regions of both pathogens also holds for genes located on the virulence-determining linear plasmid of *R. fascians*.

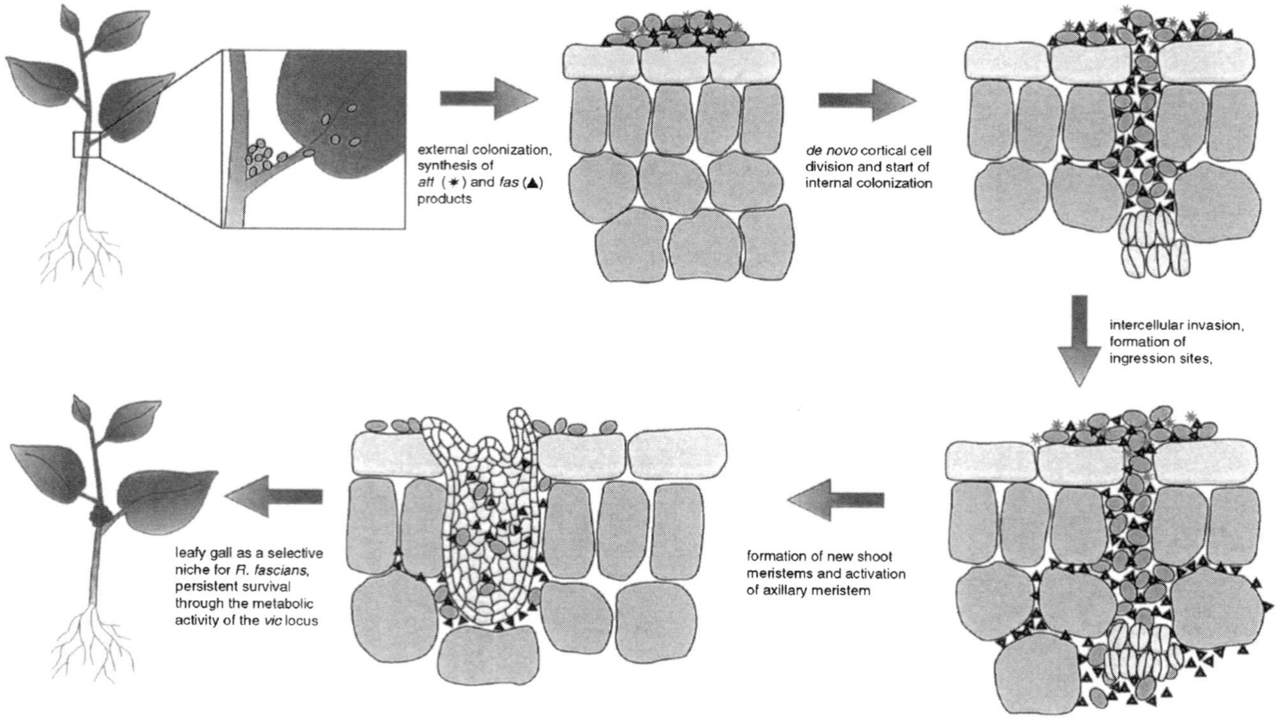

Fig. 2. Schematic representation of the infection cycle of *R. fascians*.

References

1. Akiyoshi D E, Klee H, Amasino R M, Nester E W, Gordon M P (1984) T-DNA of *Agrobacterium tumefaciens* encodes an enzyme of cytokinin biosynthesis. Proc Natl Acad Sci USA 81:5994-5998.
2. Akiyoshi D E, Regier D A, Gordon M P (1987) Cytokinin production by *Agrobacterium* and *Pseudomonas* spp. J Bacteriol 169:4242-4248.
3. Amann R, Kühl M (1998) *In situ* methods for assessment of microorganisms and their activities. Curr Opin Microbiol 1:352-358.
4 Amann R I, Ludwig W, Schleifer K-H (1995) Phylogenetic identification and in situ detection of individual microbial cells without cultivation. Microbiol Rev 59:143-169.
5. Armstrong D J, Scarbrough E, Skoog F, Cole D L, Leonard N J (1976) Cytokinins in *Corynebacterium fascians* cultures. Isolation and identification of 6-(4-hydroxy-3-methyl-*cis*-2-butenylamino)-2-methyl-thiopurine. Plant Physiol 58:749-752.
6. Baker K F (1950) Bacterial fasciation disease of ornamental plants in California. Plant Dis. Rep. 34:121-126.
7. Balázs E, Sziráki I (1974) Altered levels of indoleacetic acid and cytokinin in geranium stems infected with *Corynebacterium fascians*. Acta Phytopathol Acad Sci Hung 9:287-292.
8. Barry G F, Rogers S G, Fraley R T, Brand L (1984) Identification of a cloned cytokinin biosynthetic gene. Proc Natl Acad Sci USA 81:4776-4780.
9. Beattie G A, Lindow S E (1995) The secret life of foliar bacterial pathogens on leaves. Annu Rev Phytopathol 33:145-172.
10. Bell K S, Philp J C, Aw D W J, Christofi N (1998) The genus *Rhodococcus*. J Appl Microbiol 85:195-210.
11. Berg A, de Kok A (1997) 2-Oxo acid dehydrogenase multienzyme complexes. The central role of the lipolyl domain. Biol Chem 378:617-634.
12. Bradbury J F (1986) *Rhodococcus* Zopf 1891. Pages 185-187 in: Guide to Plant Pathogenic Bacteria, Bradbury J F, ed. CAB International Mycological Institute, Slough, UK.
13. Brandl M T, Lindow S E (1998) Contribution of indole-3-acetic acid production to the epiphytic fitness of *Erwinia herbicola*. Appl Env. Microbiol. 64:3256-3263.
14. Brown N A (1927) Sweet pea fasciation, a form of crowngall. Phytopathology 17:29-30.
15. Buchmann I, Marner F-J, Schröder G, Waffenschmidt S, Schröder J (1985) Tumour genes in plants: T-DNA encoded cytokinin biosynthesis. EMBO J 4:853-859

16. Burr T J, Katz B H, Abawi G S, Crosier D C (1991) Comparison of tumorigenic strains of *Erwinia herbicola* isolated from table beet with *E. h. gypsophilae*. Plant Dis 75:855-858.
17. Chen C-m (1997) Cytokinin biosynthesis and interconversion. Physiol Plant 101:665-673.
18. Chun J, Kang S O, Hah Y C, Goodfellow M (1996) Phylogeny of mycolic acid-containing actinomycetes. J Ind Microbiol 17:205-213
19. Clark E, Manulis S, Ophir Y, Barash I, Gafni Y (1993) Cloning and characterization of *iaaM* and *iaaH* from *Erwinia herbicola* pathovar *gypsophilae*. Phytopathology 83:234-240.
20. Cornelis G, Van Gijsegem F (2000) Assembly and function of type III secretory systems. Annu Rev Microbiol 54:735-774.
21. Cornelis K (2000) Behaviour of the phytopathogenic bacterium *Rhodococcus fascians* on plants. PhD dissertation. Ghent University, Belgium.
22. Cornelis K, Ritsema T, Nijsse J, Holsters M, Goethals K, Jaziri M (2001) The plant pathogen *Rhodococcus fascians* colonizes the exterior and interior of the aerial parts of plants. Mol Plant-Microbe Interact 14:599-608.
23. Cornelis K, Maes T, Jaziri M, Holsters M, Goethals K (2002) Virulence genes of the phytopathogen *Rhodococcus fascians* show specific spatial and temporal expression patterns during plant infection. Mol Plant-Microbe Interact 15:398-403.
24. Crespi M, Messens E, Caplan A B, Van Montagu M, Desomer J (1992) Fasciation induction by the phytopathogen *Rhodococcus fascians* depends upon a linear plasmid encoding a cytokinin synthase gene. EMBO J 11:795-804.
25. Crespi M, Vereecke D, Temmerman W, Van Montagu M, Desomer J (1994) The *fas* operon of *Rhodococcus fascians* encodes new genes required for efficient fasciation of host plants. J Bacteriol 176:2492-2501.
26. De Buck S, De Wilde C, Van Montagu M, Depicker A (2000) Determination of the T-DNA transfer and the T-DNA integration frequencies upon cocultivation of *Arabidopsis thaliana* root explants. Mol Plant-Microbe Interact 13:658-665.
27. de O Manes C-L, Van Montagu M, Prinsen E, Goethals K, Holsters M (2001) De novo cortical cell division triggered by the phytopathogen *Rhodococcus fascians* in tobacco. Mol Plant-Microbe Interact 14:189-195.
28. Desomer J, Crespi M, Van Montagu M (1991) Illegitimate integration of non-replicative vectors in the genome of *Rhodococcus fascians* upon electrotransformation as an insertional mutagenesis system. Mol Microbiol 5:2115-2124.

29. Desomer J, Dhaese P, Van Montagu M (1988) Conjugative transfer of cadmium resistance plasmids in *Rhodococcus fascians* strains. J Bacteriol 170:2401-2405.

30. Desomer J, Dhaese P, Van Montagu M (1990) Transformation of *Rhodococcus fascians* by high-voltage electroporation and development of *R. fascians* cloning vectors. Appl Environ Microbiol 56:2818-2825.

31. Desomer J, Vereecke D, Crespi M, Van Montagu M (1992) The plasmid-encoded chloramphenicol resistance protein of *Rhodococcus fascians* is homologous to the transmembrane tetracycline efflux proteins. Mol Microbiol 6:2377-2385.

32. Dowson W J (1942) On the generic name of the Gram-positive bacterial plant pathogens. Trans Brit Myc Soc 25:311-314.

33. Eason J R, Jameson P E, Bannister P (1995) Virulence assessment of *Rhodococcus fascians* strains on pea cultivars. Plant Pathol 44:141-147.

34. Eason J R, Morris R O, Jameson P E (1996) The relationship between virulence and cytokinin production by *Rhodococcus fascians* (Tilford 1936) Goodfellow 1984. Plant Pathol 45:323-331.

35. El-Wakil M, Blakeny E (1980) Quantitative analysis of free amino acids in either leafy gall induced by *Corynebacterium fascians* or its tissue culture. Egypt J Phytopathol 12:145-148.

36. Embley T M, Stackebrandt E (1994) The molecular phylogeny and systematics of the actinomycetes. Annu Rev Microbiol 48:257-289.

37. Faivre-Amiot A (1967) Quelques observations sur la présence de *Corynebacterium fascians* (Tilford) Dowson dans les cultures maraichères et florales en France. Phytiatrie-Phytopharmacie 16:165-176.

38. Gafni Y, Kunik T, Ophir Y (1995) Scanning electron microscopy of the interactions between *Erwinia herbicola* pv. *gypsophilae* and *Gypsophila paniculata*. Phytoparasitica 23:345-350.

39. Galán J E, Collmer A (1999) Type III secretion machines: bacterial devices for protein delivery into host cells. Science 284:1322-1333.

40. Galuszka P, Frébort I, Šebela P, Jacobsen S, Peč P (2001) Cytokinin oxidase or dehydrogenase? Mechanism of cytokinin degradation in cereals. Eur J Biochem 268:450-461.

41. Gardan L, Bollet C, Abu Ghorrah M, Grimont F, Grimont P A D (1992) DNA relatedness among the pathovar strains of *Pseudomonas syringae* subsp. *savastanoi* Janse (1982) and proposal of *Pseudomonas savastanoi* sp. nov. Int J System Bacteriol 42:606-612.

42. Gardan L, David C, Morel M, Glickmann E, Abu-Ghorrah M, Petit A, Dessaux Y (1992) Evidence for a correlation between auxin production and host plant species among strains of *Pseudomonas syringae* subsp. *savastanoi*. Appl Env. Microbiol 58:1780-1783.

43. George E F, ed. (1993) Plant Propagation by Tissue Culture. Part 1: The Technology. 2nd ed. Exegetics, Edington, UK.
44. Glass N L, Kosuge T (1988) Role of indoleacetic acid-lysine synthetase in regulation of indoleacetic acid pool size and virulence of *Pseudomonas syringae* subsp. *savastanoi*. J Bacteriol 170:2367-2373.
45. Goethals K, Vereecke D, Jaziri M, Van Montagu M, Holsters M (2001) Leafy gall formation by *Rhodococcus fascians*. Annu Rev Phytopathol 39:27-52.
46. Goodfellow M (1984) Reclassification of *Corynebacterium fascians* (Tilford) Dowson in the genus *Rhodococcus*, as *Rhodococcus fascians* comb. nov. System Appl Microbiol 5:225-229.
47. Gross D C, Vidaver A K, Keralis M B (1979) Indigenous plasmids from phytopathogenic *Corynebacterium* species. J Gen Microbiol 115:479-489.
48. Grossman K (1992) Plant growth retardants: their mode of action and benefit for physiological research. Pages 788-797 in: Progress in Plant Growth Regulation (Current Plant Science and Biotechnology in Agriculture, Vol 13), Karssen C M, van Loon L C, Vreugdenhil D, eds. Kluwer Academic Publishers, Dordrecht, The Netherlands.
49. Heinemeyer W, Buchmann I, Tonge D W, Windass J D, Alt-Moerbe J, Weiler E W, Botz T, Schröder J (1987) Two *Agrobacterium tumefaciens* genes for cytokinin biosynthesis: Ti plasmid-coded isopentenyltransferases adapted for function in prokaryotic or eukaryotic cells. Mol Gen Genet 210:156-164.
50. Helgeson J P, Leonard N J (1966) Cytokinins: identification of compounds isolated from *Corynebacterium fascians*. Proc Natl Acad Sci USA 56:60-63.
51. Hinnebusch J, Tilly K (1993) Linear plasmids and chromosomes in bacteria. Mol Microbiol 10:917-922.
52. Höner zu Bentrup K, Miczak A, Swenson D L, Russell D G (1999) Characterization of activity and expression of isocitrate lyase in *Mycobacterium avium* and *Mycobacterium tuberculosis*. J Bacteriol 181:7161-7167.
53. Houba-Hérin N, Pethe C, d'Alayer J, Laloue M (1999) Cytokinin oxidase from *Zea mays*: purification, cDNA cloning and expression in moss protoplasts. Plant J 17:101-112
54. Iacobellis N S, Caponero A, Evidente A (1998) Characterization of *Pseudomonas syringae* ssp. *savastanoi* strains isolated from ash. Plant Pathol 47:73-83.
55. Iacobellis N S, Sisto A, Surico G, Evidente A, DiMaio E (1994) Pathogenicity of *Pseudomonas syringae* subsp. *savastanoi* mutants defective in phytohormone production. J Phytopathol 140:238-248.

56. Goethals K, El Jaziri M, Van Montagu M (1998) Plant micropropagation and germplasm storage. Patent Application No. PCT/EP98/0117 (WO 98/36635).
57. Kahn, M C (1930) A growth cycle of the human tubercle bacillus as determined by single-cell studies. Tubercle 11:202.
58. Kerscher L, Oesterhelt D (1982) Pyruvate : ferredoxin oxidoreductase - new findings on an ancient enzyme. Trends Biochem Sci 7: 371-374.
59. Klämbt D, Thies G, Skoog F (1966) Isolation of cytokinins from *Corynebacterium fascians*. Proc Natl Acad Sci USA 56:52-59.
60. Kunow J, Linder D, Thauer R K (1995) Pyruvate:ferredoxin oxidoreductase from the sulfate-reducing *Archaeglobus fulgidus*: Molecular composition, catalytic properties, and sequence alignments. Arch Microbiol 163:21-28.
61. Lacey M S (1936) Further studies on a bacterium causing fasciation of sweet peas. Ann Appl Biol 23:743-751.
62. Lacey M S (1939) Studies on a bacterium associated with leafy galls, fasciations and "cauliflower" disease of various plants. Part III. Further isolations, inoculation experiments and cultural studies. Ann Appl Biol 26:262-278.
63. Lacey M S (1961) The development of filter-passing organisms in *Corynebacterium fascians* cultures. Ann Appl Biol 49:634-644.
64. Lawson E N, Gantotti B V, Starr M P (1982) A 78-megadalton plasmid occurs in avirulent strains as well as virulent strains of *Corynebacterium fascians*. Curr Microbiol 7:327-332.
65. Lelliott R A (1966) The plant pathogenic coryneform bacteria. J Appl Bacteriol 29:114-118.
66. Lichter A, Barash I, Valinsky L, Manulis S (1995) The genes involved in cytokinin biosynthesis in *Erwinia herbicola* pv. gypsophilae: characterization and role of gall formation. J Bacteriol 177:4457-4465.
67. Lichter A, Manulis S, Sagee O, Gafni Y, Gray J, Meilan R, Morris R O, Barash I (1995) Production of cytokinins by *Erwinia herbicola* pv. *gypsophilae* and isolation of a locus conferring cytokinin biosynthesis. Mol Plant-Microbe Interact 8:114-121.
68. Lorenz M C, Fink G R (2001) The glyoxylate cycle is required for fungal virulence. Nature (London) 412:83-86.
69. Luehrsen K, Woese C R, Wolters J, Stackebrandt E (1989) Nucleotide sequence of 5S ribosomal RNA of *Rhodococcus fascians*. Nucleic Acids Res 17:p. 5378.
70. Maes T (2001) The *att* locus of the plant-pathogen *Rhodococcus fascians*. Ph D. thesis, Ghent University.
71. Maes T, Vereecke D, Ritsema T, Cornelis K, Ngo Thi Thu H, Van Montagu M, Holsters M, Goethals K (2001) The *att* locus of *Rhodococcus fascians* strain D188 is essential for full virulence on

tobacco through the production of an autoregulatory compound. Mol Microbiol 42:13-28

72. Manulis S, Haviv-Chesner A, Brandl M T, Lindow S E, Barash I (1998) Differential involvement of indole-3-acetic acid biosynthetic pathways in pathogenicity and epiphytic fitness of *Erwinia herbicola* pv. *gypsophilae*. Mol Plant-Microbe Interact 11:634-642.
73. Matzk A, Mantell S, Schiemann J (1996) Localization of persisting agrobacteria in transgenic tobacco plants. Mol Plant-Microbe Interact 9:373-381.
74. McKinney J D, Höner zu Bentrup K, Muñoz-Elias E J, Miczak A, Chen B, Chan W-T, Swenson D, Sacchettini J C, Jacobs W R Jr, Russell D G (2000) Persistence of *Mycobacterium tuberculosis* in macrophages and mice requires the glyoxylate shunt enzyme isocitrate lyase. Nature (London) 406:735-738.
75. Meins F Jr (1989) HABITUATION: heritable variation in the requirement of cultured plant cells for hormones. Annu Rev Genet 23:395-408.
76. Merrell D S, Camilli A (1999) The *cadA* gene of *Vibrio cholerae* is induced during infection and plays a role in acid tolerance. Mol Microbiol 34:836-849.
77. Miller H J, Janse J D, Kamerman W, Muller P J (1980) Recent observations of leafy gall in Liliaceae and some other families. Neth J Plant Pathol 86:55-68.
78. Mor H, Manulis S, Nizan-Koren R, Zuk M, Barash I (1999) Characterization of the *hrp* gene cluster and the *dspEF* operon on the pPATH of Erwinia herbicola pv. gypsophilae. Abstract presented at the 9th International Congress on Molecular Plant-Microbe Interactions, Amsterdam (The Netherlands), July 25-30, p. 170 (#16.6).
79. Morris R O, Bilyeu K D, Laskey J G, Cheikh N N (1999) Isolation of a gene encoding a glycosylated cytokinin oxidase from maize. Biochem Biophys Res Commun 255:328-333.
80. Muller Y A, Lindqvist Y, Furey W, Schulz G E, Jordan F, Schneider G (1993) A thiamin diphosphate binding fold revealed by comparison of the crystal structures of transketolase, pyruvate oxidase and pyruvate decarboxylase. Structure 1:95-103.
81. Murai N, Skoog F, Doyle M E, Hanson R S (1980) Relationships between cytokinin production, presence of plasmids, and fasciation caused by strains of *Corynebacterium fascians*. Proc Natl Acad Sci USA 77:619-623.
82. Neveling U, Bringer-Meyer S, Sahm H (1998) Gene and subunit organization of bacterial pyruvate dehydrogenase complexes. Biochim Biophys Acta 1385:367-372.
83. Nizan R, Barash I, Valinsky L, Lichter A, Manulis S (1997) The presence of *hrp* genes on the pathogenicity-associated plasmid of

the tumorigenic bacterium *Erwinia herbicola* pv. *gypsophilae*. Mol Plant-Microbe Interact 10:677-682.

84. Nizan-Koren R, Manulis S, Mor H, Iraki N M, Barash I (1999) Characterization of the *hrp* regulon in Erwinia herbicola pv. gypsophilae. Abstract presented at the 9th International Congress on Molecular Plant-Microbe Interactions, Amsterdam (The Netherlands), July 25-30, p. 170 (#16.7).

85. O'Keefe D P, Harder P A (1991) Occurrence and biological function of cytochrome P450 monooxygenases in the actinomycetes. Mol Microbiol 5:2099-2105.

86. O'Keefe D P, Gibson K J, Emptage M H, Lenstra R, Romesser J A, Litle P J, Omer C A (1991) Ferredoxins from two sulfonylurea herbicide monooxygenase systems in *Streptomyces griseolus*. Biochemistry 30:447-455.

87. Oduro K A, Munnecke, D E (1975) Persistence of pea cotyledons induced by Corynebacterium fascians. Phytopathology 65 1114-1116.

88. Park Y-K, Bearson, B, Bang, S H, Bang, I S, Foster, J W (1996) Internal pH crisis, lysine decarboxylase and the acid tolerance response of *Salmonella typhimurium*. Mol Microbiol 20:605-611.

89. Picardeau M, Vincent V (1997) Characterization of large linear plasmids in mycobacteria. J Bacteriol 179:2753-2756.

90. Pieulle L, Guigliarelli B, Asso M, Dole F, Bernadac A, Hatchikian E C (1995) Isolation and characterization of the pyruvate-ferredoxin oxidoreductase from the sulfate-reducing bacterium *Desulfovibrio africanus*. Biochim Biophys Acta 1250:49-59.

91. Pisabarro A, Correia A, Martín J F (1998) Pulse-field gel electrophoresis analysis of the genome of *Rhodococcus fascians*: genome size and linear and circular replicon composition in virulent and avirulent strains. Curr Microbiol 36:302-308.

92. Pisabarro A, Correia A, Martín J F (1998) Characterization of the *rrnB* operon of the plant pathogen *Rhodococcus fascians* and targeted integrations of exogenous genes at *rrn* loci. App Environ Microbiol 64:1276-1282.

93. Powell G K, Morris R O (1986) Nucleotide sequence and expression of a *Pseudomonas savastanoi* cytokinin biosynthetic gene: homology with *Agrobacterium tumefaciens tmr* and *tzs* loci. Nucleic Acids Res 14:2555-2565.

94. Powell G K, Hommes N G, Kuo J, Castle L A, Morris R O (1988) Inducible expression of cytokinin biosynthesis in *Agrobacterium tumefaciens* by plant phenolics. Mol Plant-Microbe Int 1:235-242.

95. Rademacher W (1991) Biochemical effects of plant growth retardants. Pages 169-199 in: Plant Biochemical Regulators (Books

in soils, plants, and the Environment), Gausman H W, ed. Marcel Dekker, New York, NY.

96. Rainey F A, Burghardt J, Kroppenstedt R M, Klatte S, Stackebrandt E (1995) Phylogenetic analysis of the genera *Rhodococcus* and *Nocardia* and evidence for the evolutionary origin of the genus *Nocardia* from within the radiation of *Rhodococcus* species. Microbiology 141:523-528.

97. Rathbone M P, Hall R H (1972) Concerning the presence of the cytokinin, N^6-(Δ^2-isopentenyl)adenine in cultures of *Corynebacterium fascians*. Planta 108:93-102.

98. Roberto F F, Klee H, White F, Nordeen R, Kosuge T (1990) Expression and fine structure of the gene encoding N^ϵ-(indole-3-acetyl)-L-lysine synthetase from *Pseudomonas savastanoi*. Proc Natl Acad Sci USA 87:5797-5801.

99. Roussaux J (1965) Etude préliminaire des modifications induites chez le pois express Alaska par le *Corynebacterium fascians* (Tilford) Dowson. Rev Gén Bot 72:21-53.

100. Roussaux J (1975) Stimulation and inhibition reactions in plants infected by *Corynebacterium fascians* (Tilford) Dowson. Marcellia 38:305-310.

101. Sariaslani F S, Omer C A (1992) Actinomycete cytochromes P-450 involved in oxidative metabolism: biochemistry and molecular biology. Crit Rev Plant Sci 11:1-16.

102. Scarbrough E, Armstrong D J, Skoog F, Frihart C R, Leonard N J (1973) Isolation of *cis*-zeatin from *Corynebacterium fascians* cultures. Proc Natl Acad Sci USA 70:3825-3829.

103. Schmid S R, Linder P (1992) D-E-A-D protein family of putative RNA helicases. Mol Microbiol 6:283-292.

104. Silverstone S E, Gilchrist D G, Bostock R M, Kosuge T (1993) The 73-kb pIAA plasmid increases competitive fitness of *Pseudomonas syringae* subspecies *savastanoi* in oleander. Can J Microbiol 39:659-664.

105. Stange R R Jr, Jeffares D, Young C, Scott D B, Eason J R, Jameson P E (1996) PCR amplification of the *fas-1* gene for the detection of virulent strains of *Rhodococcus fascians*. Plant Pathol 45:407-417.

106. Temmerman W (2000) The role of the *fas* locus in leafy gall formation by *Rhodococcus fascians*. Ph D. dissertation. Ghent University, Belgium.

107. Temmerman W, Vereecke D, Dreesen R, Van Montagu M, Holsters M, Goethals K (2000) Leafy gall formation is controlled by *fasR*, an AraC-type regulatory gene, in *Rhodococcus fascians*. J Bacteriol 182:5832-5840.

108. Temmerman W, Ritsema T, Simón-Mateo C, Van Montagu M, Mironov V, Inzé D, Goethals K, Holsters M (2001) The *fas* locus of

the phytopathogen *Rhodococcus fascians* affects mitosis of tobacco BY-2 cells. FEBS Lett 492:127-132.
109. Thimann K V, Sachs T (1966) The role of cytokinins in the "fasciation" disease caused by *Corynebacterium fascians*. Am J Bot 53:731-739.
110. Tilford P E (1936) Fasciation of sweet peas caused by *Phytomonas fascians* n. sp. J Agric Res 53:383-394.
111. Vasse J, Frey P, Trigalet A (1995) Microscopic studies of intercellular infection and protoxylem invasion of tomato roots by *Pseudomonas solanacearum*. Mol Plant-Microbe Int 8:241-251.
112. Vereecke D (1997) Leafy gall induction by *Rhodococcus fascians*. Ph D. Thesis. University of Gent, Belgium.
113. Vereecke D, Burssens S, Simón-Mateo C, Inzé D, Van Montagu M, Goethals K, Jaziri M (2000) The *Rhodococcus fascians*-plant interaction: morphological traits and biotechnological applications. Planta 210:241-251.
114. Vereecke D, Cornelis K, Temmerman W, Jaziri M, Holsters M, Goethals K (2002) Characterization of a chromosomal locus that affects the pathogenicity of *Rhodococcus fascians*. J Bacteriol 184:1112-1120.
115. Vereecke D, Messens E, Klarskov K, De Bruyn A, Van Montagu M, Goethals K (1997) Patterns of phenolic compounds in leafy galls of tobacco. Planta 201:342-348.
116. Werbrouck S P O, Debergh P C (1996) Imidazole fungicides and paclobutrazol enhance cytokinin-induced adventitious shoot proliferation in Araceae. J Plant Growth Regul 15:81-85.
117. Werbrouck S P O, Redig P, Van Onckelen H A, Debergh P C (1996) Gibberellins play a role in the interaction between imidazole fungicides and cytokinins in Araceae. J Plant Growth Regul 15:87-93.
118. Whitty C D, Hall R H (1974) A cytokinin oxidase in *Zea mays*. Can J Biochem 52:781-799.
119. Wilson E E, Magie A R (1963) Physiological, serological, and pathological evidence that *Pseudomonas tonelliana* is identical with *Pseudomonas savastanoi*. Phytopathology 53:653-659.
120. Zutra D, Cohen J, Gera A, Loebenstein G (1994) Association of *Rhodococcus* (*Corynebacterium*) *fascians* with the stunting-fasciation syndrome of carnation in Israel. Acta Horticul 377:319-3

Genomic Architecture and Evolution of NBS-LRRs

Steven B. Cannon and Nevin D. Young

With the advent of modern genomic tools, dozens of plant disease resistance (R) genes of known specificity have been cloned and characterized. For many, the complete nucleotide sequence is known, multiple alleles have been described, and the potential role of the corresponding protein product in signal transduction is being revealed (for reviews, see 4,11,13,23,31,41,51). There are several different types of R proteins and they all fall into a few structural categories. One type of R protein consists of a leucine-rich repeat (LRR) bound to a transmembrane domain (22). This group includes *Cf2* and *Cf9* of tomato, which are known to provide resistance to different races of *Cladosporium fulvum*. Likewise, a single example of a serine threonine kinase, *Pto*, confers resistance to *Pseudomonas syringae* (28). The rice gene *Xa21* codes for a R protein that is a combination of both an extracellular LRR and an intracellular kinase (42). However, the most abundant type of plant R protein and the subject of this review chapter is the large and diverse family known as "nucleotide binding site, leucine rich repeats" (NBS-LRRs). The NBS-LRR family is especially well elaborated in plants, but largely absent from organisms in other kingdoms. Understanding the molecular evolution and genomic organization of NBS-LRRs will be essential to our understanding of plant-microbe interactions. At the same time, studying the NBS-LRR family promises to reveal important general features in genomic architecture and evolution of large protein families in angiosperms.

Because R proteins are so important in plant biology — and the study of NBS-LRRs so fascinating — there have been many excellent reviews of this subject area (4,11,13,23,31,41,51). These reviews highlight the structural domains that comprise NBS-LRRs, the possible role of the LRR domain in recognition, and the defense response pathways in which NBS-LRR proteins seem to participate. With this in mind, our chapter focuses on the genomic architecture and molecular evolution of NBS-LRRs, topics that have not been reviewed so widely in the past. In this chapter, we will briefly describe the structure of NBS-LRRs, then examine in detail the organization of NBS-LRR genes in the *Arabidopsis thaliana* genome. In reviewing the genomic organization of NBS-LRRs, we pose the questions: what are the relationships between the genomic structure and evolution of this gene family and how well can *Arabidopsis* NBS-LRRs serve as a model for this gene family in other angiosperms?

The NBS-LRR Family

Based on what we know today, the NBS-LRR family is the largest group of plant R proteins, including at least 20 known R proteins from eight different species (13). Hundreds of additional plant NBS-LRR homologues have also been isolated and sequenced, though their functions remain unknown. Sequence analysis of NBS-LRR proteins reveals they all posses a putative nucleotide binding domain, thought to be involved in signal transduction (30,37). The NBS domain consists of short amino acid motifs that are highly conserved among family members, interspersed among sequences that are far more divergent. Conserved motifs within the NBS show sequence similarity to motifs within nematode CED-4 and mammalian Apaf-1, both of which are required in certain types of protease-mediated apoptosis (26,43). Moreover, the NBS domain of *Arabidopsis RPP5* (conferring resistance to *Peronospora parasitica*) is known to interact with a predicted plasma membrane-anchored molecule that may regulate levels of guanosine tetra- and pentaphosphate (48). These compounds are effector molecules of the prokaryote stringent response, so potentially they could play a similar role plants. While many lines of evidence point to a role in signal transduction by the NBS domain, a different structural interpretation has also been suggested (40). In this alternative model, the sequence region comprising the putative NBS can be modeled as a receiver domain common to many proteins of His-Asp phosphotransfer pathways.

Carboxy-terminal to the NBS domain is a second distinctive region known as the leucine-rich repeat (LRR) domain. LRRs are found in a vast array of proteins other than plant R proteins (21). LRRs consist of imperfect amino acid segments folded into solvent exposed ß-strand ß-turn structures (21). There is some evidence that this domain binds to pathogen "avirulence" (Avr) proteins (pathogen proteins required for infection that also seem to be recognized by the plant to initiate a defense response). Although evidence of direct interaction between Avr and plant R proteins has been hard to come by, the Avr protein from the rice pathogen *Magnaporthe grisea* has been shown to bind specifically to the LRR of the *Pi-ta* NBS-LRR gene (20). Point mutations in either the *Pi-ta* LRR or the Avr-*Pita* protein result in loss of resistance in the plant. Recently, an alternative model for NBS-LRR interaction with pathogen Avr proteins has been proposed (11). In this model, known as the guard hypothesis, NBS-LRRs are envisioned to physically associate with the cellular targets of pathogen Avr proteins. Once the Avr protein interacts with its host target, the complex would be recognized by an NBS-LRR (or other type of R protein), activating the defense response. If true, this might explain the puacity of direct evidence for interactions between LRRs and Avr factors.

Meyers *et al.* (29) found an alternating pattern of conservation and hypervariability within the LRR regions of lettuce *Dm3*, tomato *I2C*, tomato *Mi*, rice *Xa21,* and flax *L* and *M*. Variability was highest for the nucleotides coding for amino acids around two conserved aliphatic residues in the LRR consensus. Based on the ratio of synonymous to non-synonymous amino acid substitutions, these results indicated that these sites experienced diversifying selection. The number of LRR repeats frequently differs among family members. Among sequences at the *Cf5* locus of tomato, for example, the number of LRR repeats ranges from 25 to 38 (12). Chimeric proteins derived from alleles at the *L* locus of flax exhibited the pathogen specificity of either the donor LRR domain or entirely novel specificities (14). Taken together, these observations suggest LRR domains undergo high rates of change related to the evolution of pathogen recognition.

NBS-LRR proteins generally exhibit one of two different conserved domains N-terminal to the NBS region. One class of NBS-LRR proteins posses a domain with homology to both Toll of *Drosophila* and interleukin (IL) receptor-like proteins of mammals (18). This domain is generally referred to as the "TIR" domain. Toll, IL-1R and related proteins are known to play a role in non-specific cellular immunity in animals, potentially by participation in signal transduction pathways. The TIR domain of plant R proteins may also play a role in pathogen recognition. In a study of 13 alleles of the flax resistance gene *L*, variation in the TIR domain was associated with changes in pathogen recognition (15).

A second class of plant NBS-LRRs lacks the N-terminal TIR and instead contains amino acid motifs that resemble coiled-coils (CC) (37). CCs are bundles of two to five helices with a distinctive packing of amino acid side chains at the helix-helix interface (27). The CC structure typically exhibits a seven residue repeat organization with the hydrophobic side chains of two of the amino acids forming an interface for interactions between coils. Leucine zippers are members of this broader class of structural elements. TIR- and non-TIR-NBS-LRRs can also be distinguished by the amino acid motifs found within the NBS domain itself (30,37).

Structural differences between TIR- and non-TIR-NBS-LRR sequences seem to be related to a functional role in defense response. Two different *Arabidopsis* mutations, *eds1* (38) and *ndr1* (9), have separately been shown to reduce defense responses to pathogens. The *ndr1* gene encodes a putative transmembrane protein of unknown function (9), while *eds1* encodes a putative lipase (15). Analysis of these mutants indicates that TIR-NBS-LRR sequences operate through an *eds1*-dependent pathway, while at least some non-TIR-NBS-LRR sequences operate through a *ndr1*-pathway (1). Conceivably, the amino-terminal TIR or CC domains and/or related motifs within the NBS play a role in the bifurcation in the signal transduction pathway.

NBS-LRRs of *Arabidopsis thaliana*

As in nearly every aspect of plant biology, the completion of the *Arabidopsis thaliana* genome sequence (3) has transformed our understanding of NBS-LRRs. For the first time it is possible to create a complete "inventory" of *Arabidopsis* NBS-LRR genes. This inventory provides a basis for comprehensively examining the coding and flanking regions of all *Arabidopsis* NBS-LRR genes, cataloguing them into subfamilies, revealing their chromosomal positions and genomic context, and developing far-reaching tools for transcript profiling, proteomic analysis, and gene tagging. An essential step in making this type of information useful to biologists has been the development of easily accessible bioinformatic resources. Today, with just a few "clicks of the mouse", all of the Arabidopsis NBS-LRR nucleotide and amino acid sequences can be retrieved (33), the entire genomic architecture of *Arabidopsis* NBS-LRRs can be displayed (32), as can phylogenetic trees and sequence alignments of the NBS-LRR family (32, 8).

So what have we learned about R genes from access to the complete *Arabidopsis* genome sequence? First of all, it has been possible to construct a detailed census of *Arabidopsis* NBS-LRRs, although the process of developing such a census gives an indication of the complexity of NBS-LRRs. Depending upon the criteria used to define an NBS-LRR, there are approximately 150-160 genes in this sequence family in *Arabidopsis*. (By comparison, the rice genome is estimated to contain approximately 600 NBS-LRR genes, all lacking the TIR domain (17). In *Arabidopsis*, some NBS-LRRs have N- or C-terminal truncations or unusual configurations. The *Arabidopsis* Genome Initiative (3) reports 100 TIR-NBS genes, 85 with LRRs and 15 without, and 49 non-TIR-NBS genes, 43 with LRRs and six without. Two of the TIR-NBS-LRRs contain a WRKY domain (a possible transcription factor domain) and one TIR-NBS-LRR includes a protein kinase domain (3). The MIPS *Arabidopsis thaliana* group (33) includes several predicted genes not found in the *Arabidopsis* Genome Initiative (3) report, bringing the count in that database to 161.

Based on studies of *Arabidopsis* NBS-LRR genes, it is also clear they are not uniformly distributed throughout the genome (Fig. 1). Different *Arabidopsis* chromosomes have strikingly different numbers of NBS-LRRs: 49 full-length copies on chromosome 1; 2 on chromosome 2; 16 on chromosome 3; 28 on chromosome 4; and 55 on chromosome 5 (3). The majority of the NBS-LRRs are found in clusters. If "tandem" clusters are defined as collections of NBS-LRRs that are each separated by no more than 100 kbp, then 58% (92 of 158) fall within tandem clusters of two to eight members. Even singleton NBS-LRRs tend to be physically linked to other NBS-LRRs. If clusters are instead defined by separations between NBS-LRRs of less than 500 kbp, then 77% (122 of 158) fall within clusters. Fewer than 25 truly "isolated" NBS-LRRs are found in *Arabidopsis* (defined as being at least 1 Mbp from another NBS-LRR), including the phenotypically defined *RPM1* gene. Gene clusters can be remarkably rich in NBS-LRRs. One region extending 4.5 Mbp on chromosome 5 contains 47

NBS-LRRs, consisting mostly of TIR-NBS-LRRs plus a smaller number of non-TIR-NBS-LRRs and some truncated copies.

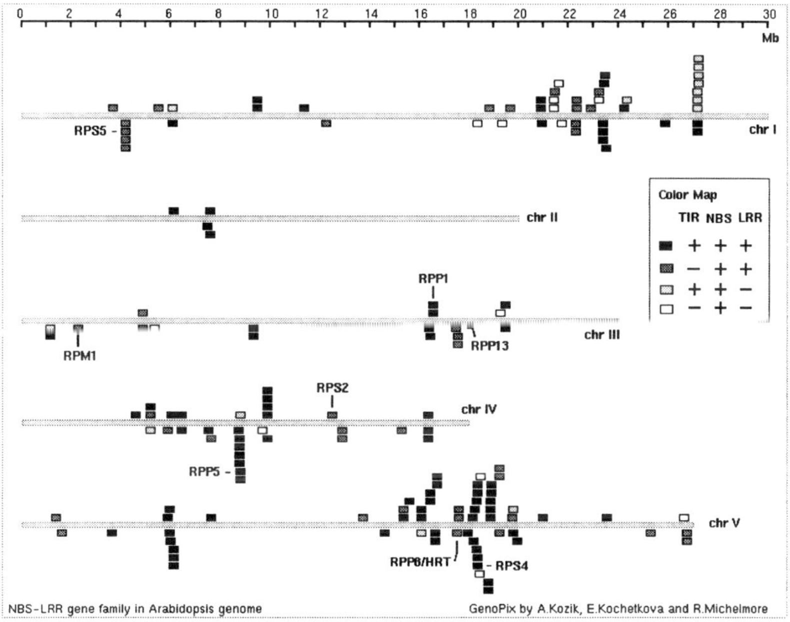

Figure 1. Physical location of *Arabidopsis thaliana* sequences related to NBS-encoding plant R-genes. Printed with permission of Michelmore et al., (32), and available at http://niblrrs.ucdavis.edu/. Chromosomal positions of all NBS and NBS-like sequences are as shown, based on MIPS annotation tables (33). Each small rectangle indicates the presence of a predicted protein. Genes above chromosomes have "Watson" orientation, genes below chromosomes have "Crick" orientation. Known resistance genes are indicated, with genes cloned from ecotypes other than Columbia in parentheses. Each protein was assessed for conserved TIR, NBS and LRR domains using the Pfam database); the presence of these domains is indicated by different shades shown in the legend.

Another important outcome of the complete sequencing of the *Arabidopsis* genome has been the finding of extensive genome duplication and rearrangement (3,49). Vision *et al.* (49) inferred four ancient rounds of polyploidy or large-scale segmental duplication, followed by extensive rearrangements and losses. The resulting *Arabidopsis* genome is therefore a mosaic of multiple, fragmented, and often overlaid duplication blocks. As discussed below, this may help to explain many features of NBS-LRR gene family architecture in *Arabidopsis*, including the duplication and expansion of some NBS-LRR clusters and the loss or expansion of some sequence types in the *Arabidopsis* NBS-LRR phylogeny. The extent of fragmentation and rearrangement in the *Arabidopsis* genome also implies that *Arabidopsis* will probably not be useful in positional cloning of NBS-LRRs outside the Brassicaceae, though small microsyntenic blocks on the order of a few 100 kbp have been observed between *Arabidopsis* and tomato (24), soybean (16), and even rice (47).

Genomic organization and evolutionary mechanics

The genomic organization of NBS-LRR genes provides an indication of how diversity is generated and maintained in this important gene family. Amplification of clusters through tandem duplication is a common feature. For example, a comparison of the complex *RPP5* locus in *Arabidopsis* reveals eight *RPP5* homologs or fragments in ecotype Columbia and ten in Landsberg *erecta*, suggesting expansion or contraction of the clusters during the relatively short evolutionary time span separating these ecotypes (34). This comparison also provides evidence of extensive intragenic sequence exchange within the cluster. At this locus, just as in the *Cf9/Cf4* locus in tomato (39) and the *Dm3* locus in lettuce (29), recombination within the LRR has led to variation in number of repeats within the domain. While recombination provides a mechanism for generation of diversity, extensive gene conversion and recombination could also lead to homogenization within a cluster, at least in the absence of mechanisms to counteract such homogenization. At the *Cf9/Cf4* locus (composed of genes with membrane-anchored LRR domains), divergent intergenic sequences may play a role in suppressing rapid gene conversion within clusters of similar R genes (39). The same mechanism could, in principle, be important in NBS-LRR clusters.

If clusters arise through rounds of local tandem duplications, it might be expected that R-gene clusters would generally be comprised of highly similar genes. Although this is often the case, as in the *RPP5* cluster (34), the *M* locus in flax (2), and the *Rp1* locus in maize (10,44), it is also true that many R-gene clusters are composed of heterogeneous, highly divergent sequences. For example, the largest tandem cluster on *Arabidopsis* chromosome 5 contains at least nine highly divergent sequence types, including the phenotypically defined TIR sequence *RPS4* and the non-TIR sequence *RPP8*. Other mixed clusters have been observed in soybean (19,35), *Medicago truncatula* (52), tomato (36), and rice, barley, and millet (25,50). Furthermore, when highly divergent R-gene homologs are found in close proximity, they frequently occur together elsewhere in the genome (Fig. 1). Indeed, the repeated occurrence of similar mixtures of divergent R-gene homologs in multiple clusters is consistent with a history of chromosomal breakages, duplications, and rearrangements, rather than frequent ectopic translocations of these genes. Moreover, the origin of R-gene clusters can often be traced by combining phylogenetic and chromosomal duplication information. For example, NBS-LRRs from two divergent non-TIR clades (one containing the *RPS5* gene) occur in the north and south arms of chromosome 1 of *Arabidopsis*, within two segmental duplication blocks (blocks 8a and 8b in Vision *et al.*, 49). The NBS-LRR sequences in block 8b, in turn, appear to have been brought near TIR sequences in an adjacent duplication block that has a corresponding partner in the large NBS-LRR cluster on chromosome 5 (blocks 34a and 34b). The arrangement and degree of heterogeneity (or homogeneity) of clusters probably have important consequences for R-gene evolution. Rates of intergenic sequence exchange within NBS-LRR clusters and among similar sequences is much higher than between clusters or between dissimilar NBS-LRRs within a cluster (A. Baumgarten, R. Spangler, G. May, personal communication). This observation suggests a mechanism for generating R gene diversity: both heterogeneous clusters as well as clusters that *become* duplicated due to polyploidy or chromosome breakage and rearrangement are free to diverge under lowered rates of intergenic sequence exchange.

Making use of R-genes to combat crop pathogens clearly requires an understanding of the related evolutionary mechanics of plant R and pathogen Avr proteins. In addition to recombination within clusters, high rates of allelism have been observed at some R-gene loci, such as the flax *L* locus (14) and the *Arabidopsis RPS2* locus (7). At the flax *L* locus, for example, ten of eleven identified alleles express different flax rust resistance specificities (14). This suggests maintenance of divergent alleles in a population through frequency-dependent selection, in which complete fixation of a particular R-gene allele is unlikely because it would mean the loss of alleles needed to recognize rare Avr gene products in the pathogen population. It is worth noting that most R-gene loci have not been extensively sampled to determine the extent of allelism, and the large number of alleles at the flax L locus may not be typical. Nevertheless, among *Arabidopsis* R-genes for which allelism has been studied, alleles are not young and loci are not monomorphic (5,45). This supports a frequency dependent model, rather than a model of plant-pathogen "arms races" and selective sweeps. In chitinases (proteins involved in defense, but unrelated to NBS-LRRs) the evidence does support accelerated evolution in an "arms race" model, with higher rates of amino-acid substitution in the active site. This presumably indicates evolution in response to new pathogen chitinase inhibitors (6). It seems likely that the appropriate model for the evolutionary dynamics of any particular R-gene will depend on many factors, including locus structure, pathogen virulence, and pathogen and plant population structures. The strongest evidence for most NBS-LRR genes, however, supports a frequency-dependent model, a finding that has practical importance for plant breeders and genetic engineers who must take into account diverse and rapidly evolving pathogen populations.

Evolutionary history of the NBS-LRR family

The evolutionary history of the NBS-LRR family has been studied quite extensively. The results clearly support a division of NBS-LRRs into separate TIR and non-TIR groups (30,37,8). Features in the NBS, as well as the presence or absence of the TIR or CC domains, unambiguously distinguish sequence types in this gene superfamily (30,37). Surprisingly, TIR-NBS-LRRs are undetectable and probably absent in the Poaceae (30,37). Efforts to uncover TIRs in both public and private databases of grass sequences have uniformly failed, while non-TIR-NBS-LRR sequences are found in all angiosperm species examined. Targeted PCR amplification experiments have added further support to these observations (37). Because TIR-containing NBS-LRR sequences have been discovered among Gymnosperms, and proteins with TIRs are known to exist in animals, it seems likely that the common ancestor of angiosperms and gymnosperms contained both types of NBS-LRR sequences, with the branch leading to modern grasses (maybe all monocots) subsequently losing the TIR class.

Beyond the deep TIR/non-TIR division, phylogenetic studies of NBS-LRR genes from diverse taxa demonstrate several important features. First, the non-TIR subfamily has greater sequence diversity than the TIR subfamily, and can be divided into at least four ancient, multi-plant-family clades. Two of these clades contain both eudicot and gymnosperm sequences, and three contain both dicot and monocot sequences (8). The deeply divided phylogeny of NBS-LRRs indicates that the gene superfamily diversified early in the history of plant evolution, and argues for caution in extrapolating functional information from known R genes to divergent R gene homologues.

While early divergences among NBS-LRR genes predated the separation of extant plant families, more recently evolved clades are frequently populated by sequences from single taxonomic families. In a detailed phylogenetic analysis of tomato and other Solanaceous NBS-LRR sequences, Pan et al. (36) observed that sequences from different Solanaceous species are well distributed among branches of the tomato phylogenetic tree. This suggests that these NBS-LRRs probably arose from common ancestors that existed before speciation within the Solanaceae.

Potato and tomato sequences form tight clusters on the phylogenetic tree and some tomato NBS-LRRs are more closely related to potato than other tomato-derived sequences. Potentially these NBS-LRRs represent sequence orthologs or sequences derived from relatively

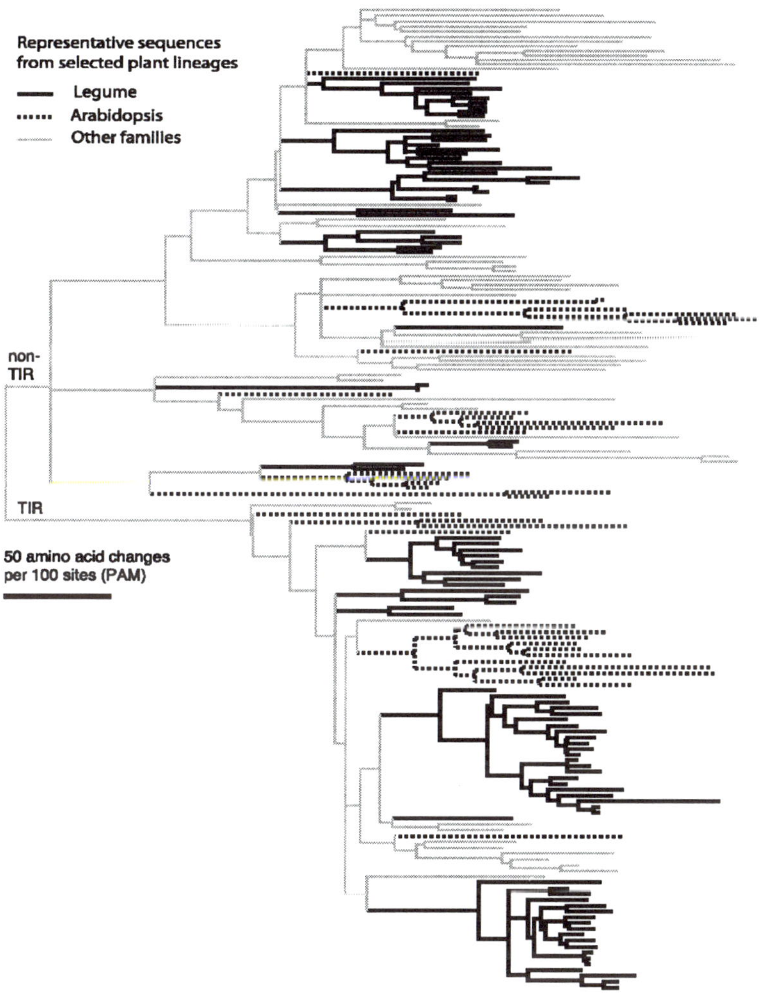

Figure 2. Phylogenetic tree of representative NBS-LRR sequences from selected plant lineages, showing the TIR and non-TIR subfamilies. Dotted lines show placement of sequences representing major *Arabidopsis thaliana* lineages. Solid bold lines show sequences from eleven legume species. Gray lines show sequences sampled from other diverse plant families, including monocots (non-TIR only). Sequences from well-sampled legume species (primarily *Glycine max* and *Medicago truncatula*) are found together in most legume-specific clades, but are distantly separated from *Arabidopsis* sequences. The tree was calculated using the NBS domain, and is based on a parsimony topology with maximum likelihood branch lengths. From supplement to (8), available at http://www.tc.umn.edu/~cann0010/CannonEtAl_R_genes.html.

recent common ancestors. Even after dozens of *Arabidopsis* NBS-LRRs were added to the phylogenetic tree, all branches remained family-specific. From this, the authors inferred that major gene duplication events occurred during dicot divergence into various taxa, followed by recent radiation from common ancestors.

Within any major R-gene clade, particular taxa can be dramatically over or under-represented relative to sequences from other taxa, suggesting preferential expansions or losses of certain R-gene types (8). The most dramatic example is the apparent loss of the TIR sequence subfamily from Poaceae. Though less dramatic, a non-TIR clade that appears to have undergone extensive diversification in Fabaceae (legumes) is represented by only two sequences in *Arabidopsis* (AT3G14460 and AT3G14470), while a TIR clade that has undergone dramatic diversification in *Arabidopsis* (the *RPP1*-containing clade, conferring resistance to *Peronospora parasitica*, and at least 50 homologues) has no close homologues identified to date in any other plant family (Fig. 2). In fact, *Arabidopsis* TIR-type sequences appear to have generally undergone an expansion relative to non-TIR sequences (with approximately a 2:1 ratio), a pattern not been observed in counts of R genes from other well-sampled plant taxa.

These findings underscore several points of theoretical and practical interest: the NBS-LRR gene family is diverse and rapidly changing, with diversification or complete loss of important sequence types in some plant lineages. Thus, no single species, including *Arabidopsis*, is likely to serve as a model for all sequence types in distantly related plant species. This observation may have functional significance, as lineage-specific NBS-LRR genes exhibit functionality only in restricted taxa. For example, the cloned R genes, *Bs2* from pepper and *RPS2* from *Arabidopsis,* both function in only in their respective related species (46). Nonetheless, nearly every branch of the TIR and non-TIR trees contains at least one R gene of known specificity, so most NBS-containing sequences are related to known R genes and may encode functional R proteins. This is especially significant because so many NBS-LRR sequences reported to date have been isolated by PCR amplification using degenerate primers and therefore have no direct connection (yet) to actual resistance phenotypes.

Perspectives on the NBS-LRR Family

Access to the complete genome sequence of *Arabidopsis* emphasizes just how important the analysis of complex gene families will be to our understanding of biological function and evolution. NBS-LRRs represent one of the best-characterized sequence families in plants today. Still, a great deal remains to be learned about their function, organization, and evolution. The true biological roles of NBS-LRR domains remain largely hypothetical or, at best, suggested through circumstantial evidence.

Powerful conceptual frameworks for understanding the driving forces of diversification within NBS-LRRs have been proposed, but only much more genome sequence and re-sequencing of R gene haplotypes can provide the information needed to reveal the underlying mechanisms. Hundreds (perhaps thousands) of NBS-LRR family members have been partially sequenced and several NBS-LRR gene clusters have been completed sequenced. Yet we still do not know whether the NBS-LRRs of *Arabidopsis*, other dicots, monocots, or green plants generally undergo the same kind of evolutionary histories or adopt the same type of genomic architecture. Clearly, a thorough understanding of the NBS-LRR gene family will provide important insights into both plant-pathogen interactions and the overall evolution of plant genomes.

Acknowledgements

We thank Dr. Deborah Samac for her valuable suggestions on the manuscript, Dr. Georgiana May, Dr. Russ Spangler, and Andy Baumgarten for scientific discussions and unpublished data, and Dr. Richard Michelmore for permission to reprint a figure from the University of California-Davis "*Arabidopsis* Resistance Gene" web site.

References

1. Aarts N, Metz M, Holub E, Staskawicz B J, Daniels M J, Parker JE (1998) Different requirements for EDS1 and NDR1 by disease resistance genes define at least two R gene-mediated signaling pathways in *Arabidopsis*. Proc. Natl. Acad. Sci. USA 95:10306-10311.
2. Anderson PA, Lawrence GJ, Morrish BC, Ayliffe MA, Finnegan EJ, Ellis JG (1997) Inactivation of the flax rust resistance gene M associated with loss of a repeated unit within the leucine-rich repeat coding region. Plant Cell 9: 641-651.
3. *Arabidopsis* Genome Initiative (2000) Analysis of the genome sequence of the flowering plant *Arabidopsis thaliana*. Nature 408. 796-815.
4. Bent A F (1996) Plant disease resistance genes: function meets structure. Plant Cell 8:1757-1771.
5. Bergelson J, Kreitman M, Stahl EA, Tian D (2001) Evolutionary dynamics of plant R-genes. Science 292: 2281-2285.
6. Bishop JG, Dean AM, Mitchell-Olds, T (2000) Rapid evolution in plant chitinases: molecular targets of selection in plant-pathogen coevolution. Proc. Natl. Acad. Sci. USA 97:5322-55327.
7. Caicedo AL, Schaal BA, Kunkel, B. N. (1999) Diversity and molecular evolution of the RPS2 resistance gene in *Arabidopsis thaliana*. Proc. Natl. Acad. Sci. USA 96:302-306.

8. Cannon SB, Zhu H, Baumgarten AM, Spangler R, May G, Cook DR, Young ND (2002) Diversity, distribution, and ancient taxonomic relationships within the TIR and non-TIR NBS-LRR resistance gene subfamilies. Jour. Molec. Evol. 54:548-562. URL: http://www.tc.umn.edu/~cann0010/CannonEtAl_R_genes.html

9. Century KS, Shapiro AD, Repetti PP, Dahlbeck D, Holub E, Staskawicz BJ (1997) NDR1, a pathogen-induced component required for *Arabidopsis* disease resistance. Science 278:1963-1965.

10. Collins N, Drake J, Ayliffe M, Sun Q, Ellis J, Hulbert S, Pryo T (1999) Molecular characterization of the maize Rp1-D rust resistance haplotype and its mutants. Plant Cell 11: 1365-1376.

11. Dangl JS, Jones J DG (2001) Plant Pathogens and integrated defense responses to infection. Nature 411: 826-833.

12. Dixon M S, Hatzixanthis K, Jones D A, Harrison K, Jones JDG. (1998) The tomato Cf-5 disease resistance gene and six homologs show pronounced allelic variation in leucine-rich repeat copy number. Plant Cell 10:1915-1925.

13. Ellis J, Jones D (1998) Structure and function of proteins controlling strain-specific pathogen resistance in plants. Curr. Op. Plant Biol. 1:288-293.

14. Ellis JG, Lawrence GJ, Luck JE, Dodds PN (1999). Identification of regions in alleles of the flax rust resistance gene L that determine differences in gene-for-gene specificity. Plant Cell 11: 495-506.

15. Falk A, Feyes B, Frost LN, Jones J DG, Daniels MJ, Parker JE (1999) EDS1, an essential component of R gene-mediated disease resistance in *Arabidopsis* has homology to eukaryotic lipases. Proc. Natl. Acad. Sci. USA 96:3292-3297.

16. Foster-Hartnett D, Mudge J, Danesh D, Yan H, Denny R, Young ND A detailed comparative genomic analysis of a 10 centimorgan region on soybean molecular linkage group 'G'. Genome, in press.

17. Goff SA, Ricke D, Lan T-H, et al. (2002) A draft sequence of the rice genome (*Oryza sativa* L. ssp. *japonica*). Science 296:92-100.

18. Hoffmann JA, Kafatos FC, Janeway CA, Ezkowitz RAB (1999) Phylogenetic perspectives in innate immunity. Science 284:1313-1317.

19. Jeong SC, Jayes AJ, Biyashev RM, Saghai Maroof MA (2001) Diversity and evolution of a non-TIR-NBS sequence family that clusters to a chromosomal "hotspot" for disease resistance genes in soybean. Theor. Appl. Genet. 103:406-414.

20. Jia Y, McAdams SA, Bryan GT, Hershey HP, Valent B (2000) Direct interaction of resistance gene and avirulence gene products confers rice blast resistance. EMBO J. 19: 4004-4014.

21. Jones DA, Jones JDG. (1997) The role of leucine-rich repeat proteins in plant defences. Adv. Bot. Res. 24:90-167.
22. Jones DA, Thomas CM, Hammond-Kosack KE, Balint-Kurti PJ, Jones JDG. (1994) Isolation of the tomato Cf-9 gene for resistance to *Cladosporium fulvum* by transposon tagging. Science 266:789-793.
23. Jones JDG (2001) Putting knowledge of plant disease resistance genes to work. Curr. Op. Plant Biol. 4: 281-287.
24. Ku H-M, Vision T, Liu J, Tanksley SD (2000) Comparing sequenced segments of the tomato and *Arabidopsis* genomes: Large-scale duplication followed by selective gene loss creates a network of synteny. Proc. Natl. Acad. Sci. USA 97:9121–9126.
25. Leister D, Kurth J, Laurie DA, Yano M, Sasaki T, Devos K, Graner A, Schulze-Lefert P (1998) Rapid reorganization of resistance gene homologues in cereal genomes. Proc. Natl. Acad. Sci. USA 95: 370-375
26. Li P, Nijhawan D, Budihardjo I, Srinvasula SM, Ahmad M, Alnemri E S, Wang X (1997) Cytochrome c and dATP-dependent formation of Apaf-1/caspase-9 complex initiates an apoptotic protease cascade. Cell 91:479-487.
27. Lupas A (1996) Coiled coils: New structures and new functions. Trends Biochem. Sci. 21:375-382.
28. Martin GB, Brommonschenkel SH, Chunwongse J, Frary A, Ganal M W, Spivey R, Wu T, Earle ED, Tanksley SD (1993) Map-based cloning of a protein kinase gene conferring disease resistance in tomato. Science 262:1432-1436.
29. Meyers BC, Shen KA, Rohani P, Gaut BS, Michelmore RW (1998) Receptor-like genes in the major resistance locus of lettuce are subject to divergent selection. Plant Cell 10:1833-1846.
30. Meyers BC, Dickerman AW, Michelmore RW, Pecherer RM, Sivaramakrishnan S, Sobral BW, Young ND (1999) Plant disease resistance genes encode members of an ancient and diverse protein family within the nucleotide-binding superfamily. Plant J. 20: 317-332.
31. Michelmore R (2000) Genomic approaches to plant disease resistance. Curr. Op. Plant Biol. 3: 125-131.
32. Michelmore R, Bent A, Hulbert S, Leach J et al. (2001) "Functional and comparative genomics of disease resistance gene homologs" web page. URL: *http://niblrrs.ucdavis.edu*
33. MIPS *Arabidopsis thaliana* group (2001) "AT_RGenes db resistance gene resource" web page. URL: http://mips.gsf.de/proj/thal/
34. Noël L, Moores TL, van der Biezen EA, Parniske M, Daniels MJ, Parker JE, Jones JDG (1999) Pronounced intraspecific haplotype

divergence at the RPP5 complex disease resistance locus of *Arabidopsis*. Plant Cell 11: 2099-2112.

35. Penuela S, Danesh D, Young ND (2002) Targeted isolation, sequence analysis, and physical mapping of nonTIR NBS-LRR genes in soybean. Theor. Appl. Genet. 104:261-272.
36. Pan Q, Liu YS, Budai-Hadrian O, Sela M, Carmel-Goren L, Zamir D, Fluhr R (2000a) Comparative genetics of nucleotide binding site-leucine rich repeat resistance gene homologues in the genomes of two dicotyledons: tomato and *Arabidopsis*. Genetics 155:309-322.
37. Pan Q, Wendel J, Fluhr R (2000b) Divergent evolution of plant NBS-LRR resistance gene homologues in dicot and cereal genomes. J. Mol. Evol. 2000 50: 203-213.
38. Parker JE, Holub EB, Frost LN, Falk A, Gunn ND, Daniels M J (1996) Characterization of eds1, a mutation in *Arabidopsis* suppressing resistance to *Peronospora parasitica* specified by several different RPP genes. Plant Cell 8:2033-2046.
39. Parniske M, Jones JDG (1999) Recombination between diverged clusters of the tomato Cf-9 plant disease resistance gene family. Proc. Natl. Acad. Sci. USA 96: 5850-5855.
40. Rigden DJ, Mello LV, Bertioli DJ (2000) Structural modeling of a plant disease resistance gene product domain. Prot. Struc., Func. & Genet. 41:133-143.
41. Ronald PC (1998) Resistance gene evolution. Curr. Op. Plant Biol. 1:294-298.
42. Song W-Y, Wang G-L, Chen L-L, Kim H-S, Holsten T, Wang T, Zhai W-X, Zhu L-H, Fanquet C, Ronald P (1995) A receptor kinase-like protein encoded by the rice disease resistance gene, Xa21. Science 270:1804-1806.
43. Srinivasula SM, Ahmad M, Fernandes-Alnemri T, Alnemri ES (1998) Autoactivation of procaspase-9 by Apaf-1-mediated oligomerization. Mol. Cell 1:949-957.
44. Sun Q, Collins NC, Ayliffe M, Smith SM, Drake J, Pryor T, Hulbert S H. (2001) Recombination between paralogues at the Rp1 rust resistance locus in maize. Genetics 158: 423-438.
45. Stahl EA, Dwyer G, Mauricio R, Kreitman M, Bergelson J (1999) Dynamics of disease resistance polymorphism at the Rpm1 locus of *Arabidopsis*. Science 400:667-671.
46. Tai TH, Dahlbeck D, Clark ET, Gajiwala P, Pasion R, Whalen MC, Stall RE, Staskawicz BJ (1999) Expression of the Bs2 pepper gene confers resistance to bacterial spot disease in tomato. Proc. Natl. Acad. Sci. USA 96: 14153-14158.
47. van der Biezen EA, Sun J, Coleman MJ, Bibb M J, Jones JDG (2000) *Arabidopsis* RelA/SpoT homologs implicate (p)ppGpp in plant signaling. PNAS 97: 3747-3752.

48. van Dodeweerd A-M, Hall CR, Bent EG, Johnson SJ, Bevan MW, Bancroft I (1999) Identification and analysis of homoeologous segments of the genomes of rice and *Arabidopsis thaliana*. Genome 42: 887-892.
49. Vision T, Brown DG, Tanksley SD (2000) The origins of genomic duplications in *Arabidopsis*. Science 290: 2114-2117.
50. Wei F, Gobelman-Werner K, Morroll SM, Kurth J, Mao L, Wing R, Leister D, Schulze-Lefert P, Wise RP (1999) The Mla (powdery mildew) resistance cluster is associated with three NBS-LRR gene families and suppressed recombination within a 240-kb DNA interval on chromosome 5S (1HS) of barley. Genetics 153: 1929-1948.
51. Young ND (2000) The genetic architecture of resistance. Curr. Opin. Plant Biol. 3: 285-290.
52. Zhu H, Cannon SB, Young ND, Cook DR Phylogeny and genomic organization of the TIR and non-TIR NBS-LRR resistance gene family in *Medicago truncatula*. Molec. Plant-Microbe Interact. In press.

Transporters Involved in Communication, Attack or Defense in Plant-Microbe Interactions

Janet L. Taylor

One of the great challenges ahead in the post-genomics era will be gaining an understanding of the structures and functions of integral membrane proteins. Proportionally few membrane proteins have been characterized since they are difficult to purify. However, as the number of sequenced genomes increases so does the available sequence data on putative membrane proteins increase. Therefore, we can make sequence comparisons between known membrane proteins and literally thousands of candidate proteins. This will allow us to build more detailed structural models for these proteins. The models can then be tested in membrane reconstitution experiments. This advancement in our understanding of membrane structure/function will no doubt open a new era in plant-microbe interaction research, since the plasma membranes of both plant and microbe are key determinants of the outcome of the interaction.

Among the most important of the membrane proteins are those that function in uptake or efflux. In this chapter I will bring together the available information on transporters that function in signaling, attack or defense in plant-microbe interactions. Transporters involved in nutrient uptake are not included.

Transporter Function and Distribution

Transporters are involved in a large number of vital functions in both prokaryotic and eukaryotic cells (102). They promote entry of all essential nutrients, control metabolite concentrations in cells through excretion and extrude drugs/toxic substances. Transporters also mediate uptake and efflux of ions from the cytoplasm to maintain the concentration differential necessary for enzyme activity. Additionally, they are responsible for the secretion of small molecules, proteins, complex carbohydrates, and lipids that function in communication, antigen presentation, sporulation, protection and pathogenesis.

Of the estimated 5600 protein coding genes of *Saccharomyces cerevisiae*, at least 320 encode putative or established transporters involved in small molecule transport (122). Functions are known for 140 of these proteins. Approximately the same number of genes in *Escherichia coli* code for transporter components. For the multicellular organisms *Arabidopsis thaliana* (L.) Heynh. and *Caenorhabditis elegans* the estimated numbers of genes for transporters is 600 and 700, respectively. A tabulation of the transporters found in the genomes from more than 20 organisms can be found at the World Wide Web site (http://www-biology.ucsd.edu/ ~ipaulsen/transport/)

Transporter Classification

Considering the large numbers and complexity of transporters Saier (102) and co-workers have proposed a transporter classification (TC) system that was reviewed and recommended for adoption by a panel of experts for the International Union of Biochemistry and Molecular Biology. The classifications are based on both structure and phylogeny. The detailed description of the TC system can be found at the World Wide Web site (http://www-biology.ucsd.edu/~msaier/transport).

Each transporter is assigned a five-digit TC number that represents class, subclass, family, subfamily and finally substrate or range of substrates. The classes are: [1] channels and pores, [2] electrochemical potential-driven transporters, [3] primary active transporters, [4] group translocators, [8] accessory factors involved in transport and [9] incompletely characterized transport systems. Yet to be discovered novel types of transporters will be placed in classes 5 – 7. The class and subclass assignments are based on mode of transport and energy-coupling source.

For assignment to the same family, proteins must display a region of 60 or more amino acid residues in comparable parts of their sequence that have a comparison score in excess of nine standard deviations. The probability of this degree of sequence similarity occurring by chance is less than 10^{-19}. It is also unlikely that this degree of sequence similarity could have arisen from convergent evolution. The application of these criteria leads to the assignment of known transporters to about 250 families (103).

In this chapter the focus is mainly on members of three superfamilies of transporters that have been shown to function in or are associated with plant-microbe interaction. These families are the ATP-binding cassette (ABC) transporters (TC3.A.1) of the primary active transporter class, the Major Facilitator Superfamily (MFS) (TC2.A.1) and the Resistance-Nodulation-Cell Division (RND) superfamily (TC2.A.6) both from the electrochemical potential-driven transporter class.

ATP-Binding Cassette Transporters

The ABC family of transporters (TC3.A.1), also referred to as traffic ATPases (82), is the largest known protein family. The first complete sequence of genes encoding an ABC transporter was reported in 1982 (43). It is now known that almost 5% of the *E. coli* genome encodes components of ABC transporters. A search of the protein database at NCBI in October 2001 with the keyword ABC transporter retrieved 10,971 entries. The vast majority of the ABC proteins are primary membrane translocators but some also function as ion channels, channel regulators, receptors, proteases and sensors (107, 7).

ABC transporters responsible for uptake of substrates from the external environment are thus far confined to prokaryotes but efflux pumps are found in both prokaryotes and eukaryotes. Currently, the ABC superfamily is divided into 22 uptake permease families, 21 prokaryotic efflux system families and 11 families of eukaryotic efflux pumps (103). However, there are several bacterial ABC transporters that demonstrate bi-directional transport (123), such as the general amino acid permease of *Rhizobium leguminosarum* (129). ABC transporters move a vast array of different substrates including, ions, heavy metals, carbohydrates, vitamins, numerous drugs, amino acids, phospholipids, steroids, glucocorticoids, bile acids, mycotoxins, antibiotics, pigments, peptides and whole proteins. *Mycoplasma genitalium*, thought to have the smallest genome of any self-replicating organism does not contain homologues of drug efflux pumps. This finding suggests that while these types of transporters may provide a selective advantage, they are not essential for survival (92).

STRUCTURE

All ABC transporters have a similar molecular architecture composed of two nucleotide-binding domains (ABC) and two transmembrane domains (TMD) with several predicted membrane spanning segments each (MSS) (42). The ABC domain is composed of approximately 250 amino acids and has three conserved motifs. The Walker A and Walker B motifs are found in all nucleotide binding proteins (128). A third motif called the ABC signature or C motif is found only in ABC transporters. The ABC domains of transporters are located on the inside face of membranes (43).

Saurin and co-workers (106) performed a phylogenetic analysis on 197 ABC domain sequences. Surprisingly, the unrooted tree had two main branches, one composed of all uptakes systems and the other composed of efflux systems. The authors proposed that the differentiation occurred only once in history, probably before the separation of prokaryotes and eukaryotes. Additional correlation was found between the substrate specificity and the ABC domain classification. This is surprising since there is no conclusive data indicating a direct interaction of substrate with an ABC domain.

The first data on the tertiary structure of an ABC domain of a transporter came with the crystallization of the *HisP* gene product (48). This *HisP* encodes the ABC domains of the histidine permease of *Salmonella typhimurium*. The HisP monomer in the crystal was roughly L-shaped with two thick arms. The proteins, bound to ATP crystallized as a dimer with the short arms of the L lying parallel to each other. Each peptide was composed of a combination of β-strands and α-helices. The overall fold of the structure was different from any known protein but had limited similarities to parts of *E. coli* RecA and bovine F_1-ATPase. The structure of the HisP crystal was consistent with the biochemical and genetic data collected on the protein in association with the other subunits of this transporter.

The usual number of MSS in the TMD of an ABC transporter is six. In prokaryotes, different genes encode the ABC and TMD. As stated earlier, the functional transporter consists of two ABC domains and two TMDs. In eukaryotes, two different gene structures are found. Firstly, the half-transporter where one gene encodes one ABC domain and one TMD in a single polypeptide. The functional transporter is a homodimer. In the other gene structure two ABC domains and two TMDs are encoded in a single polypeptide (42). The domain arrangement varies from one transporter to another with the ABC located either N-terminally or C-terminally to the TMD. These protein structures are generally designated as $(ABC\text{-}MSS_6)_2$ and $(MSS_6\text{-}ABC)_2$, respectively. Certain ABC transporters have additional domains or associated peptides that serve regulatory or other auxiliary functions.

All transporters in Gram-negative bacteria that mediate uptake associate with a substrate-binding protein located in the periplasmic space also referred to as a periplasmic binding protein (PBP). Results from experiments with reconstituted uptake systems in liposomes indicated that the substrate-binding protein acts as a signal transducer to initiate transport (18). ABC transporters of Gram-negative bacteria that export proteins require not only a PBP but also an outer membrane protein to facilitate passage (88).

MULTIDRUG EFFLUX PUMPS

Among the ABC transporters that function as multidrug efflux pumps the most intensely studied are Pdr5p (pleiotropic drug resistance) (TC3.A.1.205) of *S. cerevisiae* and the mammalian P-glycoprotein (P-gp) (TC3.A.1.201). These two transporters and others from a range of organisms are capable of exporting multiple drugs of dissimilar structures. For P-gp, Seelig and co-workers (110) suggested that the spatial separation of electron donor groups determined substrate recognition. The mammalian P-gp encoded by *MDR1* (multidrug resistance) is particularly important from a medical standpoint. Overexpression of P-gp in cancer cells leads to resistance to many chemical therapeutics. Long term exposure to the drugs apparently also selects for genetic variants of P-gp that have altered substrate specificity (24).

SUBSTRATE RECOGNITION

A number of studies have been done to determine the amino acids involved in substrate recognition by the multidrug efflux pumps. *S. cerevisiae* Pdr5p $(ABC\text{-}MSS_6)_2$ confers resistance to cycloheximide, several rhodamines, various azole fungicides and numerous other compounds. Mutant proteins were obtained that no longer recognized some of these substrates but retained recognition of others (28, 29). Sequence analysis of the various mutants indicated that mutations in either of the ABCs, in predicted extracellular loop 6 between MSS11 and 12 or in predicted MSS10 altered drug substrate specificity. A mutation in MSS10, S1360F, also abolished Pdr5p inhibition by the drug FK506.

The C1427Y mutation in extracellular loop 6 caused Pdr5p to be retained in the endoplasmic reticulum (ER). In contrast, a P-gp mutant lacking all cysteines was still inserted into the plasma membrane. However, mutations of several glycines in predicted cytoplasmic loops of P-gp did lead to ER retention (74).

The double mutation T1460I/V1467I in predicted extracellular loop 6 of Pdr5p led to loss of resistance to cycloheximide and two azole fungicides but resistance to rhodamines was retained (29). Mutants of P-gp with alterations in predicted extracellular loop 6 also display altered substrate specificity (132).

However, the structure of these pumps does not appear to be the sole determinant of substrate specificity. Kaur and Bachhawat (60) found that both the drug specificity and the transport efficiency of Pdr5p were altered in ergosterol mutants of *S. cerevisiae*. Similar studies on reconstituted P-gp in liposomes indicated that the membrane lipid composition affected ATP hydrolysis (100).

A recent study of P-gp utilizing radioligand-binding indicated that the protein has at least three substrate binding sites (77). One of these sites also binds drugs that modulate P-gp activity but are not transported. A fourth site was identified that only bound modulators. The authors proposed that each site has a high- and low-affinity state for its ligand that exist in equilibrium. Furthermore, they suggested that allosteric interactions among sites could shift the equilibrium in the states of any one particular site. The distance between the binding sites identified is unknown. It may be that they make up individual domains in a single large binding pocket (111).

STRUCTURE

On the basis of the hydropathy profile, the MSS in P-gp were predicted to be α-helical (55). This structure has become the most accepted model for ABC transporters but recently another model was presented

(52). This model of P-gp was based on computer prediction algorithms, the hydropathic profile and secondary structure analysis. The model proposes that the transporter is formed into two membrane-embedded sixteen-strand β-barrels attached by short loops to two six-helix bundles underneath each barrel. Jones and George (53) also proposed an alternative model for the ABC domain in which the C-motif of one ABC participates in ATP-binding in the adjacent ABC domain.

The three-dimensional structure of P-gp at 2.5-nanometer resolution was recently published (101). The structure was determined by electron microscopy and image analysis of purified reconstituted protein in the absence of ATP. A drawing depicting that structure is shown in Figure 1.

P-gp was revealed to be a cylinder of about ten-nanometer diameter and eight-nanometer maximum height having six-fold symmetry. Approximately three-nanometer of the height was seen as lobes on the cytoplasmic face of the membrane. The sizes of these lobes corresponded to the estimated dimensions of the ABC domains.

A cone-shaped pore (P) of about five-nanometer diameter appeared roughly in the center of P-gp as viewed from the exterior surface of the cell.

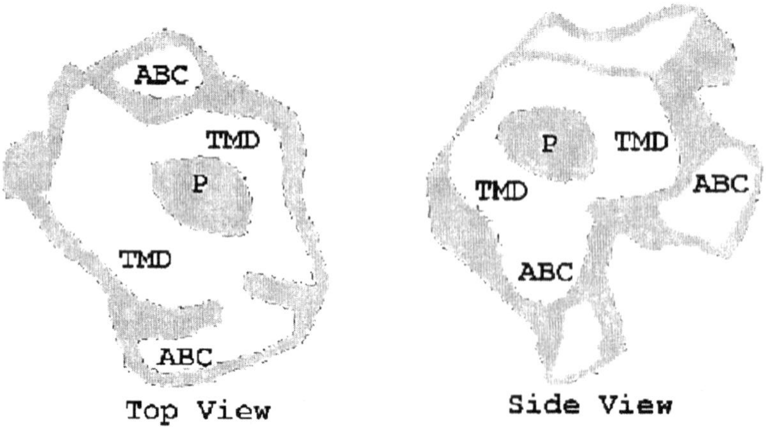

Figure 1. Line drawing depicting three-dimensional structure of P-glycoprotein at 2.5-nanometer resolution. The designations are: ATP-binding domain (ABC), transmembrane domain (TMD), pore (P). Shading indicates portions of the protein below the plane of view.

The pore was closed at the cytoplasmic face of the plasma membrane. The authors suggested that the two intracellular lobes (putative ABC domains) and the intracellular loops that join individual MSS make up the gate on the pore. On the side view of P-gp, showing the protein lying within the lipid bilayer of the membrane, another opening (P) is evident on one side of the molecule. This opening would presumably provide access for substrates to the transporter pore from within the plasma membrane. This provides an explanation for the selective transport of amphipathic compounds that can partition into the phospholipid bilayer (124).

Among the proposed models for substrate transport by MDR proteins, two are considered the most likely. The "vacuum cleaner" model proposes that the substrates enter the central domain of a channel from the membrane rather than the cytosol. This channel is closed on the cytosolic face of the membrane but open to the external face (35). In the "flippase" model of transport the substrate also contacts the transporter in the membrane and is subsequently flipped from the inner to the outer face of the membrane (44).

REGULATION OF GENE EXPRESSION

The regulation of ABC transporter gene expression has been studied in the most detail in *S. cerevisiae*. The focus of these studies was the set of transporters known as the pleiotropic drug resistance (PDR) network. The first transcriptional regulators that were identified were Pdr1p (6) and Pdr3p (19). These two proteins are closely related and belong to the binuclear Gal4p-like $Zn(II)_2Cys_6$ family of transcription factors. Mutations in *PDR1* and *PDR3* result in overexpression of several transporters. Gain-of-function alleles of *PDR1* and *PDR3* have also been identified that affect not only drug resistance phenotypes but also increase transmembrane flipping of phospholipid analogues (61). It was suggested that the factors interact with other transcriptional regulators to produce these phenotypes.

DNA binding sites for Pdr1p and Pdr3p have been identified in the promoters of target genes. The consensus motif called the pleiotropic drug resistance element (PDRE) consists of the perfect palindrome 5'-TCCGCGGA-3' (58). Variations in sequence, number and placement of the PDRE motif are found in target gene promoters but it is unknown how these variations affect gene regulation (7). However, the presence of a single degenerate PDRE in a promoter appears to be sufficient for Pdr1p/ Pdr3p regulation (59).

Recent microarray analysis of cDNAs indicated that Pdr1p and Pdr3p regulate expression of 26 genes that fall in six functional groups (23). Those groups are: [1] ABC transporters, [2] MFS transporters, [3] genes involved in lipid metabolism, [4] genes predicted to be involved in cell wall metabolism, [5] stress response genes and [6] genes of unknown function. An additional member of the $Zn(II)_2Cys_6$ family of transcription factors, Yrr1p was also found to participate in ABC transporter control.

Another family of transcription factors has also been shown to regulate the expression of ABC transporter genes in *S. cerevisiae*. This is the Yap family of b-zip proteins that are related to Gcn4p and mammalian AP-1. This family of stress response transcription factors binds to a DNA element consisting of 5'-TTAGCTAA-3' and the Gcn4p binding motif. The targets of the Yap1p are not limited to ABC transporters but include genes that are important for maintaining cell viability during oxidative stress. It is not known what role ABC transporters may play in this process except that the transporter Ycf1p functions in vacuolar sequestering of glutathione conjugates (7).

Finally, transcription factors of the high osmolarity glycerol pathway were found to regulate expression of the ABC transporter gene *PDR15* (TC3.A.1.205) (7). A picture is emerging of a complex and tightly controlled network of transcription factors that respond to different stimuli resulting in expression of ABC transporter genes. This is to be expected for a superfamily of proteins that transport diverse substrates and can dramatically affect cell permeability/ viability.

POST-TRANSLATIONAL MODIFICATION

There is also evidence that ABC transporters are regulated by post-translational modification. These studies were conducted on the best known ABC transporter, mammalian P-gp (15). The over-expression of this protein in cancer cells leads to resistance to anticancer drugs. All ABC transporters of the $(ABC\text{-}MSS_6)_2$ or $(MSS_6\text{-}ABC)_2$ type have a central linker region that can be phosphorylated by protein kinases. P-gp is phosphorylated *in vivo* by protein kinase C (PKC). Inhibitors of PKC induce intracellular drug accumulation and destroy the multidrug resistance phenotype. The inhibitor staurosporine was shown to bind to the ATP-binding site of P-gp, *S. cerevisiae* Pdr5p and *Leishmania tropica* Mdr1p (TC3.A.1.201). Therefore, protein kinase C can be considered a positive regulator of some ABC transporters. As a corollary to this finding, a type 2A-related Ser/Thr protein phosphatase from *Kluyveromyces lactis* was found to negatively regulate *Kl*Pdr5p (TC3.A.1.205) (14).

The Major Facilitator Superfamily of Transporters

MFS transporters are classified as secondary transporters (TC2.A.1) since transport is driven by membrane electrochemical potential (90, 92, 121). Most MFS transporters use a proton gradient to power transport. The superfamily contains transporters that are uniport, symport and antiport. Substrates are limited to small molecules; no oligomer larger than four amino acids or sugar residues is transported. MFS transporters function in uptake, efflux, exchange transport or facilitated diffusion.

A phylogenetic tree of MFS transporters constructed on the basis of sequence similarity splits the transporters into 17 families. These protein families correlate with the structural class of compound transported. The phylogenetic analysis also indicated that the families diverged from each other long ago, perhaps as much as two billion years ago. Of the 17 families, seven so far have been found only in prokaryotes and three only in eukaryotes.

It appears that a minimum of 12 membrane-spanning segments (MSS) is required for activity. Most MFS transporters are 400 - 600 amino acids long and have 12 MSS but there are also families of proteins that contain 14 MSS. A drawing depicting the proposed MSS arrangement of the *E. coli* lactose permease (37) MFS transporter is shown in Figure 2.

Sequence similarity between the N- and C- terminal halves of the proteins indicate that MFS transporters originated from a duplication of an ancestral gene encoding six MSS. Sequence comparison of MFS transporters in different families suggests that the C-terminal half of the proteins have evolved into the region that binds substrate and the N-terminal half is involved in energization of the transport (38). Members of

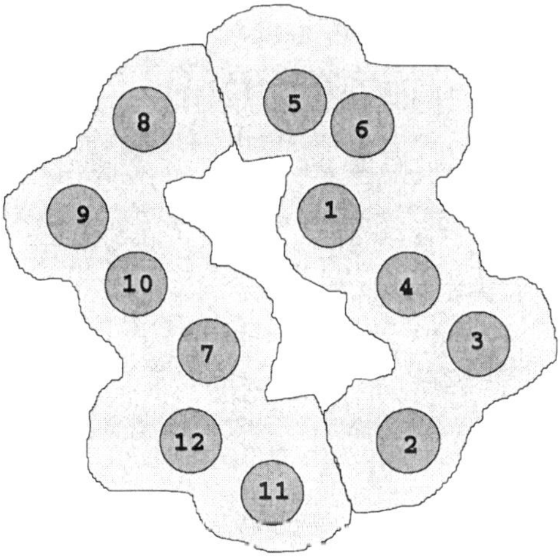

Figure 2. Proposed arrangement of transmembrane segments of a major facilitator transporter, *Escherichia coli* lactose permease, as viewed from the periplasm.

the 12 MSS family have a large intracytosolic loop located between the sixth and seventh MSS. Replacement of the hydrophilic amino acids in this loop with hydrophobic residues may have led to the creation of the two additional MSS found in the 14 MSS family.

Although, MFS transporters do not possess well-conserved domains like the nucleotide-binding domain of ABC transporters, one 13 amino acid motif has been identified. The consensus sequence of the motif is [G (RKPATY) L (GAS) (DN) (RK) (FY) G R (RK) (RKP) (LIVGST) (LIM)] and it is located between the second and third MSS (90). Based on phenotypic analysis of 28 mutants with alterations in that conserved region, it was suggested that these residues are involved in the conformational changes that accompany transport (51). However, there is also data suggesting that this motif acts as a cytoplasmic gate controlling the passage of substrate (131).

Another motif, (g x x x G P x x G G x I) found in the fifth MSS of drug antiporters is not found in symporters of the same families. Molecular modeling of this region led to speculation that the motif may determine the orientation of the unoccupied substrate-binding site and thus determines direction of transport (125).

The results of cysteine-scanning mutagenesis studies suggested that the interaction between substrate and protein involves only a few residues while transport itself requires widespread conformational changes (92). However, there are increasing amounts of data that indicate the existence of more than one drug-interaction site in the efflux transporters (123).

Resistance, Nodulation, Cell Division Transporters

Transporters of the RND superfamily (TC2.A.6), like the MFS, are secondary transporters (92, 121). All substrate efflux by these transporters is likely the result of proton antiport. RND transporters are found in bacteria, archaea and eukaryotes (116). The proteins are divided into seven families. Those families are: [1] heavy metal exporters (TC2.A.6.1), [2] drug and other hydrophobic compound efflux (TC2.A.6.2), [3] lipooligosaccharide secretion (TC2.A.6.3), [4] SecDF (TC2.A.6.4), auxiliary components of the type II secretory pathway, [5] antibiotic export (TC2.A.6.5), [6] sterol homeostasis (TC2.A.6.6), and [7] unknown function (TC2.A.6.7). The first three families are confined mostly to Gram-negative bacteria.

The transporters are generally composed of a single large polypeptide of 700 - 1300 amino acid residues. They share a common topology consisting of 12 membrane-spanning segments and two large periplasmic loops of approximately 300 amino acids each located between MSS 1 and 2 and MSS 7 and 8 (34). A drawing depicting the proposed topology is shown in Figure 3.

It is believed that the structure is the result of an internal duplication of the ancestral gene. Four conserved motifs are found in these proteins. The **A** (G x s x v T v x F x x g t D x x x A q v q V q n k L q x A x p x L P x x V q x q g x x v x k) and **D** (S i N t l T l f g l v l a i G L l v D D A I V v V E N v e R v l a e) motifs in the N-terminal half of the proteins and the **B** (a l v l s a V F l P m a f f g G x t G x i y r q f s i T x v s A m a l S v x v a l t l t P A l c A) and **C** (G k x l x e A x x x a a x x R L R P I L M T s L a f i l G v l P l a i a t G x A G a) motifs in the C-terminal half of the transporters. No functional roles for these motifs have as yet been assigned. In the Gram-negative bacteria the extracytoplasmic loops are proposed to interact with a membrane fusion protein (MFP) connecting the inner and outer membranes and an outer membrane factor (OMF) protein that spans the outer membrane.

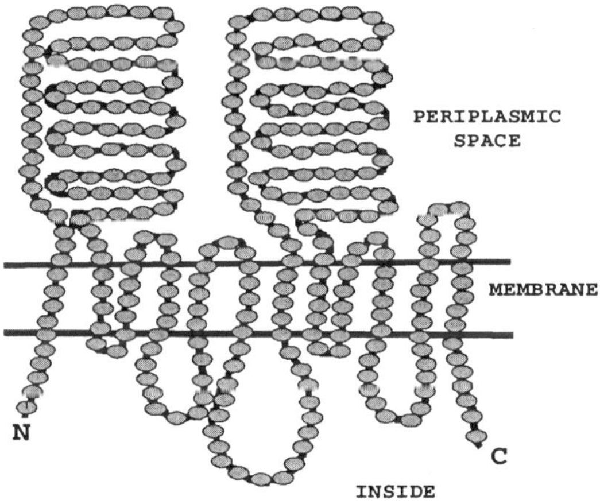

Figure 3. Proposed topology of resistance, nodulation, cell division transporters of families 1-3.

The SecD and SecF proteins of family 4 found in bacteria and archaea vary greatly in length but hydropathy plots indicate a structure similar to families 1-3. Family 5, antibiotic export, is confined to Gram-positive bacteria, mostly those of high G + C content, and only one member has been functionally characterized. The hydropathy plot of these proteins again indicates 12 MSS and two periplasmic loops, the N-terminal loop being much smaller than the C-terminal loop.

The proteins in family 6, sterol homeostasis, are functionally diverse, acting as receptors, enzymes and possibly transporters. The mammalian proteins that are classified in this family include HMG-CoA reductase, Nieman-Pick type C protein 1, SREBP cleavage-activating protein (SCAP) and Patched, a target of the hedgehog signal protein. The proposed topologies are equally diverse indicating as few as 8 MSS for HMG-CoA reductase and SCAP to as many as 14 MSS for Nieman-Pick type C protein (66). The proteins assigned to family 7, unknown function, come from archaea and spirochetes. The hydropathy plots of half-length sequences indicated 6 MSS with a large loop between MSS 1 and 2 and smaller loop between MSS 4 and 5 (116).

Transporters in Bacteria

Bacterial transporters classified in the ABC, MFS, and RND superfamilies have been shown to participate in interactions with plants. These transporters function in communication between plant and bacterium, in attachment, in nutrient uptake, in secretion of pathogenicity factors, in chemotaxis and in resistance to toxic compounds.

Rhizobium

Mutations in the n4 region of the nod box locus of *R. meliloti* caused a three to nine day delay in nodulation of *Medicago sativa* L. (5). There was also a 60% reduction in the number of nodules per plant at 12 days post-inoculation. Sequencing of the region revealed a single operon composed of six genes whose expression was induced by the plant compound luteolin. Based on sequence homology or lack thereof the open reading frames (ORF) were designated in order *nodM*, *nolF*, *nolG*, *nolH*, *nolI* and *nodN*. At the time no database homology could be found for the *nolF* - *nolI* ORFs. In 1994, Saier and co-workers (104) aligned the amino acid sequences of *nolG* - *nolI* with members of the RND transporter superfamily. The *nol*G, *nolH* and *nolI* (TC2.A.6.3) sequences corresponded to the N-terminal, central and C-terminal portions, respectively, of RND transporters. The sequence of *nolF* aligned with membrane fusion proteins that are an auxiliary component of these transporter systems. No further functional analysis of the transporter system has been published. But it is speculated that NolFGHI participates in the export of the lipooligosaccharide nod factor (36).

There is evidence that another transporter is involved in secretion of lipo-chitin oligosaccharides (LCO) in rhizobia (12). Disruption of *nodI* or *nodJ* in *R. etli* resulted in intracellular accumulation of LCO and a phenotype of delayed and reduced numbers of nodules on *Phaseolus vulgaris* L. The nodI and nodJ together constituted an ABC transporter (TC3.A.1.102) (99). This is a half-transporter that likely functions as a homodimer, nodI is the ABC domain and nodJ is the TMD domain.

Formation of normal nitrogen-fixing nodules is also dependent on another transporter of the ABC superfamily. Mutations in the *ndvA* (TC3.A.1.108.1) locus of *R. meliloti* caused delayed formation of small white nodules that were not invaded by the mutant bacterium and thus did not fix nitrogen (113). These mutant bacteria did not produce extracellular β-(1, 2) glucan and displayed decreased attachment and motility.

Although, rhizobia and leguminous plants have a symbiotic interaction, all is not strictly friendly in this relationship. Invasion of root hairs by rhizobia triggers a mild plant defense response that includes production of phytoalexins, salicylic acid and other phenolic compounds. The exopolysaccharides and lipopolysaccharides produced by rhizobia apparently provide some protection from these plant defense compounds.

The secretion of the acidic exopolysaccharide succinoglycan (EPS I) is essential for effective nodulation of alfalfa by *R. meliloti*. Here again an ABC transporter was found to function in the transport (9). The gene, *exsA*, encodes the transporter (TC9.A.1.2.1) and it is located next to the *exo* gene cluster of *R. meliloti*. Mutations in *exsA* resulted in a decreased ratio of high molecular weight to low molecular weight EPS I.

Apparently, exsA is not the only ABC transporter that participates in EPS I production. Mutants of *prsD* in *R. leguminosarum* bv. *trifolii* induced non-nitrogen-fixing nodules on *Trifolium pratense* L. (81). The prsD ABC transporter (TC3.A.1.110.3) resembled protease exporters from *Erwinia* and *Pseudomonas* species (65). The results indicated that *prsD* mutants produced an increased amount of EPS I with an abnormal degree of polymerization (81).

The production of functional O-antigen lipopolysaccharide (LPS) by *R. etli* also requires the services of an ABC transporter (68). The genes *wzt* and *wzm* encode the ABC domain and the TMD, respectively, of the transporter (TC3.A.1.103). Strains with a mutant transporter induced small white nodules that did not fix nitrogen. The authors suggested that this transporter is responsible for translocation of O-antigen across the inner plasma membrane.

Now there is evidence that a drug resistance transporter also protects *R. etli* during establishment of symbioses (33). The genes *rmrA* and *rmrB* encode a transporter system (TC2.A.1.3.18) of the major facilitator superfamily. Based on sequence similarity RmrA is a membrane fusion protein while RmrB constitutes the transmembrane component of the transporter system. Mutants of *rmrA* formed 40% fewer nodules in bean while *rmrB* mutants showed a smaller decrease in nodule formation. In addition, these mutants displayed sensitivity to phaseollin, phaseollidin, naringenin, coumaric acid and salicylic acid.

Recently, the complete genome sequence was determined for *Mesorhizobium loti* strain MAFF303099 (57). The bacterium was found to contain a chromosome of approximately seven million base pairs (bp) and two plasmids of around 350,000 bp, MLa, and 208,000 bp, MLb. In the chromosome was a region of 611,000 bp that is likely the site of a symbiotic island. Analysis of codon usage in the island and the plasmids suggested that they originated in another organism. Among the genes on pMLa were 40 encoding various components of ABC transporter systems while pMLb contained five genes for these systems.

AGROBACTERIUM

The most intensely studied transport system of *Agrobacterium* species is the one involved in DNA transfer to plant cells. This system is classified as a type IV secretion system (TC3.A.7) and is discussed in detail elsewhere in this volume.

Before an *Agrobacterium* strain can initiate plant infection it must effectively colonize the rhizosphere or plant surface. Mutant analysis indicated that a transporter of the RND superfamily participates in competitive colonization (89). The three genes *ifeA*, *ifeB* and *ifeR* encode the components of this transport system (TC2.A.6.2.3). Mutations in *ifeA* resulted in a competitive disadvantage for the mutant compared to wild type bacteria. Mutant strains accumulated the isoflavonoid coumestrol while the wild type did not. This result suggested that the transporter mediates resistance to plant secondary metabolites.

Rhizobium and *Agrobacterium* species have a very close phylogenetic relationship. Therefore, it is not surprising that *A. tumefaciens* possesses a homologue of *ndvA* designated *chvA* (76% amino acid sequence identity) (TC3.A.1.108.1). Like *ndvA*, mutations in *chvA* block β-(1, 2) glucan export (11). The *chvA* mutants failed to attach to plant cells and thus did not initiate crown gall tumor formation.

At least one other ABC transport system has a role in *Agrobacterium* attachment to plant cells (79, 80). The loci that encode the transporter system are designated *attA1*, *attA2*, *attB*, *attC* and *attE*. Strains carrying mutations in any of these loci failed to attach to plant cells and consequently were avirulent. However, incubating the mutants in a medium that, prior to filter sterilization, had held wild-type bacteria and plant cells did complement the mutations. The result suggested that this ABC transporter system is involved in mediating a signaling compound exchange.

Successful DNA transformation of plant cells by *Agrobacterium* species requires the expression of plasmid encoded virulence genes. Virulence gene expression is controlled by an apparent two-component regulatory system composed of virA and virG. An ABC transporter, resembling the bacterial drug resistance family, was recently found to be involved in control of virulence gene expression. The gene *chvD* encodes the ABC domain of the transporter system (TC3.A.1.105) (73). Mutants of *chvD* had reduced virulence that could be complemented by constitutive expression of *virG*. The mutants also grew poorly in rich medium but had normal growth in minimal medium. The authors speculated that this transporter system may reduce intracellular concentrations of toxic compounds.

Plant cells transformed by *Agrobacterium* produce amino acids and sugar derivatives called opines. The opines are chemo-attractants for the bacterium. Periplasmic binding proteins such as AccA and OccJ that are components of ABC transporters of the permease family mediated the chemo-attraction (63). The genes encoding the transporter systems are located on the Ti plasmids. The gene designations are derived from the opine to which the proteins bind. In pTiA6 the other components of the system are encoded by *occQMPJ* (TC3.A.1.3.5) (120), in pTiC58 the genes are *accABCDE* (TC3.A.1.5.4) (62) and in pTiR10 the genes are *ophABCDE* (TC3.A.1.11.3) (32). For *A. tumefaciens* C58 the transporter system is also responsible for uptake of the antibiotic agrocin 84.

ERWINIA

Maceration of plant tissue by the phytopathogenic bacterium *Erwinia chryanthemi* results mainly from the breakdown of pectin in the cell wall. The bacterium secretes a set of endo-pectate lyases that initiate pectin degradation into oligogalacturonides (OGN) of various lengths. The final degradation of these oligomers takes place inside the bacterium. Two transporters are responsible for the uptake of the OGNs (46, 47). The *togM*, *togN*, *togA* and *togB* genes encode an ABC transporter (TC3.1.1.11) that is highly similar to the products of the *ogtABCD* operon from *Yersinia pestis* and *Klebsiella pneumoniae* (46). TogM and N are the TMDs of the transporter while TogA is the ATP-binding domain. The presence of an N-terminal signal sequence on TogB suggests that it is the periplasmic ligand-binding protein. Expression of the TogMNAB transporter in *E. coli* resulted in OGN uptake. TogMNAB mutants retained the ability to grow on various OGNs indicating transporter redundancy. However, the mutants had longer lag phases than wild type on polygalacturonate. Additionally, the mutants showed reduced attraction to OGNs suggesting that TogB acts as a chemoreceptor. Finally, chicory leaves infected with the mutants showed 25% less rotting than with wild type bacteria. The mutant bacterial population in the leaves was also 32% less than wild type.

The second transporter shown to participate in OGN uptake is TogT (47). The protein is a member of the glycoside-pentoside-hexuronide (GPH) family (TC2.A.2.51) of cation symporters. A *togT* mutant grew normally on various OGNs. However, a *togT*, *togMNAB* double mutant was unable to use polygalacturonate or shorter oligomers as carbon sources. Like the *togMNAB* mutant, the *togT* mutant caused less rotting and had reduced population size in leaves. The effect of the double mutations was additive.

The bacterium also secretes two metalloproteases designated B and C. The proteases are synthesized as inactive precursors with short N-terminal extensions that are auto catalytically cleaved in the external environment. The secretion of these proteases does not require signal peptides but is accomplished by an ABC transporter (69). The genes that encode the transporter system are *prtD*, *prtE* and *prtF*. PrtD contains the ABC and TMD of the transporter. PrtE is apparently the MFP that facilitates transfer across the periplasmic space to PrtF. Sequence homology to TolC indicates that PrtF (TC1.B.17.1.2) is the OMP that provides passage to the external environment.

The production of additional virulence factors by the bacterium is required for pathogenicity. The area of the *E. chrysanthemi* genome that encodes these virulence factors was identified through transposon mutagenesis. Recent molecular analysis of this area revealed an operon that is involved in iron acquisition and resistance to oxidative stress (85). Based on sequence similarity to database entries, the genes *sufABCDE* and *sufS* are predicted to participate in iron-sulfur metabolism. Sequence comparison also revealed that *sufC* likely encodes an ABC domain. No TMD appeared to be encoded in the operon. Functional analysis of the operon confirmed the predictions. Mutations in all but *sufD* caused increased intracellular concentrations of free iron. The authors proposed that a high free iron concentration would lead to overproduction of activated oxygen species. An increased sensitivity to paraquat in *sufC* and *sufD* mutants supported this hypothesis. Mutations in *sufC* also resulted in bacteria that could not systemically infect *Saintpaulia ionantha* H. Wendl. or macerate chicory leaves.

The ABC domains/transporters described above function in attack of the host plant but the bacterium must also be able to defend itself. Another ABC transporter was found to function in defense against antimicrobial peptides. The *sap* operon was first identified in *S. typhimurium* (91). These five genes encoded an ABC transporter (TC3.A.1.5.5) that conferred resistance to the antimicrobial peptides melittin and protamine. The *sapA* gene encoded the periplasmic binding protein, *sapB* and *sapC* encoded the TMDs of the transporter and *sapD* and *sapF* encoded the ABC domains.

The *sap* operon has a homologue in *E. chrysanthemi* with 71% amino acid sequence similarity (75). Mutations in this operon resulted in sensitivity to wheat α-thionin and potato snakin-1 antimicrobial peptides. Unlike in *S. typhimurium* the mutants were not more sensitive to protamine. The mutants also showed reduced virulence on potato tubers with an average 37% decrease in lesion necrotic area compared to wild type bacteria.

PSEUDOMONAS

Pseudomonas syringae pv. *syringae* produces cyclic lipodepsipeptide toxins syringomycins (syr) and syringopeptins (syp). These toxins cause necrosis in host plants by disrupting ion transport and plasma membrane electrical potential. The toxins are virulence factors. A functional SyrD protein is required for production of syringomycin (98). A *syrD* mutant was 70% less virulent than a wild type bacterium. Based on sequence similarity *syrD* (TC3.A.1.113.1) is predicted to encode a single

ABC and TMD and presumably functions as a homodimer. Very little syringomycin was present in culture supernatants or cell pellets of *syrD* mutants. This result indicated that SyrD is the efflux pump for syringomycin. The mutants also had a reduced amount of the syringomycin synthase complex. These data imply the existence of a concentration dependent feedback control mechanism.

The genes involved in syringopeptin biosynthesis are adjacent to the syringomycin gene cluster (108). The *syp* gene cluster contains an ABC transporter homolog designated *ybjZ* (TC3.A.1). A transposon insertion in this gene knocks out secretion of both syr and syp.

Certain strains of *P. putida* promote emergence and growth of many crop species. For growth promotion to occur, the bacterium must first colonize the rhizosphere. The first step in root colonization is seed adherence. Transposon mutagenesis was used to locate loci in *P. putida* involved in seed attachment (30). Analysis of the transposon flanking sequences indicated that two of the loci encoded transporters. The *mus-13* locus had sequence similarity to an *E. coli* peptide transport protein, CstA, that is induced during carbon starvation. The *mus-21* locus had sequence similarity to glutathione-regulated potassium efflux pumps. These proteins are classified in the secondary transporter class. In addition to decreased attachment the *mus-21* mutant was more sensitive to β-lactam antibiotics.

In another study, the phenotypic changes in *P. putida* associated with adherence were analyzed by 2D gel electrophoresis and cDNA subtraction (105). Among the proteins that were down-regulated during adherence was a homolog of the ABC transporter PotF (TC3.A.1.11.2). A reduced amount of this protein was also seen after addition of homoserine lactone. In contrast, the gene for the ABC transporter PotB (TC3.A.1.11.1) was up-regulated. As well, the expression of the *mex* gene encoding an RND efflux pump and the *ybaL* gene, a probable potassium efflux transporter, increased during adherence.

The efficient use of nutrients present in seed exudates is another determinant of bacterial colonization. Bayliss and co-workers (8) examined induction of gene expression by seed exudates in *P. putida*. One gene that showed this induction pattern was designated *seiA*. A *seiA* mutant could not compete with wild type in co-culture. Database sequence comparison with *seiA* showed similarity to broad specificity sugar transporters (TC3.A.1.1) in the ABC superfamily. The authors proposed that the SeiA transporter system mediates uptake of glucosamine and other sugars in *P. putida*.

The *P. putida* strain 06909 can suppress the growth of the root-rot fungus *Phytophthora parasitica* Dastur. Mutagenesis indicated that siderophore production and hyphal adhesion were important in achieving suppression. Recently, Lee and Cooksey (67) looked for other genes that were important to successful colonization of *P. parasitica* hyphae by *P. putida*. They isolated five unique clones that represented genes only expressed during fungal colonization. One ORF showed high sequence similarity to bacterial ABC-type uptake permeases (TC3.A.1). Data indicated that the gene's promoter was induced during fungal colonization. No induction was observed in various culture medium or after addition of known permease substrates. Another clone contained a gene with similarity to an OMP that might act in concert with the transporter.

Transporters in Fungi

Fungal plant pathogens inflict major yield losses in crops annually. Transporters of the MFS subclass are virulence factors in many of these pathogens. ABC transporters also play major roles in pathogenicity by protecting fungi against toxic plant metabolites and fungicides. It is likely that transporters in both subclasses protect some fungi against their own toxins.

Botrytis

Botrytis cinerea (Pers. ex Fr.) [teleomorph: *Botryotinia fuckeliana* (deBary) Whetzel] is a broad host range phytopathogen that causes gray mold. Fungicide treatment is an important component of the disease control strategy. Some grapevine field isolates of the fungus were found to show cross-resistance to several anilinopyrimidine and dicarboximide fungicides in an energy dependent manner (13). These data imply that an ABC transporter may mediate the fungicide resistance. Recently laboratory mutants displaying cross-resistance to multiple azole fungicides were found to have increased basal amounts of transcript for an ABC transporter designated BcatrD (TC3.A.1.205) (41).

A number of genes for ABC and MFS transporters have been cloned from *B. cinerea*. Analyses of gene expression in the wild type and phenotypes of gene disruptants are being used to elucidate their functions. The first two genes identified, *BcatrA* and *BcatrB*, encoded ABC transporters with the structure $(ABC\text{-}MSS_6)_2$ (TC3.A.1.205) (20). Both genes showed a low amount of expression in germlings in liquid culture. Expression of *BcatrA* increased after cycloheximide treatment of germlings and a small increase of expression was also seen after hydrogen peroxide treatment. Disruption of *BcatrA* did not appear to affect either fungicide sensitivity or virulence on common host plants. On the other hand, disruption of *BcatrB* had a number of consequences.

Expression of *BcatrB* was weakly induced by the fungicides tebuconazole and cycloheximide (109). Much stronger induction was observed with the fungicide fenpiclonil and the phytoalexins pisatin from pea and resveratrol from grapevine. The fungicide and phytoalexin sensitivity and the virulence of two gene replacement mutants were tested. No difference in sensitivity to cycloheximide, vinclozolin, or imazalil was observed in the mutants. However, a small increase in sensitivity to the fungicide fenpiclonil was seen. As for the phytoalexins, the mutants were not more sensitive to pisatin than the wild type but they were significantly more sensitive to resveratrol. The increased sensitivity to this grapevine phytoalexin correlated with reduced virulence on detached grapevine leaves. There was a statistically significant reduction in lesion diameter observed for the mutants compared to the wild type isolate.

The BcatrB transporter also appears to play a role in resistance to the fungicide fludioxonil (126). The sensitivity of the gene replacement mutants to fludioxonil was comparable to the fenpiclonil sensitivity. A very slight increase in sensivity to tebuconazole and other azole fungicides was also observed for the mutants. The sensitivity to fludioxonil correlated with an increased accumulation of the radiolabelled compound in mycelia from mutants.

The authors also identified 12 new sequences with similarity to ABC transporters and three sequences with similarity to MFS transporters in a *B. cinerea* expressed sequence tags (EST) library constructed from mycelia grown under nitrogen starvation conditions. The topology of the ABC transporters varied as follows: $(ABC\text{-}MSS_6)_2$ (TC3.A.1.205) for *BcatrC*, *BcatrD*, *BcatrL* and *BcatrK* (=BMR1), $(MSS_6\text{-}ABC)_2$ (TC3.A.1.201) for *BcatrN*, MSS_6-ABC for *BcatrH* and *BcatrI*, $[MSS_4\text{-}(MSS_6\text{-}ABC)_2]$ for *BcatrE*, *BcatrF* and *BcatrG*. *BcatrJ* and *BcatrM* had similarity to bacterial ABC transporters. The *Bcmfs1*, *Bcmfs2* and *Bcmfs4* genes sequence had similarity to MFS transporters of the drug proton antiporter family with either 12 (TC2.A.1.2) or 14 (TC2.A.1.3) MSS. In fungicide treatments transcript amounts increased for *BcatrG*, *BcatrJ* and *BcatrK* after fludioxonil addition, cyprodinil increased *BcatrB*, *BcatrD*, *BcatrF*, *BcatrG*, *BcatrK* and *Bmfs1*, iprodione induced *BcatrB* and trifloxystrobin induced *BcatrG*, *BcatrN* and *Bcmfs4*.

NECTRIA

The isolation of fungicide resistant strains is, of course, not confined to *B. cinerea*. After UV treatment of conidia 120 fenarimol resistant isolates of *Nectria haematococca* Berk. & Broome were obtained (56). Fenarimol, like many other fungicides, is an inhibitor of the cytochrome P450-dependent sterol 14α-demethylation (DMI) step of ergosterol biosynthesis. Progeny testing of crosses of 50 mutants selected for further study indicated 8 independent loci involved in the fungicide resistance. A mutation in the gene designated *fen*-7 caused a decrease in accumulation of radiolabelled fenarimol in mycelia. Treatment of the *fen*-7 mutant with inhibitors of plasma membrane ATPase activity increased accumulation of the fungicide in the mycelia. The results imply the existence of an ABC transporter or transporters involved in fungicide resistance in this fungus. The *fen*-7 mutation may knockout a negative regulator of transcription, similar to *S. cerevisiae* Pdr1p and Pdr3p.

Further support for ABC transporter involvement in DMI fungicide resistance in *N. haematococca* was provided by a recent report (1). UV mutagenesis was used to generate tebuconazole resistant mutants. The results of genetic crosses of these DMI-resistant mutants indicated at least three loci, Teb1, Teb2 and Teb3, were involved in the phenotype. An energy-dependent efflux system was implicated in the resistance mechanism of Teb1 mutants. The cross-resistance of the Teb2 and Teb3 mutants also implied a transporter system. Interestingly, mutations in Teb2 and Teb3 had pleiotropic effects, yielding reduced sporulation, growth rate and pigment production in Teb2 mutants and altered spore viability in Teb3 mutants.

An ABC transporter or transporters may also be involved in phytoalexin tolerance in *N. haematococca*. Isolates of mating population VI of the fungus were found to have an inducible tolerance to the phytoalexins pisatin, medicarpin and phaseollin (22). The isolates also showed tolerance to the antibiotic amphotericin B and partial tolerance to the isoflavonoid biochanin A. The tolerance was not the result of a detoxification process but did require active metabolism. In a later study (21) into the mechanism of this tolerance, it was found that tolerance correlated with reduced retention of pisatin in mycelium. The authors proposed that the tolerance was the result of plasma membrane modification to exclude pisatin influx. However, the data do not exclude the possibility that tolerance is the result of increased transporter activity. At the time of this writing only one sequence (accession AAK18809) encoding a putative drug facilitator was available for *N. haematococca*.

PENICILLIUM

Blue mold rot of oranges is caused by *Penicillium italicum* Wehmer. Field isolates of the fungus were found that showed resistance to several DMI fungicides (25). The mycelia of the isolates did not appear to take up the fungicides. The low-level resistance to fenarimol appeared to require the presence of an energy-dependent efflux system (39). Cross-resistance to fungicides was also observed in *Aspergillus nidulans* (Eidam) G. Wint. and *Ustilago avenae* (Pers.) Rostr. In *A. nidulans*, the ABC transporter AtrB was found to mediate resistance to all classes of fungicides and other toxic compounds (4).

The fungus *P. digitatum* (Pers.:fr.) Sacc. causes citrus green mold. A study of DMI-resistant field isolates of the fungus revealed an increased basal amount of transcript for an ABC transporter (86). These isolates showed cross-resistance to cycloheximide, 4-nitroquiniline-N-oxide (4NQO) and acriflavine A. A gene, *PMR1*, encoding an ABC transporter of topology $(ABC\text{-}MSS_6)_2$ (TC3.A.1.205) was cloned and characterized.

Disruptions of *PMR1* in a DMI-resistant isolate resulted in an increased sensitivity to the fungicides fenarimol and bitertanol, now comparable to wild type. However, the sensitivities to pyrifenox, cycloheximide, 4NQO and acriflavine A did not increase significantly, suggesting the existence of additional transporters with overlapping specificity. The *PMR1* mutants grew normally and produced similar symptoms to the parental strain after fruit inoculation.

Notwithstanding the above results, the most recent functional analysis of PMR1 in DMI-sensitive strains indicates that the transporter determines baseline sensitivity to DMI fungicides (40). However, the higher resistance observed in the field isolates was due to a duplication of a transcriptional enhancer in the gene for the cytochrome P450-dependent sterol 14α-demethylase, not to increased transcription of *PMR1*.

MYCOSPHAERELLA

Mycosphaerella graminicola (Fuckel) J. Schrot in Cohn [anamorph: *Septoria tritici* (Desm.) Roberge] is a serious pathogen of wheat worldwide. A field isolate with DMI-resistance was identified (54). The resistance was not the result of either target-site alteration or metabolic breakdown of the fungicide. However, the resistant isolate showed reduced accumulation of radiolabelled triadimenol compared to the wild type. This result could be due to a decreased influx or increased efflux of the fungicide. The data suggested that transporters are also involved in fungicide resistance in this fungus.

Five ABC transporter genes have been cloned from *M. graminicola*. The derived amino acid sequence of all five indicate a protein topology of $(ABC\text{-}MSS_6)_2$ (TC3.A.1.205). The expression patterns of the *MgAtr1* and *MgAtr2* genes suggested that these transporters are involved in fungal protection against plant defense compounds (133). In yeast-like cells *MgAtr1* gene expression was induced by the plant secondary metabolites eugenol, quercetin, reserpine, resveratrol, psoralen and tomatine. This increase in transcript amount was not observed in mycelia. In contrast, the only plant secondary metabolite that up-regulated *MgAtr2* gene expression was eugenol and only in mycelia not in yeast-like cells. No disruptants of *MgAtr1* or *MgAtr2* were found among 369 transformants screened, so no additional functional analysis was included in this report.

A poster and abstract describing further work on the *M. graminicola* ABC transporters was presented at the XXI Fungal Genetics Conference (De Waard, personal communication). The poster is available through the internet at www.dpw.wageningen-ur.nl/fyto/ABC_Mgr.pdf. It reported that no expression of *MgAtr3* was detected by Northern analysis under any of the conditions tested. Expression of *MgAtr4* was highly induced by imazalil, eugenol, palmitic acid, psoralen, progesterone and lanosterol in yeast-like cells. In mycelia, *MgAtr4* gene expression was highly induced by cycloheximide, imazalil, linoleic acid, cyproconazole, psoralen and progesterone. In yeast-like cells, *MgAtr5* gene expression was highly induced by cycloheximide, imazalil, neomycin and psoralen. In mycelia, psoralen induced the largest amount of transcript for *MgAtr5*.

Functional analysis of *MgAtr1*, *MgAtr2*, *MgAtr4* and *MgAtr5* was carried out in *S. cerevisiae*. The recipient strain had disruptions in multiple ABC transporters. The transformants for all four genes were resistant to a number of fungicides and plant secondary metabolites. Further functional analysis of the genes was done through gene disruption. The disruption of all four genes in *M. graminicola* was obtained by *Agrobacterium*-mediated transformation. Only *MgAtr4* mutants showed reduced virulence on wheat.

FUSARIUM

Fusarium sporotrichioides Sherb. produces potent sesquiterpenoid phytotoxins called trichothecenes. Many of the genes involved in the biosyntheses of these complex molecules are found in gene clusters. Trichothecenes are non-specific toxins that appear to inhibit the peptidyltransferase step in eukaryotic protein synthesis. Therefore, the fungus would require a mechanism of self-protection. One possible mechanism of self-protection could be a specific efflux system. Among the genes in the trichothecene biosynthetic cluster is *TRI12*. The *TRI12* gene encodes a protein with high similarity to MFS transporters of the 14 MSS drug resistance family (TC2.A.1.3) (2).

After disruption of *TRI12* only 3% of the wild type amount of T-2 toxin was observed in the mutants' culture supernatant. The mutants were also more sensitive to growth inhibition by the trichothecene diacetoxyscirpenol (DAS) than wild type. However, transformation of a *S. cerevisiae pdr5* mutant with *TRI12* did not protect the recipient from the toxic effects of DAS. So it is unlikely that *TRI12* is the sole determinant of trichothecene self-protection.

COCHLIOBOLUS

Isolates of race 1 of *Cochliobolus carbonum* R. R. Nelson produce a peptide phytotoxin called HC-toxin. The toxin synthase is a large multifunctional enzyme that is encoded by a gene designated *HTS1*. The gene occurs in two copies and is present only in race 1 of *C. carbonum*. Adjacent to each copy of *HTS1* is *TOXA*, a gene whose derived amino acid sequence is highly similar to MFS transporters (TC2.A.1.2) (97). The hydropathy profile of TOXA indicated 10 – 13 MSS. All attempts to disrupt both copies of the gene failed. The authors propose that TOXA is the specific efflux transporter for HC-toxin and that it is essential for survival.

CERCOSPORA

Cercospora kikuchii (Matsumoto & Tomoyasu) M. W. Gardner is a pathogen of soybean that produces the polyketide toxin cercosporin. Cercosporin is activated by light and can react with O_2 through energy transfer to form singlet oxygen (17). Mutants of *C. kikuchii* that are deficient in cercosporin production are non-pathogenic on soybean so the toxin is a pathogenicity factor (118). Cercosporin is another non-specific toxin requiring the fungus to have a method for self-protection.

Callahan and co-workers (10) showed that light induced expression of a gene encoding an apparent MFS transporter. The gene with an ORF of 1821bp was designated *CFP*. A hydropathy plot of the predicted protein indicated 14 MSS (TC2.A.1.3). Three *CFP* mutants were generated by gene disruption and characterized. The mutants showed normal growth rate and viability on potato dextrose agar. However, they produced less than 5% the amount of cercosporin produced by the parental isolate. The radial growth rate of the mutants was also reduced by 42 – 47% compared to the parent in the presence of 10 μM cercosporin. In addition, the mutants showed greatly reduced virulence on soybean compared to the parental strain. These data further supported the hypothesis that cercosporin is a pathogenicity factor.

Southern blot analysis of *CFP* in *C. kikuchii* indicated that it is a single copy gene (117). Transformation leading to multiple copies of the gene increased transcript accumulation at least three-fold. A two-fold increase in cercosporin secretion accompanied the *CFP* over-expression. However, neither resistance to cercosporin or virulence on soybean was changed in the transformants.

In *S. cerevisiae* another transporter has been implicated in defense against cercosporin and other singlet oxygen-generating photosensitizers (127). In this study, the cercosporin-sensitive yeast strain YPH98 was transformed with clones of the *S. cerevisiae* ABC transporter genes *PDR5* and *SNQ2* and the MFS transporter genes *SGE1* and *ATR1*. Only transformants expressing *SNQ2* (TC3.A.1.205) from a high copy number plasmid were able to grow on medium containing 5 μM cercosporin.

MAGNAPORTHE

Magnaporthe grisea (T. T. Hebert) Yaegashi & Udagawa is the causal organism of rice blast disease. This ascomycete fungus has been the subject of extensive genetic and molecular studies. On the whole genome scale, random insertional inactivation was carried out and the transformants were screened for pathogenicity on rice cultivar CO-39 (119). The transformant designated TF7-3131 showed much reduced pathogenicity on this rice cultivar. A probe derived from the rescued plasmid from TF7-3131 was used to screen a *M. grisea* genomic library. A

BLAST search with the derived amino acid sequence of the selected clone revealed high similarity to several fungal ABC transporters.

The proposed topology of Abc1p is (ABC-$MSS_6)_2$ (TC3.A.1.205). Sequence comparison indicated that the insertion in TF7-3131 had occurred in the putative promoter of *ABC1*. Subsequently, transformation with a construct carrying an insertion in the coding region of *ABC1* was performed. Several disruption and deletion mutants were obtained and characterized. The new mutants showed the same reduced pathogenicity as TF7-3131 on rice and barley. Additionally, no viable fungal material could be recovered from the infected leaves.

Observation of the infection process of the mutants revealed appressoria that failed to produce infection hyphae. In an effort to identify substrates of the Abc1p, the mutants and the parental strain were fed various compounds in spore germination and radial growth assays. No difference in sensitivities to cycloheximide, chloramphenicol, several DMI fungicides, brefeldin A, 4NQO, or the rice phytoalexin sakuranetin was detected between mutants and parent. However, several of these compounds did induce expression of *ABC1*. In TF7-3131 cycloheximide induced only about a four-fold increase in transcript amount while in the Guy-11 parent there was a 200-fold increase. The exact functional role of Abc1p in *M. grisea* pathogenicity remains to be determined.

GIBBERELLA

Gibberella pulicaris (Fr.:fr.) Sacc. is a necrotrophic fungus that causes dry rot disease in potatoes. The fungus enters the tuber through wounds. Very recently, an ABC transporter was found to participate in the tolerance of the fungus to the phytoalexin rishitin and to contribute to virulence (31).

RNA was isolated from mycelium that was exposed to rishitin for two to four hours. A cDNA library was constructed from the mRNA and differentially screened. Two partial cDNAs with homology to ABC transporters were isolated in this screen. Both cDNAs were found to correspond to one 4,576 bp ORF that encoded a predicted protein of 1,491 amino acids. This protein had 65% identity to the *ABC1* of *M. grisea*. The *G. pulicaris* gene was designated *Gpabc1* (TC3.A.1).

Mutants for *abc1* were obtained by gene disruption through homologous recombination. Growth of the mutants on agar containing rishitin was reduced by 90% compared to wild type. Potato tuber disks were inoculated with the mutants and wild type and fungal growth was observed over time. At five days post-inoculation the wild type and control transformant had colonized more than half the tuber disk. In contrast, the *abc1* mutants showed only slight growth. Complementation of the disrupted gene with a wild type copy restored the mutants' ability to grow on both rishitin and potato tuber disks.

LEPTOSPHAERIA

Leptosphaeria maculans (Desm.) Ces. et de Not. [anamorph: *Phoma lingam* (Desm.) Tode ex Fr.] causes blackleg disease in several crucifers. My laboratory has been studying this fungus in collaboration with Dr. M. S. C. Pedras, Dept. of Chemistry, University of Saskatchewan, for a number of years. Dr. Pedras has shown that *L. maculans* produces a host-selective toxin, phomalide (96), and several non-specific toxic epipolythiodioxopiperazines, sirodesmins (95). Additionally, the fungus is able to detoxify the *Brassica* phytoalexin brassinin (93) and other *Brassica* phytoalexins (94). For our part, we have cloned a number of different transporter genes that may function in concert with these chemical compounds in fungal pathogenicity.

Phomalide is only produced for a short time after spore germination in culture. The toxin is a cyclic depsipeptide and is likely synthesized on a large multifunctional enzyme. We isolated a cDNA representing a gene whose expression parallels phomalide production. The derived amino acid sequence of the apparent full length cDNA was highly similar to database entries for peptide transporters (TC2.A.17). These proteins are classified among the MFS transporters. In a departure from the usual pattern, the hydropathy profile of our protein indicated only six MSS, equivalent to a half-size transporter. However, recent sequence analysis of the genomic clone revealed a potential coding region, designated *PTR1*, for a transporter with 12 MSS. The cDNA sequence corresponded to the putative first exon of the genomic clone, continuing through a predicted intron and ending before the start of the second exon. Given this alignment it is unlikely that the cDNA is the result of a cloning artifact. We are currently making a detailed investigation into the expression of the gene.

In addition to *LmPTR1*, we are presently characterizing two ABC transporters (115). The genes designated *ABC1* and *ABC2* had 36% overall similarity to each other. The derived amino acid sequences were 1431 and 1501 residues in length, respectively. Based on the hydropathy profiles the topology of these transporters is predicted to be $(ABC\text{-}MSS_6)_2$ (TC3.A.1.205). The *ABC2* gene complemented a *S. cerevisiae pdr5* strain for cycloheximide resistance and a *snq2* strain for 4NQO resistance. In contrast, *ABC1* did not complement either mutant yeast strain for drug resistance. Interestingly, overexpression of these genes in *S. cerevisiae* appeared to be deleterious since no transformants were obtained with constructs made in two-micron plasmid-based vectors. We believe that the high amount of protein produced had a deleterious effect on membrane permeability.

We tested the effect of various compounds on expression of *ABC1* and *ABC2* (115). No expression of the genes was detected in minimal medium at 48 h post-inoculation. Dr. Pedras kindly provided us with the brassinin phytoalexin analogue methyl-4-chlorobenzyldithiocarbamate and sirodesmin PL. Expression of *ABC1* was strongly induced by treatment with the brassinin analogue or miconazole, a moderate induction was observed with sirodesmin PL. Cycloheximide did not induce *ABC1* expression. For *ABC2*, strong induction was seen with cycloheximide and sirodesmin PL. Miconazole was a moderate inducer of *ABC2* expression and the brassinin analog was a very weak inducer. Only *ABC1* expression was detected in leaf lesions 10 days post-infection. We have recently obtained an *ABC1* gene disruptant through *Agrobacterium*-mediated transformation that will be used for further functional analysis.

Transporters in Plants

As stated earlier the number of proteins estimated to be directly involved in transport of molecules across membranes in *A. thaliana* is 600 (122). Few of these proteins have been characterized. The majority of plant transporters that function in microbe interactions protect against toxic metabolites. However, transporters with roles in ethylene or salicylic acid signaling are also known. In addition, a plant gene encoding a putative MFS transporter is implicated in legume-rhizobia interaction. A cDNA with similarity to ABC transporters was also identified in rice in a screen for defense-related genes (130). Finally, transgenic plants expressing heterologous ABC transporters have increased tolerance to mycotoxins.

HORDEUM

The detoxification of xenobiotics by plants is a subject of increasing interest, particularly for application in soil remediation. The detoxification process is generally divisible into three phases: [1] an oxidation, reduction or hydroxylation step to create a functional group on the toxic compound, [2] conjugation of the compound to glutathione or malonyl or glucosyl moieties, and [3] storage in the central vacuole (49).

Over the last decade the mechanism governing the vacuolar uptake of glutathione-S –conjugates (GS) has been investigated. Martinoia and co-workers (78) found that uptake of GS-conjugates of N-ethylmaleimide or metolachlor in isolated barley mesophyll cells was dependent on Mg-ATP. The uptake of any particular GS-conjugate was inhibited by any other suggesting that a single carrier was responsible. The non-hydrolysable ATP analogue adenylyl imidodiphosphate also inhibited uptake indicating that ATP hydrolysis was necessary for transport.

Further investigations into transport of GS-conjugates were carried out in mung bean, red beet, corn, and *A. thaliana*. (72). The results of this study confirmed the earlier findings and provided additional data on the nature of the transporter. The uptake of conjugates was inhibited by vanadate, vinblastine and verapamil, which are all inhibitors of P-type

ATPases. The uncouplers of the transtonoplast proton gradient, carbonylcyanide 4-trifluoromethoxyphenylhydrazone, gramicidin-D or ammonium chloride did not inhibit uptake. It was also found that the purified vacuolar membrane vesicles from all these plants behaved the same. The authors concluded that transport of GS-conjugates into vacuoles is solely dependent on energy supplied by Mg-ATP rather than on proton-electrochemical potential difference.

ARABIDOPSIS

A gene encoding the transporter responsible for vacuolar uptake of GS conjugates was cloned from *A. thaliana*. The gene, *AtMRP1* was identified using degenerate oligonucleotides based on the human and yeast homologues (76). As expected the gene encodes a protein with high similarity to ABC transporters (TC3.A.1.207). The predicted topology of this transporters is $(MSS_6\text{-}ABC)_2$. The functionality of MRP1 was demonstrated by complementation of a *S. cerevisiae ycf1*Δ strain. Transport of S-(2,4-dinitrophenyl) glutathione in vacuolar membrane-enriched vesicles was restored in the transformants. Comparison of the biochemical characteristics of the transformants with mung bean vacuolar membrane vesicles established their functional equivalence. The results supported the conclusion that *AtMRP1* encodes a plant GS-conjugate vacuole transporter.

The first plant ABC transporter gene was cloned from *A. thaliana* several years before *AtMRP1* identification (27). The clones were isolated from a genomic library screened with oligonucleotides encoding amino acids from the ABC domains of *E. coli* HlyB and human P-gp. Restriction enzyme analysis and probe hybridization indicated two loci. One locus encoding 1286 amino acids was characterized and the gene was designated *Atpgp1*. Similar to P-gp, the hydropathy profile predicted the topology $(MSS_6\text{-}ABC)_2$ (TC3.A.1.201). Southern blot analysis indicated that *Atpgp1* was single copy but it had faint cross-hybridization with a second locus as expected. RNA transcribed from *Atpgp1* was found in leaves, roots, flower buds, open flowers, and inflorescence axes (peduncles). The amount of transcript found in the peduncles was approximately five-fold more than in the other tissues. No substrates for this ABC transporter have as yet been identified.

Two *A. thaliana* genes involved in resistance to toxic compounds have been identified. The genes *ALF5* (26) and *DTX1* (71) encode proteins with similarity to the multidrug antimicrobial toxic compound extrusion (MATE) family of transporters (TC2.A.66.1). These integral membrane proteins are drugs: Na^+ antiporters that consist of 12 MSS.

The *ALF5* gene was identified in a spontaneous mutant that showed aberrant lateral root formation when grown on Bacto agar (26). Similar abnormal morphology was observed in the presence of commercial preparations of polyvinylpyrrolidone (PVP) and pyrrolidinone. The effect was due to contaminants in the agar, PVP and pyrrlidinone rather than to the compounds themselves. The exact natures of the contaminants are not yet known.

Positional cloning was used to isolate *alf5*. The gene was strongly expressed in root epidermis and cortex. The expression of *ALF5* in *S. cerevisiae* resulted in resistance to tetramethylammonium chloride. A BLAST search of the *A. thaliana* genome revealed 54 additional candidates for MATE transporters. The authors proposed that *ALF5* plays a role in vacuolar sequestering or cellular efflux of toxic compounds found in soil.

Among the additional candidates for MATE transporters was a gene now designated as *AtDTX1*. The *DTX1* gene was identified in a functional screen of the *A. thaliana* CD4-7 cDNA library (71). An *E. coli KAM3* mutant was used as the recipient. This mutant is sensitive to many drugs that are substrates of the bacterial *AcrAB* multidrug efflux system. The expression of the *AtDTX1* cDNA in the *E. coli* mutant restored resistance to norfloxacin. The cDNA was also able to mediate efflux of ethidium bromide and the plant alkaloid berberine.

Imaging of a GFP-DTX1 fusion protein by confocal microscopy in transgenic *A. thaliana* indicated that the transporter is located in the plasma membrane. The expression of *DTX1* appeared to be ubiquitous. However, larger amounts of the mRNA accumulated in the flower and stem in comparison to leaf and root. The authors suggest that *DTX1* is involved in multidrug and heavy metal resistance in plants.

A number of plant hormones participate in the responses to microbes. Among those hormones are salicylic acid and ethylene. As a model system, extensive investigations of hormone signaling pathways have been done in *A. thaliana*. Thus far one transporter involved in salicylic acid (SA) signaling and two transporters involved in ethylene signaling have been identified.

EDS5 is another member of the MATE family of transporters (TC2.A.66.1) (87). An *eds5* mutant previously called *sid1* does not accumulate SA or *PR1* transcript after pathogen infection and it is hypersusceptible. The *EDS5* gene was isolated through positional cloning. The gene contained an ORF of 1632 bp encoding a putative protein of 543 amino acids. Salicylic acid, UV-C light and inoculation with virulent or avirulent *P. syringae* induced expression of *EDS5*. The *EDS5* transcript accumulation after UV-C light exposure and inoculation with certain pathogens was dependent on the *PAD4*, *EDS1* and *NDR1* genes. The transported substrates of EDS5 remain unknown.

The RAN1 transporter involved in ethylene signaling has similarity to copper-transport P-type ATPases (45). The P-type ATPase transporters form a superfamily in the active transporter class (TC3.A.3). The common structural features of these transporters are [1] N-terminal metal-binding motifs, [2] a phosphatase domain, [3] a transduction domain, [4] a phosphorylation domain, and [5] an ATP-binding domain. The proteins contain eight putative MSS. Positional cloning in a *ran1* mutant was used to identify the gene. The mutant displayed an ethylene response in the presence of the ethylene antagonist trans-cyclooctene suggesting a defect in ethylene perception.

RAN1 was able to complement a *S. cerevisiae ccc2* mutant that was defective in copper transport. These transporter types are located in the post-Golgi compartment where they deliver copper ions to the secretory pathway for incorporation into secreted or membrane-bound proteins. These results support the hypothesis that ethylene receptors require coordination of a transition metal for hormone binding.

The other transporter found to be involved in ethylene signaling is EIN2 (3). Mutations in *EIN2* caused complete ethylene insensitivity. An *ein2* mutant also failed to express the pathogen-response gene *PDF1.2* after jasmonate treatment. The genetic data indicated that *EIN2* mediates a step in the signaling pathway between Raf-like protein kinase CTR1 and EIN3/EIL transcription factors.

As above, *EIN2* was isolated using the positional cloning approach. The gene is predicted to encode a 1294 amino acid protein. The N-terminal half of the protein is highly hydrophobic and the hydropathy profile indicated 12 MSS. The C-terminal half of the protein is predominantly hydrophilic. A BLAST search with the derived amino acid sequence showed similarity to transporters in the Nramp family of divalent cation secondary transporters (TC2.A.55). No metal-transporting activity was detected in *Xenopus* oocytes, a yeast *mif* mutant or baculovirus-infected insect cells expressing *EIN2*. The authors proposed that the N-terminal half of EIN2 functions as a membrane-bound receptor while the C-terminal half interacts with other signal pathway components such as CTR1 and ETR1.

SPIRODELA

Another plant hormone involved in response to abiotic and biotic stress is abscisic acid (ABA). Treatment of the aquatic plant *Spirodela polyrhiza* (L.) Schleid. with ABA induces formation of dormant bud-like structures termed turions. One transcript that was induced by treatment with ABA had an ORF of 4323 bp (112). The gene from which the transcript was derived was designated *TUR2*. The protein encoded by *TUR2* displayed high similarity to ABC transporters. The predicted topology of the protein is $(ABC\text{-}MSS_6)_2$ (TC3.A.1.205).

TUR2 was expressed in low amounts in untreated plants. An increased amount of transcript was evident at 30 min following ABA treatment and it reached a maximum of seven-fold induction by 2 h. The transcript amount began to decline slowly after a few hours. Cold treatment induced a slow increase in transcript amount peaking at seven days with little subsequent decline.

The induction of turion formation by ABA can be counteracted by kinetin treatment. Simultaneous treatment with ABA and kinetin had little effect on *TUR2* transcript amount at 2 h. However, at 24 h and 72 h after the treatment the transcript amount was significantly reduced compared to ABA treatment alone. It was also found that cycloheximide and 100 mM NaCl induced *TUR2* expression but expression was not induced by 10 μM 2,4-D.

Southern blot analysis indicated that *TUR2* was a single copy gene but some faint hybridization suggested that a related gene might be present. A BLAST search with the cDNA sequence revealed similarity to several rice and *A. thaliana* ESTs. The authors proposed that TUR2 and its homologues function in efflux of toxic cellular compounds produced during stress. It is likely that the same transporter functions during biotic as well as abiotic stress.

CHENOPODIUM

Chenopodium spp. show a hypersensitive response (HR) to a broad range of viruses including tobacco mosaic virus (TMV) and tobacco rattle virus (TRV) (16). This HR appears to be triggered by the attempted movement of a virus from an infected cell. As expected, the HR is accompanied by the induction of a number of genes. Some of these genes were identified through cDNA-AFLP differential display and quantitative RT-PCR. Among the cDNA clones isolated were two that had similarity to ABC transporters.

The cDNA clone designated DESCA4 was similar to the *S. polyrhiza* ABC transporter (TC3.A.1.205) described above. The transcript amount of DESCA4 in TMV-infected *C. giganteum* (D.) Don at four days after infection (DAI) was 21-fold more than the amount in mock-infected tissue. It appeared to decline slowly after that time point. The transcript amount at four DAI with TRV was seven-fold greater than in the control. In *C. quinoa* Willd. four DAI with TMV the transcript amount of DESCA4 was 52-fold greater than in the control. This transporter may be involved in efflux of toxic compounds produced during programmed cell death (PCD).

The cDNA clone designated DESCA10 showed similarity to *AtMRP1* (TC3.A.1.207). The increase in DESCA10 transcript amount in *C. giganteum* triggered by virus infection was less than that observed for DESCA4. The maximum induction after TMV infection was 5.6-fold and after TRV infection it was 4.1-fold. No induction was detected in *C. quinoa* after TMV infection. It may be that generation and/or transport of GS-conjugates into vacuoles is not greatly utilized during PCD.

LOTUS

Since it was demonstrated that transporters have several roles in mediating nitrogen-fixing nodule formation from the bacterial side it is not surprising that they also make contributions from the plant side. Szczyglowski and co-workers (114) identified nodule-specific transcripts associated with late stages of nodule development and/or functions in *Lotus corniculatus* L. var. *japonicus* Regel.

The gene from which two of the transcripts were derived was designated *NOD70*. The larger of the two transcripts appeared to contain an unspliced intron. The resulting peptide showed similarity to MFS transporters of the oxalate/formate exchange family (TC2.A.1.11). The smaller transcript, which was less abundant in nodules, represented the spliced mRNA. The resulting two peptides would correspond to the N- and C-terminal halves of the transporter. Southern blot analysis indicated that *LjNOD70* belonged to a small gene family. The authors proposed that NOD70 is involved in translocation of carbon substrates in *L. japonicus* nodules. This hypothesis is based on the finding that nodules of broad bean contain high concentrations of oxalate postulated to serve as a carbon substrate for nitrogen fixation.

NICOTIANA

Based on the hypothesis that ABC transporters might be involved in secretion of defense compounds, Jasiński and co-workers (50) examined *de novo* protein synthesis in *Nicotiana plumbaginifolia* Viv. cell cultures treated with the terpenoid sclareolide. This compound is an analogue of sclareol, an antifungal metabolite found on tobacco leaf surfaces. Twelve hours after sclareolide treatment a 160-kd protein appeared on SDS-PAGE gels. Amino acid sequence data was collected from peptide cleavage products and used for design of degenerate oligonucleotides.

A full-length cDNA was eventually obtained and found to encode a protein with high similarity to TUR2. Therefore, *Np*ABC1 is predicted to have the structure $(ABC\text{-}MSS_6)_2$ (TC3.A.1.205). The transcript of *ABC1* was enhanced in cell cultures after both sclareolide and sclareol treatment. Immunolocalization of ABC1 in leaves placed it in the epidermis and sclareol infiltration increased the amount of protein present in this tissue. More detailed localization placed the transporter in the plasma membrane. Analyses of cell cultures treated with a labeled sclareol analogue showed that loss of cell-associated radioactivity correlated with induction of ABC1. Treatment with ATP synthesis inhibitors increased cell-associated radioactivity indicating that efflux was energy dependent.

EXPRESSION OF HETEROLOGOUS TRANSPORTERS IN PLANTS

Since ABC transporters like *S. cerevisiae* Pdr5p have broad substrate specificity they could potentially be used to increase plant resistance to various toxins. Two investigations into this potential use were recently reported (83, 84). Tobacco transformed with *PDR5* was tested for resistance to the trichothecene mycotoxin deoxynivalenol (DON) (83). In leaf disk regeneration assays transformants were more resistant to DON than controls. In addition, a three-fold higher concentration of DON was needed to yield 50% inhibition of radiolabelled methionine incorporation into protein in transformants than in controls.

The other investigation into using Pdr5p for protection against a mycotoxin utilized a seed germination assay and the trichothecene 4,15-diacetoxyscirpenol (DAS) (84). Again tobacco was used as the recipient but in this case another gene, *TRI101* encoding a potential trichothecene detoxification enzyme, was also tested separately. The percent germination of DAS-treated seeds expressing either *PDR5* or *TRI101* was significantly higher than the controls with vector alone. No difference in percent germination was observed between *PDR5* and *TRI101* transformants until the DAS concentration reached 20 µM. At this concentration the percent germination was slightly higher for the *TRI101* transformants. The potential usefulness of this approach in generating field resistance in the *Fusarium* host plants wheat and barley remains to be determined but the outlook is promising.

Effects of Agricultural Chemicals and Plant Secondary Metabolites on Various Transporters

The *S. cerevisiae* pleiotropic drug resistance network is the most-characterized network of transporters. It is composed of the transcriptional regulators Pdr1p and Pdr3p, the transporters Pdr5p, Snq2p, and Yor1p and a group of as yet little characterized gene products. In an effort to better define the substrate range of these transporters 349 compounds were tested in various mutants (64). Among the compounds tested were several herbicides and plant secondary metabolites. All three transporters mediated resistance to various urea derivative herbicides. Yor1p also mediated resistance to the anilide herbicide propanil. Pdr1p and Pdr3p controlled resistance to the acaricide dicofol. None of the network modified the reaction to propham. Yor1p in particular was found to mediate resistance to the plant flavonoids, fisetin, myricetin, quercetin and together with Pdr5p to baicalein.

Although the substrate range for multi-drug resistance (MDR) pumps is quite broad, upon examination a common pattern is evident. The substrates with few exceptions are amphipathic cations. These compounds, made up of a strong positively charged group and strong non-polar group would be expected to accumulate in the cell due to confinement by the membrane potential difference. Therefore, it's not surprising that a defense mechanism evolved early.

What are some of the natural products that selected for the evolution of MDR pumps? This topic was the subject of a recent study (70). The transportability of isoquinoline alkaloids from plants was investigated. These compounds were chosen because of their resemblance to known MDR substrates. In particular, berberine and palmatine from *Ranunculales* species were tested for antimicrobial activity in a wild type and a *norA* (2.A.1.2.10) mutant strain of *Staphylococcus aureus*. The minimum inhibitory concentration (MIC) of palmatine was at least four-fold greater for the wild type than for the transporter mutant. The MIC of berberine was 20-fold greater for the wild type than for the *norA* mutant. Sensitivity in the mutant was increased even further with the addition of the MDR inhibitor INF271. *S. cerevisiae* became equally sensitive to berberine in the presence of INF271 (MIC - 120 μg/ ml vs. 1 μg/ ml).

The next question addressed was whether plants produce MDR inhibitors that act synergistically with these cationic antibiotics. An extract prepared from *Mahonia fremontii* (Torr.) Fedde was found to contain two different MDR inhibitors that acted synergistically with the berberine. The first of these MDR inhibitors to be identified is 5'-methoxyhydnocarpin-D, a flavonolignan.

The author proposed that plants further supplement this defensive arsenal with compounds that alter membrane permeability, specifically the saponins. The saponins form a complex with and then remove ergosterol from membranes. As stated earlier, substrate specificity and transport efficiency is altered in yeast ergosterol mutants (60). Therefore, the protection against plant-produced toxic compounds afforded by the fungal MDR pumps may be lost after saponin removal of ergosterol.

Concluding Remarks and Future Prospects

The transporters involved in plant-microbe interaction that were described in this chapter are listed, based on classification, in Table 1. The vast majority of these transporters are classified in the ABC superfamily. This is not surprising since it is the largest family of known proteins. Among the ABC transporters so far proposed to be involved in plant-microbe interaction the majority are drug resistance efflux pumps. Because both the plant and pathogenic microbe are engaged in attack and defense this observation is also not surprising. In the future, use of a combination of targeted mutation along with metabolic profiling will no doubt reveal the action of many more transporters in plant microbe-interaction.

Expanding our knowledge of transporter gene regulation will be another goal of future research. Here the ABC transporters of *M. graminicola* present an interesting picture. There were significant differences in the compounds that induced the same gene's expression in the yeast-like versus the filamentous morphological states of the fungus. The Southern blot analysis indicated that the genes were single copy. Thus the transcriptional differences were not the result of induction of different members of a gene family. Instead, the results may indicate that different transcriptional regulators exist for the same gene in alternate morphological states.

However, there is an alternative explanation for the disparity in compounds that induced transporter gene expression between yeast-like and filamentous morphologies. It may be that the plasma membrane composition is sufficiently different in the two morphological states that membrane permeability is affected. The interaction between membrane lipid composition and transporter function is another exciting subject for future research. For example, are there alterations in membrane composition during plant and microbe interaction that modify transporter action? Does plant cell wall modification during defense affect transporters in the underlying plasma membrane?

Kim Lewis (70) pointed out another exciting area for focus in future transporter research. That area is the search for natural substrates and inhibitors for multidrug resistance pumps. These compounds are a largely untapped resource that have applications in plant and human health. Could we acquire MDR inhibitors through our diet that would improve the efficacy of cancer therapeutics? Would engineering plants with new or additional MDR inhibitors increase disease resistance or increase the efficacy of systemic fungicides?

Finally, analyses of transporter activity could add an exciting new dimension to pathogen recognition research. There are any number of interesting questions to address. What compounds/ oligomers secreted by attacking microbes activate transporters? Are any of these compounds/ oligomers taken up through transporter action? Are there transporters in plants that take up fungal avirulence gene products? Do elicitors act solely on plasma membrane-bound receptors or are they internalized through transporter action?

Acknowledgements

I would like to thank Drs. M. A. De Waard, G. Stacey and N. T. Keen for critical review of this manuscript. I am also grateful to J. Condie for her hard work on the *L. maculans* ABC transporters. Finally, I thank Dr. S. R. Abrams for her input and G. Berry for her assistance in the preparation of this review.

Table 1. Transporters involved in plant-microbe interaction

TRANSPORTER TYPE	ORGANISM	FUNCTION (PUTATIVE)	GENES	ACCESSIONS
ABC (TC3.A.1)	*Rhizobium etli*	Oligosaccharide secretion	*nodIJ*	AY029295
		(O-antigen translocation)	*wzt, wzm*	AF182824
	R. meliloti	β-(1,2) glucan secretion	*ndvA*	M20726
		Exopolysaccharide (EPS) secretion	*exsA*	Z50189
	R. leguminosarum bv. *trifolii*	EPS secretion	*prsD*	X98117
	Agrobacterium tumefaciens	β-(1,2) glucan secretion	*chvA*	M24198
		(Signal compound secretion)	*attA1A2BCE*	U59485
		(Toxic compound efflux)	*chvD*	AY027490
		Opine uptake	*occQMPJ, accABCDE, ophABCDE*	M77784, AF10180, NC003064
	Erwinia chrysanthemi	Metalloprotease secretion	*prtDEF*	X53253
		(Toxic metabolite efflux)	*sufC*	AJ301654
		Antimicrobial peptide resistance	*sapABCDF*	AJ222649

ABC	*Erwinia chrysanthemi*	Oligogalacturonide uptake	*togT* *togMNAB*	AJ305143 AJ305144
	Pseudomonas syringae pv. *syringae*	Syringomycin and syringopeptin secretion	*syrD* *ybjZ*	M97223 AE000198
		(Oligosaccharide uptake)	*seiA*	U75905
		Polyamine transport	*potF2* *potB*	PA3608
	Botrytis cinerea	(Drug resistance)	*atrA,B,C,D,E,F,G, H,I,J,K,L,M,N*	Z68906 (A), AJ006217 (B), AF241315 (C), AJ272521 (D), AF238224 (E), AF238230 (F), AJ278038 (G), AF241313 (H), AF238229 (I), AF238228 (J), AF238227 (K), AF238226 (N)
	Aspergillus nidulans	Drug resistance	*atrB*	Z68905
	Penicillium digitatum	Drug resistance	*pmr1*	AB010442
	Mycosphaerella graminicola	Drug resistance Toxic compound efflux	*ATR1,2,3,4,5*	AJ243112 (1), AJ243113 (2), AF364105 (3), AF329852 (4), AF364104 (5)
	Saccharomyces cerevisiae	Drug resistance	*snq2*	X66732
		Drug resistance	*pdr5*	L19922
	Magnaporthe grisea	(Toxic compound efflux)	*abc1*	AF032443
ABC	*Gibberella*	Toxic compound efflux	*abc1*	AJ306607

	pulicaris			
	Leptosphaeria maculans	Drug resistance (Toxic compound efflux)	*abc1,2*	
	Arabidopsis thaliana	Glutathione conjugate (GS) vacuolar uptake	*mrp1*	AF044031
		(Drug resistance)	*pgp1*	X61370
	Spirodela polyrhiza	(Toxic metabolite efflux)	*tur2*	Z70524
	Chenopodium spp.	(Toxic metabolite efflux)	DESCA4	BI534449
		(GS-conjugate vacuolar uptake)	DESCA10	BI534444
	Nicotiana plumbaginifolia	(Toxic metabolite efflux)	*abc1*	AJ404328
MFS (TC2.A.1)	*R. meliloti*	Drug resistance	*rmrAB*	AF233286
	B. cinerea	(Drug resistance)	*mfs1,2,4*	AF238225
	Fusarium sporotrichioides	Trichothecene efflux	*tri12*	AF011355
	Cochliobolus carbonum	(HC-toxin efflux)	*toxA*	L48797
	Cercospora kikuchii	Cercosporin efflux	*cfp*	AF091042
	L. maculans	(peptide transport)	*ptr1*	
	Lotus japonicus	(Carbon substrate transport)	*nod70*	AF031243
RND (TC2.A.6)	*R. meliloti*	(NOD factor secretion)	*nolFGHI*	X58632
	P. putida	(Drug resistance)	*mez*	PA0425

	A. tumefaciens	(Drug resistance)	*ifeABR*	AF039653
MATE (TC2.A.66)	*A. thaliana*	(Drug resistance)	*alf5* *dtx1*	AF337954 AAD28687
		(Signaling)	*eds5*	AF416569
P-type ATPase (TC3.A.3)		(Copper transport)	*ran1*	AF091112
Nramp (TC2.A.55)		(Sensor protein)	*ein2*	AF141203
Secondary (TC2.A)	*P. putida*	(peptide transport)	*mus-13*	AF249736
		(cation efflux)	*mus-21*	-
		(K^+ efflux)	*ybaL*	PA5518

References

1. Akallal R, Debieu D, Lanen C, Daboussi MJ, Fritz R, Malosse C, Bach J, Leroux P (1998) Inheritance and mechanisms of resistance to tebuconazole, a sterol C14-demethylation inhibitor, in *Nectria haematococca*. Pestic. Biochem. Physiol. 60:147-166.
2. Alexander NJ, McCormick SP, Hohn TM (1999) TRI12, a trichothecene efflux pump from *Fusarium sporotrichioides*: gene isolation and expression in yeast. Mol. Gen. Genet. 261:977-984.
3. Alonso JM, Takashi H, Roman G, Nourizadeh S, Ecker JR (1999) EIN2, a bifunctional transducer of ethylene and stress responses in *Arabidopsis*. Science 284:2148-2152.
4. Andrade AC, Del Sorbo G, Van Nistelrooy JGM, De Waard MA (2000) The ABC transporter AtrB from *Aspergillus nidulans* mediates resistance to all major classes of fungicides and some natural toxic compounds. Microbiology 146:1987-1997.
5. Baev N, Endre G, Petrovics G, Banfalvi Z, Kondorosi A (1991) Six nodulation genes of *nod* box locus 4 in *Rhizobium meliloti* are involved in nodulation signal production: *nodM* codes for D-glucosamine synthetase. Mol. Gen. Genet. 228:113-124.
6. Balzi E, Wang M, Leterme S, Van Dyck L, Goffeau A (1994) PDR5, a novel yeast multidrug resistance conferring transporter controlled by the transcription regulator PDR1. J. Biol. Chem. 269:2206-2214.
7. Bauer BE, Wolfger H, Kuchler K (1999) Inventory and function of yeast ABC proteins: about sex, stress, pleiotropic drug and heavy metal resistance. Biochim. Biophys. Acta 1461:217-236.
8. Bayliss C, Bent E, Culham DE, MacLellan S, Clarke AJ, Brown G L, Wood JM (1997) Bacterial genetic loci implicated in the *Pseudomonas putida* GR12-2R3 – canola mutualism: identification of an exudate-inducible sugar transporter. Can. J. Microbiol. 43:809-818.
9. Becker A, Küster H, Niehaus K, Pühler A (1995) Extension of the *Rhizobium meliloti* biosynthesis gene cluster identification of the *exsA* gene encoding an ABC transporter protein and the *exsB* gene which probably codes for a regulator of succinoglycan biosynthesis. Mol. Gen. Genet. 249:487-497.
10. Callahan TM, Rose MS, Meade MJ, Ehrenshaft M, Upchurch RG 1999. *CFP*, the putative cercosporin transporter of *Cercospora kikuchii*, is required for wild type cercosporin production, resistance and virulence on soybean. Mol. Plant-Microbe Interact. 12:901-910.
11. Cangelosi GA, Martinetti G, Leigh JA, Lee CC, Theines C, Nester EW (1989) Role of *Agrobacterium tumefaciens* ChvA Protein in Export of β-1,2-glucan. J. Bacteriol. 171:1609-1615.

12. Cardenas L, Dominguez J, Santana O, Quinto C (1996) The role of the *nodI* and *nodJ* genes in the transport of Nod metabolites in *Rhizobium etli*. Gene 173:183-187.
13. Chapeland F, Fritz R, Lanen C, Gredt M, Leroux P (1999) Inheritance and mechanisms of resistance to anilinopyrimidine fungicides in *Botrytic cinerea (Botryotinia Fuckeliana)*. Pestic. Biochem. Physiol. 64:85-100.
14. Chen XJ (2001) Activity of the *Kluyveromyces lactis* Pdr5 multidrug transporter is modulated by the Sit4 Protein Phosphatase. J. Bacteriol. 183: 3939-3948.
15. Conseil G, Perez-Victoria JM, Jault JM, Gamarro F, Goffeau A, Jofmann J, Di Pietro A (2001) Protein kinase C effectors bind to multidrug ABC transporters and inhibit their activity. Biochemistry 40:2564-2571.
16. Cooper B (2001) Collateral gene expression changes induced by distinct plant viruses during the hypersensitive resistance reaction in *Chenopodium amaranticolor*. Plant J. 26:339-349.
17. Daub ME, Hangarter R P (1983) Light-induced production of singlet oxygen and superoxide by the fungal toxin, cercosporin. Plant Physiol. 73:855-857.
18. Davidson AL, Shuman HA, Nikaido H (1992) Mechanism of maltose transport in *Escherichia coli*: transmembrane signaling by periplasmic binding proteins. Proc. Natl. Acad. Sci. USA 89:2360-2364.
19. Delaveau T, Delahodde A, Carvajal E, Subic J, Jacq C (1994) *PDR3*, a new yeast regulatory gene, is homologous to *PDR1* and controls the multidrug resistance phenomenon. Mol. Gen. Genet. 244:501-511.
20. Del Sorbo GD, Schoonbeek H-J, De Waard MA (2000) Fungal transporters involved in efflux of natural toxic compounds and fungicides. Fungal Genet. Biol. 30:1-15.
21. Denny TP, Matthews PS, VanEtten HD (1987) A possible mechanism of nondegradative tolerance of pisatin in *Nectria haematococca* MP VI. Physiol. Mol. Plant Pathol. 30:93-107.
22. Denny TP, VanEtten HD (1983) Characterization of an inducible, nondegradative tolerance of *Nectria haematococca* MP VI to phytoalexins. J. Gen. Microbiol. 129:2903-2913.
23. DeRisi J, van den Hazel B, Marc P, Balzi E, Brown P, Jacq C, Goffeau A (2000) Genome microarray analysis of transcriptional activation in multidrug resistance yeast mutants. FEBS Lett. 470:156-160.
24. Devine SE, Melera P W (1994) Diversity of multidrug resistance in mammalian cells. J. Biol. Chem. 269:6133-6139.
25. De Waard MA, Van Nistelrooy JGM (1984) Differential accumulation of fenarimol by a wild-type isolate and fenarimol-

resistant isolates of *Penicillium italicum*. Neth. J. Plant Path. 90:143-153.

26. Diener AC, Gaxiola RA, Fink GR (2001) Arabidopsis *ALF5*, a multidrug efflux transporter gene family member, confers resistance to toxins. Plant Cell 13:1625-1637.
27. Dudler R, Hertig C (1992) Structure of an *mdr*-like gene from *Arabidopsis thaliana*. J. Biol. Chem. 267:5882-5888.
28. Egner R, Bauer BE, Kuchler K (2000) The transmembrane domain 10 of the yeast Pdr5p ABC antifungal efflux pump determines both substrate specificity and inhibitor susceptibility. Mol. Microbiol. 35:1255-1263.
29. Egner R, Rosenthal FE, Kralli A, Sanglard D, Kuchler K (1998) Genetic separation of FK506 susceptibility and drug transport in the yeast Pdr5 ATP-binding cassette multidrug resistance transporter. Mol. Biol. Cell 9:523-543.
30. Espinosa-Urgel M, Salido A, Ramos J L (2000) Genetic analysis of functions involved in adhesion of *Pseudomonas putida* to seeds. J. Bacteriol. 182:2363-2369.
31. Fleiβner A, Sopalia C, Weltring K-M (2002) An ATP-binding cassette multidrug-resistance transporter is necessary for tolerance of *Gibberella pulicaris* to phytoalexins and virulence on potato tubers. Mol. Plant-Microbe Interact. 15:102-108.
32. Fuqua C, Winans SC (1996) Localization of OccR-activated and TraR-activated promoters that express two ABC-type permeases and the traR gene of Ti plasmid pTiR10. Mol. Microbiol. 20:1199-1210.
33. González-Pasayo R, Martinez-Romero E (2000) Multiresistance genes of *Rhizobium etli* CFN42. Mol. Plant-Microbe Interact. 13:572-577.
34. Gotoh N, Kusumi T, Tsujimoto H, Wada T, Nishino T (1999) Topological analysis of an RND family transporter, MexD of *Pseudomonas aeruginosa*. FEBS Lett. 458:32-36.
35. Gottesman MM, Pastan I (1993) Biochemistry of multidrug resistance mediated by the multidrug transporter. Annu. Rev. Biochem. 62:385-427.
36. Göttfert M (1993) Regulation and function of rhizobial nodulation genes. FEMS Microbiol. Rev. 10:39-63.
37. Green AL, Anderson EJ, Brooker RJ (2000) A revised model for the structure and function of the lactose permease. J. Biol. Chem. 275:23240-23246.
38. Griffith JK, Baker ME, Rouch DA, Page MG, Skurray RA, Paulsen I T, Chater KF, Baldwin SA, Henderson PJ (1992) Membrane transport proteins: implications of sequence comparisons. Curr. Opin. Cell Biol. 4:684-695.

39. Guan J, Kapteyn JC, Kerkenaar A, De Waard MA (1992) Characterisation of energy-dependent efflux of imazalil and fenarimol in isolates of *Penicillium italicum* with a low, medium and high degree of resistance to DMI-fungicides. Neth. J. Plant Path. 98:313-324.
40. Hamamoto H, Nawata O, Hasegawa K, Nakaune R, Lee Y J, Makizumi Y, Akutsu K, Hibi T (2001) The role of the ABC transporter gene *PMR1* in demethylation inhibitor resistance in *Penicillium digitatum*. Pestic. Bioch. Physiol. 70:19-26.
41. Hayashi K, Schoonbeek H-J, Sugiura H, De Waard M A (2001) Multidrug resistance in *Botrytis cinerea* associated with decreased accumulation of the azole fungicide oxpoconazole and increased transcription of the ABC transporter gene *BcatrD*. Pestic. Biochem. Physiol. 70:168-179.
42. Higgins CF (1992) ABC transporters: From microorganisms to man. Annu. Rev. Cell Biol. 8:67-113.
43. Higgins CF (2001) ABC transporters: physiology, structure and mechanism – an overview. Res. Microbiol. 152:205-210.
44. Higgins CF, Gottesman MM (1992) Is the multidrug transporter a flippase? Trends Biochem. Sci. 17:18-21.
45. Hirayama T, Kieber JJ, Hirayama N, Kogan M, Guzman P, Nourizadeh S, Alonso J M, Dailey W P, Dancis A, Ecker JR (1999) RESPONSIVE-TO-ANTAGONIST1, a Menkes/Wilson disease-related copper transporter, is required for ethylene signaling in *Arabidopsis*. Cell 97:383-393.
46. Hugouvieux-Cotte-Pattat N, Blot N, Reverchon S (2001) Identification of TogMNAB, an ABC transporter which mediates the uptake of pectic oligomers in *Erwinia chrysanthemi* 3937. Mol. Microbiol. 41:1113-1123.
47. Hugouvieux-Cotte-Pattat N, Reverchon S (2001) Two transporters, TogT and TogMNAB, are responsible for oligogalacturonide uptake in *Erwinia chrysanthemi* 3937. Mol. Microbiol. 41:1125-1132.
48. Hung L-W, Wang IX, Nikaido K, Liu P-Q, Ames GF-L, Kim S-H (1998) Crystal structure of the ATP-binding subunit of an ABC transporter. Nature 396:703-707.
49. Ishikawa T (1992) The ATP-dependent glutathione S-conjugate export pump. Trends Biochem. Sci. 17:463-468.
50. Jasiński M, Stukkens Y, Degand H, Purnelle B, Marchand-Brynaert J, Boutry M (2001) A plant plasma membrane ATP binding cassette-type transporter is involved in antifungal terpenoid secretion. Plant Cell 13:1095-1107.
51. Jessen-Marshall AE, Paul NJ, Brooker RJ (1995) The conserved motif, GXXX(D/E)(R/K)XG[X](R/K)(R/K), in hydrophilic loop 2/3 of the lactose permease. J. Biol. Chem. 270:16251-16257.

52. Jones PM, George AM (1998) A new structural model for P-glycoprotein. J. Membr. Biol. 166:133-147.
53. Jones PM, George AM (1999) Subunit interactions in ABC transporters: towards a functional architecture. FEMS Microbiol. Lett. 179:187-202.
54. Joseph-Horne T, Hollomon D, Manning N, Kelly SL (1996) Investigation of the sterol composition and azole resistance in field isolates of *Septoria tritici*. Appl. Environ. Microbiol. 62:184-190.
55. Juranka, PF, Zastawny RL, Ling V (1989) P-glycoprotein: multidrug-resistance and a superfamily of membrane-associated transport proteins. FASEB J. 3:2583-2592.
56. Kalamarakis AE, De Waard MA, Ziogas BN, Georgopoulos SG (1991) Resistance to fenarimol in *Nectria haematococca* var. *cucurbitae*. Pestic. Biochem. Physiol. 40:212-220.
57. Kaneko T, Nakamura Y, Sato S, Asamizu E, Kato T, Sasamotao S, Watanabe A, Idesawa K, Ishikawa A, Kawashima K, Kimura T, Kishida Y, Kiyokawa C, Kohara M, Matsumoto M, Matsuno A, Mochizuki Y, Nakayama S, Nakazaki N, Shimpo S, Sugimoto M, Takeuchi C, Yamada M, Tabata S (2000) Complete genome structure of the nitrogen-fixing symbiotic bacterium *Mesorhizobium loti*. DNA Research 7:331-338.
58. Katzmann DJ, Burnett PE, Golin J, Mahe Y, Moye-Rowley WS (1994) Transcriptional control of the yeast *PDR5* gene by the *PDR3* gene product. Mol. Cell Biol. 14:4653-4661.
59. Katzmann DJ, Hallstrom TC, Voet M, Wysock W, Golin J, Volckaert G, Moye-Rowley W S (1995) Expression of an ATP-binding cassette transporter-encoding gene (*YOR1*) is required for oligomycin resistance in *Saccharomyces cerevisiae*. Mol. Cell Biol. 15:6875-6883.
60. Kaur R, Bachhawat AK (1999) The yeast multidrug resistance pump, Pdr5p, confers reduced drug resistance in *erg* mutants of *Saccharomyces cerevisiae*. Microbiology 145:809-818.
61. Kean LS, Grant AM, Angeletti C, Mahe Y, Kuchler K, Fuller RS, Nichols JW (1997) Plasma membrane translocation of fluorescent labeled phosphatidylethanolamine is controlled by transcription regulators, PDR1 and PDR3. J. Cell Biol. 138:255-270.
62. Kim H, Farrand SK (1997) Characterization of the *acc* operon from the nopaline-type Ti plasmid pTiC58, which encodes utilization of agrocinopines A and B and susceptibility to agrocin 84. J. Bacteriol. 179:7559-7572.
63. Kim H, Farrand SK (1998) Opine catabolic loci from *Agrobacterium* plasmids confer chemotaxis to their cognate substrates. Mol. Plant-Microbe Interact. 11:131-143.

64. Kolaczkowski M, Kolaczkowska A, Luczynski J, Witek S, Goffeau A (1998) *In vivo* characterization of the drug resistance profile of the major ABC transporters and other components of the yeast pleiotropic drug resistance network. Microbial Drug Resist. 4:143-158.
65. Krol J, Skorupska A (1997) Identification of genes in *Rhizobium leguminosarum* bv *trifolii* whose products are homologous to a family of ATP-binding proteins. Microbiology 143:1389-1394.
66. Lange Y, Steck TL (1998) Four cholesterol-sensing proteins. Curr. Opin. Struct. Biol. 8:435-439.
67. Lee S-W, Cooksey DA (2000) Genes expressed in *Pseudomonas putida* during colonization of a plant-pathogenic fungus. Appl. Environ. Microbiol. 66:2764-2772.
68. Lerouge I, Laeremans T, Verreth C, Vanderleyden J, Van-Soom C, Tobin A, Carlson RW (2001) Identification of an ATP-binding cassette transporter for export of the O-antigen across the inner membrane in *Rhizobium etli* based on the genetic, functional, and structural analysis of an lps mutant deficient in O-antigen. J. Biol. Chem. 276:17190-17198.
69. Létoffé S, Delepelaire P, Wandersman C (1990) Protease secretion by *Erwinia chrysanthemi*: the specific secretion functions are analogous to those of *Escherichia coli* α-haemolysin. EMBO J. 9:1375-1382.
70. Lewis K (2001) In search of natural substrates and inhibitors of MDR pumps. J. Mol. Microbiol. Biotechnol. 3:247-254.
71. Li L, He Z, Pandey GK, Tsuchiya T, Luan S (2002) Functional cloning and characterization of a plant efflux carrier for multidrug and heavy metal detoxification. J. Biol. Chem. 277:5360-5368.
72. Li Z-S, Zhao Y, Rea PA (1995) Magnesium adenosine 5'-triphosphate-energized transport of glutathione-S-conjugates by plant vacuolar membrane vesicles. Plant Physiol. 107:1257-1268.
73. Liu Z, Jacobs M, Schaff DA, McCullen CA, Binns AN (2001) ChvD, a chromosomally encoded ATP-binding cassette transporter-homologous protein involved in regulation of virulence gene expression in *Agrobacterium tumefaciens*. J. Bacteriol. 183:3310-3317.
74. Loo TW, Clarke DM (1995) Membrane topology of a cysteine-less mutant of human P-glycoprotein. J. Biol. Chem. 270:843-8.
75. López-Solanilla E, Garcia-Olmedo F, Rodriguez-Palenzuela P (1998) Inactivation of the *sapA* to *sapF* locus of *Erwinia chrysanthemi* reveals common features in plant and animal bacterial pathogenesis. Plant Cell 10:917-924.
76. Lu Y-P, Li Z-S, Rea PA (1997) *AtMRP1* gene of *Arabidopsis* encodes a glutathione *S*-conjugate pump: Isolation and functional

definition of a plant ATP-binding cassette transporter gene. Proc. Natl. Acad. Sci. USA 94:8243-8248.
77. Martin C, Berridge G, Higgins CF, Mistry P, Charlton P, Callaghan R (2000) Communication between multiple drug binding sites on P-glycoprotein. Mol. Pharmacol. 58:624-632.
78. Martinoia E, Grill E, Tommasini R, Kreuz K, Amrhein N (1993) ATP-dependent glutathione *S*-conjugate 'export' pump in the vacuolar membrane of plants. Nature 364:247-249.
79. Matthysse AG (1987) Characterization of nonattaching mutants of *Agrobacterium tumefaciens*. J. Bacteriol. 169:313-323.
80. Matthysse AG, Yarnall H, Boles SB, McMahan S (2000) A region of the *Agrobacterium tumefaciens* chromosome containing genes required for virulence and attachment to host cells. Biochem. Biophys. Acta 1490:208-212.
81. Mazur A, Weilbo J, Krol J, Kopcinska J, Lotocka B, Golinowski W, Skorupska A (1998) Molecular characterization and symbiotic importance of *prsD* gene of *Rhizobium leguminosarum* bv. *trifolii* TA1. Acta Biochimica Polonica 45:1067-1073.
82. Mimura CS, Admon A, Hurt KA, Ames GF-L (1990) The nucleotide-binding site of HisP, a membrane protein of the histidine permease. J. Biol. Chem. 265:19535-19542.
83. Mitterbauer R, Karl T, Lemmens M, Kuchler K, Adam G (2000) Resistance to mycotoxins: a role for ABC transporter proteins in plant-pathogen interactions. Pages 352-355 in: Biology of Plant-Microbe Interactions Vol. 2. P. J. G. M. DeWit, T. Bisseling and W. J. Stiekema, eds. International Society for Molecular Plant-Microbe Interactions, St. Paul, MN.
84. Muhitch MJ, McCormick SP, Alexander NJ, Hohn TM (2000) Transgenic expression of the *TRI*101 or *PDR*5 gene increases resistance of tobacco to the phytotoxic effects of the trichothecene 4,15-diacetoxyscirpenol. Plant Sci. 157:201-207.
85. Nachin L, Hassouni M E, Loiseau L, Expert D, Barras F (2001) SoxR-dependent response to oxidative stress and virulence of *Erwinia chrysanthemi*: the key role of SufC, an orphan ABC ATPase. Mol. Microbiol. 39:960-972.
86. Nakaune R, Adachi K, Nawata O, Tomiyama M, Akutsu K, Hibi T (1998) A novel ATP-binding cassette transporter involved in multidrug resistance in the phytopathogenic fungus *Penicillium digitatum*. Appl. Environ. Microbiol. 64:3983-3988.
87. Nawrath C, Heck S, Parinthawong N, Métraux J-P (2002) EDS5, an essential component of salicylic acid-dependent signaling for disease resistance in *Arabidopsis*, is a member of the MATE transporter family. Plant Cell 14:275-286.
88. Nikaido H, Saier Jr. M H (1992) Transport proteins in bacteria: common themes in their design. Science 258:936-942.

89. Palumbo JD, Kado CI, Phillips DA (1998) An isoflavonoid-inducible efflux pump in *Agrobacterium tumefaciens* is involved in competitive colonization of roots. J. Bacteriol. 180:3107-3113.
90. Pao SS, Paulsen IT, Saier Jr. MH (1998) Major facilitator superfamily. Microbiol. Mol. Biol. Rev. 62:1-34.
91. Parra-Lopez C, Baer MT, Groisman EA (1993) Molecular genetic analysis of a locus required for resistance to antimicrobial peptides in *Salmonella typhimurium*. EMBO J. 12:4053-4062.
92. Paulsen IT, Brown MH, Skurray RA (1996) Proton-dependent multidrug efflux systems. Microbiol. Rev. 60:575-608.
93. Pedras MS, Khan AQ, Taylor JL (1997) Phytoalexins from Brassicas: overcoming plants' defenses. Pages 155-166 in: Phytochemicals for Pest Control. P. A. Hedin, R. M. Hollingworth, E. P. Masler, J. Miyamoto, and D. G. Thompson, eds. American Chemical Society, Washington, DC.
94. Pedras MS, Okanga FI (1999) Strategies of cruciferous pathogenic fungi: detoxification of the phytoalexin cyclobrassinin by mimicry. J. Agric. Food Chem. 47:1196-1202.
95. Pedras MS, Séguin-Swartz G, Abrams SR (1990) Minor phytotoxins from the blackleg fungus *Phoma lingam*. Phytochemistry 29:777-782.
96. Pedras MS, Taylor JL, Nakashima TT (1993) A novel chemical signal from the "Blackleg" fungus: beyond phytotoxins and phytoalexins. J Org. Chem. 58:4778-4780.
97. Pitkin JW, Panaccione DG, Walton JD (1996) A putative cyclic peptide efflux pump encoded by the TOXA gene of the plant-pathogenic fungus *Cochliobolus carbonum*. Microbiology 142:1557-1565.
98. Quigley NB, Mo Y-Y, Gross DC (1993) SyrD is required for syringomycin production by *Pseudomonas syringae* pathovar *syringae* and is related to a family of ATP-binding secretion proteins. Mol. Microbiol. 9:787-801.
99. Reizer J, Reizer A, Saier Jr. MH (1992) A new subfamily of bacterial ABC-type transport systems catalyzing export of drugs and carbohydrates. Protein Sci. 1:1326-1332.
100. Romsicki Y, Sharom FJ (1998) The ATPase and ATP-binding functions of P-glycoprotein-modulation by interaction with defined phospholipids. Eur. J. Biochem. 256:170-178.
101. Rosenberg MF, Callaghan R, Ford RC, Higgins CF (1997) Structure of the multidrug resistance P-glycoprotein to 2.5 nm resolution determined by electron microscopy and image analysis. J. Biol. Chem. 272:10685-10694.
102. Saier Jr. MH (2000) A functional-phylogenetic classification system for transmembrane solute transporters. Microbiol. Mol. Biol. Rev. 64:354-411.

103. Saier Jr. MH, Paulsen IT (2001) Phylogeny of multidrug transporters. Cell & Dev. Biol. 12:205-213.

104. Saier Jr. MH, Tam R, Reizer A, Reizer J (1994) Two novel families of bacterial membrane proteins concerned with nodultaion, cell division and transport. Mol. Microbiol. 11:841-847.

105. Sauer K, Camper AK (2001) Characterization of phenotypic changes in *Pseudomonas putida* in response to surface-associated growth. J. Bacteriol. 183:6579-6589.

106. Saurin W, Hofnung M, Dassa E (1999) Getting in or out: early segregation between importers and exporters in the evolution of ATP-binding cassette (ABC) transporters. J. Mol. Evol. 48:22-41

107. Schneider E, Hunke S (1998) ATP-binding-cassette (ABC) transport systems: functional and structural aspects of the ATP-hydrolyzing subunits/domains. FEMS Microbiol. Rev. 22:1-20.

108. Scholz-Schroeder BK, Soule JD, Lu S-E, Grgurina I, Gross DC (2001) A physical map of the syringomycin and syringopeptin gene clusters localized to an approximately 145-kb DNA region of *Pseudomonas syringae* pv. *syringae* strain B301D. Mol. Plant-Microbe Interact. 14:1426-1435.

109. Schoonbeek H, Del Sorbo G, De Waard MA (2001) The ABC transporter BcatrB affects the sensitivity of *Botrytis cinerea* to the phytoalexin resveratrol and the fungicide fenpiclonil. Mol. Plant-Microbe Interact. 14:562-571.

110. Seelig A, Blatter XL, Wohnsland F (2000) Substrate recognition by P-glycoprotein and the multidrug resistance-associated protein MRP1: a comparison. Int. J. Clin. Pharmacol. Ther. 38:111-121.

111. Shapiro AB, Fox K, Lam P, Ling V (1999) Stimulation of P-glycoprotein-mediated drug transport by prazosin and progesterone: Evidence for a third drug-binding site. Eur. J. Biochem. 259:841-50.

112. Smart CC, Fleming AJ (1996) Hormonal and Environmental regulation of a plant PDR5-like ABC transporter. J. Biol. Chem. 271:19351-19357.

113. Stanfield SW, Ielpi L, O'Brochta D, Helsinki DR, Ditta GS (1988) The *ndvA* gene product of *Rhizobium meliloti* is required for β-(1→2) glucan production and has homology to the ATP-binding export protein HlyB. J. Bacteriol. 170:3523-3530.

114. Szczyglowski K, Kapranov P, Hamburger D, de Bruijn FJ (1998) The *Lotus japonicus LjNOD70* gene encodes a protein with similarities to transporters. Plant Mol. Biol. 37:651-661.

115. Taylor JL, Condie J (2000) Characterization of ABC transporters from the fungal phytopathogen *Leptosphaeria maculans*. Pages 71-76 in: Biology of Plant-Microbe Interactions, Vol. 2. P. J. G.

M. DeWit, T. Bisseling, and W. J. Stiekema, eds. International Society for Molecular Plant-Microbe Interactions. St. Paul, MN.

116. Tseng T-T, Gratwick KS, Kollman J, Park D, Nies DH, Goffeau A, Saier Jr. MH (1999) The RND permease superfamily: An ancient, ubiquitous and diverse family that includes human disease and development proteins. J. Mol. Microbiol. Biotechnol. 16:107-125.

117. Upchurch RG, Rose MS, Eweida M (2001) Over-expression of the cercosporin facilitator protein, *CFP*, in *Cercospora kikuchii* up-regulates production and secretion of cercosporin. FEMS Microbiol. Letts. 204:89-93.

118. Upchurch RG, Walker DC, Rollins JA, Ehrenshaft M, Daub ME (1991) Mutants of *Cercospora kikuchii* altered in cercosporin synthesis and pathogenicity. Appl. Environ. Microbiol. 57:2940-2945.

119. Urban M, Bhargava T, Hamer JE (1999) An ATP-driven efflux pump is a novel pathogenicity factor in rice blast disease. EMBO J. 18:512-521.

120. Valdivia RH, Wang L, Winans SC (1991) Characterization of a putative periplasmic transport system for octopine accumulation encoded by *Agrobacterium tumefaciens* Ti Plasmid pTiA6. J. Bacteriol. 173:6398-6405.

121. Van Bambeke F, Balzi E, Tulkens PM (2000) Antibiotic efflux pumps. Biochem. Pharmacol. 60:457-470.

122. Van Belle D, Andre B (2001) A genomic view of yeast membrane transporters. Curr. Opin. Cell Biol. 13:389-398.

123. Van Veen HW (2001) Towards the molecular mechanism of prokaryotic and eukaryotic multidrug transporters. Cell & Dev. Biol. 12:239-245.

124. Van Veen HW, Higgins CF, Konings WN (2001) Multidrug transport by ATP binding cassette transporters: a proposed two-cylinder engine mechanism. Res. Microbiol. 152:365-374.

125. Varela MF, Sansom CE, Griffith JK (1995) Mutational analysis and molecular modelling of an amino acid sequence motif conserved in antiporters but not symporters in a transporter superfamily. Mol. Membr. Biol. 12:313-319.

126. Vermeulen T, Schoonbeek H, De Waard MA (2001) The ABC transporter BcatrB from *Botrytis cinerea* is a determinant of the activity of the phenylpyrrole fungicide fludioxonil. Pest Manag. Sci. 57:393-402.

127. Ververidis P, Davrazou F, Diallinas G, Georgakopoulos D, Kanellis A K, Panopoulos N (2001) A novel putative reductase (Cpd1p) and the multidrug exporter Snq2p are involved in resistance to cercosporin and other singlet oxygen-generating

photosensitizers in *Saccharomyces cerevisiae*. Curr. Genet. 39:127-136.

128. Walker JC, Saraste M, Runswick M J, Gay N J (1982) Distantly related sequences in the α- and β-subunits of ATP synthase, myosin, kinases and other ATP-requiring enzymes and a common nucleotide binding fold. EMBO J. 8:945-951.

129. Walshaw DL, Poole PS (1996) The general L-amino acid permease of *Rhizobium leguminosarum* is an ABC uptake system that also influences efflux of solutes. Mol. Microbiol. 21:1239-1252.

130. Xiong L, Lee M-W, Qi M, Yang Y (2001) Identification of defense-related rice genes by suppression subtractive hybridization and differential screening. Mol. Plant-Microbe Interact. 14:685-692.

131. Yamaguchi A, Someya Y, Sawai T (1992) Metal-tetracycline/H+ antiporter of *Escherichia coli* encoded by transposon Tn10. The role of a conserved sequence motif, GXXXXFXGRR, in a putative cytoplasmic loop between helices 2 and 3. J. Biol. Chem. 267:19155-19162.

132. Zhang L, Sachs CW, Fu HW, Fine RL, Casey PJ (1995) Characterization of prenylcysteines that interact with P-glycoprotein and inhibit drug transport in tumor cells. J. Biol. Chem. 270:22859-22865.

133. Zwiers L-H, De Waard MA (2000) Characterization of the ABC transporter genes *MgAtr1* and *MgAtr2* from the wheat pathogen *Mycosphaerella graminicola*. Fungal Genet. Biol. 30:115-125.

Ustilago Pathogenicity

Scott E. Gold

Fungal Pathogenesis

Fungal plant pathogens are responsible for enormous annual losses of marketable food and fiber. The smut fungi as a group constitute an important agricultural problem and, in some crops, are occasionally responsible for local yield losses exceeding 25% [115]. Yield loss due to corn smut, caused by *Ustilago maydis*, is generally below 2% because of available partially resistant varieties [117]. However, due to the high value of maize grown in the U.S. a loss of 1% is equal to approximately $190 million per year in this country alone.

Interactions between fungi and plants that lead to colonization and disease require fungal virulence factors [93] and programmed development by the fungus and plant. For example some rust fungi recognize topographical features of leaf surfaces and respond by producing infection structures called appressoria [2]. Once penetration of the leaf surface has occurred the fungus and plant both participate in the formation of the fungal haustorium-plant cell interface [70]. In corn smut, gall formation also clearly requires specific fungal and plant development and communication between both organisms. Most other smut fungi grow systemically in the plant host with stealth, producing symptoms only by replacement of the seed with their spores.

Ustilago molecular biology has primarily been studied using *U. maydis* as the species of focus. About one dozen active laboratories around the world are currently employing a number of approaches to analyze the genetics of fungal mating, morphogenesis and fungal-plant interactions in the *U. maydis*-maize pathosystem. Additionally, several laboratories study the related *U.* hordei-barley interaction. To date most research effort has focused on the characterization of genes involved in completion of the *U. maydis* life and disease cycles. Additional work in *U. hordei* helps to corroborate and extend these results. The plant side of these interactions has received little research effort thus far. There is a great deal of additional research carried out on *U. maydis* in relation to specific physiological functions. Some of these include studies on mycoviruses [26, 54, 66, 84], fungicide resistance [22, 23, 38, 51-53, 71, 105], genetic recombination [31-33, 45, 46, 82, 98] processes including the work generating the famous Holliday model of recombination [45, 98], none of which will be further described here. Several of these topics have recently been reviewed (A.D. Martinez-Espinoza, M. Garcia-Pedrajas and S.E.G. Fungal Genetics and Biology, In Press).

Ustilago as a Model Organism

Ustilago maydis is a frequently used model organism in studies of fungal mating type, morphogenesis and pathogenicity. This fungus provides an ideal system for study because of its facile sexual cycle and available molecular genetic tools. It is completely dependent on the host for growth of the dikaryon and for production of sexual spores. Plant development is impacted by infection and the host responds to fungal colonization by producing highly modified gall structures indicating that signals received from the pathogen are important in disease development. The obligate nature of the sexual cycle has been an area of speculation in terms of what specific requirements are present in the plant but absent in culture. Related to this, a recent report suggests that coculture of the *U. maydis* dikaryon with maize callus can generate genetic recombinants [91]. Although the mechanism of this recombination is not currently documented, this work has the potential to open the door to the characterization of plant derived signals inducing *U. maydis* sexual development and/or genetic recombination.

In addition to *U. maydis*, the small grain pathogen *U. hordei* is a fairly well studied relative and shows a high level of conservation with *U. maydis* with regard to mechanisms of genetic control [3, 6-8, 67, 68, 78, 108]. The results with these two organisms as well as those from research on the more distantly related Holobasidiomycetes (Hymenomycetes, [1]) such as *Coprinus cinereus* and *Schizophyllum commune* [24, 58] indicate the general applicability of findings from research on *U. maydis* to the genetics of the genus, the order, and in many cases the phylum Basidiomycota. Genetic research with *U. hordei* continues to provide insight into common mechanisms of development and pathogenicity in the genus. Tools developed for *U. maydis* are generally readily transferable to research on *U. hordei* and vice versa.

One of the reasons *U. maydis* is commonly studied is its excellent transformation system in which 10^4 transformants per microgram DNA are attainable [110, 114]. Due to both ectopic and homologous integration events, transformants with gene introductions or disruptions can be obtained fairly efficiently [34, 59]. Additionally, the availability of vectors carrying an autonomously replicating sequence (ARS) allows non-integrative transformation and simplifies plasmid recovery in Escherichia coli [110]. Additional tools for molecular genetic manipulation have been developed for use with *U. maydis*. These include drug resistance markers that allow for selection of transformants and progeny with multiple gene modifications [38], reporter genes [88, 104, 112], as well as collections of interesting mutants [19, 35, 73, 75].

Direct Identification of Pathogenicity genes

There are an increasing number of clear examples of genes required for full virulence in this group of fungi, especially in *U. maydis*. The majority of these genes have not however been isolated as pathogenicity mutants, but rather based on processes predicted to correlate with pathogencity such as mating and morphogenetic changes. In *U. maydis* screens for pathogenicity mutants have been hampered because most loss of function mutations are recessive and compensated for upon formation of the dikaryon by mating with wild-type strains. Additionally, the construction of compatible strains with unknown mutations is technically unfeasible because crosses to generate compatible haploid mutants are very labor intensive. However, with the development of new genetic techniques efforts have been launched to directly isolate pathogenicity genes. Using restriction enzyme mediated integration (REMI) mutagenesis of a solopathogenic haploid strain (described in greater detail later in this chapter) it was possible to identify 10-20 *U. maydis* mutants out of a collection of 1000 that were unable to induce symptoms in corn seedlings [19]. Some of the non-pathogenic mutants were auxotrophs [48].

Ustilago maydis Morphogenesis, Mating and Pathogenicity

In wild-type *U. maydis-Zea mays* interactions, growth form and pathogenicity are inextricably linked. Filamentous growth appears to be necessary but not sufficient for pathogenic development [14]. Haploid strains are saprophytic budding cells that are easily cultured. The filamentous cell type in *U. maydis* is normally established through mating interactions governed by two genetic loci called *a* and *b* (reviewed in [9]). Budding haploid cells are compatible to fuse and form a stable dikaryon only if they carry alleles with different specificities at both the *a* and *b* loci Cell fusion is controlled by the a mating-type locus [109], which has two alternative forms (*a1* and *a2*) and, as described in detail below, heterozygosity at the multiallelic *b* locus is required for the production of a stable filamentous dikaryon (Figure 1) and pathogenicity [86]. The dikaryon, formed upon mating of compatible haploids, is the pathogenic cell type; it is filamentous and an obligate biotroph [25]. The control exerted by the *b* locus and environmental signals can lead to similar morphologies in vitro, however heterozygosity at the b locus is required for pathogenicity. Synthetic diploid strains indicate that once mating has occurred the *a* locus is dispensable for pathogenicity [11] but heterozygosity does seem to enhance the rate of gall formation to a minor degree [81].

Figure 1. *2b* or not *2b*, that is the question. The upper portion of the photo shows an a1b1 strain overlaid with an *a2b2* strain yielding the white filamentous dikaryotic growth of the compatible mating reaction. The bottom portion shows an *a1b1* strain overlaid with an *a2b1* strain yielding yeast growth. These results are indicative of the feature that 2 different *b* alleles are essential for the formation of the filamentous pathogenic dikaryon.

The filamentous dikaryon causes a localized infection on maize plants typified by the formation of large tumors (galls) on any above ground part of the plant [25]. The fungus enters host tissue by penetrating the cuticle and plant cells directly; it then ramifies intra- and later intercellularly through the host tissue [13, 99, 101]. In the field the most obvious symptoms are seen on the ears (Figure 2). The infection of kernels occurs via the silks (stigmas) [100]. Interestingly, pollination shortens the period of susceptibility of silks to infection by *U. maydis* [28] probably due to stigma abscission. Hyphae proliferate within gall tissue and, as galls mature, the nuclei of the dikaryon fuse and the diploid teliospores are formed [13]. Upon dispersal from the host plant, the diploid teliospores germinate, form promycelia (short filamentous multicelled basidia) and undergo meiosis to yield budding haploid basidiospores [1, 9]. Infection repeats after spores overwinter within gall tissue on the soil surface. Teliospores are water repellent and thus more readily spread by wind and rain splash or even insects [25]. The basidiospores can further divide indefinitely producing masses of haploid sporidia that may potentially be spread further by the forces mentioned above [25]. It is unclear if sporidia significantly contribute to disease spread by transport to other plants.

The master control genes of mating and pathogenicity, the *a* and *b* mating type genes, have been characterized [21, 34, 56, 57, 95]. At the *a*

Figure 2. Severely infected maize ear with enlarged corn smut galls.

locus, the *a1* and *a2* allelic sequences are idiomorphs [34]. The *a* locus possesses *mfa* and *pra*, two tightly linked genes that encode secreted pheromone and membrane spanning pheromone receptors, respectively [21]. In addition to its function as a mating attraction system, dikaryon heterozygosity at the *a* locus (in addition to heterozygosity at *b*) also contributes to the in vitro production of the post mating dikaryotic filamentous form through an autocrine response in which the pheromones and receptors of opposite allelic specificity are present within the same cell and therefore may continually interact [11, 103].

Genetic and biochemical data indicate that the interaction between the *U. maydis* pheromones and receptors is quite similar to the events in the *Saccharomyces cerevisiae* paradigm [10]. The pheromone encoded by the *mfa* gene is thought to interact directly with the pheromone receptor product encoded by the *pra* gene of the opposite *a* mating specificity [103]. The downstream events generating the final response to pheromone presumably involve components similar to those encountered in *S. cerevisiae*. In *S. cerevisiae* signal transduction from the pheromone-receptor interaction to the final cellular responses involves trimeric G proteins and a MAP kinase cascade with the final phosphorylation and activation of two critical proteins. These proteins are the Ste12p transcription factor, which when activated regulates transcription of target genes, and Far1p which causes cell cycle arrest by inhibition of the kinase activity of the G1 cyclin complex Cdc28-Cln [10, 113]. In *U. maydis*, published and unpublished data suggest that none of the four cloned Gα subunits of the trimeric G proteins are directly involved in transmission of the pheromone signal [60, 87], while a *ras1* gene, as is the case in *Schizosaccharomyces pombe* [97], may be involved (N. Lee and J. Kronstad, personal communication). A gene designated *prf1* encodes an HMG family transcription factor that links the pheromone response pathway to the expression of the b locus and thus to pathogenicity [42]. The *prf1* protein has potential phosphorylation sites for both a MAP kinase (presumably *ubc3/kpp2*, see below) and for the cyclic AMP dependent protein kinase [49, 81]. The putative MAP kinase phosphorylation sites appear important for the biological function of the protein [81]. The *prf1* gene is required for pathogenicity due to its essential function in the regulation of the b mating type genes. This was shown clearly by the fact that constitutive expression of the the b genes restores pathogenicity in *prf1* mutants [42].

The *b* mating type locus encodes two homeodomain containing proteins that interact when produced from different alleles [36, 50, 121]. These proteins are believed to regulate the transcription of a set of target genes that directly or indirectly control morphogenetic transitions and pathogenicity. The b locus controls events after cell fusion necessary for establishment of the infectious filamentous dikaryon. The two *b* locus encoded products have been designated bEast (*bE*) and bWest (*bW*) [36]. The alignment of the predicted amino acid sequences of several alleles of the *bE* and *bW* genes revealed that each contains a variable N-terminal region, a central homeodomain-like motif and a conserved C-terminal region [36, 57, 95]. Recognition mediated by the products of the *b* genes has been a topic of research focus for understanding self/nonself recognition because there are at least 25 different specifities at the b locus, any of which can function properly with any nonself allele [86, 96]. The interaction of the *bE* product from one allele of the *b* locus with the *bW* product from another establishes a novel regulatory protein that triggers formation of the infectious dikaryon [36]. For example, *bW1* and *bE2* gene products form a functional heterodimer while those of *bW1* and *bE1* do not [50]. Specificity is mediated by a 40 amino acid region in the variable N-terminal region of *bE* as demonstrated by the construction of chimeric alleles of *bE1* and *bE2* and chimeric alleles of *bW1* and *bW2* [121] that can be further divided into two subdomains, heterozygosity at either of which is sufficient for compatibility [76]. Point and insertional mutation analysis led to a model suggesting cohesive (hydrophobic or polar) interactions of the amino acid R-groups in determination of the ability of inter-allelic interaction of the *bE* and *bW* polypeptides [50]. The lack of such contacts yields an ineffective combination. A similar mechanism for the interaction of *b* type homeodomain proteins (referred to as A in these organisms) occurs in Holobasidiomycete mating systems [5, 24, 62]. In *U. hordei* mating is controlled by a single genetic locus (MAT), which is controlled by two alleles, MAT-1 and MAT-2. At the MAT locus are genes equivalent to those of both the a and *b* loci of *U. maydis* [7]. Additionally, the *a* and *b* genes are genetically tightly linked [7]. This genetic linkage and consequent lack of recombination is the cause for the bipolar mating system in this fungus. The mating type locus spans a 500-kb region suppressed in recombination located on the largest chromosome of *U. hordei* [64]. Work aimed at identifying targets of *b* in *U. maydis* has been initiated [18]. *lga2*, a gene of unknown function [111] located within the *a2* idiomorph is directly and positively regulated by the *b*-heterodimer [89]. Additional triggers, aside from mating type, for inducing dimorphic transitions have been identified. Such stimuli include nutritional status, exposure to air, medium pH and cellular cAMP concentration. As discussed later the study of these inductive triggers has provided additional information related to the connections of growth form and pathogenicity in *Ustilago*.

Solopathogenic strains have been generated by a number of means. Forced diploids heterozygous at the *b* mating type locus are pathogenic [11, 56]. These diploids, however, anecdotally appear to be less virulent than dikaryotic cells [56, 77]. Solopathogenic haploids have been constructed by introduction of complementary alleles at the *b* locus with or without addition of a complementary allele at *a* [20, 35, 63]. These haploid strains provide a way to study the effects of mutations without the need to produce mutations in compatible strains or homozygous mutant diploids. The relative virulence of solopathogenic haploids versus the wild-type dikaryon has not been addressed but again anecdotally appear significantly reduced (J.D. Egan and S.E.G, unpublished). Single-chain b fusion proteins containing the homeodomains of *bE* and *bW* separated by a flexible "kinker" region also have been expressed in a haploid strain deleted for b and yield solopathogens [90].

Candidate gene approaches based on hypotheses related to mechanisms of mating and morphogenesis in other fungi identified genes in *U. maydis*. Such genes include the *U. maydis fuz7* gene, a homolog of the *S. cerevisiae ste7* MAP kinase kinase [12], G protein alpha subunit encoding genes [87], and a kinesin motor protein encoding gene [107]. In general mutation of these genes has indicated predicted functions in *U. maydis*. In the case of the Gα encoding genes however, of four genes isolated only one had an observed mutant phenotype. This gene (*gpa3*) is involved in cAMP signaling and generates a weak filamentous phenotype when deleted. Interestingly, a filamentous *U. hordei* haploid deletion mutant called fil1 [78] that could be converted back to budding growth by addition of cAMP was identified. The *fil1* gene was identified by transformation based complementation and the gene was identified as encoding a Gα [67]. Sequence comparison indicates that fil1 is the *U. hordei* paralog to the *U. maydis gpa3* gene (S.E.G., unpublished). The *U. hordei* and *U. maydis* genes were reported nearly simultaneously and both appear to function in similar manners in the cAMP pathway indicating the similarity in genetic mechanisms for these two *Ustilago* species. Initially it was believed the *U. maydis gpa3* gene played a direct role in pheromone signaling but later it was determined that this was a secondary effect due to the crosstalk in the cAMP and MAP kinase pathways [60].

The cAMP and Map Kinase Pathways Regulate Dimorphism and Pathogenicity in *U. maydis*

The dimorphic transition has been helpful for the identification of genes that influence the ability of the fungus to alternate between budding and filamentation. Because filamentous growth is central to the ability to cause disease it is a reasonable hypothesis that genes necessary for filamentation will likely be critical for pathogenicity. Because of the efficient transformation system, forward genetic approaches based on plasmid complementation have proven successful.

Much of the work described below is based on an initial report that described haploid *U. maydis* mutants that display a constitutively filamentous phenotype [14]. Colonies of these mutants become covered with white aerial mycelium, in contrast to the flat gray yeast morphology of colonies formed by wild-type parental cells. Interestingly, one of the mutations (*rem1-1*) was found to block pathogenicity even though the cells displayed a filamentous morphology similar to that of the infectious dikaryon. Analysis of this mutant indicated that filamentous growth is insufficient for pathogenicity in *U. maydis*. Complementation of the rem1-1 mutation with a cosmid library and subsequent disruption experiments with the isolated gene also yielded mutants with a filamentous growth morphology reminiscent of the dikaryon (Figure 3; [37]). Sequence analysis of the complementing region of the cosmid clone [37] revealed a homolog of adenylate cyclase [27]. The *rem1* designation was therefore replaced with *uac1* for <u>*U*</u>*stilago* <u>a</u>denylate <u>c</u>yclase.

Strains disrupted in *uac1* were restored to a budding phenotype when transformed with the wild-type *uac1* gene [37]. Addition of exogenous cAMP had a profound effect on the morphology of wild-type cells and on the filamentous mutant carrying a disruption in the *uac1* gene. Cyclic AMP restored budding growth to the filamentous mutant and altered bud site selection and mother-daughter separation in wild-type cells. Budding growth was restored in mutants that contain various extragenic suppressors of the defect in adenylate cyclase.

The defective gene in one of these suppressor mutants was found to encode a regulatory subunit of cAMP dependent protein kinase (rPKA). The mutation in this gene, designated *ubc1* (<u>*U*</u>*stilago* <u>b</u>ypass of <u>c</u>yclase), also attenuated filamentous growth resulting from mating interactions and from exposure to air [37]. Recently, however, we have found that the functional *ubc1* gene is not required for acid pH induced filamentation (A.D. Martínez-Espinoza, J. Ruiz-Herrera and S.E.G., unpublished).

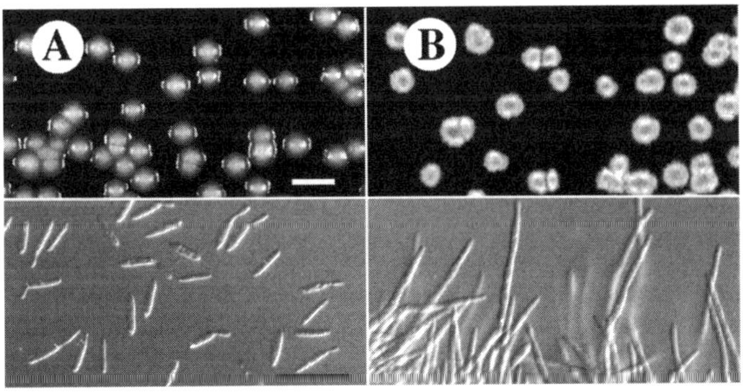

Figure 3. Fungal dimorphism displayed by *Ustilago maydis* on solid (top panels) and in liquid media (bottom panels). Panel A shows the colony morphology (top) and budding morphology (bottom) of the wild-type haploid strain. Panel B shows the colony morphology (top) and filamentous morphology (bottom) of the *uac1*- (1/9) disruption mutant haploid strain unable to synthesize cAMP. The morphology depicted in B is similar to that displayed by the haploid fungus in response to low pH and also similar to the heterozygous (at the *a* and *b* mating type loci) dikaryon produced after mating. Bars are 2 mm (white) and 25 μm (black).

Taken together these results indicate that the adenylate cyclase gene is required for normal budding growth while the regulatory subunit of protein kinase A is required for the filamentous growth displayed by a strain mutated in the adenylate cyclase gene [37]. Unlike *uac1* mutants, mutants defective in *ubc1* are able to infect the host, however, they cannot induce gall formation nor complete their life cycle [39].

Putting together the pathogenicity data collected for *uac1* [14] and *ubc1* [39] mutants, a view of a pathway to disease development emerges. Mutants in *uac1* (with low cAMP content and low PKA activity) are completely nonpathogenic suggesting that specific substrates of the catalytic subunit of PKA must be phosphorylated to allow colonization. In contrast, mutants in the regulatory subunit of PKA are able to colonize the host. However, gall formation does not occur suggesting that PKA substrates must favor a lesser degree of phosphorylation for the transmission of fungal signal molecules that induce gall development. Thus, a cyclic AMP dependent protein kinase controlled switch appears to be important in the pathogenicity of *U. maydis* such that increased PKA activity is required for initial plant infection while reduced activity is required for a transition to gall formation and possibly sporulation [39]. The presumed modifications of PKA activity to various intermediate levels in a set of mutants suggests that the frequency of production and the structure of plant galls is influenced by signaling involving the cAMP pathway [61]. Strains with increasing activity of the cAMP pathway were found to induce fewer galls. These strains included wild-type, and mutants in *gpa3,* the G-protein α subunit involved in cAMP signaling, and multiple mutants in *ubc1*. The more defective the *ubc1* allele, the lower the proportion of plants that produced galls. Interestingly, plants infected with compatible constitutive Gpa3 ($gpa3_{Q206L}$) mutant strains, with a presumed moderate increase in cAMP pathway activity generate shoot like galls as opposed to the typical wild-type amorphous galls, but like *ubc1* mutants do not sporulate. This indicates that gall formation per se is insufficient to trigger teliospore formation.

Through a continuation of this forward genetic approach a collection of *ubc* mutants, suppressed for the filamentous phenotype caused by the *uac1* disruption mutation, has been analyzed. These suppressor mutant strains are all budding yeasts but have various subtle phenotypes. Four ubc genes (*ubc2, ubc3, ubc4*, and *ubc5*) in addition to *ubc1* have now been characterized. The *ubc3, ubc4* and *ubc5* genes encode a MAP kinase (MAPK), MAP kinase kinase kinase (MAPKKK) and the previously identified *fuz7* MAP kinase kinase (MAPKK), respectively and are all most similar to members of the pheromone responsive MAP kinase cascade involved in fungal mating and morphogenesis [4, 75, 76]. This result indicates an interplay between the cAMP dependent and MAP kinase pathways which has also been found in several other fungi [41, 49, 55, 60, 69, 83, 120]. Using a PCR based candidate gene approach Muller et al. [81] also reported the isolation of the MAPK gene *ubc3*, which they called *kpp2*.

The *ubc2* gene is under further investigation because it is essential for pathogenesis and appears to encode a novel adaptor protein involved in the pheromone responsive MAP kinase cascade. Its involvement in pheromone response is suggested because the *ubc2* mutant is unresponsive to mating pheromone [77]. Additionally, the *ubc4* gene functions as a multi-copy suppressor of a temperature sensitive *ubc2* mutant, suggesting a potential interaction between these gene products [75]. The Ubc2 protein has no clear ortholog in the databases but possesses four domains known in other systems to be involved in protein-protein interactions. These include a SAM (sterile alpha motif) domain [85], a RA (Ras association or Ras binding) domain [47] and two SH3 (*src* homology 3) domains [74, 79]. Some of these domains are present in adaptor proteins associated with pheromone response pathways in *S. pombe* and *S. cerevisiae*. The temperature sensitive allele of *ubc2* has a missense mutation within the SAM domain, consistent with an interaction with the Ubc4 MAPKKK [77]. Deletion of the SAM domain eliminates Ubc2 function.

In a parallel approach, mutations that suppress the filamentous phenotype of a mutant in the primary functional PKA catalytic subunit gene, *adr1* [30], have been isolated. One gene (*hgl1*) that was identified by this approach [29] also complements a subset of the *ubc* mutants (S.E.G, unpublished). The Hgl1 protein is a possible transcription factor and shows eight potential PKA phosphorylation sites and can be phophorylated by Adr1 in vitro indicating that it may be a direct PKA substrate in vivo. *hgl1* mutants induce large galls in maize kernels, but the galls remain white due to the complete lack of teliospore formation.

The PKA and MAPK pathways are involved in post-translational regulation of morphogenesis in *U. maydis*. A model of the cAMP and MAPK pathways in *U. maydis* is depicted in Figure 4. The involvement of these pathways in fungal morphogenesis is now well documented in a number of species. The crosstalk between the MAP kinase and the cAMP signal transduction cascades is not unique to *U. maydis* or to the fungi, but is a common feature of eukaryotes. In the fungi such crosstalk has been shown to be important for pseudohyphal growth in *S. cerevisiae*, mating in *S. pombe*, dimorphic phase regulation and pathogenicity in *Candida albicans*, morphogenesis, mating and virulence in *Cryptococcus neoformans*, and mating dimorphism, appressorium formation and virulence in the riceblast fungus *Magnaporthe grisea* as well as in the mating and virulence in *U. maydis* described above (Reviewed in [65]). Interestingly, there appears to be a reversal of morphogenetic outcomes in dimorphic species between the basidiomycetes and the ascomycetes in response to cAMP levels. High cAMP pathway activity generates filamentous growth in *C. albicans* and *S. cerevisiae* but budding growth in *U. maydis* [92].

The relationship between morphogenesis and protein phosphorylation is a central theme of ongoing *Ustilago* research. Ultimately we might expect these studies to converge on the regulation of the cytoskeleton. Polarized growth of fungal cells involves deposition of secretory vesicles carrying cell wall manufacturing components to the cell tip [15]. The cytoskeleton coordinates cell wall synthesis and actin appears to be the most important cytoskeletal component in these processes (reviewed in [116]). Actin is thought to play a role in cytoplasmic migration and organelle positioning as it coordinates cell wall synthesis. Importantly, actin distribution correlates with wall expansion and exocytosis. Microtubules, on the other hand, were thought not to play a significant role in polarization of fungal cells [116]. Recently however, it has been shown that *kin2* a gene encoding kinesin, a microtubule associated motor protein, is critical for hyphal extension of dikaryotic *U. maydis* cells [106, 107]. This is proposed to be due to the inability of *kin2* defective cells to produce vacuoles that function to force the cytoplasm to the cell apex [107].

To identify downstream genes that are regulated by

morphogenesis and/or cAMP or MAP kinase pathways, substractive hybridization methods have been employed. A gene encoding cellulase was identified by subtractive hybridization as being specifically expressed in a filamentous diploid as opposed to a non-filamentous derivative mutant diploid [94]. My laboratory is currently involved in EST based differential expression projects. We employ a Suppressive Subtraction Hybridization PCR (SSHP) with a kit produced by Clontech (Palo Alto, CA), called the PCR-Select cDNA Subtraction KitTM (http://www.clontech.com/index.html). We have focused on three conditions of interest employing genetic strains we have developed. This work is intended to identify genes specifically upregulated in either 1) the filamentous or 2) budding growth form of culture grown *U. maydis* or 3) fungal and plant genes transcriptionally induced in the interaction leading to the production of galls and sproulation. We assess the roles of selected fungal genes through disruption mutant analysis.

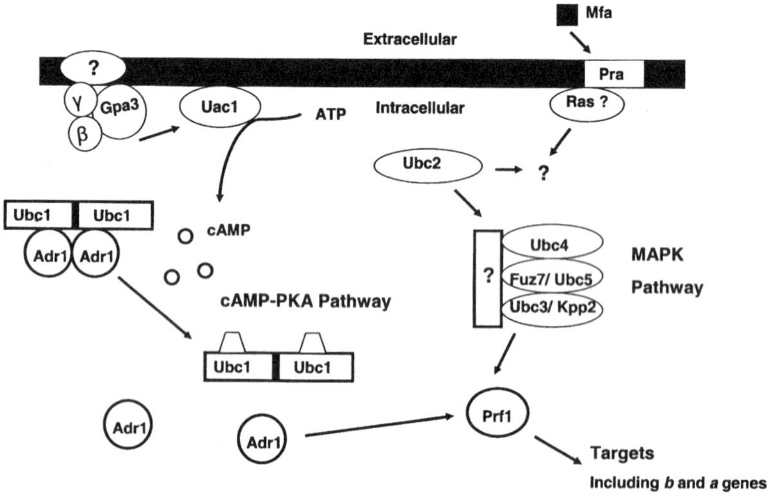

Figure 4. Interaction of the PKA and MAP kinase pathways. Current information indicates that the cAMP and MAP kinase pathways impinge on postranslational modification of the transcription factor Prf1. This is likely not the only target of these kinases however. Ras is hypothesized to interact with the MAP kinase pathway, potentially through Ubc2. Some current models suggest that Fuz7/Ubc5 is in a different MAP kinase pathway.

The SSHP method works by subtracting clones derived from common transcripts between a tester (desired condition) and a driver (similar undesired condition) such that the derived subtracted cDNA library represents clones derived from transcripts more highly expressed specifically in the tester condition. In the above listed conditions of interest the respective tester and driver combinations are 1) filamentous growth versus budding growth; 2) budding growth versus filamentous growth; 3) wild-type infected maize versus *ubc1* infected maize.

The cDNA subtraction method complements the mutagenesis approaches described above. This work is expected to enhance the identification of genes that are relevant to dimorphism and are regulated at the transcriptional level. Additionally, unlike the standard mutant analysis that we have been carrying out, this approach should also allow identification of essential genes, mutations in which cause lethality in haploids, and genes for which there is functional redundancy such that single mutations do not yield an obviously altered phenotype. Identifying these genes is critical for a full understanding of the process of dimorphism and pathogenicity. Our goal is to identify genes that are expressed in a pattern of interest in both the pathogen and the host. We plan to test the function of the most interesting genes by generating disruption mutations in the fungus and by identifying insertional mutants in maize by dovetailing with public or private research efforts on maize.

To date we have isolated fragments of approximately 40 genes that come through an initial screen for sequences transcriptionally upregulated in filaments as opposed to budding cells. Approximately half of these clones show significant homology to database sequences. The most common clone that we identified was the *rep1* gene that was previously described as a cell wall protein specifically found in filamentous cells [119]. This transcript is abundant in northern blots of filamentous cells while it is not detectable in RNA from budding cells. One differentially expressed gene that we are studying has significant amino acid similarity to the *Neurospora crassa cpc-2*, yeast *CPC2* and *Aspergillus nidulans cpcB* gene products [43, 44, 80]. The *U. maydis* homolog is upregulated in filaments approximately 8-fold over budding cells (M. Garcia-Pedrajas and S.E.G unpublished). This gene is of interest to us particularly because it plays an important role in *N. crassa* and in *A. nidulans* sexual development; mutants in both fungi are affected in female structure development and are effectively sterile [44, 80]. Because of the intimate connection between pathogenicity and sexual development in *U. maydis* it is logical for us to test the role of this gene in these processes. Disruption of the *U. maydis cpc2* ortholog (called *uhf1*) has no visible effect on in vitro mating but reduces virulence and yields strains that become dark after several days in culture (K.E. Snyder and S.E.G, unpublished). Because we know that the cAMP dependent protein kinase and MAP kinase pathways are central in *U. maydis* morphogenesis, it seems logical that protein phosphatases should likewise be involved in countering the signals of protein phosphorylation sent by these kinases.

With this in mind we hypothesized that calcineurin (protein phosphatase 2B) was a good candidate to, at least partially, serve this function. Our preliminary data indicate a role for calcineurin (PP2B) in this process (J.D. Egan and S.E.G, unpublished). Calcineurin disruption mutants have a multiple budding phenotype reminiscent of *ubc1* mutants (Figure

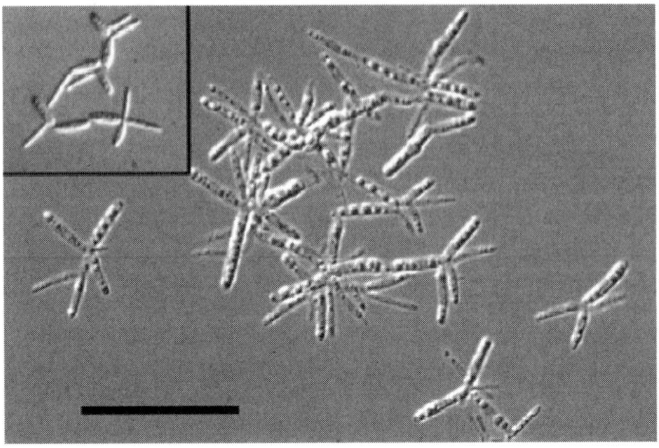

Figure 5. Mutants disrupted in *ubc1* and *ucn1* have related morphology. The ucn1 disruption mutant grows in stellate clusters. This phenotype is somewhat similar but not identical to the *ubc1* disruption mutant strain (inset, upper left). This result indicates that some cellular processes may employ both the cAMP dependent protein kinase and the calcineurin phosphatase in their regulation. However, the fact that the phenotypes are not exactly the same indicates that some processes are not shared. Bars is 50 μm.

5). This suggests potential regulation of the protein phosphorylation status of at least some common substrate proteins by both PKA and calcineurin in *U. maydis*.

Plant-Pathogen Interaction Specific Gene Expression

The communication between the fungus and the host is still a relatively poorly studied area in the *U. maydis*-maize pathosystem. Maize plants respond to infection by wild-type *U. maydis* by producing galls on any above ground plant parts. The biochemical origin of this response is not well characterized but alterations in phytohormone levels are suspected. In particular the auxin indole acetic acid (IAA) concentrations have been the focus of hypotheses. It has long been clear that *U. maydis* is capable of synthesizing IAA while, interestingly, the non-gall forming smut pathogen U. nigra apparently is unable to synthesize auxin [118]. A gene (*iad1*) encoding a purified acetaldehyde dehydrogenase (able to convert indole-3-acetaldehyde to indole-3-acetic acid) was isolated [16]. It was shown that highly reduced amounts of IAA were produced by iad1 deletion mutants when grown with specific carbon sources, however, there was no observed effect on pathogenicity or gall formation. A second relatively minor indole-3-acetaldehyde dehydrogenase was also detected in culture grown *U. maydis* and this isozyme could potentially compensate for the loss of *iad1* in planta [16]. The relative production of IAA in culture varies dramatically between strains tested and interestingly, wild-type haploid strains produced higher levels of IAA than did solopathogenic haploid or diploid strains [72]. Chemical and UV induced mutants have been generated that are deficient in IAA production [102]. In a follow-up study a null mutant was generated that produced no IAA in vitro [40]. However, progeny from a cross between the IAA null and wild type yielded progeny with varying intermediate levels of IAA production. This is consistent with multiple mutations combining in the null mutant to yield an IAA non-producer. In this work it was further found that a compatible pairing between the null mutant and one of its very weak IAA producer progeny (ca. 15-20% IAA production compared to a wild-type cross) were reduced in pathogenicity such that nearly 30% of plants inoculated showed no symptoms [40]. Other crosses generally had less than 10% symptomless plants. However, 25% of the plants inoculated with the reduced IAA producers still produced galls. There was not a strict correlation between in vitro IAA synthesis and virulence. Therefore this work is consistent with a role for fungal IAA in *U. maydis* pathogenicity but is not conclusive. Thus the role of pathogen versus plant produced auxins in this system remains unresolved.

Because the dikaryon of *U. maydis* is an obligate biotroph, it is assumed that the plant host provides a special environment where a specific set of fungal genes can be expressed. The gene *mig1* (maize-induced gene) was identified using the differential display technique comparing in planta gene expression to that in culture. Fusion to GFP indicated that *mig1* is up-regulated during plant infection but deletion of the gene indicates that it is not required for fungal development in the plant [17]. Fusion of the putative signal peptide containing N-terminus of Mig1 to GFP suggested that Mig1 is likely a secreted protein.

To date very little attention has been focused on the plant side of the interaction. Several plant gene fragments were also identified in the differential display experiments identifying *mig1* but these genes were not described [17]. My laboratory is at an early stage of a project employing the SSHP approach described above to isolate transcripts that are of either plant or fungal origin. We have generated a library of several thousand putatively differential clones that we have begun to characterize (M. García-Pedrajas and S.E.G.).

Genomic Approaches

Until very recently it has been difficult to obtain funding for sequencing of agriculturally important fungal genomes in the *U*.S.A. The recent Initiative for Future Agriculture and Food Systems, sponsored by the *U*.S. Department of Agriculture together with funds from the National Science Foundation is providing the first significant public funds for genomic sequencing of a few fungal plant pathogens. However, work on the *Ustilago maydis* genome sequencing has not received public funding. Over the past few years two private corporations have completed *U. maydis* genome projects. These projects were carried out by the German based LION Bioscience AG, Heidelberg, with funding from Bayer Corporation and by the *U*.S. based corporation, Exelixis. To my knowledge only one public research group has free access to the LION database. Others however are now able to arrange access for specific agreed upon purposes. The Exelixis Corporation has established collaborative agreements with select public sector researchers. A public database of the *U. maydis* genome is highly warranted as many researchers still find access to sequence data problematic. A white paper developed by the American Phytopathological Society lists twenty-six fungal and oomycete species warranting prioritized genomic sequencing. *U. maydis* is ranked 4th of the fungi on this list. Several initiatives are being launched to address the current lack of public plant pathogenic fungal genomic data. The Whitehead Institute at MIT is launching a major effort to sequence many fungal genomes and funding is being sought. On the current proposed lists of fungi under consideration for sequencing are several plant pathogens including *U. maydis*.

Conclusions

Ustilago maydis provides an excellent model for the study of fungal development and host-pathogen interactions. There are many powerful tools that have been generated to assist researchers in their studies on *Ustilago* species. There are several research groups focused on various aspects of the biology of these fungi that have contributed significantly to our understanding. As described in this chapter mating, morphogenesis and pathogenicity have been the major foci of research attention to date. Much of the effort has indicated the intertwined nature of signaling pathways that crosstalk to influence all of these processes.

The genomics era promises more rapid and comprehensive analysis of the biology of *U. maydis* in all areas of interest. However, a cohesive international effort has not been mounted for publicly funded genomic sequencing. Access to the private sector genomic sequence data is a problem for most public sector researchers. When there is wide access to the *U. maydis* genomic sequence research approaches to understanding the biology of this fascinating plant pathogenic fungus will become even more powerful.

References

1. Alexopoulus C J, Mims C W, Blackwell M (1996) Introductory Mycology. Wiley, New York.
2. Allen E A, Hazen B E, Hoch H C, Kwon Y, Leinhos G M E, Staples R C, Stumpf M A, Terhume B T (1991) Appressorium formation in response to topographical signals by 27 rust species. Phytopathology 81:323-331.
3. Anderson C M, Willits D A, Kosted P J, Ford E J, Martinez-Espinoza A D, Sherwood J E (1999) Molecular analysis of the pheromone and pheromone receptor genes of *Ustilago hordei*. Gene 240:89-97.
4. Andrews D L, Egan J D, Mayorga M E, Gold S E (2000) The *Ustilago maydis ubc4* and *ubc5* genes encode members of a MAP kinase cascade required for filamentous growth. Mol Plant-Microbe Interact 13:781-786.
5. Asante-Owusu R N, Banham A H, Bohnert H U, Mellor E J, Casselton L A (1996) Heterodimerization between two classes of homeodomain proteins in the mushroom *Coprinus cinereus* brings together potential DNA-binding and activation domains. Gene 172:25-31.
6. Bakkeren G, Kronstad J W (1993) Conservation of the *b* mating-type gene complex among bipolar and tetrapolar smut fungi. Plant Cell 5:123-136.
7. Bakkeren G, Kronstad J W (1994) Linkage of mating-type loci distinguishes bipolar from tetrapolar mating in basidiomycetous smut fungi. Proc Natl Acad Sci USA 91:7085-7089.
8. Bakkeren G, Kronstad J W (1996) The pheromone cell signaling components of the *Ustilago* a mating-type loci determine intercompatibility between species. Genetics 143:1601-1613.
9. Banuett F (1995) Genetics of *Ustilago maydis*, a fungal pathogen that induces tumors in maize. Annu Rev Genet 29:179-208.
10. Banuett F (1998) Signalling in the yeasts: an informational cascade with links to the filamentous fungi. Microbiol Mol Biol Rev 62:249-274.
11. Banuett F, Herskowitz I (1989) Different a-Alleles of *Ustilago maydis* are necessary for maintenance of filamentous growth but not for meiosis. Proc Natl Acad Sci USA 86:5878-5882.
12. Banuett F, Herskowitz I (1994) Identification of *fuz7*, a *Ustilago maydis* MEK/MAPKK homolog required for a-locus-dependent

and -independent steps in the fungal life cycle. Genes Dev 8:1367-1378.

13. Banuett F, Herskowitz I (1996) Discrete developmental stages during teliospore formation in the corn smut fungus, *Ustilago maydis*. Development 122:2965-2976.
14. Barrett K J, Gold S E, Kronstad J W (1993) Identification and complementation of a mutation to constitutive filamentous growth in *Ustilago maydis*. Mol Plant-Microbe Interact 6:274-283.
15. Bartnicki-Garcia S, Lippman E (1969) Fungal morphogenesis: cell wall construction in *Mucor rouxii*. Science 165:302-304.
16. Basse C W, Lottspeich F, Steglich W, Kahmann R (1996) Two potential indole-3-acetaldehyde dehydrogenases in the phytopathogenic fungus *Ustilago maydis*. Eur J Biochem 242:648-656.
17. Basse C W, Stumpferl S, Kahmann R (2000) Characterization of a *Ustilago maydis* gene specifically induced during the biotrophic phase: Evidence for negative as well as positive regulation. Mol Cell Biol 20:329-339.
18. Bolker M, Bohlman R, Kamper J, Reichmann M, Schauwecker F, Spellig T, Urban M, Kahmann R (1994) The genetic regulation of mating and dimorphism in *Ustilago maydis*. Abstract, Fifth International Mycological Congress, Vancouver, Canada, 1994.
19. Bolker M, Bohnert H U, Braun K H, Gorl J, Kahmann R (1995) Tagging pathogenicity genes in *Ustilago maydis* by restriction enzyme-mediated integration (REMI). Mol Gen Genet 248:547-552.
20. Bolker M, Genin S, Lehmler C, Kahmann R (1995) Genetic-regulation of mating and dimorphism in *Ustilago maydis*. Can J Bot-Rev 73:S320-S325.
21. Bolker M, Urban M, Kahmann R (1992) The a mating type locus of *U. maydis* specifies cell signaling components. Cell 68:441-450.
22. Broomfield P L E, Hargreaves J A (1992) A single amino-acid change in the iron-sulfur protein subunit of succinate-dehydrogenase confers resistance to carboxin in *Ustilago maydis*. Curr Genet 22:117-121.
23. Butters J A, Hollomon D W (1996) Molecular analysis of azole fungicide resistance in a mutant of *Ustilago maydis*. Pesticide Sci 46:278-280.
24. Casselton L A, Olesnicky N S (1998) Molecular genetics of mating recognition in basidiomycete fungi. Microbiol Mol Biol Rev 62:55-70.
25. Christensen J J (1963) Corn smut caused by *Ustilago maydis*. Monograph No. 2. American Phytopathological Society, Saint Paul.

26. Clausen M, Krauter R, Schachermayr G, Potrykus I, Sautter C (2000) Antifungal activity of a virally encoded gene in transgenic wheat. Nat Biotech 18:446-449.
27. Danchin A (1993) Phylogeny of adenylyl cyclases. Adv Second Messenger Phosphoprotein Res 27:109-162.
28. du Toit L J, Pataky J K (1999) Effects of silk maturity and pollination on infection of maize ears by *Ustilago maydis*. Plant Disease 83:621-626.
29. Durrenberger F, Laidlaw R D and Kronstad J W (2001) The *hgl1* gene is required for dimorphism and teliospore formation in the fungal pathogen *Ustilago maydis*. Mol Microbiol 41: 337-348.
30. Durrenberger F, Wong K, Kronstad J W (1998) Identification of a cAMP-dependent protein kinase catalytic subunit required for virulence and morphogenesis in *Ustilago maydis*. Proc Natl Acad Sci USA 95:5684-5689.
31. Ferguson D O, Holloman W K (1996) Recombinational repair of gaps in DNA is asymmetric in *Ustilago maydis* and can be explained by a migrating D-loop model. Proc Natl Acad Sci USA 93:5419-5424.
32. Ferguson D O, Rice M C, Rendi M H, Kotani H, Kmiec E B, Holloman W K (1997) Interaction between *Ustilago maydis* REC2 and RAD51 genes in DNA repair and mitotic recombination. Genetics 145:243-251.
33. Fotheringham S, Holloman W K (1990) Pathways of transformation in *Ustilago maydis* determined by DNA conformation. Genetics 124:833-843.
34. Froeliger E H, Leong S A (1991) The a mating-type alleles of *Ustilago maydis* are idiomorphs. Gene 100:113-122.
35. Giasson L, Kronstad J W (1995) Mutations in the *myp1* gene of *Ustilago maydis* attenuate mycelial growth and virulence. Genetics 141:491-501.
36. Gillissen B, Bergemann J, Sandmann C, Schroeer B, Bolker M, Kahmann R (1992) A two-component regulatory system for self/non self recognition in *Ustilago maydis*. Cell 68:647-657.
37. Gold S, Duncan G, Barrett K, Kronstad J (1994) cAMP regulates morphogenesis in the fungal pathogen *Ustilago maydis*. Genes Dev 8:2805-2816.
38. Gold S E, Bakkeren G, Davies J E, Kronstad J W (1994) Three selectable markers for transformation of *Ustilago maydis*. Gene 142:225-230.
39. Gold S E, Brogdon S M, Mayorga M E, Kronstad J W (1997) The *Ustilago maydis* regulatory subunit of a cAMP-dependent protein kinase is required for gall formation in maize. Plant Cell 9:1585-1594.

40. Guevara-Lara F, Valverde M E, Paredes-Lopez O (2000) Is pathogenicity of *Ustilago maydis* (huitlacoche) strains on maize related to in vitro production of indole-3-acetic acid? World J Microbiol Biotechnol 16:481-490.
41. Hamer J E, Talbot N J (1998) Infection-related development in the rice blast fungus *Magnaporthe grisea*. Curr Opin Microbiol 1:693-697.
42. Hartmann H A, Kahmann R, Bolker M (1996) The pheromone response factor coordinates filamentous growth and pathogenicity in *Ustilago maydis*. EMBO J 15:1632-1641.
43. Hoffmann B, Mosch H U, Sattlegger E, Barthelmess I B, Hinnebusch A, Braus G H (1999) The WD protein Cpc2p is required for repression of Gcn4 protein activity in yeast in the absence of amino-acid starvation. Mol Microbiol 31:807-822.
44. Hoffmann B, Wanke C, LaPaglia S K, Braus G H (2000) c-Jun and RACK1 homologues regulate a control point for sexual development in *Aspergillus nidulans*. Mol Microbiol 37:28-41.
45. Holliday R (1961) Induced mitotic crossing-over in *Ustilago maydis*. Genet Res 2:231-248.
46. Holliday R (1964) Mechanism for gene conversion in fungi. Genet Res 5:282-304.
47. Inoue K, Yamada H, Akasaka K, Hermann C, Kremer W, Maurer T, Doker R, Kalbitzer H R (2000) Pressure-induced local unfolding of the Ras binding domain of RalGDS. Nat Struct Biol 7:547-550.
48. Kahmann R, Basse C (1999) REMI (Restriction Enzyme Mediated Integration) and its impact on the isolation of pathogenicity genes in fungi attacking plants. Euro J Plant Pathol 105:221-229.
49. Kahmann R, Basse C, Feldbrugge M (1999) Fungal-plant signalling in the *Ustilago maydis*-maize pathosystem. Curr Opin Microbiol 2:647-650.
50. Kamper J, Reichmann M, Romeis T, Bolker M, Kahmann R (1995) Multiallelic recognition: nonself-dependent dimerization of the *bE* and *bW* homeodomain proteins in *Ustilago maydis*. Cell 81:73-83.
51. Keon J P, James C S, Court S, Baden-Daintree C, Bailey A M, Burden R S, Bard M, Hargreaves J A (1994) Isolation of the *Erg2* gene, encoding sterol delta(8)-]delta(7) isomerase, from the rice blast fungus *Magnaporthe grisea* and its expression in the maize smut pathogen *Ustilago maydis*. Curr Genet 25:531-537.
52. Keon J P, White G A, Hargreaves J A (1991) Isolation, characterization and sequence of a gene conferring resistance to the systemic fungicide carboxin from the maize smut pathogen, *Ustilago maydis*. Curr Genet 19:475-481.

53. Keon J P R, Hargreaves J A (1996) An *Ustilago maydis* mutant partially blocked in P45014DM activity is hypersensitive to azole fungicides. Fungal Genet Biol 20:84-88.
54. Kinal H, Park C M, Berry J O, Koltin Y, Bruenn J A (1995) Processing and secretion of a virally encoded antifungal toxin in transgenic tobacco plants - evidence for a Kex2p pathway in plants. Plant Cell 7:677-688.
55. Kronstad J, De Maria A D, Funnell D, Laidlaw R D, Lee N, de Sa M M, Ramesh M (1998) Signaling via cAMP in fungi: interconnections with mitogen-activated protein kinase pathways. Arch Microbiol 170:395-404.
56. Kronstad J W, Leong S A (1989) Isolation of two alleles of the *b* locus of *Ustilago maydis*. Proc Natl Acad Sci USA 86:978-982.
57. Kronstad J W, Leong S A (1990) The *b* mating-type locus of *Ustilago maydis* contains variable and constant regions. Genes Dev 4:1384-1395.
58. Kronstad J W, Staben C (1997) Mating type in filamentous fungi. Annu Rev Genet 31:245-276.
59. Kronstad J W, Wang J, Covert S F, Holden D W, McKnight G L, Leong S A (1989) Isolation of metabolic genes and demonstration of gene disruption in the phytopathogenic fungus *Ustilago maydis*. Gene 79:97-106.
60. Kruger J, Loubradou G, Regenfelder E, Hartmann A, Kahmann R (1998) Crosstalk between cAMP and pheromone signalling pathways in *Ustilago maydis*. Mol Gen Genet 260:193-198.
61. Kruger J, Loubradou G, Wanner G, Regenfelder E, Feldbrugge M, Kahmann R (2000) Activation of the cAMP pathway in *Ustilago maydis* reduces fungal proliferation and teliospore formation in plant tumors. Mol Plant-Microbe Interact 13:1034-1040.
62. Kues U, Richardson W V, Tymon A M, Mutasa E S, Gottgens B, Gaubatz S, Gregoriades A, Casselton L A (1992) The combination of dissimilar alleles of the A alpha and A beta gene complexes, whose proteins contain homeo domain motifs, determines sexual development in the mushroom Coprinus cinereus. Genes Dev 6:568-577.
63. Laity C, Giasson L, Campbell R, Kronstad J (1995) Heterozygosity at the *b* mating-type locus attenuates fusion in *Ustilago maydis*. Curr Genet 27:451-459.
64. Lee N, Bakkeren G, Wong K, Sherwood J E, Kronstad J W (1999) The mating-type and pathogenicity locus of the fungus *Ustilago hordei* spans a 500-kb region. Proc Natl Acad Sci U S A 96:15026-31.
65. Lengeler K B, Davidson R C, D'souza C, Harashima T, Shen W-C, Wang P, Pan X, Waugh M, Heitman J (2000) Signal

transduction cascades regulating fungal development and virulence. Microbiol Mol Biol Rev 64:746-785.
66. Li N Y, Erman M, Pangborn W, Duax W L, Park C M, Bruenn J, Ghosh D (1999) Structure of *Ustilago maydis* killer toxin KP6 alpha-subunit - A multimeric assembly with a central pore. J Biol Chem 274:20425-20431.
67. Lichter A, Mills D (1997) Fil1, a G-protein alpha-subunit that acts upstream of cAMP and is essential for dimorphic switching in haploid cells of *Ustilago hordei*. Mol Gen Genet 256:426-435.
68. Lichter A, Mills D (1998) Control of pigmentation of *Ustilago hordei*: the effect of pH, thiamine, and involvement of the cAMP cascade. Fungal Genet Biol 25:63-74.
69. Madhani H D, Fink G R (1998) The control of filamentous differentiation and virulence in fungi. Trends Cell Biol 8:348-353.
70. Manners J M (1989) The Host - haustorium interface in powdery mildews. Aust J Plant Physiol 16:45-52.
71. Markoglou A N, Ziogas B N (1999) Genetic control of resistance to fenpropimorph in *Ustilago maydis*. Plant Pathol 48:521-530.
72. Martinez V M, Osuna J, ParedesLopez O, Guevara F (1997) Production of indole-3-acetic acid by several wild-type strains of *Ustilago maydis*. World J Microbiol Biotechnol 13:295-298.
73. Martinez-Espinoza A D, León C G E, Ruiz-Herrera J (1997) Monomorphic nonpathogenic mutants of *Ustilago maydis*. Phytopathology 87:259-265.
74. Mayer B J, Eck M J (1995) SH3 domains. Minding your p's and q's. Curr Biol 5:364-367.
75. Mayorga M E, Gold S E (1998) Characterization and molecular genetic complementation of mutants affecting dimorphism in the fungus *Ustilago maydis*. Fung Genet Biol 24:364-376.
76. Mayorga M E, Gold S E (1999) A MAP kinase encoded by the *ubc3* gene of *Ustilago maydis* is required for filamentous growth and full virulence. Mol Microbiol 34:485-497.
77. Mayorga M E, Gold S E (2001) The *ubc2* gene of *Ustilago maydis* encodes a putative novel adaptor protein required for filamentous growth, pheromone response and virulence. Mol Microbiol 41:1365-1379.
78. McCluskey K, Agnan J, Mills D (1994) Characterization of genome plasticity in *Ustilago hordei*. Curr Genet 26:486-493.
79. Morton C J, Campbell I D (1994) SH3 domains. molecular 'velcro'. Curr Biol 4:615-617.
80. Muller F, Kruger D, Sattlegger E, Hoffmann B, Ballario P, Kanaan M, Barthelmess I B (1995) The *Cpc-2* gene of Neurospora crassa encodes a protein entirely composed of WD-repeat segments that is involved in general amino-acid control and female fertility. Mol Gen Genet 248:162-173.

81. Muller P, Aichinger C, Feldbrugge M, Kahmann R (1999) The MAP kinase *kpp2* regulates mating and pathogenic development in *Ustilago maydis*. Mol Microbiol 34:1007-1017.
82. Onel K, Koff A, Bennett R L, Unrau P, Holloman W K (1996) The REC1 gene of *Ustilago maydis*, which encodes a 3'->5' exonuclease, couples DNA repair and completion of DNA synthesis to a mitotic checkpoint. Genetics 143:165-174.
83. Pan X W, Heitman J (1999) Cyclic AMP-dependent protein kinase regulates pseudohyphal differentiation in *Saccharomyces cerevisiae*. Mol Cell Biol 19:4874-4887.
84. Park C M, Banerjee N, Koltin Y, Bruenn J A (1996) The *Ustilago maydis* virally encoded KP1 killer toxin. Mol Microbiol 20:957-963.
85. Ponting C P (1995) SAM: a novel motif in yeast sterile and Drosophila polyhomeotic proteins. Protein Sci 4:1928-1930.
86. Puhalla J E (1970) Genetic studies on the *b* incompatibility locus of *Ustilago maydis*. Genet Res Camb 16:229-232.
87. Regenfelder E, Spellig T, Hartmann A, Lauenstein S, Bolker M, Kahmann R (1997) G proteins in *Ustilago maydis*: transmission of multiple signals? EMBO J 16:1934-1942.
88. Richard G, Bailey J A, Keon J P R, Hargreaves J A (1992) Development of a Gus reporter gene system for the maize pathogen *Ustilago maydis*. Physiol Mol Plant Pathol 40:383-393.
89. Romeis T, Brachmann A, Kahmann R, Kamper J (2000) Identification of a target gene for the *bE-bW* homeodomain protein complex in *Ustilago maydis*. Mol Microbiol 37:54-66.
90. Romeis T, Kamper J, Kahmann R (1997) Single-chain fusions of two unrelated homeodomain proteins trigger pathogenicity in *Ustilago maydis*. Proc Natl Acad Sci USA 94:1230-1234.
91. Ruiz-Herrera J, Leon-Ramirez C, Cabrera-Ponce J L, Martinez-Espinoza A D, Herrera-Estrella L (1999) Completion of the sexual cycle and demonstration of genetic recombination in *Ustilago maydis* in vitro. Mol Gen Genet 262:468-472.
92. Sanchez-Martinez C, Perez-Martin J (2001) Dimorphism in fungal pathogens: *Candida albicans* and *Ustilago maydis*—similar inputs, different outputs. Curr Opin Microbiol 4:214-221.
93. Schafer W (1994) Molecular mechanisms of fungal pathogenicity to plants. Ann Rev Phytopath 32:461-477.
94. Schauwecker F, Wanner G, Kahmann R (1995) Filament-specific expression of a cellulase gene in the dimorphic fungus *Ustilago maydis*. Biol Chem Hoppe Seyler 376:617-625.
95. Schulz B, Banuett F, Dahl M, Schlesinger R, Schafer W, Martin T, Herskowitz I, Kahmann R (1990) The *b* alleles of *U. maydis*, whose combinations program pathogenic development, code for

polypeptides containing a homeodomain-related motif. Cell 60:295-306.

96. Silva J (1972) Alleles at the *b* incompatibility locus in Polish and North American populations of *Ustilago maydis* (DC) Corda. Physiol Plant Pathol 2:333-337.

97. Sipiczki M (1988) The role of sterility genes (*ste* and *aff*) in the initiation of sexual development in Schizosaccharomyces pombe. Mol Gen Genet 213:529-534.

98. Smith T (1999) Holliday model of recombination. Nat Struct Biol 6:908-909.

99. Snetselaar K M, Mims C W (1992) sporidial fusion and infection of maize seedlings by the smut fungus *Ustilago maydis*. Mycologia 84:193-203.

100. Snetselaar K M, Mims C W (1993) Infection of maize stigmas by *Ustilago maydis* - light and electron-microscopy. Phytopathology 83:843-850.

101. Snetselaar K M, Mims C W (1994) light and electron-microscopy of *Ustilago maydis* hyphae in maize. Mycological Res 98:347-355.

102. Sosa-Morales M E, Guevara-Lara F, Martinez-Juarez V M, Paredes-Lopez O (1997) Production of indole-3-acetic acid by mutant strains of *Ustilago maydis* (maize smut huitlacoche). App Microbiol Biotechnol 48:726-729.

103. Spellig T, Bolker M, Lottspeich F, Frank R W, Kahmann R (1994) Pheromones trigger filamentous growth in *Ustilago maydis*. EMBO J 13:1620-1627.

104. Spellig T, Bottin A, Kahmann R (1996) Green fluorescent protein (GFP) as a new vital marker in the phytopathogenic fungus *Ustilago maydis*. Mol Gen Genet 252:503-9.

105. Steffens J J, Pell E J, Tien M (1996) Mechanisms of fungicide resistance in phytopathogenic fungi. Curr Opin Biotechnol 7:348-355.

106. Steinberg G (2000) The cellular roles of molecular motors in fungi. Trends Microbiol 8:162-168.

107. Steinberg G, Schliwa M, Lehmler C, Bolker M, Kahmann R, McIntosh J R (1998) Kinesin from the plant pathogenic fungus *Ustilago maydis* is involved in vacuole formation and cytoplasmic migration. J Cell Sci 111:2235-2246.

108. Thomas P L (1991) Genetics of Small-Grain Smuts. Ann Rev Phytopath 29:137-148.

109. Trueheart J, Herskowitz I (1992) The *a* locus governs cytoduction in *Ustilago maydis*. J Bacteriol 174:7831-3.

110. Tsukuda T, Carleton S, Fotheringham S, Holloman W K (1988) Isolation and characterization of an autonomously replicating sequence from *Ustilago maydis*. Mol Cell Biol 8:3703-3709.

111. Urban M, Kahmann R, Bolker M (1996) The biallelic *a* mating type locus of *Ustilago maydis*: Remnants of an additional pheromone gene indicate evolution from a multiallelic ancestor. Mol Gen Genet 250:414-420.
112. Urban M, Kahmann R, Bolker M (1996) Identification of the pheromone response element in *Ustilago maydis*. Mol Gen Genet 251:31-37.
113. Valdivieso M H, Sugimoto K, Jahng K Y, Fernandes P M, Wittenberg C (1993) FAR1 is required for posttranscriptional regulation of *CLN2* gene expression in response to mating pheromone. Mol Cell Biol 13:1013-1022.
114. Wang J, Holden D W, Leong S A (1988) Gene transfer system for the phytopathogenic fungus *Ustilago maydis*. Proc Natl Acad Sci USA 85:865-869.
115. Weise M V (1987) Compedium of wheat diseases. APS Press, St. Paul.
116. Wessels J G H (1994) Developmental regulation of fungal cell-wall formation. Ann Rev Phytopath 32:413-437.
117. White DG (1999) Compendium of Corn Diseases. APS Press, St. Paul.
118. Wolf F T (1952) The production of indole acetic acid by *Ustilago* zeae, and its possible significance in tumor formation. Proc Natl Acad Sci USA 38:106-111.
119. Wosten H A, Bohlmann R, Eckerskorn C, Lottspeich F, Bolker M, Kahmann R (1996) A novel class of small amphipathic peptides affect aerial hyphal growth and surface hydrophobicity in *Ustilago maydis*. EMBO J 15:4274-4281.
120. Xu J R, Hamer J E (1996) MAP kinase and cAMP signaling regulate infection structure formation and pathogenic growth in the rice blast fungus *Magnaporthe grisea*. Genes Dev 10:2696-2706.
121. Yee A R, Kronstad J W (1993) Construction of chimeric alleles with altered specificity at the *b* incompatibility locus of *Ustilago maydis*. Proc Natl Acad Sci USA 90:664-668.

Mechanisms of Biological Control of Phytopathogenic Fungi by *Pseudomonas* spp.

Thomas F.C. Chin-A-Woeng, Ben J.J. Lugtenberg, and Guido V. Bloemberg

Microbiological control

EXPLOITING THE NATURAL ABILITY OF SOILS TO SUPPRESS DISEASE

The existence of soils and composts with the natural ability to suppress plant diseases prompted researchers to investigate the mechanisms by which these effects are mediated (9; 35; 89; 110; 129; 226). At the beginning of the twentieth century, it was shown that *Fusarium graminearum* or *Helminthosporium sativum*-conducive soils could be converted into suppressive soils by addition of less than 5% of soil suppressive for these pathogens. The transfers were often associated with an increase in numbers of antagonistic microorganisms in the target soil. In many cases plant growth-promoting effects correlated with the presence of certain soil-borne bacterial strains. These bacteria are generally termed plant growth-promoting rhizobacteria (PGPR) (129). In particular the presence of populations of fluorescent *Pseudomonas* species was correlated with disease suppression (219; 240; 270). The ecological balance in naturally suppressive soils favorable to crop plants is now often considered to be a concerted action of several microorganisms with their own mode of action against pathogens, often in conjunction with the host plant (148; 200).

Modern day crop protection relies heavily on the use of chemical pesticides (47). PGPRs being exploited in agriculture as biological pesticides, for instance by coating bacteria onto seeds, have resulted in protection against phytopathogens and consequently, in improvement of plant growth. Seed coating with biocontrol bacteria in potato, radish, sugar beet, and fruits has been shown to increase crop yield (23; 89; 222; 244). Biopesticides can be used either as an alternative to agrochemicals or in combination with chemical pesticides, thereby lowering the doses of chemicals needed to eliminate the disease. The study of mechanisms of microbiological control has been driven by the increased concern for health and the environmental hazards associated with the use of many of the traditional chemical pesticides. This has resulted in the need for new approaches to control agricultural plant diseases that allow greater sustainability. In recent years, with the increase in the costs of production of new chemical pesticides and stricter safety rules on the use of agrochemicals, this field of research has gained new momentum with the development of new and more powerful microbiological, genetic, and biochemical tools. These tools provide the means to investigate in detail the mechanisms through which plant-beneficial interactions are achieved.

This chapter will focus on the use of *Pseudomonas* species as biocontrol agents and the essential traits needed to exploit them as efficient biopesticides. Root colonization and the possession of at least one mechanism to establish plant protection appear to be important factors in the selection process for biocontrol agents. Both rhizosphere colonization and plant protection are complex processes in which many molecular mechanisms are involved. The model organisms *P. fluorescens* WCS365, for which numerous colonization traits and genes have been unraveled, and *P. chlororaphis* PCL1391, which produces a phenazine derivative as a crucial factor for plant protection will be used to illustrate some of these aspects.

PREREQUISITES FOR BIOCONTROL

In disease-suppressive soils the pathogen is not necessarily completely eliminated from the soil. However, the disease symptoms are suppressed or absent (9; 219). After application of microbial control agents to the seed, these microorganisms must (*i*) inhibit growth of the target pathogen to reduce infection by the pathogen and (*ii*) proliferate on the appropriate plant root surface. The presence of biocontrol microbes, either present naturally or introduced exogenously onto the seed, results in a number of interactions with the surrounding organisms, through which — either directly or indirectly — growth or the negative action of the pathogen is reduced. This may be the result of a direct interaction between biocontrol bacterium and pathogen but can also be mediated through the host plant such as by induced systemic resistance (ISR) (258). Furthermore, microbes also interact directly with the host plant via the root system on which they propagate. For growth, the biocontrol microbes are highly dependent upon nutrients provided by the plants in the form of root exudates. One may expect heavy competition for nutrients between the biocontrol agent and the indigenous microflora in the rhizosphere of the host plant. The effectiveness of a biocontrol strain may even depend upon the genotype of the host plant, e.g. as a result of different root exudate compositions (105; 235-237).

The use of *Pseudomonas* spp. as biocontrol agents

A variety of rhizobacteria with biological control activities has been described and these bacteria use diverse mechanisms to protect crops (63; 70; 161; 164). Potential biocontrol agents include *Pseudomonas* (269), *Bacillus* (98; 205; 206; 231), and *Streptomyces* species (80). Although numerous commercial biocontrol strains are already being marketed (Table 1), there is much interest in the development of new biocontrol agents to optimize the suppressive ability and to extend the area of application and the range of target pathogens to be controlled.

Many fluorescent pseudomonads are known to be able to exhibit inhibitory activity towards phytopathogens. Their plant-growth promoting potentials that make them appropriate for use as horticultural and agricultural biocontrol agents have been studied extensively over the past three decades. In many disease suppressive soils fluorescent *Pseudomonas* spp. were found to be plant disease control agents. A number of traits make *Pseudomonas* spp. particularly suitable for application as biocontrol agents. *Pseudomonas* bacteria (*i*) can use many exudate compounds as a nutrient source (166), (*ii*) are abundantly present in natural soils, in particular on plant root systems indicative for their adaptive potential (216), (*iii*) have a high growth rate relative to many other rhizosphere bacteria, (*iv*) possess various and diverse mechanisms for controlling plant growth and diseases including the production of a wide range of antagonistic metabolites (94), (*v*) are easy to grow under laboratory conditions and in batch cultures, and (*vi*) can subsequently be reintroduced into the rhizosphere by seed bacterization (162; 209), (*vii*) are susceptible to mutation and modification using available genetic tools, and (*viii*) are generally genetically accessible. The currently known mechanisms underlying biocontrol by PGPR strains, with emphasis on *Pseudomonas* spp., will be outlined in the remainder of this chapter.

BIOCONTROL MECHANISMS OF *PSEUDOMONAS* BIOCONTROL STRAINS

The strategies through which biocontrol agents protect plants against root diseases caused by pathogens are generally divided into four categories (248): (*i*) competition for niches and nutrients (niche exclusion), (*ii*) predation, (*iii*) antibiosis, and (*iv*) induction of a plant defense response (induced systemic resistance or ISR).

Competition for niches and nutrients. One of the mechanisms thought to play a role in biocontrol is the ability of PGPRs to establish themselves in niches or rapidly compete for nutrients that are shared with the pathogen. Failure of a pathogen to compete effectively with the biocontrol strain and utilize the available nutrient sources will disable the propagation of the pathogen. The most nutrient-rich and likely niche for both biocontrol agent and pathogen to occupy is the rhizosphere, particularly the intracellular junctions between root epidermal cells, the places where high concentrations of exudate are thought to be leaking from the root (17; 18; 40; 213).

The extent to which bacteria are able to colonize the root surface is limited to a small percentage of the totally available surface area, and probably corresponds to those places at which elevated amounts of nutrients are available (19; 40). *Pseudomonas* spp. colonize the tomato root system in micro-colonies located at the junctions of epidermal plant cells (19; 40). Likewise, the fungal pathogen *Fusarium oxysporum* f. sp. *radicis-lycopersici* colonizes the tomato root surface at the same locations as *Pseudomonas* biocontrol bacteria (140; 164). The supposed overlap of ecological niches of biocontrol agent and deleterious microorganism presumably leads to competition for these restricted sites. Experimental support for this hypothesis was obtained in a tomato/*Fusarium oxysporum* f. sp. *radicis-lycopersici* system using an autofluorescent protein-marked fungus and biocontrol bacteria to detect them microscopically in the rhizosphere (unpublished results) (164). Already established (pre-emptive competitive exclusion) or aggressively colonizing biocontrol bacteria can prevent the establishment and subsequent deleterious effects of the pathogen. A classical example of niche exclusion is the control of leaf frost injury caused by *P. syringae* that has an ice nucleation protein on its cell surface. Application of an ice-nucleation-minus mutant prevents damage caused by the establishment of the pathogenic wild type (151-153). The speed with and extent to which biocontrol bacteria aggressively colonize the root system is assumed to be a very important biocontrol trait. *Pseudomonas fluorescens* strain WCS365 forms micro-colonies on the tomato root one day after seed inoculation (Bolwerk *et al.*, unpublished data).

The competition for niches may in fact reflect a competition for nutrients such as carbon, nitrogen sources, and iron (2; 24; 82; 150). These compounds were shown to be involved in mechanisms through which biocontrol strains can reduce the ability of fungal pathogens to propagate in the soil (99; 158). The best-known example of competition for nutrients is limitation by iron. Iron is an essential cofactor for growth of all organisms. However, the amount of solubilized Fe^{3+} available to the organisms in soils is low at neutral and alkaline pH, leading to limitation of Fe^{3+}. Organisms can take up ferric iron ions using siderophores that are secreted by cells and bind to ferric iron ions to form a complex. Fluorescent *Pseudomonas* species grown under Fe^{3+} limitation are capable of producing large amounts of water-soluble siderophores that function as high affinity iron chelators. The siderophore/iron complexes re-enter the cell via specialized cell surface-located uptake systems and thus provide a route for iron uptake under low-iron conditions. The ability to produce efficient siderophores can be combined with the ability to take up related

Table 1. Commercial biological control products for use against soil-borne crop diseases based on bacterial inoculants

Product	Biocontrol organism	Target pathogen or disease	Crop	Manufacturer
Bacillus				
Epic	*Bacillus subtilis*	*Rhizoctonia solani*, *Fusarium* spp., *Alternaria* spp., and *Aspergillus* spp. that attack roots	Cotton, legumes	Gustafson, Inc., Dallas, TX, USA
Kodiak, Kodiak HB, Kodiak AT	*Bacillus subtilis*	*Rhizoctonia solani*, *Fusarium* spp., *Alternaria* spp., and *Aspergillus* spp. that attack roots	Cotton, legumes	Gustafson, Inc., Dallas, TX, USA
Rhizo-Plus, Rhizo-Plus Konz	*Bacillus subtilis* FZB24	*Rhizoctonia solani*, *Fusarium* spp., *Alternaria* spp., *Sclerotinia*, *Verticillium*, *Streptomyces scabies*	Field (potatoes, corn), vegetables, and ornamental plants	KFZB Biotechnik GmbH, Berlin, Germany
Serenade	*Bacillus subtilis*	Powdery mildew, downy mildew, *Cercospora* leaf spot, early blight, late blight, brown rot, fire blight, and others	Cucurbits, grapes, hops, vegetables, peanuts, pome fruits, stone fruits, and others	AgraQuest, Inc., Davis, CA, USA
System 3	*Bacillus subtilis* GB03 and chemical pesticides	Seedling pathogens	Barley, beans, cotton, peanut, pea, rice, and soybean	Helena Chemical Co., TN, USA
Streptomyces				
Mycostop	*Streptomyces griseoviridus* strain K61	*Fusarium* spp., *Alternaria brassicola*, *Phomopsis* spp., *Botrytis* spp., *Pythium* spp., and *Phytophthora* spp. that cause seed, root, and stem rot, and wilt disease	Field, ornamental, and vegetable crops	Kemira Agro Oy, Helsinki, Finland
Pseudomonas				
BlightBan A506	*Pseudomonas fluorescens* A506	Frost damage, *Erwinia amylovora*, and russet-inducing bacteria	Almond, apple, apricot, blueberry, cherry, peach, pear, potato, strawberry, tomato	Plant Health Technologies, CA, USA
Conquer	*Pseudomonas fluorescens*	*Pseudomonas tolassii*	Mushrooms	Mauri Foods, North Ryde, Australia

Table 1 (*continued*).

Product	Biocontrol organism	Target pathogen or disease	Crop	Manufacturer
Victus	*Pseudomonas fluorescens* strain NCIB 12089	*Pseudomonas tolasii* that causes bacterial blotch disease	Mushrooms	Sylvan Spawn Laboratory, Kittanning, PA, USA
Bio-save 100, Bio-save 1000	*Pseudomonas syringae* ESC-10	*Botrytis cinerea*, *Penicillium* spp., *Mucor pyroformis*, *Geotrichum candidum*	Pome fruit (Bio-save 100) and citrus (Bio-save 1000)	EcoScience Corp., Produce Systems Div., Orlando, FL, USA
Bio-save 110	*Pseudomonas syringae* ESC-11	*Botrytis cinerea*, *Penicillium* spp., *Mucor pyroformis*, *Geotrichum andidum*	Pome fruit	EcoScience Corp., Produce Systems Div., , Orlando, FL, USA
PSSOL	*Pseudomonas solanacearum* (non-pathogenic)	*Pseudomonas solanacearum*	Vegetables	Natural Plant Protections, France
Cedomon	*Pseudomonas chlororaphis*	*Drechslera teres*, *Tilletia caries*	Cereals	BioAgri, Sweden
Burkholderia				
Deny	*Burkholderia cepacia*	*Rhizoctonia*, *Pythium*, *Fusarium*, nematodes	Alfalfa, barley, beans, clover, peas, sorghum, vegetables, wheat	CTT Corp., USA
Blue Circle	*Burkholderia cepacia*	*Rhizoctonia*, *Pythium*, *Fusarium*	Vegetables	CTT Corp., USA
Intercept	*Burkholderia cepacia*	*Rhizoctonia solani*, *Fusarium* spp., *Pythium* sp.	Maize, vegetables, cotton	Soil Technologies Corp., Fairfield, IA, USA
Agrobacterium				
Galltrol-A	*Agrobacterium radiobacter* strain 84	Crown gall disease caused by *Agrobacterium tumefaciens*	Fruit, nut, and ornamental nursery stock	AgBioChem, Inc., Orinda, CA, USA
Nogall, Diegall	*Agrobacterium radiobacter*	*Agrobacterium tumefaciens*	Trees	Bio-Care Technology Pty. Ltd., Somersby, Australia
Norbac 84C	*Agrobacterium radiobacter* strain K84	Crown gall disease caused by *Agrobacterium tumefaciens*	Fruit, nut, and ornamental nursery stock	New BioProducts, Inc., Corvallis, OR, USA

siderophores from other organisms (134; 135; 207; 266). Since bioavailability of Fe^{3+} in certain soils is limited, the ability to scavenge iron gives the biocontrol organism a selective advantage over pathogens or deleterious organisms that produce less efficient iron binding and uptake systems. Experimental evidence for such a mechanism in biocontrol was obtained using siderophore-minus mutants that were less suppressive to pathogens than the isogenic parental strain (10).

Parasitism and predation. Bacteria and fungi are capable of producing lytic enzymes such as chitinases, β(1,3)-glucanases, cellulases, lipases, and proteases. Some of these enzymes attack fungal pathogens by degrading fungal cell wall constituents such as glucans and chitins. This process results in the destruction of pathogen structures or propagules. Biocontrol bacteria producing chitinase (72; 73; 212; 228), protease (69; 74), cellulase (34), or β-glucanases (124; 214) were shown to suppress plant diseases. The enzymes kill the pathogen, allowing the use of the degradation products by the biocontrol agent. In addition, these enzymes may act synergistically with other antifungal metabolites (AFMs) (61; 67; 160).

Antifungal metabolites produced by PGPR. The best-studied mechanism through which PGPRs can inhibit pathogen growth is the production of secondary metabolites. Pseudomonads produce a wide array of AFMs (48; 147; 187; 248). These compounds are usually small organic molecules that inhibit growth or metabolism of other microorganisms (Table 2). The first support for the hypothesis that antifungal metabolites are involved in biological control came from a correlation of pathogen inhibition *in vitro* and disease suppression *in vivo* (85). Direct evidence for the role of antifungal metabolites in biocontrol came from studies of genetically altered mutants defective in their antagonistic potential (85; 248). In biocontrol of black root rot of tobacco, caused by *Thielaviopsis basicola*, a mutant of the wild-type *P. fluorescens* CHA0 was isolated, which does not produce the antibiotic 2,4-diacetylphloroglucinol (DAPG; Table 2). This mutant strain suppressed black root rot to a distinctly lesser extent than the wild type (60; 127; 128). Likewise, suppression of *Gaeumannomyces graminis* var. *tritici* by *P. fluorescens* strain 2-79, producing the antibiotic phenazine-1-carboxylic acid (Table 2), *P. aureofaciens* strain 30-84, additionally producing 2-hydroxyphenazine-1-carboxylic acid and 2-hydroxyphenazine, and *P. chlororaphis* PCL1391, producing phenazine-1-carboxamide, was correlated with the *in situ* production of the antifungal factor(s) (39; 200; 247). Other well-known compounds with antibiotic action produced by pseudomonads include pyrrolnitrin (6; 115; 116), pyocyanin (11; 12; 83), pyoluteorin (116), and oomycin A (117) (Table 2). Pyrrolnitrin is involved in biocontrol activity towards fungal pathogens (108; 112; 115; 122; 177; 178). Pyoluteorin is an aromatic polyketide antibiotic suppressing a number of plant pathogens including *Pythium*. Biocontrol strains *P. fluorescens* strain CHA0 and Pf-5, which produce pyoluteorin, also were shown to suppress this pathogen (95; 116; 170; 171). Cyclic lipopeptides such as viscosinamide (182) and tensin (183) produced by *Pseudomonas fluorescens* have antifungal activity against *Rhizoctonia solani* and *Pythium ultimum* (250). The antifungal factor responsible for the ability of *Burkholderia cepacia* BC11 to control the damping-off of cotton is also a lipopeptide (125). Volatiles such as hydrogen cyanide (HCN) (263), formed by *Pseudomonas*, and ammonia, formed by *Enterobacter* spp., were shown to be biocidal metabolites. Since HCN influences plant growth directly, the exact role and mechanism of HCN in biocontrol remains unclear. Ammonia has been implicated in the control of plant-pathogenic fungi and nematodes (114; 189; 253). The biosynthetic genes for most of the secondary metabolites discussed above have been identified and the biosynthetic pathways for these compounds have been at least partially or completely elucidated (41; 81; 97; 125; 136; 143; 186; 262).

Induced systemic resistance. After contact with a necrotizing pathogen or a non-pathogenic biocontrol bacterium, a state of physiological immunity can be induced in plants whereby they are protected against subsequent fungal, viral, or bacterial attacks (systemic resistance). Remote action, long-lasting resistance, and protection against a large range of other pathogens are characteristic. Physical and chemical defense responses are activated within the host plant by the inducing agent(s), resulting in partial or complete resistance to the disease. This resistance occurs by restricting or blocking the ability of the pathogen to produce disease in the host plant. The immunity caused by infection with a necrotizing agent is known as systemic acquired resistance (SAR). At the physiological level, salicylic acid accumulates and the production of pathogenesis-related (PR) proteins is induced (62; 120). Certain root-colonizing bacteria and fungi are also capable of inducing resistance to a variety of diseases in several types of plants in a fairly unique relationship. The plant defense mechanism induced by non-pathogenic biocontrol bacteria is known as induced systemic resistance (ISR) (145; 222; 257-259). ISR mediated by *Pseudomonas* spp. was observed in carnation against *F. oxysporum* f. sp. *dianthi* (68), in cucumber against *Colletotrichum orbiculare* (265) and cucumber mosaic virus (208), in bean against halo blight (4), in tobacco against tobacco necrosis virus (169), and in radish against *F. oxysporum* f. sp. *raphani* (146). ISR can be activated also by biotic agents such as lipopolysaccharides, siderophores, or flagella (145; 145). In contrast to its wild type, a pyocyanin mutant of *P. aeruginosa* 7NSK2 is unable to induce resistance to *Botrytis cinerea*. It was hypothesized that salicylic acid produced on roots is converted to the siderophore pyochelin and that

Table 2. Metabolites produced by pseudomonads implicated in control of plant diseases

	Antifungal metabolite	*Pseudomonas* spp.	Affected pathogen	Host plant	Reference
1.	Acetylphloroglucinols, e.g. 2,4-diacetyl-phloroglucinol 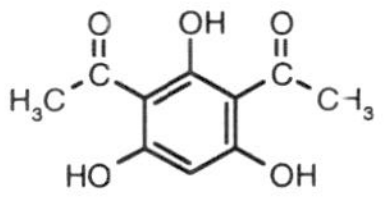	*P. fluorescens*	*Gaeumannomyces gramini* var. *tritici*	wheat	Keel et al., 1992; Vincent et al., 1991 (127; 262)
		Pseudomonas spp.	*Pythium ultimum*	sugar beet	Fenton et al., 1992 (81)
		P. fluorescens	*Thielaviopsis basicola*	tobacco	Keel et al., 1990 (128)
		P. auranticca	*Fusarium oxysporum*	wheat	Pidoplichko and Garagulya, 1974 (197)
2.	Oomycin A Structure to be determined	*P. fluorescens*	*Pythium ultimum*	cotton	Howie and Suslow, 1991 (117)
3.	Phenazine-1-carboxylic acid 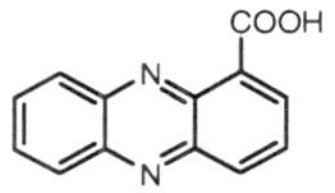	*P. fluorescens* *P. aureofaciens*	*Gaeumannomyces gramini* var. *tritici*	wheat	Pierson et al., 1996; Thomashow et al., 1990 (200; 249)
4.	Phenazine-1-carboxamide 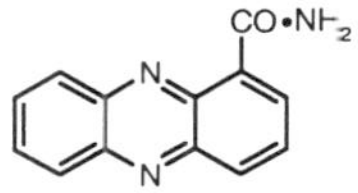	*P. chlororaphis*	*Fusarium oxysporum* f. sp. *radicis-lycopersici*	tomato	Chin-A-Woeng et al., 1998 (39)
5.	Pyocyanine 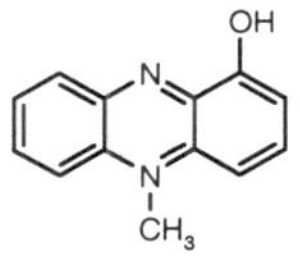	*P. aeruginosa*	*Septoria tritici*	wheat	Flaishman et al., 1990 (83)

Table 2 (*continued*)

	Antifungal metabolite	*Pseudomonas* spp.	Affected pathogen	Host plant	Reference
6.	Anthranilate 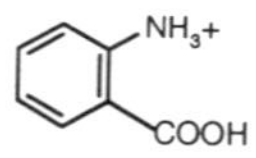	*P. aeruginosa*	*Fusarium oxysporum* f. sp. *ciceris*	chickpea	Anjaiah et al., 1998 (5)
7.	Pyoluteorin 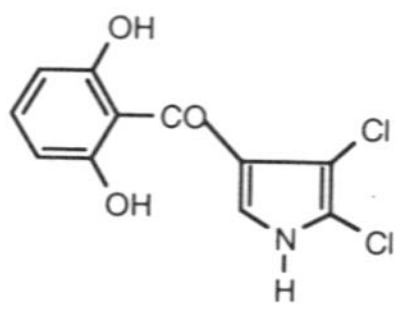	*P. fluorescens*	*Pythium ultimum*	cucumber, cotton	Howell and Stipanovic, 1980; Maurhofer et al., 1992 (116; 171)
8.	Pyrrolnitrin 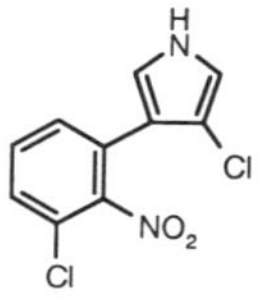	*P. fluorescens*	*Rhizoctonia solani*	cotton	Howell and Stipanovic, 1979; Howell and Stipanovic, 1980 (115; 115; 116)
		P. cepacia	*Aphanomyces cochliodes*	sugar beet	Homma, 1994 (112)
		P. fluorescens	*Pyrenophora tritici-repens*	wheat	Pfender et al., 1993 (196)
9.	Hydrogen cyanide	*P. fluorescens*	*Thielaviopsis basicola*	tobacco	Voisard et al., 1989 (263)

Table 2 (*continued*)

	Antifungal metabolite	*Pseudomonas* spp.	Affected pathogen	Host plant	Reference
10.	Pyoverdine 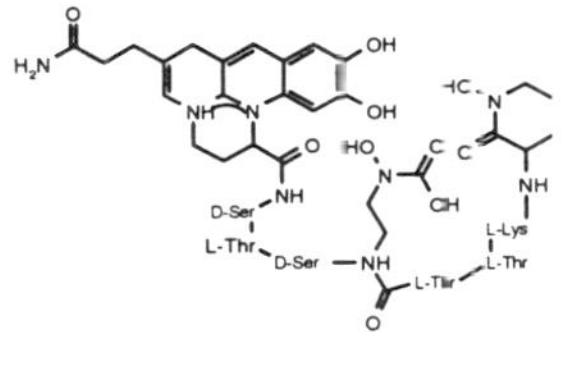	*P. fluorescens* *P. putida*	Pythium ultimum *Fusarium oxysporum*	cotton carnation, radish	Loper, 1988 (157) Lemanceau et al., 1992; Lemanceau et al., 1993 (148; 149)
11.	Pyochelin 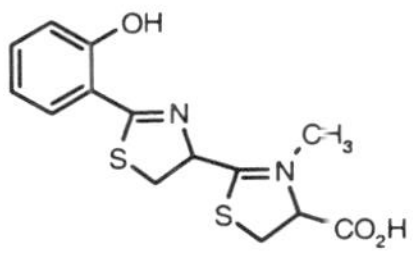	*P. aeruginosa*	*Pythium splendens*	tomato	Buysens et al., 1994 (25)

the combination of pyochelin and pyocyanin results in the production of active oxygen species that cause cell damage, which subsequently leads to induced resistance (7). ISR induced by non-pathogenic bacteria is not identical with systemic acquired resistance (SAR), the classical response induced upon challenge by a pathogen. SAR induced by plant pathogens is characterized by accumulation of salicylic acid and production of PR proteins in the plant, whereas jasmonic acid and ethylene production are involved in the ISR response (109; 203). Often two physiologically different responses with distinct signaling pathways can be observed in the same plant system when challenged either by induction of the classical response or ISR. The ISR and SAR pathways are mutually compatible, with no significant cross-talk between them. Moreover, simultaneous activation of the two pathways resulted in an additive effect in the level of protection against pathogens (251; 260). It is also thought that ISR is associated with closer contact between inducing agent and the host plant (261).

Root colonization by *Pseudomonas*

Microbial proliferation associated with the root is generally referred to as root colonization (51). Root colonization functions as the delivery system of AFMs to protect the root. In general, shortly after seeds coated with biocontrol bacteria are sown, biocontrol bacteria must compete with the native microflora. After introduction of inoculant bacteria into soils, the inoculant population usually declines progressively (13). When a biocontrol strain has to achieve a desired effect, it must establish itself for several months at a high level in the rhizosphere.

Not all isolates showing pathogen inhibition *in vitro* provide disease control or colonize the root surface effectively. One explanation for this discrepancy is that many of these isolates are not rhizosphere competent. The inability of the introduced biocontrol agent to establish itself effectively in the rhizosphere has been suggested to be the cause of several inconsistent field trials (22; 268). In several field trials colonization was indicated to be the limiting step for biocontrol (221; 268). Colonization of the plant root is considered to be essential for the success of applications for beneficial purposes and suppression of plant diseases. Novel procedures to select for efficient root-colonizing bacterial strains combined with other beneficial activities such as degradation of polyaromatic hydrocarbons have been developed (137), showing that selection of efficient strains is possible (Kuiper *et al.*, in press). For reliable application of biocontrol agents it is crucial to understand the traits and genes involved in efficient rhizosphere colonization (163; 243).

TRAITS IMPORTANT FOR EFFICIENT COLONIZATION

It is assumed that various bacterial traits contribute to the ability of a bacterial strain to colonize the rhizosphere and loss of such a trait can reduce the ability to establish itself effectively in the rhizosphere and hence also reduce its beneficial effects. A number of traits suspected to be important for root colonization were investigated extensively. One of the factors appeared to be motility. Flagella-less *Pseudomonas* strains, when tested in direct competition with the wild type after application on seeds, are severely impaired in colonization of the root tip of potato (264) and tomato (52; 55; 233). Non-motile Tn5 transposon mutants of strain PCL1391, antagonistic for *Fusarium oxysporum* f. sp. *radicis-lycopersici*, were at least one thousand-fold impaired in competitive tomato root tip colonization against its wild type (38).

Chemotaxis towards seed exudate was suggested to be the first step in establishment of bacterial seed and root colonization (220). A *cheA*$^-$ chemotaxis mutant of *P. fluorescens* WCS365 appears to be strongly reduced in competitive root colonization, both in a gnotobiotic system as well as in non-sterile potting soil (de Weert *et al.*, unpublished results).

Agglutination and attachment of *Pseudomonas* cells to plant roots are likely to be of importance for colonization. Compounds qualifying for these roles are adhesins, fimbriae, pili, cell surface proteins, and polysaccharides. The number of fimbriae on bacterial cells of strain WCS365 correlates with the degree of attachment to tomato roots (29). The outer membrane protein OprF of *P. fluorescens* OE28.3 is involved in attachment to plant roots (58). A root-surface glycoprotein agglutinin was shown to mediate agglutination of *P. putida* isolate Corvallis (21) but had no role in long-term colonization (91; 131).

Mutants of *P. fluorescens* strains WCS365 and WCS374, and *P. putida* WCS358 lacking the O-antigen side chain of lipopolysaccharide (LPS) were shown to be impaired in colonization (50; 55; 233). The colonization defect in strains with defective LPS can be explained by assuming that for the optimal functioning of nutrient uptake systems an intact outer membrane is required.

Specific genes for the biosynthesis of amino acids and vitamin B1 and for utilization of root exudate components such as organic acids are also important for colonization of strain WCS365 on tomato roots (232) (Wijfjes *et al.* unpublished results). *Pseudomonas chlororaphis* PCL1391 mutants auxotrophic for phenylalanine were at least one thousand-fold less in population on the tomato root tip in competition with the wild type (38). Putrescine is an important root exudate component of which the uptake rate must be carefully regulated. *Pseudomonas fluorescens* mutants with increased uptake have a decreased growth rate resulting in a decreased competitive colonization ability (138).

Other putative colonization factors include generation time (233), osmotolerance (159), resistance to predators (45; 96), host plant cultivar (268), and soil type (8).

Other genes for which their role in colonization are not readily obvious were identified with mutant analysis after screening random Tn*5* mutants of *P. fluorescens* WCS365 in competition with the parental strains (164). These colonization genes include the *nuoD* gene, which is part of a 14-gene operon encoding NADH dehydrogenase NDH-1 (Camacho *et al.*, in press). The biocontrol strain WCS365 possesses two NADH dehydrogenases, and apparently the absence of NDH-1 cannot be adequately compensated for by the other NADH dehydrogenase under rhizosphere conditions resulting in sub-optimal growth of these strains on the root.

A two-component regulatory system consisting of the *colS* and *colR* genes, that have homology to sensor kinases and response regulators, respectively, (52) also was shown to be involved in efficient root colonization of strain WCS365. It was concluded that an environmental stimulus is important for colonization but the nature of the signal as well as of the target genes is still to be elucidated (55).

The *sss* gene, encoding a protein of the lambda integrase gene family of site-specific recombinases, which also includes XerC and XerD, is necessary for adequate root colonization of *P. fluorescens* WCS365 (54). It was postulated that a certain bacterial sub-population, which expresses an as yet unknown cell surface component regulated by site-specific recombinases, is important for competitive colonization of strain WCS365. Mutation of an *sss/xerD* homologue in biocontrol strain PCL1391 resulted in a mutant severely impaired in root tip colonization both in a sterile sand system as well as in potting soil (38). In addition, introduction of the colonization operon containing the *sss* homologous operon into wild-type strains *P. fluorescens* strains F113 and WCS307 led to an enhanced colonization ability and enabled strain WCS307 to accomplish biocontrol through improved colonization (51; 51; 53; 54). The production of secondary metabolites is hypothesized to confer a selective advantage in the persistence in soil and the rhizosphere. The contribution to the ecological competence of strains was indeed shown for the phenazine-producing strains *P. fluorescens* 2-79 and *P. aureofaciens* strain 30-84 using Tn*5* mutants impaired in phenazine biosynthesis. Phenazine-minus strains had a reduced survival and a diminished ability to compete with the resident microflora (174). However, production of the antifungal factor 2,4-diacetylphloroglucinol in *P. fluorescens* strain F113 did not influence its persistence in the soil (31).

ROLE OF ROOT COLONIZATION IN BIOCONTROL

When bacteria are applied in relatively high numbers to seeds before planting, the applied microbial fungicides could affect inhibition of soil fungi only within a short term, and in effect act as a chemical. Bacterial inoculants become more powerful agents than chemicals when they multiply on the root and colonize the root system resulting in protection for longer periods. In several field trials the bacterial population size was shown to be the limiting step for biocontrol (221; 268).

The degree of colonization required for biocontrol may also be dependent on the mechanism used by a biocontrol agent to perform its action. For a strain which uses antibiosis one must assume that good colonization is needed to deliver antifungal metabolites over the entire root system covering potential sites of infections, whereas for a strain which acts through ISR smaller numbers of bacteria may be sufficient to elicit a successful response of the host plant.

With the identification of essential root colonization genes (165), mutants in these genes in the biocontrol strain *P. chlororaphis* PCL1391 were constructed and the effect of a lower colonization efficiency on biocontrol was measured. Motility-impaired mutants and a phenylalanine auxotrophic mutant were one thousandfold impaired in colonization, whereas a mutant in an *sss/xerD* homologous gene was tenfold impaired when tested in competition with its wild type. Concomitantly with their lower colonization rates in soil and an unchanged production of the essential antifungal metabolite, biocontrol was abolished in an *F. oxysporum* f. sp. *radicis-lycopersici* system (38), showing that root colonization is another essential trait for the action of this strain. On the other hand, the biocontrol of tomato foot and root rot by *P. fluorescens* WCS365 is presumably based upon the induction of system resistance of the plant (90). Mutations in various colonization genes did not decrease the biocontrol abilities of this strain, suggesting that colonization only plays a limited or no role in ISR-based plant protection (53).

Root-colonizing ability could not only be important in biocontrol, but also in other applications of microbial inoculants of seeds, i.e. biofertilizers, phytostimulators, and phytoremediators, in which the effectiveness of an inoculant is likely to be dependent on the establishment of a minimum population size.

It is also noteworthy that many colonization traits important for biocontrol also play a role in colonization of animal tissues by bacteria (36; 64; 163; 211; 267). Similarly, phenazine derivatives do not only kill fungi but the phenazine derivative pyocyanin produced by *P. aeruginosa*, for example, is involved in killing of animal cells and tissues (167). The two established biocontrol traits of *P. chlororaphis* PCL1391, colonization and production of phenazine antibiotics, are bacterial traits that also play a role in colonization of animal tissues and in killing of animal cells, respectively, and therefore we suggest that these bacterial traits are important in interactions with widely different eukaryotes.

Phenazine antibiotics produced by *Pseudomonas*

ROLE OF PHENAZINE DERIVATIVES IN BIOCONTROL

In the first part of the twentieth century it was already reported that pseudomonads producing phenazine derivatives could protect plants against diseases. However, with the resurgence of interest in biocontrol in the beginning of the 1980s, driven in part by trends in agriculture toward greater sustainability and an increased concern about the use of chemical pesticides, the interest in the phenazine class of compounds also increased. Phenazine-1-carboxylic acid (PCA) is a derivative often produced by *Pseudomonas* biocontrol strains (5), among which are *P. fluorescens* 2-79 (247) and *P. aeruginosa* 30-84 (198), and *P. chlororaphis* PCL1391 (39). Phenazines encompass a large family of heterocyclic nitrogen-containing molecules with broad-spectrum antibiotic activity that are synthesized almost exclusively by bacteria. Their production has been reported in *Pseudomonas*, *Streptomyces*, *Nocardia*, *Sorangium*, *Brevibacterium*, and *Burkholderia* species (254). More than 50 naturally occurring phenazine derivatives have been described and many have been chemically synthesized. The best-known derivatives produced by *Pseudomonas* spp. are pyocyanin, iodinin, phenazine-1-carboxylic acid, and hydroxy-phenazines (Table 3). Phenazines are brightly colored pigments and some play a pivotal role in biological control (39; 247).

Phenazine-1-carboxylic acid also plays a role in ecological fitness (174). The ability to synthesize particular phenazine pigments, e.g. pyocyanin, was used as an important taxonomic feature in conventional microbial systematics (147). Phenazines were found to be toxic to a wide range of organisms including bacteria, fungi, and algae (252), but their mechanism of action is poorly understood. It is thought that they diffuse across, or insert into, the membrane, undergo redox cycling in the presence of various reducing agents and molecular oxygen, resulting in the uncoupling of oxidative phosphorylation and the generation of toxic intracellular superoxide radicals (O_2^-) and hydrogen peroxide (H_2O_2), leading to oxidative cell injury and death (103; 167; 254). The higher activity of superoxide dismutases of the pyocyanin-producing *P. aeruginosa* which would provide protection against the action of phenazines supports this idea (103; 104).

Currently, only a limited number of phenazine derivatives, including phenazine-1-carboxylic acid (PCA) and phenazine-1-carboxamide (PCN), also known as chlororaphin (254), have been shown to be involved in biocontrol. Mutants of *P. fluorescens* 2-79 impaired in phenazine-1-carboxylic acid biosynthesis provided

Table 3. Naturally occurring phenazine derivatives produced by *Pseudomonas* spp.

Chemical structure	Phenazine derivative	Reference
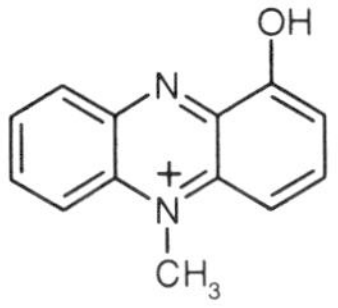	pyocyanin	Fordos, 1860 (84)
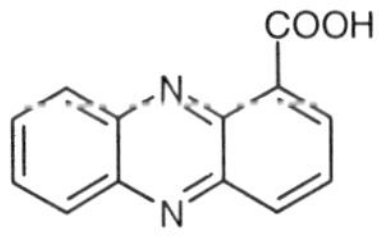	phenazine-1-carboxylic acid	Kluyver, 1956 (130)
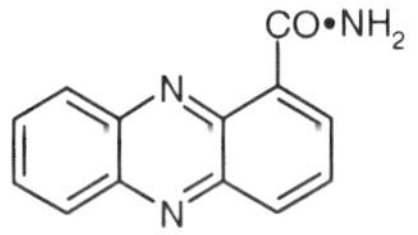	phenazine-1-carboxamide	Birkofer, 1947 (16)
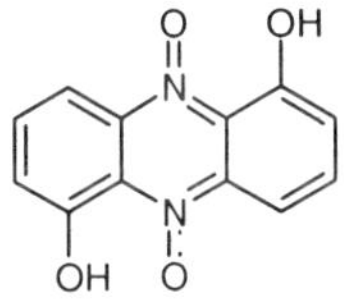	iodinin	Bell and Turner, 1973 (15)
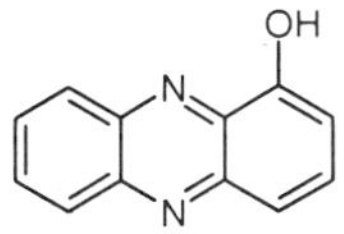	1-hydroxyphenazine	Schoental, 1941 (225)

significantly less control of take-all than the wild type on wheat seedlings (247). In a tomato-*Fusarium* foot and root rot system the phenazine-1-carboxamide-producing wild-type *P. chlororaphis* strain PCL1391 reduced the number of diseased plants from 78% in the untreated control to 33%. In contrast, strain PCL1119 (*phzB*::Tn5), an isogenic derivative impaired in phenazine-1-carboxamide biosynthesis, did not suppress disease formation (39).

The conditions under which phenazine derivatives are active can also be different (254). The PCA-producing strains *P. fluorescens* 2-79 (247) and *P. aureofaciens* 30-84 (198) showed no significant biocontrol activity in a *F. oxysporum* f. sp. *radicis-lycopersici* assay, whereas the PCN-producing strain PCL1391 inhibited this pathogen under the same conditions. *In vitro* antifungal activity of PCN was at least ten times higher than that of PCA at pH levels 5.7 or higher, whereas both compounds behaved similarly under acidic conditions (39). This suggests that antifungal activity of PCA is related to the concentration of protonated PCA, suggesting that as the soil pH or rhizosphere pH increases, the anionic form of PCA predominates. These observations are consistent with studies in which the PCA-producing *P. fluorescens* strain 2-79 was tested on pH-controlled agar medium against the wheat pathogen *G. graminis* var. *tritici* (20). Transfer of the *phzH* gene, which is involved in converting the carboxylic moiety in a carboxamide moiety, under control of the *tac* promoter to the PCA-producing biocontrol strains *P. fluorescens* 2-79 (247) and *P. aureofaciens* 30-84 (198) enabled these strains to produce PCN. The introduction of the *phzH* gene under control of the *tac*-promoter enabled these strains to efficiently suppress tomato foot and root rot. In this way the biocontrol efficiency of these bacterial strains could be extended by introduction of a single gene (41).

Also other differences in physical properties may influence the activities *in vivo*, e.g. hydroxylated phenazines are more soluble in water than their unhydroxylated counterparts. For many other phenazine derivatives their activity in biocontrol remains to be investigated.

BIOSYNTHESIS OF PHENAZINE

Although the first thorough studies of the biosynthetic pathways of phenazines took place in the late seventies, the biochemical details of most individual reactions are still unknown. Shikimic acid was established to be a precursor of phenazines (121) (Fig. 1A), and chorismate was identified as the branch point from the aromatic biosynthetic pathway using mutants blocked at various steps in this pathway (28; 156). Phenazine-1,6-dicarboxylic acid was proposed to be a common precursor to all naturally occurring phenazines (26; 27). Ring assembly was shown to take place via a diagonally symmetrical pairing of shikimate derivatives in the case of iodinin (111). Some strains are able to produce more than one phenazine derivative e.g. *P. aeruginosa* strains Mac 436 and PAO1 produce pyocyanin, phenazine-1-carboxylic acid, and PCN (33). PCA is considered to be the precursor for many phenazine derivatives (27; 179). Recent data indicate that particular conversion steps to other phenazine products are the result of additional modification by specific enzymes whereas other conversions occur spontaneously.

Genetic data on the synthesis of some of these derivatives have shed more light on the biochemistry of these compounds. Pierson *et al.* characterized production in *P. aureofaciens* strain 30-84 genetically by identifying a cluster of five genes, *phzFABCD*, required for phenazine-1-carboxylic acid production (198). Based on homologies with enzymes in *Escherichia coli*, functions were assigned to the enzyme products in the basal phenazine biosynthetic pathway (Fig. 1A). The *phzC* gene product has homology with 3-deoxy-D-arabinoheptulosonate-7-phosphate (DAHP) synthases and is thought to by-pass the action of household DAHP synthetases that direct the synthesis of the intermediate shikimic acid. PhzD and PhzE are homologous to 2,3-dehydro-2,3-dihydroxybenzoate synthetases (isochorismatase) and the anthranilate synthetase TrpE, respectively. Since the conversion of chorismic acid to phenazine-1,6-dicarboxylic acid is thought to occur via the intermediate

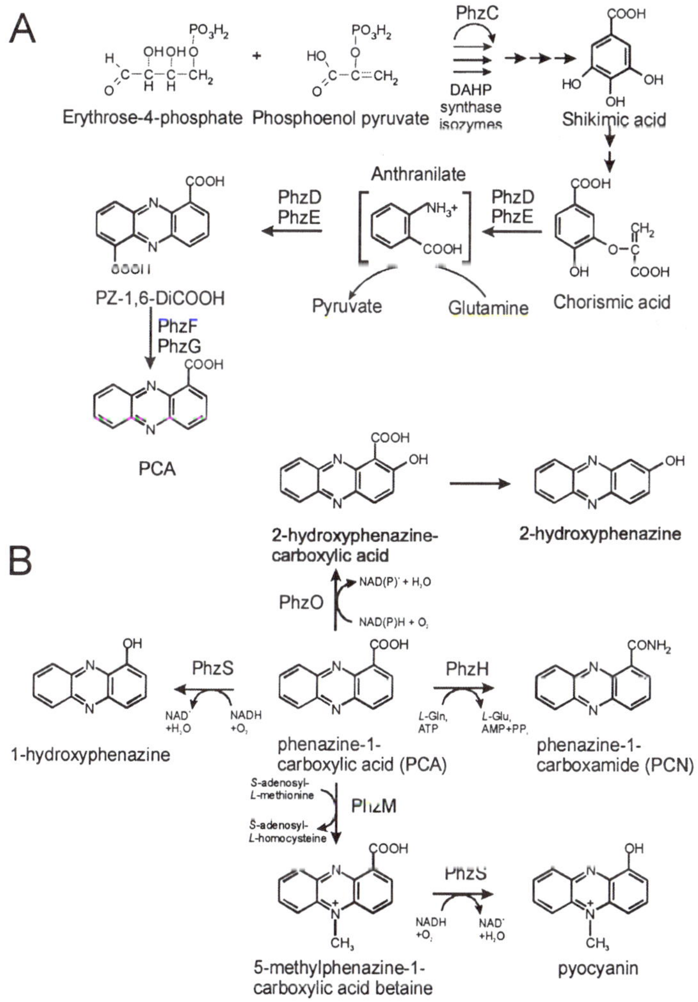

Fig. 1. Proposed phenazine biosynthetic pathway in *Pseudomonas* spp. for microbial phenazines. Panel A. Biosynthesis of phenazine-1-carboxylic acid (PCA). Panel B. Biosynthesis of derivatives of phenazine-1-carboxylic acid. For explanation see text.

3-hydroxyanthranilate, PhzD and PhzE were hypothesized to form one enzyme complex converting chorismic acid to the first phenazine derivative, phenazine-1,6-dicarboxylic acid (173; 201). PhzF and PhzG are thought to play a role in the next step, the conversion of phenazine-1,6-dicarboxylic acid to PCA. The phenazine biosynthetic clusters of *P. fluorescens* 2-79 and *P. chlororaphis* PCL1391 consist of the *phzABCDEFG* and *phzABCDEFGH* genes, respectively. The proteins encoded by *phzA* and *phzB*, found in the biosynthetic operon in *P. fluorescens* 2-79 (173) and *P. chlororaphis* (41), and later identified in *P. aureofaciens* 30-84 and designated *phzX* and *phzY*, both predicted 163-amino acids, were suggested to stabilize a putative multi-enzyme complex formed by PhzD and PhzE (173; 198).

In *P. aeruginosa* PAO1 two complete sets of the core *phzABCDEFG* genes have been identified on the chromosome (172; 239). The nucleotide sequences are 98.3% identical to each other at nucleotide level, with most sequence divergence occurring in the first part of the *phzA1B1* and *phzA2B2* genes. The second gene cluster *phzA2B2C2D2E2F2G2* is located 2.6 Mb from the first cluster. In contrast to *P. fluorescens* 2-79, *P. aureofaciens* 30-84, and *P. chlororaphis* PCL1391, the genes for quorum sensing regulation of phenazine biosynthesis are not located upstream of the core genes but elsewhere in the genome. The *lux* box-like element in the putative promoter region of *phzA1* was not present upstream of *phzA2*, indicating that the second cluster might not be regulated by quorum sensing.

The *phzABCDEFG* genes are now considered to be the core genes for biosynthesis of phenazine-1-carboxylic acid. The nucleotide sequences of the core genes of *P. fluorescens* 2-79 (173) *P. aureofaciens* 30-84 (198), *P. chlororaphis* PCL1391, and *P. aeruginosa* PAO1 (239) are very homologous (70-95% identity). In addition to these core genes, a number of phenazine-modifying enzymes have been identified.

In *P. chlororaphis* PCL1391, downstream of *phzG*, the *phzH* gene was identified and shown to be required for the presence of the 1-carboxamide group of PCN, the final product in strain PCL1391. A *phzH* mutant of strain PCL1391 does not produce PCN and accumulates PCA. The deduced PhzH protein shows homology with asparagine synthetases. The N-terminal domain of PhzH has a motif that is conserved in class II glutamine amidotransferases. In addition, the catalytic cysteine (Cys^1) characteristic for the class II glutamine amidotransferase domain is also present in PhzH (41; 168). The C-terminal domain of PhzH harbors motifs characteristic for asparagine synthetases indicating that the conversion of PCA to PCN occurs via a transamidase reaction catalyzed by PhzH.

In *P. aureofaciens* 30-84 the *phzO* gene is located closely downstream of the core biosynthetic operon *phzXYFABCD* directing the synthesis of 2-hydroxyphenazine carboxylic acid (56). PhzO belongs to the family of two-component non-heme, flavin-diffusible bacterial aromatic monooxygenases. The subsequent conversion from 2-hydroxyphenazine carboxylic acid to 2-hydroxyphenazine appears to occur spontaneously in the absence of enzymes (Fig. 1B). The *phzO* gene is exclusively conserved in isolates of *P. aureofaciens* (which all produce hydroxyphenazines) indicating that the acquisition of this phenazine-modifying gene, and possibly also for *phzH*, is a fairly recent event (56).

In *P. aeruginosa* PAO1, besides *phzH*, two other phenazine-modifying enzymes *phzM* and *phzS* were characterized. The *phzM* gene is located upstream of the *phzA1B1C1D1E1F1G1* operon and transcribed divergently. It encodes a 334 amino acids protein that most closely resembles *O*-demethylpuromycin-*O*-methyltransferases with a methyltransferase motif and a *S*-adenosyl-L-methionine (SAM) binding domain (172; 190). Functional analysis revealed that the *phzM* gene product is involved in the production of pyocyanin (Fig. 1B). The *phzS* gene is located downstream from *phzG1* and encodes a 402-residue protein similar to bacterial monooxygenases. PhzS is thought to be involved in pyocyanin production as well as in the biosynthesis of 1-hydroxyphenazine in *P. aeruginosa* PAO1 (172) (Fig. 1B).

Regulation of antifungal factor production in *Pseudomonas*

Many of the antifungal factors produced by biocontrol organisms are secondary metabolites (94). In many cases the production of secondary metabolites is not only dependent on intracellular factors but also on environmental conditions. Bacteria have adopted many different mechanisms to regulate the production of antifungal factors. One of the mechanisms playing an important role in the regulation of phenazine biosynthesis in a population density dependent manner, is called quorum sensing. This regulatory mechanism involves the action of so-called LuxI and LuxR homologues and appears to be the most important regulation mechanism for phenazine biosynthesis. Quorum sensing regulation processes are often interlinked with regulation of primary metabolism and stress response. Production of antifungal metabolites is also dependent upon global regulatory systems such as the GacS-GacA system and sigma factors.

POPULATION DENSITY DEPENDENT REGULATION

Bacteria can perceive extracellular conditions using numerous sensor/kinase signal transduction pathways (93). Quorum sensing is an intercellular communication mechanism that enables a bacterium to monitor the density of its own population (14; 71; 86; 180; 215). It enables bacteria to regulate their gene expression in a population density-dependent way and adjust their physiology according to their environmental conditions, thereby coordinating the behavior of the entire cell population.

Bacteria can perceive population density information from neighboring sister cells through perception of a class of signal molecules known as autoinducers. The signals leave the cell but can diffuse back into the bacterial cell. When the intracellular signal reaches a certain threshold concentration as a result of a high population density, which can be enhanced in a closed system or confined space, it is thought to interact with and activate a transcriptional activator, a LuxR homologue (Fig. 2A) (100; 238). In Gram-positive bacterial species such as *Streptomyces*, γ-butyrolactones were found to regulate antibiotic production and sporulation in a population density-dependent way (75; 113). In *Staphylococcus aureus* an oligopeptide regulates toxic exoprotein and virulence factor secretion (123). In Gram-negative bacteria the most intensively investigated signal molecules belong to the class of *N*-acyl-L-homoserine lactones (*N*-AHLs; Fig. 2C) that modulate a diverse array of phenotypes ranging from bioluminescence to virulence and secondary metabolite production.

Diverse bacterial species are now known to regulate gene expression through these types of regulatory circuits. Many bacterial functions related to pathogenicity or symbiotic interactions with plants or animals are regulated by quorum sensing systems. Traits regulated by *N*-AHLs include bioluminescence in *Photobacterium fisheri* (238), conjugative plasmid transfer in *Agrobacterium tumefaciens* (118; 204), carbapenem antibiotic production in *Erwinia carotovora* (32; 176), swarming motility (79), capsular polysaccharide synthesis (92), biofilm formation of *P. aeruginosa* (49; 230), and production of toxins, rhamnolipids (188; 193), and exoenzymes in *P. aeruginosa* (142; 273). Also phenazine-1-carboxylic production in *P. aeruginosa* (199) and phenazine-1-carboxamide production in *P. chlororaphis* (42) appear to be regulated by quorum sensing. Under certain circumstances, bacteria acting collectively will be more efficient than individual cells such as in (*i*) a collective attack on other organisms, (*ii*) the production of a high concentration of metabolites, or (*iii*) survival by generation of distinct cell types with different abilities to adjust to environmental changes (229).

The first quorum sensing system was described in the early 1970s in the bioluminescent marine symbiont *Photobacterium fisheri* (76; 181). A culture of *P. fisheri* grown under laboratory conditions showed a lag of bioluminescence during early and mid-exponential growth, whereas a high bioluminescent activity was observed during late exponential growth and early stationary phase. The active compound that accumulated during growth in the culture medium that was able to induce bioluminescence in early growth phases was identified as *N*-(3-oxohexanoyl)-L-homoserine lactone (77).

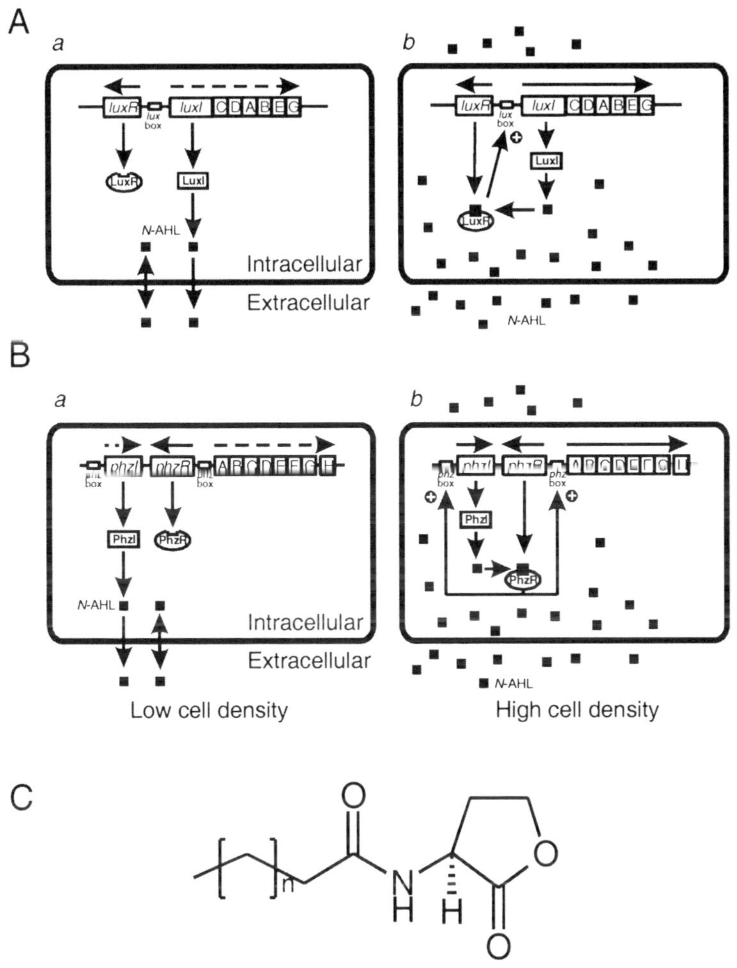

Fig. 2. Quorum sensing regulation in *Vibrio fisheri* and *Pseudomonas* spp. Panel A. Model for quorum sensing in the marine symbiont *P. fisheri*. The designations C to G represent the *lux* operon consisting of the genes *luxC* to *luxG*. *N*-acyl homoserine lactone is abbreviated *N*-AHL. a, low population density cells, b, high population density cells. For explanation, see text. Panel B. Model for quorum sensing regulation of phenazine production in *Pseudomonas chlororaphis* PCL1391. The designations A to H represent the *phz* operon consisting of the genes *phzA* to *phzH*. *N*-acyl homoserine lactone is abbreviated *N*-AHL. For explanation, see text. Panel C. General structure of *N*-acyl-L-homoserine lactones.

In their most simple form, quorum sensing systems involve two proteins belonging to the *luxI-luxR* family of response-regulators (87). The *luxI* homologue encodes an *N*-AHL-synthase that produces diffusible signal molecules derived from homoserine lactone (Fig. 2C) (87; 102; 202; 215; 255), the response to which is mediated by LuxR, a transcriptional regulator with an *N*-AHL-binding- and a DNA-binding domain. The *luxI* and *luxR* homologues identified as being involved in phenazine biosynthesis in *Pseudomonas* strains are designated *phzI* and *phzR* (42; 202; 202; 276). They appear to be essential for the expression of the *phz* biosynthetic operon.

Several systems for detection of the production of *N*-AHL molecules are available. They include bioassays based on the *Chromobacterium* Cvi (175), *Photobacterium* Lux (59; 246; 274), *Agrobacterium* Tra (46) and *Pseudomonas* Las (191) quorum sensing systems. These reporter systems allow simple detection of a broad range of *N*-AHLs and have allowed the rapid and large-scale screening of a number of bacterial strains and species for production of *N*-AHLs and facilitated the identification of *luxI* and *luxR* homologues. An extensively used biosensor is *Chromobacterium violaceum* strain CV026. This strain has a defective *N*-AHL synthase gene *cviI* and, as a result, the response regulator CviR only activates purple violacein pigment production when autoinducer is added exogenously (175).

N-AHLs produced by a diverse range of Gram-negative bacteria differ in acyl chain length, ranging from C_4 to C_{14}, and the nature of the substituent on the carbon-3 position of the acyl chains. Although the *phzI* genes of *P. aureofaciens* 30-84, *P. fluorescens* 2-79, and *P. chlororaphis* PCL1391 are very homologous, the products of the autoinducer synthase PhzI are not the same. *Pseudomonas aureofaciens* 30-84 produces *N*-butanoyl homoserine lactone (C_4-HSL) and *N*-hexanoyl-L-homoserine lactone (C_6-HSL). *Pseudomonas fluorescens* 2-79 produces at least five autoinducer signals among which are *N*-(3-hydroxyhexanoyl)-L-homoserine lactone (3-OH-C_6-HSL), *N*-(3-hydroxyoctanoyl)-L-homoserine lactone (3-OH-C_8-HSL), *N*-(3-hydroxydecanoyl)-L-homoserine lactone (OH-C_{10}-HSL), *N*-octanoyl-L-homoserine lactone (C_8-HSL), and C_6-HSL, although not all of these signals are necessarily products of PhzI. The alleged signals produced by PhzI in *P. chlororaphis* PCL1391 are C_6-HSL, C_4-HSL, and *N*-octanoyl-L-homoserine lactone (C_8-HSL). Other phenazine-producing pseudomonads that were found to produce autoinducers included *P. aureofaciens* type strain ATCC13985, *P. phenazinium* ATCC33666, and the pyocyanin-producing *P. aeruginosa* strain ATCC0927 (202).

In the *Photobacterium* quorum sensing model, the genes encoding the *N*-AHL synthase and the response regulator are present in two divergent transcriptional units. One unit contains the *N*-AHL-synthase and the genes for bioluminescence, *luxCDABEG*. The other transcriptional unit contains the *luxR* gene. The *phzI* and *phzR* genes are also present in two divergent transcriptional units. However, *phzI* is not part of the regulon controlled by PhzR. The PhzI products of *P. aureofaciens* 30-84, *P. fluorescens* 2-79, and *P. chlororaphis* PCL1391 are highly homologous and share homology with other members of the LuxI family. In *P. fluorescens* 2-79, *P. aureofaciens* 30-84, and *P. chlororaphis* PCL1391 the *phzI* and *phzR* genes are located directly upstream from the phenazine biosynthetic core genes. In *P. aeruginosa* PAO1 phenazine production is regulated by two sets of LuxI-LuxR homologues, RhlI-RhlR and LasI-LasR, the genes of which are located elsewhere in the genome.

LuxI homologues are approximately 220 amino acids in length. Protein sequence analysis shows that there is about 25-35% similarity between LuxI homologues, with a small number of residues conserved in all sequences. This makes it difficult to identify LuxI homologous proteins on the basis of sequence homology. Two regions of the protein seem to be essential for enzyme function. The C terminal region has been proposed to play a role in acylated acyl carrier protein (ACP) selection whereas the N-terminal domain contains the active site of the enzyme (102).

Some LuxI homologues can produce more than one *N*-AHL molecule, suggesting that they can use more than one fatty acid type as a substrate. LuxI has been shown to produce C_6-HSL in addition to the primary product *N*-(3-oxo-hexanoyl)-L-homoserine lactone (C_6-oxo-HSL) (139). RhlI in *P. aeruginosa* PAO1 produces C_4-HSL and C_6-HSL (273). TraI of *A. tumefaciens* produces C_6-oxo-HSL and C_6-HSL in addition to C_8-oxo-HSL and PhzI in *P. chlororaphis* produces C_6-HSL, C_4-HSL, and C_8-HSL. Although minor products may not interfere with the function of the main compound, one should take into account the fact that there may be cross-talk if autoinducer molecules produced by one organism reach and have an activity in another. One should also consider the fact that sensitivity to the distinct signals differs from one organism to another. This is reflected in the concentrations needed to activate gene expression. The concentration of 3-oxo-C_{12}-HSL required for half-maximal induction of LasR was around 1 μM (192). In contrast, the concentration of 3-oxo-C_8-HSL that was required for half-maximal activation of the bioluminescence genes in *P. fisheri* was 50 nM (126).

Until recently, it was assumed that autoinducers diffuse between the cytoplasm and the environment. This was based upon initial data obtained using radiolabeled 3-oxo-C_6-HSL in *P. fisheri* and *E. coli* (126). Based on additional experimental data, active transport may be involved in the translocation of long-chain *N*-AHLs in *P. aeruginosa* (194). A *P. aeruginosa* PAO1 mutant lacking the MexAB-OprM efflux pump accumulated autoinducer to a higher internal level than the wild type. These multi-drug efflux pumps are known to cause efflux of certain hydrophobic compounds (184). *N*-AHL signaling systems using long-chained molecules may therefore be dependent upon the function of membrane efflux pumps and the proton-motive force needed to drive these pumps.

LuxR homologues have about 20-35% similarity with other members of the group. The C-terminal DNA-binding domain present in all LuxR homologues has a helix-turn-helix motif, and is accordingly classified as belonging to the larger LysR superfamily of transcriptional regulators (87; 107). The N-terminal domain is considered to contain the *N*-AHL binding domain (234; 245). Analysis of *E. coli* strains containing wild-type and mutant *luxR* alleles suggest that LuxR functions as a homomultimer, and a region of the LuxR protein is required for multimerization. Promoters that are thought to be binding sites for LuxR-type proteins show sequences with dyad symmetry, suggesting some LuxR-type proteins bind as dimers (43).

Immunoprecipitation using antibodies against LuxR indicate that LuxR is located in membranes and not in the soluble pool of cytoplasmic proteins (133). Since LuxR homologues do not have a characteristic alpha-helical transmembrane motif, if was suggested that LuxR is an amphipathic protein associated with the inner leaflet of the cytoplasmatic membrane, with the C-terminal domain extending into the cytoplasm (133).

A number of studies investigated the specificity of autoinducer molecules for LuxR using *N*-AHL analogues. In these studies the cognate autoinducer molecule was found to be the most active inducer of the reporter systems. Acyl chain length was an important factor determining activity, allowing deviation into a slightly shorter or longer acyl chain, albeit with a lower activity (218).

The operator region of the *luxICDABEFG* genes contains a specific 20 base pairs inverted repeat sequence. This sequence, commonly referred to as a *lux* box, positioned at –40 nucleotides relative to the start of the *luxI* gene, is a binding site for LuxR and is required for transcription of the operon (87; 227). Similar inverted repeat sequences have been found in promoters of genes regulated by the *tra*, *las* (87; 87) and *phz* systems (42), although the specific sequence of the repeat and the distance from the start of the genes regulated differ considerably. The *lux*-box-like element in the promoter of *phzA* in *P. aeruginosa* was shown to be involved quorum sensing-controlled transcription (272).

The ability to produce autoinducer molecules in *E. coli* suggests that substrates for *N*-AHL synthesis are available in *E. coli* or that at least part of its biosynthetic pathway is present, although no indigenously produced *N*-AHLs have been identified in *E. coli*. Nevertheless, *E. coli* and *Salmonella typhimurium* were shown to produce compounds with autoinducer activities similar to that of autoinducer AI-2 produced by *V. harveyi*, a compound not related to *N*-AHLs (241) (180). The genes identified to be involved in the production of these compounds bear no homology to the classical *luxI-luxLM-ainS*-like genes, further indicating that this class of autoinducers is different (242). LuxI homologues such as

LasI and TraI also confer the ability to produce the corresponding signal molecules in *E. coli*. Experimental evidence was provided that the homoserine lactone moiety of *N*-AHL is derived from *S*-adenosylmethionine (SAM) or directly from homoserine lactone pools (78; 101; 119). The variable acyl chains are thought to be the products of either fatty acid biosynthesis or degradation (30).

QUORUM SENSING IN THE RHIZOSPHERE

Phenazine antibiotics were detected in extracts of the wheat rhizosphere and soil material using high pressure liquid chromatography (HPLC) (249). The PCN biosynthetic genes of *P. chlororaphis* PCL1391 were shown to be expressed in the tomato rhizosphere using a luminescent reporter (39). Coinoculation of *P. aureofaciens* 30-84 which produces the C_6-HSL restored phenazine gene expression in a *phzI* mutant to wild-type levels in the rhizosphere (275). The population density signal is required for phenazine expression in situ and apparently, interpopulation signaling is also required in the rhizosphere for expression of the phenazine biosynthetic genes. Many bacteria on the root surface are present in micro-colonies forming a biofilm and these locations are likely to be the places where bacteria can reach high cell densities on the root and the signal can accumulate (40).

Since two or more bacterial species can utilize identical or the same class of signal molecules for interspecies communication, cross talk may occur between signaling systems. Micro-colonies on the root surface can indeed consist of more than one population or strain (18; 53). In mixed biofilms of *P. aeruginosa* and *Burkholderia cepacia* in the lungs of cystic fibrosis patients unidirectional *N*-AHL signaling between the two strains was detected using Gfp-based biosensors (210).

GLOBAL REGULATION OF SECONDARY METABOLITES AND QUORUM SENSING SYSTEMS

Most of the quorum sensing systems are not acting solely population dependent but are also regulated at higher levels. One particular quorum sensing module may be regulated by another quorum sensing system. Bacteria can possess multiple quorum sensing units in which one unit resides on top of one or more other modules and in this way regulate gene expression in a cascaded way. In *P. aeruginosa*, the *lasI-lasR* regulatory pair controls the expression of the *rhlI-rhlR*, also termed *vsmI-vsmR*, quorum sensing genes (142).

The control of gene expression at the transcriptional level appears to be the major mechanism for quorum sensing systems to modulate the production of secondary metabolites. Other regulators that regulate secondary metabolite gene expression are σ sigma factors such as the housekeeping factor σ^D, heat shock factor σ^H, and the stationary phase factor σ^S. The stationary phase factor σ^S or RpoS is involved in the regulation of expression of over 30 genes that function during, or in the transition to, stationary phase. RpoS affects many regulatory genes, some of which are also involved in the regulation of the production of secondary metabolites. RpoS was shown to affect production of pyoluteorin and 2,4-diacetylphloroglucinol and biological control activity of *P. fluorescens* strain Pf-5 (217). Amplification of the *rpoD* gene encoding the housekeeping sigma factor σ^{70} of *P. fluorescens* increased the production of pyoluteorin and 2,4-diacetylphloroglucinol in *P. fluorescens* strain CHA0 several-fold and consequently improved protection of cucumber against disease caused by *P. ultimum* (224).

Specific transcriptional activators and repressors may also regulate transcription. The *phlF* gene product in *P. fluorescens* CHA0 represses the transcription of the 2,4-diacetylphloroglucinol biosynthetic operon (57).

The GacS-GacA global regulatory system (106) regulates expression of 2,4-diacetylphloroglucinol, HCN, and pyoluteorin in *P. fluorescens* strain CHA0, and pyrrolnitrin, chitinase, 2-hexyl-5-propyl resorcinol, and HCN in strain BL915 (88; 144). Also in other organisms GacS-GacA are involved in the regulation of production of antifungal metabolites. In *P. aeruginosa*, GacA controls cyanogenesis via a transcriptional activation of the *rhiI* gene and, in addition, via a post-transcriptional mechanism involving a recognition site overlapping the ribosome binding of the *hcnA* gene (195).

For a number of secondary metabolites such a post-transcriptional level of regulation has been elucidated. The translation of HCN biosynthesis and protease genes appears to operate via a translational repressor protein RsmA/PrpA. RsmA and the homologous CsrA were found to bind to cognate regulatory RNA molecules; RsmB (previously AepH), a 259-nucleotide regulatory RNA in *E. carotovora* (155), and CsrB, a 350-nucleotide regulatory RNA identified in *E. coli* (154). It was proposed that binding to RsmB and CsrB antagonizes the regulatory activity of CsrA and RsmA, respectively. The expression of RsmA/PrpA is dependent on the GacS-GacA system.

The expression of PrrB, encoding a regulatory RNA is also dependent on the GacS/GacA system. It was postulated that this non-coding regulatory RNA PrrB sequesters an RsmA-like repressor protein similar to RsmB, which in turn appears to be positively regulated by the GacS-GacA system (1).

There is also experimental evidence that *rpoS* expression is regulated directly by both quorum sensing and *gacS-gacA* two component regulatory systems. RhlR appeared essential for activation of a *rpoS-lacZ* reporter in response to C_4-HSL in *E. coli* (141). Additionally, *N*-(3-oxododecanoyl)-L-homoserine lactone (3-oxo-C_{12}-HSL) triggered stationary phase phenomena such as repression of cell growth, and change in cell shape and size when added during exponential phase growth (277). Transcription of *rpoS* in biocontrol strain *P. fluorescens* Pf5, assessed with an *rpoS-lacZ* transcriptional fusion, was positively influenced by GacS and GacA during the transition between exponential growth and the stationary phase (271). Recently, the *psrA* (*Pseudomonas* sigma regulator) gene product of *P. putida* WCS358 was shown to induce *rpoS* expression (132). In a *psrA* mutant of strain PCL1391 the *phz* genes are overexpressed resulting in a tenfold increased PCN production. The expression of *psrA* appears to be dependent upon the presence of an intact *gacS* gene (Chin-A-Woeng *et al.* 2002, submitted).

ENVIRONMENTAL CONDITIONS REGULATING SECONDARY METABOLITE BIOSYNTHESIS

The synthesis of phenazine antibiotics appears to be highly dependent on the physiological status of the bacterium, which in turn is dependent upon growth and environmental conditions. For cells of *P. chlororaphis* strain PCL1391 grown in liquid cultures, the availability of certain carbon sources and amino acids, including major root exudates components, metal ions, and oxygen status affect phenazine production positively (37).

In quorum sensing systems such as in *P. fisheri*, factors known to affect *lux* gene expression include iron, oxygen concentration, and other responses to stress conditions. Expression of *luxR* apparently requires cAMP and the cAMP-receptor-protein (CRP), for which a binding site is present in the *lux* operator, indicating the involvement of catabolite repression (255). Similarly, Vfr, a CRP-homologue, regulates the expression of *lasR* (3).

The stringent response induced by the amino acid analogue serine hydroxamate also leads to premature production of 3-oxo-C_{12}-HSL independently of population density (256).

The *qscR* gene of *P. aeruginosa* PAO1 dictates the timing of quorum-sensing-controlled gene expression by repression of *lasI*. The gene is a homologue of LasR and RhlR and could serve to ensure that quorum sensing-controlled genes are not prematurely transcribed or activated in environments where they are not useful (44). The combination of signals such as relayed by the GacS sensor kinase allows integration of population density information with other environmental or cellular information and thereby enabling bacteria to fine-tune their activities in line with prevailing conditions.

Also the presence of certain nutrients or ions can affect expression of secondary metabolite genes. Production of 2,4-diacetylphloroglucinol and monoacetylphloroglucinol (MAPG) by *P. fluorescens* CHA0 appeared to be stimulated by Zn^{2+}, NH_4Mo^{2+}, and glucose in a strain-dependent manner (66). In *P. fluorescens* F113, production of DAPG and MAPG is increased by Fe^{3+} and sucrose (73). Inorganic phosphate reduced diacetylphloroglucinol production in strain CHA0 and other strains. In *P. fluorescens* strains producing pyoluteorin, the production was stimulated by Zn^{2+} and glycerol and repressed by glucose. Co^{2+}, fructose, mannitol, and glucose increased pyochelin production. Fructose, mannitol, and a mixture of Zn^{2+} and NH_4Mo^{2+} increased production of pyrrolnitrin (66). In addition, 2,4-diacetylphloroglucinol biosynthesis in strain CHA0 is autoregulated and repressed by salicylate and pyoluteorin (223). The fungal toxin fusaric acid is also an inhibitor of DAPG biosynthesis in *P. fluorescens* CHA0 (65; 223). Only fusaric acid-producing *F. oxysporum* strains are able to suppress DAPG biosynthesis and the concentration appears to be correlated with the degree of suppression of the biosynthetic operon (185).

Future perspectives

Biopesticides continue to be a promising alternative for the use of environmentally unfriendly chemical fertilizers and pesticides. A significant number of bacterial biocontrol products based on *Pseudomonas*, *Bacillus*, *Streptomyces*, and *Agrobacterium* species have already been marketed, but novel and better performing products are still needed. The use of transcriptomics and proteomics promises to greatly speed up the identification of novel genes, which are involved in the complex mechanisms of rhizosphere colonization and plant protection, including the regulation of genes for production of secondary metabolites. Identification of promoters that are specifically expressed in the rhizosphere will allow the engineering of biopesticides with enhanced performance.

References

1. Aarons S, Abbas A, Adams C, Fenton A, O'Gara F (2000) A regulatory RNA (PrrB RNA) modulates expression of secondary metabolite genes in *Pseudomonas fluorescens* F113. *J.Bacteriol.* 182:3913-3919
2. Alabouvette C (1986) Fusarium wilt suppressive soils from the Chateaurenard region: reviews of a 10 year study. *Agronomie* 6:273-284
3. Albus A M, Pesci E C, Runyenjanecky L J, West S E H, Iglewski B H (1997) Vfr controls quorum sensing in *Pseudomonas aeruginosa*. *J.Bacteriol.* 179:3928-3935.
4. Alström S (1991) Induction of disease resistance in common bean susceptible to halo blight bacterial pathogen after seed

bacterization with rhizosphere pseudomonads. *J.Gen.Appl.Microbiol.* 37:495-501

5. Anjaiah V, Koedam N, Nowak-Thompson B, Loper J E, Höfte M, Tambong J T, Cornelis P (1998) Involvement of phenazines and anthranilate in the antagonism of *Pseudomonas aeruginosa* PNA1 and Tn*5* derivatives toward *Fusarium* spp. and *Pythium* spp. *Mol.Plant-Microbe Interact.* 11:847-854
6. Arima K, Imanaka H, Kousaka M, Fukata A, Tamura G (1964) Pyrrolnitrin, a new antibiotic substance, produced by *Pseudomonas. Agr.Biol.Chem.* 28:575-576
7. Audenaert K, Pattery T, Cornelis P, Höfte M (2001) Mechanisms of *Pseudomonas aeruginosa*-induced pathogen resistance in plants. In: Chablain P, Cornelis P (eds) *Pseudomonas* 2001 Abstracts Book. Brussels, p. 36
8. Bahme J B, Schroth M N (1987) Spatial-temporal colonization patterns of a rhizobacterium on underground organs of potato. *Phytopathology* 77:1093-1100
9. Baker K F, Cook R J (1974) *Biological control of plant pathogens.* Am.Phytopathol.Soc., St. Paul, MN
10. Bakker P A H M, Lamers J G, Bakker A W, Marugg J D, Weisbeek P J (1986) The role of siderophores in potato tuber yield increase by *Pseudomonas putida* in a short rotation of potato. *Neth.J.Plant Pathol.* 92:249-256
11. Baron S S, Rowe J J (1981) Antibiotic action of pyocyanin. *Antimicrob.Agents.Chemother.* 20:814-820
12. Baron S S, Teranova G, Rowe J J (1997) Molecular mechanism of the antimicrobial action of pyocyanin. *Curr.Microbiol.* 18:223-230
13. Bashan Y (1998) Inoculants of plant growth-promoting bacteria for use in agriculture. *Biotechnol.Adv.* 16:729-770
14. Bassler B L (1999) How bacteria talk to each other: regulation of gene expression by quorum sensing. *Curr.Opin.Microbiol.* 2:582-587
15. Bell S C, Turner J M (1973) Iodinin biosynthesis by a pseudomonad. *Biochem.Soc.T.* 1:751-753
16. Birkofer L (1947) Chlororaphin, ein weiteres farbiges Stoff-wechselprodukt des *Bacillus pyocyaneus. Chem.Ber.* 80:212-214
17. Bloemberg G V, O'Toole G A, Lugtenberg B J J, Kolter R (1997) Green fluorescent protein as a marker for *Pseudomonas* spp. *Appl.Environ.Microbiol.* 63:4543-4551
18. Bloemberg G V, Wijfjes A H, Lamers G E, Stuurman N, Lugtenberg B J (2000) Simultaneous imaging of *Pseudomonas fluorescens* WCS365 populations expressing three different autofluorescent proteins in the rhizosphere: new perspectives for

studying microbial communities. *Mol.Plant-Microbe Interact.* 13:1170-1176

19. Bowen G D, Rovira A D (1976) Microbial colonization of plant roots. *Annu.Rev.Phytopathol.* 14:121-144
20. Brisbane P G, Janik L J, Tate M E, Warren R F O (1987) Revised structure for the phenazine antibiotic from *Pseudomonas fluorescens* 2-79 (NRRL B-15132). *Antimicrob.Agents.Chemother.* 31:1967-1971
21. Buell C R, Anderson A J (1993) Expression of the *aggA* locus of *Pseudomonas putida* in vitro and in planta as detected by the reporter gene, *xylE*. *Mol.Plant-Microbe Interact.* 6:331-340
22. Bull C T, Weller D M, Thomashow L S (1991) Relationship between root colonization and suppression of *Gaeumannomyces graminis* var. *tritici* by *Pseudomonas fluorescens* strain 2-79. *Phytopathology* 81:954-959
23. Burr T J, Schroth M N, Suslow T (1978) Increased potato yield on treatment of seed pieces with specific strains of *Pseudomonas fluorescens* and *P. putida*. *Phytopathology* 68:1377-1383
24. Buyer J S, Leong J (1986) Iron transport-mediated antagonism between plant growth-promoting and plant-deleterious *Pseudomonas* strains. *J.Biol.Chem.* 261:791-794
25. Buysens S J, Poppe J, Höfte M (1994) Role of siderophores in plant growth stimulation and antagonism by *Pseudomonas aeruginosa* 7NSK2. In: Ryder M H, Stephens P M, Bowen G D (eds) Improving Plant Productivity with Rhizobacteria. CSIRO Division of Soils, Adelaide, Australia, pp. 139-141
26. Byng G S, Turner J M (1976) Isolation of pigmentation of *Pseudomonas phenazinium*. *J.Gen.Microbiol.* 97:57-62
27. Byng G S, Turner J M (1977) Incorporation of [^{14}C]shikimate into phenazines and their further metabolism by *Pseudomonas phenazinium*. *Biochem.J.* 164:139-145
28. Calhoun D H, Carson M, Jensen R A (1972) The branch point metabolite for pyocyanin biosynthesis in *Pseudomonas aeruginosa*. *J.Gen.Microbiol.* 72:581-583
29. Camacho M M (2001) Molecular characterization of type 4 pili, NDHI and PyrR in rhizosphere colonization of *Pseudomonas fluorescens* WCS365. Universiteit Leiden, Leiden, The Netherlands
30. Cao J G, Meighen E A (1989) Biosynthesis and stereochemistry of the autoinducer controlling luminescence in *Vibrio harveyi*. *J.Bacteriol.* 175:3856-3862
31. Caroll H, Moënne-Loccoz Y, Dowling D, O'Gara F (1995) Mutational disruption of the biosynthesis genes coding for the antifungal metabolite 2,4-diacetylphloroglucinol does not influence the ecological fitness of *Pseudomonas fluorescens* F113

in the rhizosphere of sugar beets. *Appl.Environ.Microbiol.* 61:3002-3007

32. Chan P F, Bainton N J, Daykin M M, Winson M K, Chhabra S R, Stewart G S A B, Salmond G P C, Bycroft B W, Williams P (1995) Molecule mediated autoinduction of antibiotic biosynthesis in the plant pathogen *Erwinia carotovora*. *Biochem.Soc.T.* 23:127.
33. Chang P C, Blackwood A C (1969) Simultaneous production of three phenazine pigments by *Pseudomonas aeruginosa* Mac 436. *Can.J.Microbiol.* 15:439-444
34. Chatterjee A, Cui Y, Liu Y, Dumenyo C K, Chatterjee A K (1995) Inactivation of *rsmA* leads to overproduction of extracellular pectinases, cellulases, and proteases in *Erwinia carotovora* subsp. *carotovora* in the absence of the starvation/cell density-sensing signal, *N*-(3-oxohexanoyl)-L-homoserine lactone. *Appl.Environ.Microbiol.* 61:1959-1967
35. Chen W, Hoitink H A J, Schmitthenner A F, Tuovinen O H (1987) Factors affecting suppression of *Pythium* damping-off in container media amended with composts. *Phytopathology* 77:755-760
36. Chiang S L, Mekalanos J J (1998) Use of signature-tagged transposon mutagenesis to identify *Vibrio cholerae* genes critical for colonization. *Mol.Microbiol.* 27:797-805
37. Chin-A-Woeng T F C (2000) Molecular basis of biocontrol of tomato foot and root rot by *Pseudomonas chlororaphis* strain PCL1391. Universiteit Leiden, Leiden, The Netherlands
38. Chin-A-Woeng T F C, Bloemberg G V, Mulders I H M, Dekkers L C, Lugtenberg B J J (2000) Root colonization by phenazine-1-carboxamide-producing bacterium *Pseudomonas chlororaphis* PCL1391 is essential for biocontrol of tomato foot and root rot. *Mol.Plant-Microbe Interact.* 13:1340-1345
39. Chin-A-Woeng T F C, Bloemberg G V, van der Bij A J, van der Drift K M G M, Schripsema J, Kroon B, Scheffer R J, Keel C, Bakker P A H M, Tichy H V, de Bruijn F J, Thomas-Oates J E, Lugtenberg B J J (1998) Biocontrol by phenazine-1-carboxamide-producing *Pseudomonas chlororaphis* PCL1391 of tomato root rot caused by *Fusarium oxysporum* f. sp. *radicis-lycopersici*. *Mol.Plant-Microbe Interact.* 11:1069-1077
40. Chin-A-Woeng T F C, de Priester W, van der Bij A J, Lugtenberg B J J (1997) Description of the colonization of a gnotobiotic tomato rhizosphere by *Pseudomonas fluorescens* biocontrol strain WCS365, using scanning electron microscopy. *Mol.Plant-Microbe Interact.* 10:79-86.
41. Chin-A-Woeng T F C, Thomas-Oates J E, Lugtenberg B J J, Bloemberg G V (2001) Introduction of the *phzH* gene of

Pseudomonas chlororaphis PCL1391 extends the range of biocontrol ability of phenazine-1-carboxylic acid-producing *Pseudomonas* spp. strains. *Mol.Plant-Microbe Interact.* 14:1006-1015

42. Chin-A-Woeng T F C, van den Broek D, de Voer G, van der Drift K M G M, Tuinman S, Thomas-Oates J E, Lugtenberg B J J (2001) Phenazine-1-carboxamide production in the biocontrol strain *Pseudomonas chlororaphis* PCL1391 is regulated by multiple factors secreted into the growth medium. *Mol.Plant-Microbe Interact.* 14:969-979
43. Choi S H, Greenberg E P (1992) Genetic dissection of DNA binding and luminescence gene activation by the *Vibrio fisheri* LuxR protein. *J.Bacteriol.* 174:4064-4069
44. Chugani S A, Whiteley M, Lee K M, D'Argenio D, Manoil C, Greenberg E P (2001) QscR, a modulator of quorum-sensing signal synthesis and virulence in *Pseudomonas aeruginosa. Proc.Natl.Acad.Sci.U.S.A* 98:2752-2757
45. Clarholm M (1984) Heterothrophic, free-living protozoa: neglected microorganisms with an important task in regulating bacterial populations. In: Klug, Reddy (eds) Current Perspectives in Microbial Ecology., pp. 321-326
46. Cook D M, Li P L, Ruchaud R, Padden S, Farrand S K (1997) Ti plasmid conjugation is independent of *vir*: Reconstitution of the *tra* functions from pTi58 as a binary system. *J.Bacteriol.* 179:1291-1297
47. Cook R J, Bruckart W L, Coulson J R, Goettel M S, Humber R A, Lumsden R D, Maddox J V, McManus M L, Moore L, Meyer S F, Quimbly Jr. P C, Stack J P, Vaughan J L (1996) Safety of microorganisms intended for pest and plant disease control: A framework for scientific evaluation. *Biocontrol* 7:333-351
48. Cook R J, Thomashow L S, Weller D M, Fujimoto D, Mazzola M, Bangera G, Kim D (1995) Molecular mechanisms of defense by rhizobacteria against root disease. *Proc.Natl.Acad.Sci.U.S.A.* 92:4197-4201
49. Davies D G, Parsek M R, Pearson J P, Iglewski B H, Costerton J W, Greenberg E P (1998) The involvement of cell-to-cell signals in the development of a bacterial biofilm. *Science* 280:295-298
50. de Weger L A, Bakker P A H M, Schippers B, van Loosdrecht M C M, Lugtenberg B J J (1989) *Pseudomonas* spp. with mutational changes in the O-antigenic side chain of their lipopolysaccharide are affected in their ability to colonize potato roots. In: Lugtenberg B J J (ed) Signal Molecules in Plants and Plant-Microbe Interactions. NATO ASI Series H, pp. 197-202

51. Dekkers L C (1997) Isolation and characterization of novel rhizosphere colonization mutants of *Pseudomonas fluorescens* WCS365. Leiden University, Leiden, The Netherlands

52. Dekkers L C, Bloemendaal C P, de Weger L A, Wijffelman C A, Spaink H P, Lugtenberg B J J (1998) A two-component system plays an important role in the root-colonizing ability of *Pseudomonas fluorescens* strain WCS365. *Mol.Plant-Microbe Interact.* 11:45-56

53. Dekkers L C, Mulders I H, Phoelich C C, Chin A W T, Wijfjes A H, Lugtenberg B J (2000) The *sss* colonization gene of the tomato-*Fusarium oxysporum* f. sp. *radicis-lycopersici* biocontrol strain *Pseudomonas fluorescens* WCS365 can improve root colonization of other wild-type *Pseudomonas* spp. bacteria. *Mol.Plant-Microbe Interact.* 13:1177-1183

54. Dekkers L C, Phoelich C C, van der Fits L, Lugtenberg B J J (1998) A site-specific recombinase is required for competitive root colonization by *Pseudomonas fluorescens* WCS365. *Proc.Natl.Acad.Sci.U.S.A.* 95:7051-7056

55. Dekkers L C, van der Bij A J, Mulders I H M, Phoelich C C, Wentwood R A R, Glandorf D C M, Wijffelman C A, Lugtenberg B J J (1998) Role of the O-antigen of lipopolysaccharide, and possible roles of growth rate and of NADH: Ubiquinone oxidoreductase (*nuo*) in competitive tomato root-tip colonization by *Pseudomonas fluorescens* WCS365. *Mol.Plant-Microbe Interact.* 11:763-771

56. Delaney S M, Mavrodi D V, Bonsall R F, Thomashow L S (2001) *phzO*, a gene for biosynthesis of 2-hydroxylated phenazine compounds in *Pseudomonas aureofaciens* 30-84. *J.Bacteriol.* 183:318-327

57. Delany I, Sheehan M M, Fenton A, Bardin S, Aarons S, O' Gara F (2000) Regulation of production of the antifungal metabolite 2,4-diacetylphloroglucinol in *Pseudomonas fluorescens* F113: genetic analysis of *phlF* as a transcriptional repressor. *Microbiology Uk* 146 Part 2:537-546

58. DeMot R, Veulemans B, Vanderleyden J (1991) Root-adhesive protein of *Pseudomonas fluorescens* OE28-3. In: Keel C, Knoller B, Défago G (eds) Plant Growth-Promoting Rhizobacteria. Progress and Prospect. International Organization for Biological and Integrated Control of Noxious Animals and Plants

59. Devine J H, Shadel G S (2000) Assay of autoinducer activity with luminescent *Escherichia coli* sensor strains harboring a modified *Vibrio fischeri lux* regulon. *Methods Enzymol.* 305:279-287

60. Défago G, Berling C H, Burger U, Haas D, Kahr G, Keel C, Voisard C, Wirthner P, Wüthrich B (1990) Suppression of black rot of tobacco and other diseases by strains of *Pseudomonas*

fluorescens. Potential applications and mechanisms. In: Hornby D, Cook R J, Henis Y, Ko W H, Schippers B, Scott P R (eds) Biological Control of Soil Borne Pathogens. CAB International, Wallingford, UK, pp. 93-108

61. Di Pietro A, Lorito M, Hayes C K, Broadway R M, Harman G E (1993) Endochitinase from *Gliocladium virens*: isolation, characterisation and synergistic antifungal activity in combination with gliotoxin. *Phytopathology* 83:308-312
62. Dong X (1998) SA, JA, ethylene and disease resistance. *Curr.Opin.Plant Biol.* 1:316-323
63. Dowling D N, O'Gara F (1994) Metabolites of *Pseudomonas* involved in the biocontrol of plant disease. *TIBTECH* 12:133-141
64. Drake D, Montie T C (1988) Flagella, motility and invasive virulence of *Pseudomonas aeruginosa*. *J.Gen.Microbiol.* 134:43-52
65. Duffy B K, Defago G (1997) Zinc improves biocontrol of *Fusarium* crown and root rot of tomato by *Pseudomonas fluorescens* and represses the production of pathogen metabolites inhibitory to bacterial antibiotic biosynthesis. *Phytopathology* 87:1250-1257
66. Duffy B K, Defago G (1999) Environmental factors modulating antibiotic and siderophore biosynthesis by *Pseudomonas fluorescens* biocontrol strains. *Appl.Environ.Microbiol.* 65:2429-2438
67. Duffy B K, Simon A, Weller D M (1996) Combination of *Trichoderma koningii* with fluorescent pseudomonads for control of take-all on wheat. *Phytopathology* 86:188-194
68. Duijff B J, Meijer J W, Bakker P A H M, Schippers B (1983) Siderophore-mediated competition for iron and induced systemic resistance of *Fusarium* wilt of carnation by fluorescent *Pseudomonas* spp. *Neth.J.Plant Pathol.* 99:277-289
69. Dunlap C, Crowley J J, Moënne-Loccoz Y, Dowling D N, de Bruijn F J, O'Gara F (1997) Biological control of *Pythium ultimum* by *Stenotrophomonas maltophilia* W81 is mediated by an extracellular proteolytic activity. *Microbiology* 143:3921-3931
70. Dunlap C, Delaney I, Fenton A, Lohrke S, Moënne-Loccoz Y, O'Gara F (1996) The biotechnology and application of *Pseudomonas* inoculants for the biocontrol of phytopathogens. In: Stacey G, Mullin B, Gresshoff P M (eds) Biology of Plant Microbe Interactions. International Society for Molecular Plant-Microbe Interactions, St. Paul, MN, pp. 441-448
71. Dunlap P V (1999) Quorum regulation of luminescence in *Vibrio fischeri*. *J.Mol.Microbiol.Biotechnol.* 1:5-12
72. Dunne C, Delaney I, Fenton A, Lohrke S, Moënne-Loccoz Y, O'Gara F (1996) The biotechnology and application of

Pseudomonas inoculants for the biocontrol of phytopathogens. In: Stacey G, Mullin B, Gresshoff P M (eds) Biology of Plant-Microbe Interactions. International Society for Molecular Plant-Microbe Interactions , St. Paul, MN, pp. 441-448

73. Dunne C, Delany I, Fenton A, O'Gara F (1996) Mechanisms involved in biocontrol by microbial inoculants. *Agronomie* 16:721-729
74. Dunne C, Moenne L Y, McCarthy J, Higgins P, Powell J, Dowling D, O'Gara F (1998) Combining proteolytic and phloroglucinol-producing bacteria for improved biocontrol of *Pythium*-mediated damping off of sugar beet. *Plant Pathol.* 47:299-307
75. Dunny G M, Leonard B A (1997) Cell-cell communication in gram-positive bacteria. *Annu.Rev.Microbiol.* 51:527-64:527-564
76. Eberhard A (1972) Inhibition and activation of bacterial luciferase synthesis. *J.Bacteriol.* 109:1101-1105
77. Eberhard A, Burlingame A L, Eberhard C, Kenyon G L, Nealson K H, Oppenheimer N J (1981) Structural identification of autoinducer of *Photobacterium fisheri* luciferase. *Biochemistry* 20:2444-2449
78. Eberhard A T, Longin T, Widrig C A, Stranick S J (1991) Synthesis of the *lux* gene autoinducer in *Vibrio fischeri* is positively autoregulated. *Arch.Microbiol.* 155:294-297
79. Eberl L, Winson M K, Sternberg C, Stewart G B, Christiansen G, Chhabra S R, Bycroft B, Williams P, Molin S, Givskov M (1996) Involvement of *N*-acyl-L-homoserine lactone autoinducers in controlling the multicellular behaviour of *Serratia liquefaciens*. *Mol.Microbiol.* 20:127-136
80. Emmert E A B, Handelsman J (1999) Biocontrol of plant disease: a (Gram-) positive perspective. *FEMS Microbiol.Lett.* 171:1-9
81. Fenton A, Stephens P M, Crowley J J, O'Callaghan M, O'Gara F (1992) Exploitation of gene(s) involved in 2,4-diacetylphloroglucinol biosynthesis to confer a new biocontrol capability to a *Pseudomonas* strain. *Appl.Environ.Microbiol.* 58:3873-3878
82. Fernando W G D, Watson A K, Paulitz T C (1996) The role of *Pseudomonas* spp and competition for carbon, nitrogen and iron in the enhancement of appressorium formation by *Colletotrichum coccodes* on velvetleaf. *Eur.J.Plant Pathol.* 102:1-7
83. Flaishman M, Eyal Z, Voisard C, Haas D (1990) Suppression of *Septoria tritici* by phenazine- or siderophore-deficient mutants of *Pseudomonas*. *Curr.Microbiol.* 20:121-124
84. Fordos J (1860). *Recueil des Travaux de la Societé d'Emulation pour les Sciences Pharmaceutiques* 3:30

85. Fravel D R (1988) Role of antibiosis in the biocontrol of plant diseases. *Annu.Rev.Phytopathol.* 26:75-91

86. Fuqua C, Winans S C, Greenberg E P (1996) Census and consensus in bacterial ecosystems: the LuxR-LuxI family of quorum sensing transcriptional regulators. *Annu.Rev.Microbiol.* 50 :727-751.:727-751.

87. Fuqua W C, Winans S C, Greenberg E P (1994) Quorum sensing in bacteria: the LuxR-LuxI family of cell density-responsive transcriptional regulators. *J.Bacteriol.* 176:269-275

88. Gaffney T D, Lam S T, Ligon J, Gates K, Frazelle A, Di Maio J, Hill S, Goodwin S, Torkewitz N, Allshouse A M, Kempf H-J, Becker J O (1994) Global regulation of expression of antifungal factors by a *Pseudomonas fluorescens* biological control strain. *Mol.Plant-Microbe Interact.* 7:455-463

89. Geels F P, Schippers B (1983) Reduction in yield depressions in high frequency potato cropping soil after seed tuber treatments with antagonistic fluorescent *Pseudomonas* spp. *Phytopath Z.* 108:207-214

90. Gerrits J P L, Weisbeek P J (1996) Induction of systemic acquired resistance by saprophytic *Pseudomonas* spp. in the model plant *Arabidopsis thaliana*. NWO-LNV Priority Progr. Crop Prot. Prog. Rep.Lunteren, The Netherlands. NWO, The Hague, pp. 13-14

91. Glandorf D C M, Sluis I, Anderson A J, Bakker P A H M, Schippers B (1994) Agglutination, adherence, and root colonization by fluorescent pseudomonads. *Appl.Environ.Microbiol.* 60:1726-1733

92. Gray K M, Pearson J P, Downie J A, Boboye B E A, Greenberg E P (1996) Cell to cell signaling in the symbiotic nitrogen fixing bacterium *Rhizobium leguminosarum*: autoinduction of a stationary phase and rhizosphere expressed genes. *J.Bacteriol.* 178:372-376.

93. Gross R, Arico B, Rappuoli R (1989) Families of bacterial signal-transducing proteins. *Mol.Microbiol.* 3:1661-1667

94. Gutterson N (1990) Microbial fungicides: recent approaches to elucidating mechanisms. *Crit.Rev.Biotechnol.* 10:69-91

95. Haas D, Keel C, Laville J, Maurhofer M, Oberhänsli T, Schnider U, Voisard C, Wuthrich B, Defago G (1991) Secondary metabolites of *Pseudomonas fluorescens* strain CHA0 involved in the suppression of root diseases. In: Hennecke H, Verma P S (eds) Advances in molecular genetics of plant-microbe interactions. Kluwer Academic Publishers, Dordrecht, The Netherlands, pp. 450-456

96. Habte M, Alexander M (1977) Further evidence for the regulation of bacterial populations in soil by protozoa. *Arch.Microbiol.* 113:181-183

97. Hammer P E, Hill D S, Lam S T, Van-Pee K H, Ligon J M (1997) Four genes from *Pseudomonas fluorescens* that encode the biosynthesis of pyrrolnitrin. *Appl.Environ.Microbiol.* 63:2147-2154

98. Handelsman J, Raffel S J, Mester E H, Wunderlich L, Grau C R (1999) Biological control of damping-off of alfalfa seedlings with *Bacillus cereus* UW85. *Appl.Environ.Microbiol.* 56:713-718

99. Handelsman J, Stabb E V (1996) Biocontrol of soilborne plant pathogens. *Plant Cell* 8:1855-1869.

100. Hanzelka B L, Greenberg E P (1995) Evidence that the N-terminal region of the *Vibrio fischeri* LuxR protein consitutes an autoinducer-binding domain. *J.Bacteriol.* 177:815-817

101. Hanzelka B L, Greenberg E P (1996) Quorum sensing in *Vibrio fischeri*: evidence that *S*-adenosylmethionine is the amino acid substrate for autoinducer synthesis. *J.Bacteriol.* 178:5291-5294.

102. Hanzelka B L, Stevens A M, Parsek M R, Crone T J, Greenberg E P (1997) Mutational analysis of the *Vibrio fischeri luxI* polypeptide: Critical regions of an autoinducer synthase. *J.Bacteriol.* 179:4882-4887

103. Hassett D J, Charniga L, Bean K, Ohman D E, Cohen M S (1992) Response of *Pseudomonas aeruginosa* to pyocyanin: mechanisms of resistance, antioxidant defenses, and demonstration of a manganese- cofactored superoxide dismutase. *Infect.Immun.* 60:328-336

104. Hassett D J, Schweizer H P, Ohman D E (1995) *Pseudomonas aeruginosa sodA* and *sodB* mutants defective in manganese- and iron-cofactored superoxide dismutase activity demonstrate the importance of the iron-cofactored form in aerobic metabolism. *J.Bacteriol.* 177:6330-6337

105. Hawes M C, Brigham L A, Wen F, Woo H H, Zhu Z (1998) Function of root border cells in plant health: Pioneers in the rhizosphere. *Annu.Rev.Phytopathol.* 36:311-327

106. Heeb S, Haas D (2001) Regulatory roles of the GacS/GacA two-component system in plant-associated and other gram-negative bacteria. *Mol.Plant-Microbe Interact.* 14:1351-1363

107. Henikoff S, Haughn G W, Calvo J M, Wallace J C (1988) A large family of bacterial activator proteins. *Proc.Natl.Acad.Sci.U.S.A.* 85:6602-6606

108. Hill D S, Stein J I, Torkewitz N R, Morse A M, Howell C R, Pachlatko J P, Becker J O, Ligon J M (1994) Cloning of genes involved in the synthesis of pyrrolnitrin from *Pseudomonas fluorescens* and role of pyrrolnitrin synthesis in biological control of plant disease. *Appl.Environ.Microbiol.* 60:78-85

109. Hoffland E, Pieterse C M J, Bik L, van Pelt J A (1995) Induced systemic resistance in radish is not associated with accumulation

of pathogenesis-related proteins. *Physiol.Mol.Plant Pathol.* 46:309-320
110. Hoitink H A J, Fahy P C (1986) Basis for the control of soilborne plant pathogens with composts. *Annu.Rev.Phytopathol.* 24:93-114
111. Hollstein U, McCamey D A (1973) Biosynthesis of phenazines. II. Incorporation of [6-^{14}C]-D-shikimic acid into phenazine-1-carboxylic acid and iodinin. *J.Org.Chem.* 38:3417
112. Homma Y (1994) Mechanisms in biological control - focussed on the antibiotic pyrrolnitrin. In: Ryder M H, Stephens P M, Bowen G D (eds) Improving plant productivity with rhizobacteria. CSIRO Division of Soils, Adelaide, Australia, pp. 100-103
113. Horinouchi S, Beppu T (1994) A-factor as a microbial hormone that controls cellular differentiation and secondary metabolism in *Streptomyces griseus*. *Mol.Microbiol.* 12:859-864
114. Howell C R, Beier R C, Stipanovic R D (1988) Production of ammonia by *Enterobacter cloacae* and its role in the biological control of *Pythium* preemergence damping-off by the bacterium. *Phytopathology* 78:1075-1078
115. Howell C R, Stipanovic R D (1979) Control of *Rhizoctonia solani* on cotton seedlings with *Pseudomonas fluorescens* and with an antibiotic produced by the bacterium. *Phytopathology* 69:480-482
116. Howell C R, Stipanovic R D (1980) Suppression of *Pythium ultimum*-induced damping-off of cotton seedlings by *Pseudomonas fluorescens* and its antibiotic, pyoluteorin. *Phytopathology* 70:712-715
117. Howie W J, Suslow T (1991) Role of antibiotic synthesis in the inhibition of *Pythium ultimum* in the cotton spermosphere and rhizosphere by *Pseudomonas fluorescens*. *Mol.Plant-Microbe Interact.* 4:393-399
118. Huang S S, Djordjevic M A, Rolfe B G (1993) Microscopic analysis of the effect of *Rhizobium leguminosarum* biovar *trifolii* host specific nodulation genes in the infection of white clovers. *Protoplasma* 172:180-190
119. Huisman G W, Kolter R (1994) Sensing starvation: a homoserine lactone-dependent signalling pathway in *Escherichia coli*. *Science* 265:537-539
120. Hunt M D, Neuenschwander U H, Delaney T P, Weymann K B, Friedrich L B, Lawton K A, Steiner H Y, Ryals J A (1996) Recent advances in systemic acquired resistance - a review. *Gene* 7:89-95
121. Ingledew W M, Campbell J J R (1969) Evaluation of shikimic acid as a precursor of pyocyanin. *Can.J.Microbiol.* 15:535-541
122. Janisiewicz W J, Roitman J (1988) Biological control of blue mold and grey mold on apple and pear with *Pseudomonas cepacia*. *Phytopathology* 78:1697-1700

123. Ji G Y, Beavis R C, Novick R P (1995) Cell density control of a staphylococcal virulence mediated by an octapeptide pheromone. *Proc.Natl.Acad.Sci.U.S.A.* 92:12055-12059

124. Jijakli M H, Lepoivre P (1998) Characterization of an exo-beta-1,3-glucanase produced by *Pichia anomala* strain K, antagonist of *Botrytis cinerea* on apples. *Phytopathology* 88:335-343

125. Kang Y, Carlson R, Tharpe W, Schell M A (1998) Characterization of genes involved in biosynthesis of a novel antibiotic from *Burkholderia cepacia* BC11 and their role in biological control of *Rhizoctonia solani*. *Appl.Environ.Microbiol.* 64:3939-3947

126. Kaplan H B, Greenberg E P (1985) Diffusion of autoinducer is involved in regulation of the *Vibrio fischeri* luminescence system. *J.Bacteriol.* 163:1210-1214

127. Keel C, Schnider U, Maurhofer M, Voisard C, Laville J, Burger U, Wirthner P, Haas D, Défago G (1992) Suppression of root diseases by *Pseudomonas fluorescens* CHA0: importance of the bacterial secondary metabolite 2,4-diacetylphloroglucinol. *Mol.Plant-Microbe Interact.* 5:4-13

128. Keel C, Wirthner P, Oberhänsli T, Voisard C, Haas D, Défago G (1990) Pseudomonads as antagonists of plant pathogens in the rhizosphere: role of the antibiotic 2,4-diacetylphloroglucinol in the suppression of black root of tobacco. *Symbiosis* 9:327-341

129. Kloepper J W (1980) Enhanced plant growth by siderophores produced by plant growth-promoting rhizobacteria. *Nature* 286:885-886

130. Kluyver A J (1956) *Pseudomonas aureofaciens* nov. spec. and its pigments. *J.Bacteriol.* 72:406-411

131. Knudsen I M B, Hockenhull J, Jensen D F, Gerhardson B, Hokeberg M, Tahvonen R, Teperi E, Sundheim L, Henriksen B (1997) Selection of biological control agents for controlling soil and seed-borne diseases in the field. *Eur.J.Plant Pathol.* 103:775-784

132. Kojic M, Venturi V (2001) Regulation of *rpoS* gene expression in *Pseudomonas*: involvement of a TetR family regulator. *J.Bacteriol.* 183:3712-3720

133. Kolibachuk D, Greenberg E P (1993) The *Vibrio fisheri* luminescence gene activator LuxR is a membrane-associated protein. *J.Bacteriol.* 175:7307-7312

134. Koster M, Ovaa W, Bitter W, Weisbeek P (1995) Multiple outer membrane receptors for uptake of ferric pseudobactins in *Pseudomonas putida* WCS385. *Mol.Gen.Genet.* 248.735-743

135. Koster M, van de Vossenberg J, Leong J, Weisbeek P J (1993) Identification and characterization of the *pupB* gene encoding an

inducible ferric-pseudobactin receptor of *Pseudomonas putida* WCS358. *Mol.Microbiol.* 8:591-601

136. Kraus J, Loper J E (1995) Characterization of a genomic region required for production of the antibiotic pyoluteorin by the biological control agent *Pseudomonas fluorescens* Pf-5. *Appl.Environ.Microbiol.* 61:849-854

137. Kuiper I, Bloemberg G V, Lugtenberg B J (2001) Selection of a plant-bacterium pair as a novel tool for rhizostimulation of polycyclic aromatic hydrocarbon-degrading bacteria. *Mol.Plant-Microbe Interact.* 14:1197-1205

138. Kuiper I, Bloemberg G V, Noreen S, Thomas-Oates J E, Lugtenberg B J J (2001) Increased uptake of putrescine in the rhizosphere inhibits competitive root colonization by *Pseudomonas fluorescens* strain WCS365. *Mol.Plant-Microbe Interact.* 14:1096-1104

139. Kuo A, Blough N V, Dunlap P V (1994) Multiple *N*-acyl-L-homoserine lactone autoinducers of luminescence in the marine symbiotic bacterium *Vibrio fischeri*. *J.Bacteriol.* 176:7558-7565.

140. Lagopodi A L, Ram A F J, Lamers G E M, Punt P J, van den Hondel C A M J J, Lugtenberg B J J, Bloemberg G V (2002) Novel aspects of tomato root colonization and infection by *Fusarium oxysporum* f. sp. *radicis-lycopersici* revealed by confocal laser scanning microscopic analysis using the green fluorescent protein as a marker. *Mol.Plant-Microbe Interact.* 15:172-179

141. Latifi A, Foglino M, Tanaka K, Williams P, Lazdunski A (1996) A hierarchical quorum sensing cascade in *Pseudomonas aeruginosa* links the transcriptional activators LasR and RhiR (VsmR) to expression of the stationary-phase sigma factor RpoS. *Mol.Microbiol.* 21:1137-1146.

142. Latifi A, Winson M K, Foglino M, Bycroft B W, Stewart G S A B, Lazdunski A, Williams P (1995) Multiple homologues of LuxR and LuxI control expression of virulence determinants and secondary metabolites through quorum sensing in *Pseudomonas aeruginosa* PAO1. *Mol.Microbiol.* 17:333-343

143. Laville J, Blumer C, von Schroetter C, Gaia V, Defago G, Keel C, Haas D (1998) Characterization of the *hcnABC* gene cluster encoding hydrogen cyanide and anaerobic regulation by ANR in the strictly aerobic biocontrol agent *Pseudomonas fluorescens* CHA0. *J.Bacteriol.* 180:3187-3196

144. Laville J, Voisard C, Keel C, Maurhofer M, Défago G, Haas D (1992) Global control in *Pseudomonas fluorescens* mediating antibiotic synthesis and suppression of black root rot of tobacco. *Proc.Natl.Acad.Sci.U.S.A.* 89:1562-1566

145. Leeman M, van Pelt J A, Denouden F M, Heinsbroek M, Bakker P A H M, Schippers B (1995) Induction of systemic resistance against *Fusarium* wilt of radish by lipopolysaccharides of *Pseudomonas fluorescens*. *Phytopathology* 85:1021-1027

146. Leeman M, van Pelt J A, Denouden F M, Heinsbroek M, Bakker P A H M, Schippers B (1995) Induction of systemic resistance by *Pseudomonas fluorescens* in radish cultivars differing in susceptibility to fusarium wilt, using a novel bioassay. *Eur.J.Plant Pathol.* 101:655-664

147. Leisinger T, Margraff R (1979) Secondary metabolites of the fluorescent pseudomonads. *Microbiol.Rev.* 43:422-442

148. Lemanceau P, Alabouvette C (1993) Suppression of fusarium wilts by fluorescent pseudomonads: mechanisms and applications. *Biocontrol Sci. Technol.* 3:219-234

149. Lemanceau P, Bakker P A H M, Kogel W J, Alabouvette C, Schippers B (1992) Effect of pseudobactin 358 production by *Pseudomonas putida* WCS358 on suppression of fusarium wilt of carnations by nonpathogenic *Fusarium oxysporum* Fo47. *Appl.Environ.Microbiol.* 58:2978-2982

150. Leong J (1986) Siderophores: their biochemistry and possible role in the biocontrol of plant pathogens. *Annu.Rev.Phytopathol.* 24:187-209

151. Lindow S E (1983) Methods of preventing frost injury caused by epiphytic ice-nucleation-active bacteria. *Plant Dis.* 67:327-333

152. Lindow S E (1983) The role of bacterial ice nucleation in frost injury to plants. *Annu.Rev.Phytopathol.* 21:363-384

153. Lindow S E, Arny D C, Upper C D (1983) Biological control of frost injury: an isolate of *Erwinia herbicola* antagonistic to ice nucleation active bacteria. *Phytopathology* 73:1097-1102

154. Liu M Y, Gui G, Wei B, Preston J F, III, Oakford L, Yuksel U, Giedroc D P, Romeo T (1997) The RNA molecule CsrB binds to the global regulatory protein CsrA and antagonizes its activity in *Escherichia coli*. *J.Biol.Chem.* 272:17502-17510

155. Liu Y, Murata H, Chatterjee A, Chatterjee A K (1993) Characterization of a novel regulatory gene *aepA* that controls extracellular enzyme production in the phytopathogenic bacterium *Erwinia carotovora* subsp. *carotovora*. *Mol.Plant-Microbe Interact.* 6:299-308

156. Longley R P, Halliwell J E, Campbell J J R, Ingledew W M (1972) The branch point of pyocyanin biosynthesis. *Can.J.Microbiol.* 18:1357-1368

157. Loper J E (1988) Role of fluorescent siderophore production in biological control of *Pythium ultimum* by a *Pseudomonas fluorescens* strain. *Phytopathology* 78:166-172

158. Loper J E, Buyer J S (1991) Siderophores in microbial interactions on plant surfaces. *Mol.Plant-Microbe Interact.* 4:5-13
159. Loper J E, Haack C, Schroth M N (1985) Population dynamics of soil pseudomonads in rhizosphere of potato (*Solanum tuberosum* L.). *Appl.Environ.Microbiol.* 49:416-422
160. Lorito M, Peterbauer C, Hayes C K, Harman G E (1994) Synergistic interaction between fungal cell wall degrading enzymes and different antifungal compounds enhances inhibition of spore germination. *Microbiology* 140:623-629
161. Lugtenberg B J J, de Weger L A, Bennett J W (1991) Microbial stimulation of plant growth and protection from disease. *Curr.Opin.Biotechnol.* 2:457-464
162. Lugtenberg B J J, de Weger L A, Schippers B (1994) Bacterization to protect seed and rhizosphere against disease. *BCPC Monograph* 57:293-302
163. Lugtenberg B J J, Dekkers L C (1999) What makes *Pseudomonas* bacteria rhizosphere competent? *Environ.Microbiol.* 1:9-13
164. Lugtenberg B J J, Dekkers L C, Bansraj M, Bloemberg G V, Camacho M, Chin-A-Woeng T F C, van den Hondel C, Kravchenko L, Kuiper I, Lagopodi A L, Mulders I, Phoelich C, Ram A, Tikhonovich I, Tuinman S, Wijffelman C, Wijfjes A (1999) *Pseudomonas* genes and traits involved in tomato root colonization. In: de Wit P J G M, Bisseling T, Stiekema W J (eds) 1999 IC-MPMI Congress Proceedings: Biology of Plant-Microbe Interactions, volume 2. International Society for Molecular Plant-Microbe Interactions, St. Paul, MN, pp. 324-330
165. Lugtenberg B J J, Dekkers L C, Bloemberg G V (2001) Molecular determinants of rhizosphere colonization by *Pseudomonas*. *Annu.Rev.Phytopathol.* 39:461-490
166. Lugtenberg B J J, Kravchenko L V, Simons M (1999) Tomato seed and root exudate sugars: composition, utilization by *Pseudomonas* biocontrol strains and role in rhizosphere colonization. *Environ.Microbiol.* 1:439-446
167. Mahajan M S, Tan M W, Rahme L G, Ausubel F M (1999) Molecular mechanisms of bacterial virulence elucidated using a *Pseudomonas aeruginosa-Caenorhabditis elegans* pathogenesis model. *Cell* 96:47-56
168. Massiere F, Badet D M (1998) The mechanism of glutamine-dependent amidotransferases. *Cell Mol.Life Sci.* 54:205-222
169. Maurhofer M, Hase C, Meuwly P, Metraux J-P, Defago G (1994) Induction of systemic resistance of tobacco to tobacco necrosis virus by the root-colonizing *Pseudomonas fluorescens* strain CHA0: Influence of the *gacA* gene and of pyoverdine production. *Phytopathology* 84:139-146

170. Maurhofer M, Keel C, Défago G (1994) Pyoluteorin production by *Pseudomonas fluorescens* strain CHA0 is involved in the suppression of *Pythium* damping-off of cress but not of cucumber. *Eur.J.Plant Pathol.* 100:221-232
171. Maurhofer M, Keel C, Schnider U, Voisard C, Haas D, Défago G (1992) Influence of enhanced antibiotic production in *Pseudomonas fluorescens* strain CHA0 on its disease suppressive capacity. *Phytopathology* 82:190-195
172. Mavrodi D V, Bonsall R F, Delaney S M, Soule M J, Phillips G, Thomashow L S (2001) Functional analysis of genes for biosynthesis of pyocyanin and phenazine-1-carboxamide from *Pseudomonas aeruginosa* PAO1. *J.Bacteriol.* 183:6454-6465
173. Mavrodi D V, Ksenzenko V N, Bonsall R F, Cook R J, Boronin A M, Thomashow L S (1998) A seven-gene locus for synthesis of phenazine-1-carboxylic acid by *Pseudomonas fluorescens* 2-79. *J.Bacteriol.* 180:2541-2548
174. Mazzola M, Cook R J, Thomashow L S, Weller D M, Pierson L S (1992) Contribution of phenazine antibiotic biosynthesis to the ecological competence of fluorescent pseudomonads in soil habitats. *Appl.Environ.Microbiol.* 58:2616-2624
175. McClean K H, Winson M K, Fish L, Taylor A, Chhabra S R, Camara M, Daykin M, Lamb J H, Swift S, Bycroft B W, Stewart G B, Williams P (1997) Quorum sensing and *Chromobacterium violaceum*: exploitation of violacein production and inhibition for the detection of *N*-acylhomoserine lactones. *Microbiology* 143:3703-3711
176. McGowan S, Sebaihia M, Jones S, Yu B, Bainton N, Chan P F, Bycroft B, Stewart G S, Williams P, Salmond G P (1995) Carbapenem antibiotic production in *Erwinia carotovora* is regulated by CarR, a homologue of the LuxR transcriptional activator. *Microbiology* 141:541-550
177. McLoughlin A J (1994) Plasmid stability and ecological competence in recombinant cultures. *Biotechnol.Adv.* 12:279-324
178. McLoughlin J, Quinn P, Betterman A, Brooklan R (1992) *Pseudomonas cepacia* suppression of sunflower wilt fungus and role of antifungal compounds in controlling the disease. *Appl.Environ.Microbiol.* 56:1760-1763
179. Messenger A J, Turner J M (1983) Phenazine-1,6-dicarboxylate and its dimethyl ester as precursors of other phenazines in bacteria. *FEMS Microbiol.Lett.* 18:64
180. Miller M B, Bassler B L (2001) Quorum sensing in bacteria. *Annu.Rev.Microbiol.* 55:165-199
181. Nealson K H, Platt T, Woodland Hastings J (1970) Cellular control of the synthesis and activity of the bacterial luminescent system. *J.Bacteriol.* 104:313-322

182. Nielsen T H, Christophersen C, Anthoni U, Sorensen J (1999) Viscosinamide, a new cyclic depsipeptide with surfactant and antifungal properties produced by *Pseudomonas fluorescens* DR54. *J.Appl.Microbiol.* 87:80-90

183. Nielsen T H, Thrane C, Christophersen C, Anthoni U, Sorensen J (2000) Structure, production characteristics and fungal antagonism of tensin - a new antifungal cyclic lipopeptide from *Pseudomonas fluorescens* strain 96.578. *J.Appl.Microbiol.* 89:992-1001

184. Nikaido H (1996) Multidrug efflux pumps of gram-negative bacteria. *J.Bacteriol.* 178:5853-5859

185. Notz R, Maurhofer M, Dubach H, Haas D, Défago G (2002) Fusaric acid-producing strains of *Fusarium oxysporum* alter 2,4-diacetylphloroglucinol biosynthetic gene expression in *Pseudomonas fluorescens* CHA0 in vitro and in the rhizosphere of wheat. *Appl.Environ.Microbiol.* 68:2229-2235

186. Nowak-Thompson B, Gould S J, Loper J E (1997) Identification and sequence analysis of the genes encoding a polyketide synthase required for pyoluteorin biosynthesis in *Pseudomonas fluorescens* Pf-5. *Gene* 204:17-24

187. O'Sullivan D J, O'Gara F (1992) Traits of fluorescent *Pseudomonas* spp. involved in suppression of plant root pathogens. *Microbiol.Rev.* 56:662-676

188. Ochsner U A, Reiser J (1995) Autoinducer-mediated regulation of rhamnolipid biosurfactant synthesis in *Pseudomonas aeruginosa.* *Proc.Natl.Acad.Sci.U.S.A.* 92:6424-6428

189. Oka Y, Chet I, Spiegel Y (1993) Control of the root nematode *Meloidogyne javanica* by *Bacillus cereus. Biocontrol Sci.Techn.* 3:115-126

190. Pattery T, Mondt K, Audenaert K, Cornelis P, Cornelis P (2001) Identification of *phzM*, a new phenazine biosynthesis gene necessary for the production of pyocyanin by *Pseudomonas aeruginosa*. In: Chablain P, Cornelis P (eds) *Pseudomonas* 2001 Abstracts Book. Brussels, p. 201

191. Pearson J P, Gray K M, Passador L, Tucker K D, Eberhard A, Iglewski B H, Greenberg E P (1994) Structure of the autoinducer required for expression of *Pseudomonas aeruginosa* virulence genes. *Proc.Natl.Acad.Sci.U.S.A.* 91:197-201

192. Pearson J P, Passador L, Iglewski B H, Greenberg E P (1995) A second *N*-acylhomoserine lactone signal produced by *Pseudomonas aeruginosa. Proc.Natl.Acad.Sci.U.S.A.* 92:1490-1494

193. Pearson J P, Pesci E C, Iglewski B H (1997) Roles of *Pseudomonas aeruginosa las* and *rhl* quorum sensing systems in

control of elastase and rhamnolipid biosynthesis genes. *J.Bacteriol.* 179:5756-5767

194. Pearson J P, Van-Delden C, Iglewski B H (1999) Active efflux and diffusion are involved in transport of *Pseudomonas aeruginosa* cell-to-cell signals. *J.Bacteriol.* 181:1203-1210

195. Pessi G, Haas D (2001) Dual control of hydrogen cyanide biosynthesis by the global activator GacA in *Pseudomonas aeruginosa* PAO1. *FEMS Microbiol.Lett.* 200:73-78

196. Pfender W F, Kraus J, Loper J E (1993) A genomic region from *Pseudomonas fluorescens* Pf-5 required for pyrrolnitrin production and inhibition of *Pyrenophora tritici-repentis* in wheat straw. *Phytopathology* 83:1223-1228

197. Pidoplichko V N, Garagulya A D (1974) Effect of antagonistic bacteria on the development of wheat root rot. *Mikrobiologische Z.* 36:599-620

198. Pierson III L S, Gaffney T, Lam S, Gong F (1995) Molecular analysis of genes encoding phenazine biosynthesis in the biological control bacterium *Pseudomonas aureofaciens* 30-84. *FEMS Microbiol.Lett.* 134:299-307

199. Pierson III L S, Keppenne V D, Wood D W (1994) Phenazine antibiotic biosynthesis in *Pseudomonas aureofaciens* 30-84 is regulated by PhzR in response to cell density. *J.Bacteriol.* 176:3966-3974

200. Pierson III L S, Pierson E A (1996) Phenazine antibiotic production in *Pseudomonas aureofaciens*: role in rhizosphere ecology and pathogen suppression. *FEMS Microbiol.Lett.* 136:101-108.

201. Pierson III L S, Thomashow L S (1992) Cloning and heterologous expression of the phenazine biosynthetic locus from *Pseudomonas aureofaciens* 30-84. *Mol.Plant-Microbe Interact.* 5:330-339

202. Pierson III L S, Wood D W, Pierson E A, Chancey S T (1998) *N*-acyl-homoserine lactone-mediated gene regulation in biological control by fluorescent pseudomonads: Current knowledge and future work. *Eur.J.Plant Pathol.* 104:1-9

203. Pieterse C M J, van Wees S C M, Hoffland E, van Pelt J A, van Loon L C (1996) Systemic resistance in *Arabidopsis* induced by biocontrol bacteria is independent of salicylic acid accumulation and pathogenesis related gene expression. *Plant Cell* 8:1225-1237.

204. Piper K R, Beck von Bodman S, Farrand S K (1993) Conjugation factor of *Agrobacterium tumefaciens* regulates Ti plasmid transfer by autoinduction. *Nature* 362:448-450

205. Pusey P L (1999) Use of *Bacillus subtillis* and related organisms as biofungicides. *Pestic.Sci.* 27:133-140

206. Pusey P L, Wilson C L (1984) Postharvest biological control of stone fruit brown rot by *Bacillus subtillis*. *Plant Dis.* 68:753-756

207. Raaijmakers J M, Sluis I, Koster M, Bakker P A H M, Weisbeek P J, Schippers B (1995) Utilization of heterologous siderophores and rhizosphere competence of fluorescent *Pseudomonas* spp. *Can.J.Microbiol.* 41:126-135

208. Raupach G S, Liu L, Murphy J F, Tuzun S, Kloepper J W (1996) Induced systemic resistance in cucumber and tomato against cucumber mosaic cucumovirus using plant growth-promoting rhizobacteria (PGPR). *Plant Dis.* 80:891-894

209. Rhodes D J, Powell K A (1994) Biological seed treatments - the development process. *BCPC Monograph* 57:303-310

210. Riedel K, Hentzer M, Geisenberger O, Huber B, Steidle A, Wu H, Hoiby N, Givskov M, Molin S, Eberl L (2001) *N*-acylhomoserine-lactone-mediated communication between *Pseudomonas aeruginosa* and *Burkholderia cepacia* in mixed biofilms. *Microbiology* 147:3249-3262

211. Rijpkema S G, Bik E M, Jansen W H, Gielen H, Versluis L F, Stouthamer A H, Guinee P A, Mooi F R (1992) Construction and analysis of a *Vibrio cholerae* delta-aminolevulinic acid auxotroph which confers protective immunity in a rabbit model. *Infect.Immun.* 60:2188-2193

212. Ross I L, Alami Y, Harvey P R, Achouak W, Ryder M H (2000) Genetic diversity and biological control activity of novel species of closely related pseudomonads isolated from wheat field soils in South Australia. *Appl.Environ.Microbiol.* 66:1609-1616

213. Rovira A D (1956) A study of the development of the root surface microflora during the initial stages of plant growth. *J.Appl.Bacteriol.* 19:72-79

214. RuizDuenas F J, Martinez M J (1996) Enzymatic activities of *Trametes versicolar* and *Pleurotus eryngii* implicated in biocontrol of *Fusarium oxysporum* f. sp. *lycopersici*. *Curr.Microbiol.* 32:151-155

215. Salmond G P C, Bycroft B W, Stewart G S A B, Williams P (1995) The bacterial 'enigma': cracking the code of cell-cell communication. *Mol.Microbiol.* 16:615-624

216. Sands D C, Rovira A D (1971) *Pseudomonas fluorescens* biotype G, the dominant fluorescent pseudomonad in South Australian soils and wheat rhizospheres. *J.Appl.Bacteriol.* 34:261-275

217. Sarniguet A, Kraus J, Henkels M D, Muehlchen A M, Loper J E (1995) The sigma factor σ^s affects antibiotic production and biological activity of *Pseudomonas fluorescens* PF5. *Proc.Natl.Acad.Sci.U.S.A.* 92:12255-12259

218. Schaefer A L, Hanzelka B L, Eberhard A, Greenberg E P (1996) Quorum sensing in *Vibrio fischeri*: probing autoinducer LuxR

interactions with autoinducer analogs. *J.Bacteriol.* 178:2897-2901.

219. Scher F M, Baker R (1980) Mechanism of biological control in a fusarium-suppressive soil. *Phytopathology* 72:1567-1573
220. Scher F M, Kloepper J W, Singleton C A (1985) Chemotaxis of fluorescent *Pseudomonas* spp. to soybean seed exudates in vitro and in soil. *Can.J.Microbiol.* 31:570-574
221. Schippers B, Lugtenberg B J J, Weisbeek P J (1987) Plant growth control by fluorescent pseudomonads. In: Chet I (ed) Innovative approaches to plant disease control. Wiley, New York, NY, pp. 19-39
222. Schippers B, Scheffer R J, Lugtenberg B J J, Weisbeek P J (1995) Biocoating of seeds with plant growth-promoting rhizobacteria to improve plant establishment. *Outlook.Agr.* 24:179-185
223. Schnider-Keel U, Seematter A, Maurhofer M, Blumer C, Duffy B, Gigot-Bonnefoy C, Reimmann C, Notz R, Défago G, Haas D, Keel C (2000) Autoinduction of 2,4-diacetylphloroglucinol biosynthesis in the biocontrol agent *Pseudomonas fluorescens* CHA0 and repression by the bacterial metabolites salicylate and pyoluteorin. *J.Bacteriol.* 182:1215-1225
224. Schnider U, Keel C, Blumer C, Troxler J, Défago G, Haas D (1995) Amplification of the housekeeping sigma factor in *Pseudomonas fluorescens* CHA0 enhances antibiotic production and improves biocontrol abilities. *J.Bacteriol.* 177:5387-5392
225. Schoental R (1941). *Brit.J.Exp.Pathol.* 22:137
226. Schroth M N, Hancock J G (1981) Disease suppressive soil and root colonizing bacteria. *Science* 216:1376-1381
227. Shadel G S, Devine J H, Baldwin T O (1990) Control of the *lux* regulon of *Vibrio fischeri*. *J.Biolumin.Chemilumin.* 5:99-106
228. Shapira R, Ordentlich A, Chet I, Oppenheim A B (1989) Control of plant diseases by chitinase expressed from cloned DNA in *Escherichia coli*. *Phytopathology* 79:1246-1249
229. Shapiro J A (1998) Thinking about bacterial populations as multicellular organisms. *Annu.Rev.Microbiol.* 52:81-104
230. Shih P C, Huang C T (2002) Effects of quorum-sensing deficiency on *Pseudomonas aeruginosa* biofilm formation and antibiotic resistance. *J.Antimicrob.Chemother.* 49:309-314
231. Silo-suh L A, Lethbridge B J, Raffel S J, He H, Clardy J, Handelsman J (1994) Biological activities of two fungistatic antibiotics produced by *Bacillus cereus* UW85. *Appl.Environ.Microbiol.* 60:2023-2030
232. Simons M, Permentier H P, de Weger L A, Wijffelman C A, Lugtenberg B J J (1997) Amino acid synthesis is necessary for tomato root colonization by *Pseudomonas fluorescens* strain WCS365. *Mol.Plant-Microbe Interact.* 10:102-106

233. Simons M, van der Bij A J, Brand J, de Weger L A, Wijffelman C A, Lugtenberg B J J (1996) Gnotobiotic system for studying rhizosphere colonization by plant growth-promoting *Pseudomonas* bacteria. *Mol.Plant-Microbe Interact.* 9:600-607

234. Sitnikov D M, Schineller J B, Baldwin T O (1995) Transcriptional regulation of bioluminesence genes from *Vibrio fischeri. Mol.Microbiol.* 17:801-812.

235. Sivasithamparam K (1998) Root cortex - The final frontier for the biocontrol of root-rot with fungal antagonists: A case study on a sterile red fungus. *Annu.Rev.Phytopathol.* 36:439-452

236. Smith K P, Goodman R M (1999) Host variation for interactions with beneficial plant-associated microbes. *Annu.Rev.Phytopathol.* 37:473-491

237. Smith K P, Handelsman J, Goodman R M (1999) Genetic basis in plants for interactions with disease-suppressive bacteria. *Proc.Natl.Acad.Sci.U.S.A.* 96:4786-4790

238. Stevens A M, Greenberg E P (1997) Quorum sensing in *Vibrio fischeri*: essential elements for activation of the luminescence genes. *J.Bacteriol.* 179:557-562

239. Stover C K, Pham X Q, Erwin A L, Mizoguchi S D, Warrener P, Hickey M J, Brinkman F S, Hufnagle W O, Kowalik D J, Lagrou M, Garber R L, Goltry L, Tolentino E, Westbrock-Wadman S, Yuan Y, Brody L L, Coulter S N, Folger K R, Kas A, Larbig K, Lim R, Smith K, Spencer D, Wong G K, Wu Z, Paulsen I T (2000) Complete genome sequence of *Pseudomonas aeruginosa* PA01, an opportunistic pathogen. *Nature* 406:959-964

240. Stutz E W, Defago G, Kern H (1986) Naturally occurring fluorescent pseudomonads involved in the suppression of black root rot of tobacco. *Phytopathology* 76:181-185

241. Surette M G, Bassler B L (1998) Quorum sensing in *Escherichia coli* and *Salmonella typhimurium. Proc.Natl.Acad.Sci.U.S.A.* 95:7046-7050

242. Surette M G, Miller M B, Bassler B L (1999) Quorum sensing in *Escherichia coli*, *Salmonella typhimurium*, and *Vibrio harveyi*: A new family of genes responsible for autoinducer production. *Proc.Natl.Acad.Sci.U.S.A.* 96:1639-1644

243. Suslow T V (1982) Role of root-colonizing bateria in plant growth. In: Lacy G, Mount M (eds) Pathogenic prokaryotes vol. 1. Academic Press, Inc., New York, NY, pp. 187-223

244. Suslow T V, Schroth M N (1982) Rhizobacteria of sugar beets: effects of seed application and root colonization on yield. *Phytopathology* 72:199-206

245. Swift S, Throup J P, Williams P, Salmond G P C, Stewart G S A B (1996) Quorum sensing: a population density component in the

determination of bacterial phenotype. *Trends Biochem.Sci.* 21:214-219.

246. Swift S, Winson M K, Chan P F, Bainton N J, Birdsall M, Reeves P J, Rees C E, Chhabra S R, Hill P J, Throup J P, et al (1993) A novel strategy for the isolation of *luxI* homologues: evidence for the widespread distribution of a LuxR:LuxI superfamily in enteric bacteria. *Mol.Microbiol.* 10:511-520
247. Thomashow L S, Weller D M (1988) Role of a phenazine antibiotic from *Pseudomonas fluorescens* in biological control of *Gaeumannomyces graminis* var. *tritici*. *J.Bacteriol.* 170:3499-3508
248. Thomashow L S, Weller D M (1995) Current concepts in the use of introduced bacteria for biological disease control: mechanisms and antifungal metabolites. In: Stacey G, Keen N T (eds) Plant-Microbe Interactions. Chapman & Hall, New York, NY, pp. 187-235
249. Thomashow L S, Weller D M, Bonsall R F, Pierson III L S (1990) Production of the antibiotic phenazine-1-carboxylic acid by fluorescent *Pseudomonas* species in the rhizosphere of wheat. *Appl.Environ.Microbiol.* 56:908-912
250. Thrane C, Harder N T, Neiendam N M, Sorensen J, Olsson S (2000) Viscosinamide-producing *Pseudomonas fluorescens* DR54 exerts a biocontrol effect on *Pythium ultimum* in sugar beet rhizosphere. *FEMS Microbiol.Ecol.* 33:139-146
251. Ton J, van Pelt J A, van Loon L C, Pieterse C M J (2002) Differential effectiveness of salicylate-dependent and jasmonate/ethylene-dependent induced resistance in *Arabidopsis*. *Mol.Plant-Microbe Interact.* 15:27-34
252. Toohey J I, Nelson C D, Krotkov G (1965) Toxicity of phenazine carboxylic acid to some bacteria, algae, higher plants, and animals. *Can.J.Bot.* 43:1151-1155
253. Truitman P, Nelson E (1992) Production of non-volatile and volatile inhibitors of *Pythium ultimum* sporangium germination and mycelial growth by strains of *Enterobacter cloacae*. *Phytopathology* 82:1120
254. Turner J M, Messenger A J (1986) Occurence, biochemistry and physiology of phenazine pigment production. *Adv.Microb.Physiol.* 27:211-275
255. Ulitzur S, Dunlap P V (1995) Regulatory circuitry controlling luminescence autoinduction in *Vibrio fischeri*. *Photochem.Photobiol.* 62:625-632.
256. van Delden C, Comte R, Bally A M (2001) Stringent response activates quorum sensing and modulates cell density-dependent gene expression in *Pseudomonas aeruginosa*. *J.Bacteriol.* 183:5376-5384

257. van Loon L C (1997) Induced resistance in plants and the role of pathogenesis-related proteins. *Eur.J.Plant Pathol.* 103:753-765
258. van Loon L C, Bakker P A H M, Pieterse C M J (1998) Systemic resistance induced by rhizosphere bacteria. *Annu.Rev.Phytopathol.* 36:453-483
259. van Peer R, Niemann G J, Schippers B (1991) Induced resistance and phytoalexin accumulation in biological control of *Fusarium* wilt of carnation by *Pseudomonas* spp. strain WCS417r. *Phytopathology* 81:728-734
260. van Wees S C M, de Swart E A, van Pelt J A, van Loon L C, Pieterse C M (2000) Enhancement of induced disease resistance by simultaneous activation of salicylate- and jasmonate-dependent defense pathways in *Arabidopsis thaliana*. *Proc.Natl.Acad.Sci.U.S.A* 97:8711-8716
261. van Wees S C M, Pieterse C M J, Trijssenaar A, van 't Westende Y A M, Hartog F, van Loon L C (1997) Differential induction of systemic resistance in *Arabidopsis* by biocontrol bacteria. *Mol.Plant-Microbe Interact.* 10:716-724
262. Vincent M N, Harrison L A, Brackin J M, Kovacevich P E, Mukerji P, Weller D M, Pierson E A (1991) Genetic analysis of the antifungal activity of a soilborne *Pseudomonas aureofaciens* strain. *Appl.Environ.Microbiol.* 57:2928-2934
263. Voisard C, Keel C, Haas D, Defago G (1989) Cyanide production by *Pseudomonas fluorescens* helps suppress black root rot of tobacco under gnotobiotic conditions. *EMBO J.* 8:351-358
264. Ward D.M (1989) Molecular probes for analysis of microbial communities. In: Characklis W G, Wilderer P A (eds) Structure and function of biofilms. John Wiley & Sons Ltd., New York, pp. 145-155
265. Wei G, Kloepper J W, Tuzun S (1991) Induction of systemic resistance of cucumber to *Colletotrichum orbiculare* by select strains of plant growth-promoting rhizobacteria. *Phytopathology* 81:1508-1512
266. Weisbeek P J, Gerrits H (1999) Iron and biocontrol. In: Stacey G, Keen N T (eds) Plants-Microbe Interactions. APS Press, St. Paul, MN, pp. 217-250
267. Weiser J N, Williams A, Moxon E R (1990) Phase-variable lipopolysaccharide structures enhance the invasive capacity of *Haemophilus influenzae*. *Infect.Immun.* 58:3455-3457
268. Weller D M (1988) Biological control of soilborne plant pathogens in the rhizosphere with bacteria. *Annu.Rev.Phytopathol.* 26:379-407
269. Weller D M, Cook R J (1983) Suppression of take-all of wheat by seed treatments with fluorescent pseudomonads. *Phytopathology* 73:463-469

270. Weller D M, Zhang B X, Cook R J (1985) Application of a rapid screening test for selection of bacteria suppressive to take-all of wheat. *Plant Dis.* 69:710-713

271. Whistler C A, Corbell N A, Sarniguet A, Ream W, Loper J E (1998) The two-component regulators GacS and GacA influence accumulation of the stationary-phase sigma factor sigma(S) and the stress response in *Pseudomonas fluorescens* Pf-5. *J.Bacteriol.* 180:6635-6641

272. Whiteley M, Greenberg E P (2001) Promoter specificity elements in *Pseudomonas aeruginosa* quorum-sensing-controlled genes. *J.Bacteriol.* 183:5529-5534

273. Winson M K, Camara M, Latifi A, Foglino M, Chhabra S R, Daykin M, Bally M, Chapon V, Salmond G P C, Bycroft B W, Lazdunski A, Stewart G S A B, Williams P (1995) Multiple *N*-acyl-L-homoserine lactone signal molecules regulate production of virulence determinants and secondary metabolites in *Pseudomonas aeruginosa*. *Proc.Natl.Acad.Sci.U.S.A.* 92:9427-9431

274. Winson M K, Swift S, Fish L, Throup J P, Jorgensen F, Chhabra S R, Bycroft B W, Williams P, Stewart G S (1998) Construction and analysis of *luxCDABE*-based plasmid sensors for investigating *N*-acyl homoserine lactone-mediated quorum sensing. *FEMS Microbiol.Lett.* 163:185-192

275. Wood D W, Gong F C, Daykin M M, Williams P, Pierson L S (1997) *N*-acyl-homoserine lactone-mediated regulation of phenazine gene expression by *Pseudomonas aureofaciens* 30-84 in the wheat rhizosphere. *J.Bacteriol.* 179:7663-7670

276. Wood D W, Pierson L S (1996) The *phzI* gene of *Pseudomonas aureofaciens* 30-84 is responsible for the production of a diffusible signal required for phenazine antibiotic production. *Gene* 168:49-53.

277. You Z, Fukushima J, Tanaka K, Kawamoto S, Okuda K (1998) Induction into the stationary growth phase on the *Pseudomonas aeruginosa* by *N*-acylhomoserine lactone. *FEMS Microbiol.Lett* 164:99-106

The *Pseudomonas syringae* Hrp (type III) Protein Secretion System: Advances in the New Millennium

James R. Alfano and Ming Guo

Introduction

Pseudomonas syringae is a gram-negative bacterial plant pathogen that is widespread in nature and is successful on an array of host plants. The interaction *P. syringae* has with plants is specific: Some strains (called pathovars) can only infect certain plant species. Clearly, much of the specificity observed in these interactions is due to the presence of *avirulence* (*avr*) genes in *P. syringae* that limit the ability of this pathogen to infect plants containing specific *Resistance* (*R*) genes (more on this below). There are over 40 different *P. syringae* pathovars based on the host that they infect. The diseases that result from these infections are a variety of blights, specks and spots that occur on many agricultural crops and, generally, produce symptoms that include chlorotic and necrotic lesions (4). Currently, the genome of *P. s. tomato* strain DC3000 is being sequenced. DC3000 is a pathogen of tomato, but it also infects the model plant *Arabidopsis thaliana,* whose genome sequence has recently been determined. Because we will soon have the genome sequence of DC3000 and a genome sequence of a host of DC3000 is known, this pathosystem represents an excellent model system to study the molecular basis of the gram-negative bacterial pathogenicity of plants.

The type III protein secretion system (TTSS) has a central role in the pathogenesis of plants and animals by many gram-negative bacteria (29, 45). TTSSs are present in plant pathogenic bacteria in the genera *Erwinia*, *Pseudomonas*, *Xanthomonas*, *Ralstonia*, and *Pantoea* and are encoded by *hrp/hrc* genes (4). Because mutants defective in type III secretion typically lose their ability to elicit the hypersensitive response (HR) in nonhost plants and to be pathogenic in host plants these systems are also referred to as hypersensitive response and pathogenicity (Hrp; pronounced phonetically as harp) systems (5). The HR is a defense-associated programmed cell death of plant cells that can occur when plant pathogens are infiltrated into resistant plant tissue. The proteins that are secreted by the TTSS are of two general classes: helper or accessory proteins, which help in the deployment of the extracellular secretion apparatus, and effector proteins, which are translocated or "injected" into host cells. Effector proteins often modulate host signal transduction pathways in a manner that favors pathogenesis (29).

The effectors that travel Hrp pathways have been referred to as Avr, Hop or Vir proteins depending on how they were initially discovered (5, 113). Because the Hop name refers to Hrp-dependent outer proteins, the prefix includes Hrp-secreted helper and effector proteins. Some research groups have named Hrp-secreted proteins with the 'Vir' prefix if a mutant lacking the specific protein is reduced in virulence. The Avr prefix indicates that the protein was originally identified because it converted a virulent pathogen to an avirulent pathogen on a test plant, hence producing an avirulence phenotype. Avirulence is a phenomenon that occurs when specific plant species or cultivars can recognize a product (i.e., an Avr signal) of a pathogen and trigger a rapid plant defense response, instead of allowing the pathogen to cause disease (55).

This review is focused on recent advances in our understanding of the Hrp system of *P. syringae*. We will focus primarily on advances reported in the new millennium. It has been a very productive period for research on the *P. syringae* Hrp system in several different research areas. Because of this we cover a menagerie of topics including the following: A description of the pathogenicity island that encodes the Hrp system; the current inventory of DC3000 Hops; progress on early genomic approaches taken with DC3000. We also include an update on the HrpZ harpin and the HrpA Hrp pilus stories, because the last 2 years have produced several major breakthroughs on our understanding of HrpZ and HrpA. Even though plant targets for Hops, including those from *P. syringae,* remain largely unknown, several clues have been uncovered about potential targets and we address some of these below. We encourage the reader to explore other excellent reviews that provide additional background on the topics covered and other topics not described here (5, 29, 39, 45, 48, 58, 78, 81, 101, 112).

THE *P. SYRINGAE* HRP PATHOGENICITY ISLAND

The Hrp apparatus is encoded by a cluster of conserved *hrp/hrc* genes in the *P. syringae* chromosome (5). This cluster is the central part of a pathogenicity island (Pai), called the Hrp Pai (Fig. 1; 3, 56). For the Hrp system to be immediately useful to *P. syringae* when it was first horizontally acquired, the accompanying DNA would also have to encode a basic set of effectors. This would insure that the large cluster of DNA would be selected for and maintained. Thus, it makes evolutionary sense that the regions flanking the *hrp/hrc* genes are enriched for effector genes. To the right of the *hrp/hrc* cluster in the Hrp Pai is a region that is conserved in *P. syringae* pathovars, called the conserved effector locus (CEL), which carries, among other genes, the well-characterized *avr* gene *avrE* and the *hrpW* gene (19, 70). HrpW and a homolog of AvrE, DspE,

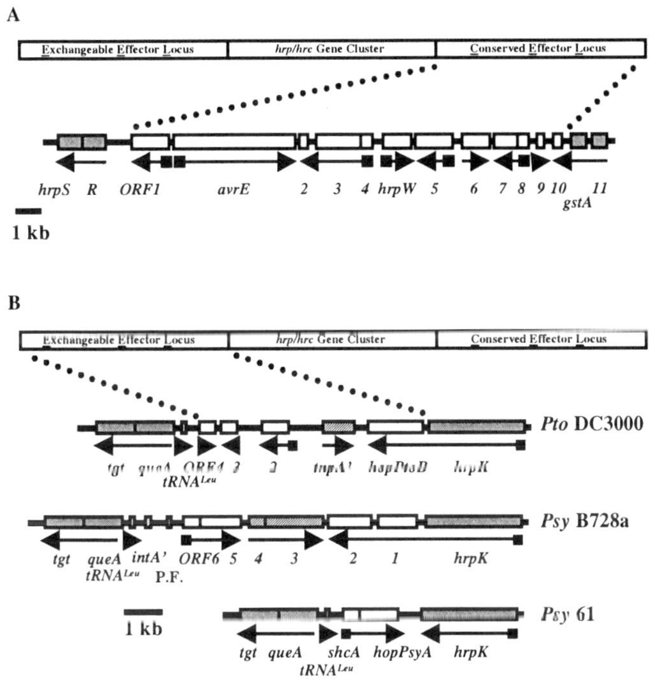

Figure 1. The conserved effector locus and the exchangeable effector locus of the *P. syringae* Hrp pathogenicity island. (A) The conserved effector locus (CEL) is bordered by the regulatory genes *hrpR* and *hrpS* on one side and *gstA* on the other. The *hrpW* gene encodes a secreted product and the avirulence gene *avrE* encodes AvrE, which is likely translocated into plant cells. The other ORFs also appear to encode Hrp-secreted proteins or act as type III chaperones (see text for details). (B) The exchangeable effector locus (EEL) of three different *P. syringae* strains is bordered by the *hrpK* gene and a *tRNA*^{leu} gene and is completely dissimilar between strains. Gray boxes denote border sequences, white boxes indicate novel genes, and striped boxes denote DNA associated with horizontal transfer. The arrows indicate predicted directions of transcription and the box at the beginning of some of the operons indicate the presence of a Hrp promoter.

from *E. amylovora* have been shown to be type III-secreted proteins (14, 19, 31, 122). Several other operons in this region have Hrp promoters and are likely to encode effectors. A *P. s. tomato* DC3000 mutant lacking a section of the CEL was unable to produce disease symptoms on tomato and bacterial growth *in planta* was greatly reduced (3). Because the CEL mutant maintained its ability to elicit an HR and secrete at least one other Avr protein, AvrPto, via its Hrp system, the inability to cause disease indicates that the deleted DNA region must encode Hop proteins that are needed for pathogenesis (instead of a general defect in the Hrp apparatus). Flanking the other side of the *hrp/hrc* cluster in *P. syringae* is a region that is completely dissimilar between even closely related *P. syringae* pathovars. This region also appears to be rich in *hop* genes, is a mosaic of different recombination events, and contains remnants of mobile DNA. Because of these characteristics the region was named the exchangeable effector locus (EEL) of the *P. syringae* Hrp Pai (3). Interestingly, the high variability of the EEL stop immediately before the *hrpK* gene at the interface between the EEL and the *hrp/hrc* cluster (see Fig. 1). The significance of the conservation of *hrpK* is unknown, however, HrpK was recently determined to be a type III-secreted protein and *P. s. tomato* DC3000 *hrpK* mutants are reduced in virulence indicating that HrpK may be an important effector (van Dijk and Alfano, manuscript submitted; 23).

The *P. s. tomato* DC3000 EEL contains several ORFs that have Hrp boxes and one ORF that has been shown to encode a protein that is secreted and translocated via the Hrp pathway (Petnicki-Ocwieja and Alfano, manuscript submitted) (Fig. 1). A *P. s. tomato* DC3000 EEL deletion mutant was only slightly affected in its ability to grow in tomato plants (3). The EELs of every pathovar examined appear to be rich in *hop* genes. For example, the EEL of *P. s. syringae* 61 contains the gene *hopPsyA*, which was shown to act as an *avr* gene on tobacco and encode a Hop (6, 109). While EELs have not been completely characterized in other pathovars of *P. syringae*, it is known that adjacent to *hrpK* in *P. s. phaseolicola* race 4 strain 1302A is the *avr* gene *avrPphE* (73). Thus, the *P. syringae* Hrp Pai consists of a conserved set of *hrp/hrc* genes that encode the Hrp secretion apparatus, a conserved CEL rich in effector genes, and a variable EEL, also rich in effector genes, which may represent a more fluid region of the Hrp Pai. The G+C content supports this because the *hrp/hrc* cluster and the CEL have a G+C% similar to the rest of the genome of *P. syringae*, whereas the EEL has a significantly lower G+C% suggesting that it was acquired sometime after the acquisition of the rest of the Hrp Pai (3).

REGULATION OF THE *P. SYRINGAE* HRP SYSTEM

The proteins that make-up the Hrp apparatus and that travel the Hrp pathway are not produced when cells are grown in rich media. However, a functional Hrp system can be induced in media and conditions that mimic the plant apoplast in terms of pH, temperature, and nutrients (47, 109, 120). A schematic showing the known regulatory elements in the *P. syringae* Hrp system is shown (Fig. 2). Essentially, the *hrp*, *hrc*, *avr*, and *hop* genes (i.e., the Hrp regulon) are activated by HrpL, a member of the ECF (extracytoplasmic function) subfamily of sigma factors (69, 119). Most genes related to the Hrp system have a *cis* element in their promoters called a "Hrp box", presumably a binding site for HrpL (49, 92, 98). The enhancer-binding proteins HrpR and HrpS activate *hrpL* transcription. However, it is unclear how HrpR and HrpS accomplish this. HrpR and HrpS are unusual members of the enhancer-binding protein class in that they both lack a receiver domain. This probably indicates that HrpR and HrpS are both constitutively active similar to the stress response regulator PspF, which also lacks this domain. Both HrpR and HrpS have σ^{54} binding domains and it was recently shown that HrpR and HrpS bind to each other *in vitro* (34, 46). The two main hypotheses that would be consistent with a

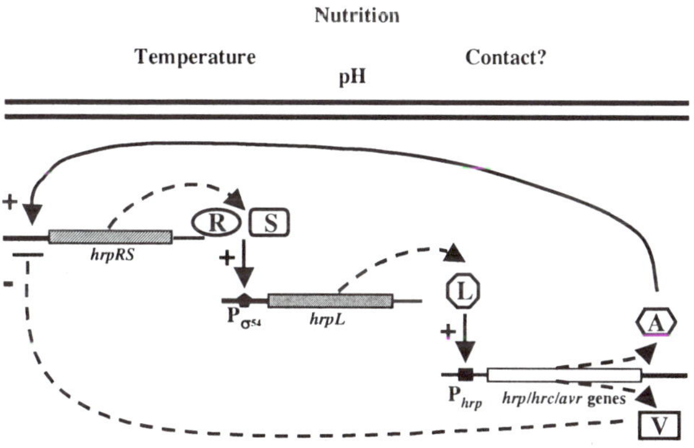

Figure 2. A regulatory cascade controls the expression of the *P. syringae* Hrp regulon. HrpR and HrpS activate the transcription of *hrpL* with the help of σ^{54}. The alternate sigma factor HrpL activates the genes that have Hrp promoters. Among the HrpL-regulated genes are *hrpV* and *hrpA*, both of which encode proteins that are involved in the regulation of the Hrp system by acting above HrpR and HrpS: HrpV represses the activation of the Hrp system, while HrpA activates it. Temperature, the nutritional status, and pH are known to act as environmental cues that effect *hrp* gene expression. Based on analogous TTSSs, contact with the plant cell likely acts as another environmental cue. The capitalized letters inside the different shapes denote the different regulatory proteins. *hrpRS*, *hrpL*, and *hrp/hrc/avr* genes are depicted as striped, stippled, or white boxes, respectively. The positive or negative symbols near the genes indicate whether the regulatory protein activates or represses the transcription of the Hrp system.

HrpR/HrpS interaction are that HrpR acts on HrpS, which then activates *hrpL* transcription or HrpR and HrpS act together as a complex to activate *hrpL*. Whichever one is right, σ^{54} is also needed because *rpoN* (the σ^{54}

gene) is required for *hrpL* expression as well as for *P. syringae* virulence (41, 42).

Two other Hrp proteins have been implicated in the regulation of the *P. syringae* Hrp system. HrpV, a protein encoded by the last gene of the *hrcC* operon, has been shown to be a negative regulator of the Hrp system that probably acts above HrpR/S in the regulatory hierarchy (87). Surprisingly, HrpA, the Hrp pilus structural protein (more on HrpA below), performs a positive regulatory role activating the Hrp regulon by affecting the expression of the *hrpRS* operon (117). The mechanism of regulation for both HrpV and HrpA is not well understood and it is likely that many other proteins are involved in regulating the Hrp regulon. One indication of this is that the Hrp system appears to be capable of sensing multiple environmental cues to determine whether the bacterium should deploy its Hrp system. Moreover, since TTSSs are contact-dependent secretion systems it is likely that *P. syringae* has a regulatory system to detect contact with the plant cell similar to the role that PrgA plays in *Ralstonia solanacearum* (1, 74).

Helper Proteins Of The *P. syringae* Hrp System

THE ENIGMATIC HRPZ HARPIN

The first protein discovered to be secreted via the Hrp system of *P. syringae* was HrpZ (40). HrpZ belongs to a group of proteins called harpins, which have the characteristic that when purified and infiltrated into many different plants elicit an HR (4). Whether HrpZ is an actual elicitor of thé HR when the bacteria deliver this protein to plant cells came into doubt because of two discoveries made several years ago. The cosmid pHIR11 carries a functional *hrp/hrc* cluster, *hopPsyA,* and *hrpZ* from *P. s. syringae* 61 and enables *P. fluorescens* and other nonpathogenic bacteria to elicit an HR on many plants. The ability of *P. fluorescens* containing pHIR11 to elicit an HR is dependent on the effector HopPsyA (2, 6). *P. fluorescens* carrying pHIR11 derivatives with mutations in *hopPsyA* retain the ability to secrete HrpZ, but no longer confer HR-eliciting activity. Thus, HopPsyA is not a required part of the Hrp apparatus and the pHIR11-dependent HR is due to HopPsyA, not HrpZ (2). The other observation that does not agree with HrpZ acting as an HR elicitor, at least not the HR seen in incompatible interactions (i.e., an Avr protein-induced HR), is that purified HrpZ preparations from different *P. syringae* pathovars do not possess the ability to elicit HRs on different plant species in a manner that would explain the specificity that occurs in *P. syringae*-plant interactions (88). How then does one reconcile the HR activity seen when purified HrpZ is infiltrated into plant tissue with the inability of bacteria that can secrete HrpZ to elicit an HR? One possible explanation is that HrpZ only acts as an elicitor when

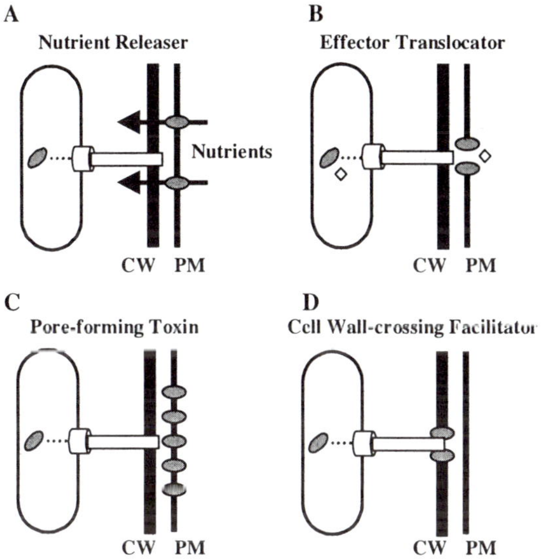

Figure 3. Potential roles for HrpZ in *P. syringae* pathogenesis. Panels A-C represent potential roles for HrpZ that are based on the observation that HrpZ possesses pore-forming activity in lipid bilayers (63). (A) HrpZ may cause the release of plant nutrients from plant cells into the apoplast. (B) HrpZ may acts as a translocator for effector proteins to cross the plant plasma membrane. A related potential role for HrpZ is that it could facilitate the "injection" of the Hrp pilus through the plasma membrane. (C) The pore-forming activity of HrpZ could have no other purpose other than to cause direct damage to the plant cell by acting as a toxin similar to the pore-forming syringomycin toxins present in many pathovars of *P. syringae*. (D) Because HrpZ has similarities with a Hrp-secreted pectate lyase (i.e., HrpW) and that it was localized to tobacco cell walls (44), it remains a possibility that HrpZ may help the Hrp pilus cross the plant cell wall. The large rod-shaped object in each panel represents a bacterial cell with a Hrp system. HrpZ is denoted by a gray oval in each panel, while the diamond represents an unnamed effector in panel B. The plant cell wall (CW) and plasma membrane (PM) are represented as a thick and a thin black line, respectively. The space immediately to the left of the CW represents the plant apoplast, whereas the space to the right of the PM represents the plant cytoplasm.

bacteria grow to high levels in plant tissue. However, since *P. fluorescens*(pHIR11) is not a plant pathogen it may not be able to grow to a high enough titer for enough HrpZ to be present in the apoplast to trigger the HR and other defenses.

Recently, researchers have made progress on understanding how purified HrpZ functions in plants. There is now evidence that HrpZ binds to tobacco plasma membranes and that the binding site is of a nonproteinaceous nature (62). This binding site appears to function as a receptor in that the HrpZ binding is specific, reversible, and saturable. Furthermore, HrpZ induces the activation of a salicyclic acid responsive mitogen-activated protein kinase (MAPK) (62). This MAPK pathway has been activated by other biotic stresses suggesting that the HrpZ response represents a bona fide plant defense pathway (121, 123). Consistent with the hypothesis that an extracellular receptor recognizes HrpZ is the observation that transgenic plants expressing HrpZ only elicit an HR-like response (i.e., necrosis) if HrpZ is fused to a secretion signal peptide that directs the secretion of HrpZ to the apoplast, where it presumably is recognized by an extracellular receptor (105). Determining how this defense pathway affects the *P. syringae* – plant interaction will be important in integrating this pathway with the more commonly studied defense responses induced by Avr proteins. Since probably all *P. syringae* pathovars have HrpZ, the HrpZ-induced defense pathway is either completely ineffective at stopping a *P. syringae* infection or the pathogens have their own strategy to suppress this defense pathway.

Plants can apparently recognize HrpZ with their innate immune system, but what is the bacterial-intended role of HrpZ? HrpZ is one of the most abundant Hrp-secreted proteins in culture supernatants (122). Thus, it is unlikely that HrpZ is translocated into plant cells, because translocated proteins (i.e., effectors) are secreted in culture in much smaller amounts. Because HrpZ was localized to the cell wall of tobacco suspension cells and that HrpZ has similarities with HrpW, a type III-secreted pectate lyase (see below), HrpZ was initially thought to act on the plant cell wall (19, 44). However, a recent study demonstrates that HrpZ forms ion-conducting pores in planar lipid bilayers (63). This reveals several intriguing potential roles for HrpZ: It could be used by the pathogen to form pores in the plasma membrane to release nutrients into the apoplast; or HrpZ may facilitate the translocation of effectors across the plasma membrane and into the plant cell in an analogous manner to translocators in animal pathogen type III systems (e.g., YopB and YopD) (79); or HrpZ could directly act as a toxin in a similar fashion as the *P. syringae* syringomycin toxins (11), which also form pores in membranes. These potential roles for HrpZ are summarized in Figure 3. It will be interesting to determine which of the potential roles noted is actually correct or if some other as-of-yet unidentified role will shed light on this enigmatic protein.

THE HRPW HARPIN CONTAINS A PECTATE LYASE DOMAIN

Another helper protein of the Hrp system is the HrpW harpin. The gene for this protein was originally identified because it was adjacent to the avirulence gene *avrE* (70). In subsequent analyses, it was shown to be a Hrp-secreted protein (19, 122). This protein has interesting properties in that the N-terminal domain shares several characteristics with HrpZ and other harpins and the C-terminal domain shares high sequence identity with pectate lysases (19). Both the N-terminal domain and the full-length protein, but not the pectate lyase domain, have HR-eliciting activity similar to other harpins. The pectate lysase domain binds to pectate, but does not have measurable pectate lyase activity. The lack of pectate lyase activity may make some sense since extensive cell wall damage triggers defense responses (37). Presumably, HrpW has cryptic pectate lyase activity that may subtly modify the plant cell wall to allow the Hrp apparatus to penetrate it and reach the plasma membrane. Interestingly, the closest fungal and bacterial pectate lyase homologs of HrpW have eight conserved cysteine molecules while HrpW has none of these (19). The lack of cysteines would preclude HrpW from forming disulfide bonds, which may indicate that HrpW needs to be in a partially unfolded state to be secreted by the Hrp apparatus.

THE *HRPA*-ENCODED HRP PILUS APPEARS TO ACT AS A CONDUIT FOR HRP-SECRETED PROTEINS

Over the last few years it has become apparent that TTSSs are dependent on a pilus for transfer of effectors to plant and animal cells (25, 32, 43, 54, 59, 91, 111). Perhaps, because the flagellar biogenesis system is essentially a strapped-down version of a TTSS and flagella are produced by the export of flagellin subunits through the growing flagellum (72), it may not be a surprise that an appendage is also associated with pathogenic TTSSs. Animal pathogen type III-associated pili appear to be of at least two different types: short and thin "needle complexes" that extend from an apparatus that resembles the flagellar basal body (59) or thicker pili that extend from the needle complexes in a sheath-like manner (95).

The first type III-associated pilus discovered in a bacterial plant pathogen was the *hrpA*-encoded Hrp pilus produced by *P. s. tomato* DC3000 (91). The *P. syringae* Hrp pilus was determined to be 6-8 nm wide and is required for pathogenicity and elicitation of the HR (91). Hrp-associated pili have now been described in both *E. amylovora* and *R. solanacearum* (54, 111). And Hrp pili have been shown to interact directly with Hrp-secreted proteins (17, 54). Because plant pathogens need to deal with another barrier to reach host cells, the plant cell wall, it makes sense that Hrp pili from the various plant pathogens appear to be longer than most of the type III pili made by animal pathogens and there is evidence that the Hrp pilus actually crosses the plant cell wall (17). Type III pili and pili associated with other secretion systems have long been predicted (but never proved) to act as conduits to transfer the substrates that travel the individual secretion pathways. In this regard, within the last year, the *P.*

syringae Hrp pilus has been clearly shown to act as a conduit for both the HrpZ harpin and the AvrPto effector proteins (53, 65). Thus, we can now better conceptualize how the Hrp apparatus and TTSSs, in general, function to deliver effector and helper proteins in or near host cells. Like other major advances, this one reveals many other new and exciting questions. Does the Hrp apparatus pierce the plant plasma membrane to deliver effectors? How does the bacterial cell orchestrate the delivery of greater than 20 proteins (see below) through a pilus pore that is probably only about 5 nm in diameter? Does this require that all of the Hrp traffic travel in a partially unfolded state? And which proteins are allowed to enter this narrow passage first? Clearly, there are several new lines of research to pursue now that we know that the Hrp pilus acts as a conduit for Hops.

P. syringae Effector Proteins

The Discovery that *P. syringae* Avr Proteins Were Translocated into Plant Cells Predates the Discovery of Avr Protein Secretion

It has only been about 6 years since researchers started acquiring evidence that bacterial Avr proteins were actually translocated (i.e., delivered) into plant cells by the Hrp system (5). This evidence was based on the fact that Avr proteins exhibit their HR-eliciting activities when they are expressed inside plant cells, but not when purified Avr proteins are infiltrated into leaf tissue, which would expose the outside of plant cells to Avr proteins. This type of evidence together with research that shows that the Avr activity of most bacterial Avr proteins is dependent on the Hrp system provided strong indirect evidence that Avr proteins were delivered into plant cells by the Hrp system (61). Using various transient *in planta* expression assays, the following *P. syringae* Avr proteins have been shown to have Avr activity inside plant cells: AvrB (33), AvrRpt2 (64), AvrPto (94, 106), AvrRpm1 (80), AvrPphE (103), AvrPphB (103), and HopPsyA (6). This list will probably become much longer as known Avr proteins are tested in this way and as more Hop proteins are identified as having Avr characteristics in certain plant species.

Demonstration that Hop Proteins Are Secreted by the *P. syringae* Hrp System

The first proteins demonstrated to be secreted in culture via the Hrp system of *P. syringae* were the helper proteins HrpZ, HrpA, and HrpW (19, 40, 91). Because Avr proteins were long thought to be secreted products several were tested for secretion in culture (61, 89), but up until the first report by Ham *et al.* (38), none were reported to be secreted. In these experiments the well-characterized Avr proteins AvrPto and AvrB were demonstrated to be secreted from *E. coli* cells containing a functional

Hrp system from *Erwinia chrysanthemi*. Soon after that, the secretion of the Avr proteins, AvrPto, AvrRpt2, and HopPsyA from their native *P. syringae* pathovars was demonstrated (77, 109). Why were Avr proteins not shown to be secreted products earlier? This is a reasonable question since researchers predicted quite early on that Avr proteins interacted with plant *R* gene products (55). There are probably several factors that slowed the discovery of Avr protein secretion. Perhaps, the most significant is that the secretion of these proteins and other effector proteins is apparently tightly controlled, probably until the bacteria make contact with plant cells. However, by optimizing the conditions and scaling-up the secretion assays many of these proteins can now be detected in culture supernatants in a Hrp-specific manner. It should be noted that the type III secretion of certain effectors (e.g., AvrB and AvrRpm1) cannot be detected in secretion assays even though they are translocated into plant cells by the Hrp system (80, 109).

Another useful strategy that has emerged to determine whether a protein travels the Hrp pathway is to fuse the candidate Hop to a N-terminally truncated Avr protein that lacks its native secretion signals. If the candidate Hop contains the secretion signals sufficient to direct the secretion and translocation of the truncated Avr protein an HR will ensue on the resistant test plant. The Avr protein that has been employed in this assay is AvrRpt2. Two groups have independently determined the secretion signals of AvrRpt2 reside in the N-terminal region and that amino acids 120-255 are sufficient to elicit an HR when transiently expressed in RPS2$^+$ plants (35, 77). As proof of principle for this assay system the Avr region of AvrRpt2 was fused to N-terminal regions of AvrRpm1 or the *Xanthomonas campestris* AvrBs2 and these heterologous secretion signals allowed the AvrRpt2 fusion proteins to be translocated into plant cells (35, 76). To facilitate the identification of Hrp-secreted proteins Guttman *et al.* (35) constructed a transposon that carried the nucleotides corresponding to amino acids 120-255 of AvrRpt2. This allowed for random transposon mutagenesis in *P. s. maculicola* ES4326 using this transposon to screen for Hrp-secreted proteins on the basis of indivdual transposon mutants gaining the ability to elicit an AvrRpt2-dependent HR (36). Because several likely helper proteins were isolated in this screen, it remains a possibility that the truncated AvrRpt2, while lacking secretion signals to direct its secretion from bacterial cells, may still possess translocation signals that can direct the translocation of an extracellular protein into plant cells. Thus, this assay may not be able to discriminate between helper proteins and effectors. Recently, a reporter system used to detect translocation of effectors from animal pathogenic type III systems has been adapted to use in plants (18). This system involves making adenylate cyclase fusions with candidate effectors and, because this enzyme is only active inside eukaryotic cells due to its dependency on calmodulin, the fusions that are active represent true effectors. This translocation system is more likely to be able to discriminate between effectors and helpers because the reporter will probably not possess cryptic type III translocation signals.

ARE SECRETION SIGNALS OF TYPE III EFFECTORS MRNA OR PROTEIN?

Much of the research characterizing the secretion signals of type III effectors has been carried out on *Yersinia* spp. effectors (i.e., Yops). The N-terminal 15 amino acids from YopE and YopH, were shown to be sufficient to direct the type III secretion of an adenylate cyclase reporter protein (93, 100). However, there is no discernable consensus secretion signal contained within the first 15 amino acids of Yops and the proteinaceous nature of the signal was put into question when evidence was reported that the secretion signal was actually carried within the mRNA message of YopE, YopN, and YopQ (8, 9, 90). Another report was unable to confirm the involvement of an mRNA signal in the *yopE* message (67). Indeed, the report emphasized that the YopE secretion signal is carried within the first 11 amino acids of YopE and amphipathicity was important for a functional secretion signal. More recently, the importance of amphipathicity in the first eight amino acids of YopE was elegantly confirmed by making every permutation of serine or isoleucine in positions 2-8 (68). The jury is still out on whether the signal is protein or RNA or both. However, two recent reviews provide contrasting viewpoints on this important, albeit controversial, research area (21, 66).

The secretion signals for the *P. syringae* effectors AvrB and AvrPto reside within the first 15 amino acids (7). Plant pathogen effectors have been entangled in the mRNA/protein signal controversy as well. Both AvrPto and the *Xanthomonas campestris* AvrBs2 proteins have been shown to possess a secretion signal present in the effector mRNA (7, 76). A recent observation made by two independent groups is that the first 50 amino acids of *P. syringae* Hops are amphipathic and rich in polar amino acids, particularly serine and glutamine (36, 85). While these may not represent secretion signals they do indicate that Hop proteins share common characteristics (more on this below). Together with the recent experiments showing the importance of amphipathicity in the secretion of *Yersinia* Yops suggest that these may be important characteristics for secretion. Moreover, additional features within the N terminus of *P. syringae* Hops further support that the secretion signal is of a proteinaceous nature. However, further research is required to resolve the controversy involving the biochemical nature of type III effector secretion signals.

TYPE III CHAPERONES ARE UTILIZED IN THE *P. SYRINGAE* HRP SYSTEM

The type III secretion of a subset of effectors from animal pathogens is assisted by type III chaperones. These proteins are small, acidic, contain predicted α-helical structure in their C termini, and are usually encoded by genes adjacent to the gene that encodes the effector that it chaperones (12, 86, 116). It is unknown how chaperones facilitate the secretion of effectors. However, many chaperones have been shown to prevent aggregation and/or proteolysis of their cognate effectors within the bacterial cell (75, 115). Recently, the crystal structure of a *Salmonella* chaperone/effector pair, SicP/SptP, was determined and the structure suggests that the chaperone may help keep the effector in a partially unfolded state, which may make the effector secretion-competent (102). There is also evidence that chaperones may give their effectors a competitive edge over other effectors for access into the type III apparatus (15). However, the role of chaperones in type III secretion appears to be multidimensional because several chaperones have recently been shown to play a regulatory role as well (24, 28, 108).

The location of chaperone genes next to their cognate effector genes makes sense evolutionarily because any required component for an effector would also need to be encoded on the horizontally transferred DNA (along with the effector gene) for it to be useful immediately (and, therefore, selected for) in the recipient bacterium. Because many bacterial plant pathogen *avr* genes have been cloned based on their avirulence activity in other pathogens or in nonpathogens carrying heterologous Hrp systems, it was speculated that bacterial plant pathogens were not as reliant on type III chaperones as animal pathogens or that the *hrp/hrc* cluster carried a more promiscuous chaperone (5). However, there were two early indications that there were type III chaperones in bacterial plant pathogens. An ORF (now named *shcA*) upstream of the *P. s. syringae* 61 effector gene *hopPsyA* shared the general characteristics of type III chaperone gene (see Fig. 1) (6). And the *Erwinia amylovora dspB* gene upstream of the *dspA* effector gene resembled chaperone genes and was required for the secretion of DspA (31). Recently, *shcA* was shown to be required for Hrp secretion of HopPsyA in culture supernatants, but not HrpZ, another Hrp-secreted protein (110). ShcA binds HopPsyA in a region within the N-terminal 166 amino acids (110). Therefore, *P. syringae* does possess type III chaperones. Indeed, the *P. syringae avr* and Hrp-related genes represented in the databases and likely *hop* genes present in the draft genome sequence of *P. s. tomato* DC3000 (more on the DC3000 draft sequence below) reveal that there are at least 9 chaperone/effector pairs in *P. syringae* (Table 1) (85, 110). Undoubtedly, type III

Table 1. Putative chaperones associated with characterized *P. syringae hop* genes or candidate *hop* genes

Chaperone or ORF name	Size (kDa)	pI	Effector or ORF name	*P. syringae* pathovar and strain	Accession number	Reference
EEL ORF6	13.2	6.3	EEL ORF5 (AvrBsT)	*syringae* B728a	AF232005	(3)
CEL ORF2	14.6	5.3	AvrE	*tomato* DC3000	AF232006	(3)
CEL ORF4	18.0	5.3	CEL ORF3	*tomato* DC3000	AF232006	(3)
CEL ORF8	19.9	6.8	CEL ORF7	*tomato* DC3000	AF232006	(3)
AvrPphF ORF1	15.6	6.1	AvrPphF ORF2	*phaseolicola* 1375A	AF231452	(107)
ORF6	14.7	6.5	ORF17	*tomato* DC3000	None	(85)
ORF13	15.6	5.5	HopPtoS1	*tomato* DC3000	None	(85)
ORF14	17.0	5.9	ORF15	*tomato* DC3000	None	(85)
ORF25	17.2	5.3	ORF26	*tomato* DC3000	None	(85)

chaperones are as prevalent in bacterial plant pathogens as they are in animal pathogens.

Type III delivery of effectors appears to be orchestrated in that certain effectors need to be delivered before other effectors into host cells. This seems to be the case because certain type III effectors from animal pathogens have opposing activities and if such effectors were delivered at the same time into host cells their activities could essentially cancel each other out (e.g., see ref. 30). Because the presence of chaperones allow effectors to exist stably in the bacterial cell without aggregating with other proteins they potentially could allow the cell to have a pool of effectors that are "good to go" into the host cell upon contact. Researchers studying the type III system in *Yersinia* have evidence that the effectors that are needed early during pathogenesis utilize chaperones (15, 66). If so, then the subgroup of plant pathogenic effectors that use chaperones may represent effectors that are needed early during plant pathogenesis.

CLUES AT DETERMINING WHAT *P. SYRINGAE* EFFECTORS ARE DOING TO FAVOR PARASITISM

The actions and targets of individual bacterial plant pathogen effectors are not well understood. However, important recent findings have provided tantalizing clues. Many of these clues are reported in greater detail in several excellent recent reviews (48, 60, 81, 101). It has been known for years that *P. syringae* is able to slow or suppress the induction of defense-related transcripts and proteins occurring during compatible interactions on susceptible plants (52, 114). The fact that virulent *P. syringae* strains can suppress defense responses appears to be, at least in part, due to the Hrp system and individual effector proteins. There are several indications reported that this occurs. For example, when the Avr protein AvrRpt2 is expressed in *Arabidopsis* it appears to suppress the RPM1-dependent defense pathway (20). Another example that is particularly well developed is the apparent suppressor activity of a virulence plasmid carried by *P. s. phaseolicola* race 7 (51, 107). The loss of this plasmid from *P. s. phaseolicola* race 7 causes the strain to elicit an HR in plants that were once fully susceptible to this strain (i.e., no HR was elicited)(51). This plasmid is known to contain several effector genes suggesting that one of them may act as a suppressor. These results also indicate that elsewhere in the genome is an *avr* gene that encodes a product that is recognized on these plants in the absence of the plasmid-encoded suppressor. Vivian and his colleagues have used a new naming system to describe such a scenario (51). The *avr* genes that are detectable in the wild type strain have been designated α *avr* genes. These *avr* genes, at least in the strain in question, have no suppressors to mask their avirulence activity. β *avr* genes, on the other hand, are only detected upon mutation or plasmid loss, which results in loss of the suppressor and unmasking of the β *avr* genes encoded avirulence activities.

The *avr* gene *avrPphF* further illustrates the potential complexity of these interactions and the α/β *avr* distinction. This *avr* gene is carried by the virulence plasmid of *P. s. phaseolicola* race 7 noted above. Bacterial strains cured of this plasmid, but containing *avrPphF in trans,* elicit an HR on plants that were normally susceptible when the strain carried the intact virulence plasmid (107). Thus, *avrPphF* is acting as a so-called β *avr* gene in this strain. Interestingly, it was determined that the *avrPphF*-associated HR was suppressed by another *avr* gene, *avrPphC*, carried on the same plasmid (107). Therefore, it is becoming apparent that these crafty bacterial pathogens have alternate strategies to overcome the evolution of a plant resistance protein that can recognize individual type III effectors (i.e., Avr proteins). One strategy that would be expected and apparently does occur in nature is loss or mutational inactivation of the recognized *avr* gene (e.g., see ref. 104). But, clearly, these pathogens can also deliver other effectors that are able to suppress specific Avr-induced defense pathways abrogating the need to disable or discard *avr* genes.

Another clue to the role of type III effectors in pathogenicity is where they localize inside the plant cell. The Avr proteins AvrRpm1, AvrB, AvrPphB, and AvrPto contain eukaryote-specific myristoylation motifs and these motifs are required for the localization of these Avr proteins to the plant plasma membrane (80, 96). The *P. s. tomato* DC3000 effectors $\text{AvrPphF}_{\text{Pto}}$ and HopPtoS1 also contain apparent myristoylation motifs (85). Thus, the plasma membrane appears to be the site of action for several *P. syringae* effectors. The *Arabidopsis* resistance protein, RPM1, which recognizes both AvrB and AvrRpm1 also localizes to the plasma membrane (16). Recently, another plasma membrane-localized *Arabidopsis* protein was identified because it interacts with RPM1 and the Avr proteins AvrRpm1 and AvrB (71). This protein, named RIN4 for RPM1-interacting protein appears to be a negative regulator of basal plant defenses and the Avr proteins may modulate the activity of RIN4 to favor bacterial pathogenesis (71). Indeed, this finding is quite significant because RIN4 may represent the first virulence target of a type III effector from bacterial plant pathogens.

Another theme that is beginning to emerge is that many broadly conserved type III effectors are cysteine proteases. There are two effectors that are broadly conserved in the TTSSs of animal and plant pathogens, YopJ/P and YopT, and both have cysteine protease activity (84, 97). YopJ is a *Yersinia* spp. type III effector that down regulates multiple signaling pathways in animal cells and can induce apoptosis in macrophages (82, 83). The net result of YopJ in host cells is the inhibition of signaling pathways that are needed for both innate and adaptive immunity. The YopJ family of cysteine proteases resembles a ubiquitin-like protease from yeast and YopJ has been shown to act on small ubiquitin-related modifier

(SUMO) tagged proteins. Thus, YopJ's activities are probably modifying specific proteins such that their signaling activities are altered or their status for degradation via the 26S proteosome is changed (82). YopJ homologs are found in several plant pathogens including *X. campestris* (22, 118), *E. amylovora* and *P. syringae* (3). Curiously, while essentially nothing is known about the involvement of this cysteine protease family in the disease of plants, the *X. campestris* AvrBsT requires the cysteine protease catalytic triad to elicit the HR in plants (84). Based on YopJ's activities in animals, the plant pathogen YopJ homologs are predicted to target the innate immune system in plants.

The YopT family of cysteine proteases is the other group that was recently reported to include several plant pathogen type III effectors (97). YopT was clearly shown to possess cysteine protease activity that acts on Rho GTPases, cleaving modifications from the C-termini (97). This activity results in changes in the actin skeleton in mammalian cells (50, 97). The plant pathogen effectors known to belong to the YopT family are *P. s. phaseolicola* AvrPphB (99), *P. s. tomato* CEL ORF7 (3), and *P. s. pisi* AvrPpiC2 (10). Do the plant pathogenic members of this family share the same targets as their animal pathogen counterparts? At first glance, this does not appear to be the case because plant pathogens remain extracellular and do not activate or suppress their uptake into host cells, a strategy used by several animal pathogens. Although, they may target a similar protein (i.e., a GTPase) involved in a different host pathway. As with the plant pathogen members of the YopJ family, nothing is known about the virulence targets of AvrPphB, CEL ORF7, or AvrPpiC2. However, the HR activity of AvrPphB, like AvrBsT, requires the catalytic triad residues of cysteine proteases (97).

P. s. tomato DC3000 Genomics

At the time of writing this chapter the draft nucleotide sequence of the *P. s. tomato* DC3000 genome is available (http://www.tigr.org/tdb/mdb/mdbinprogress.html) and the genome should be finished and closed in summer, 2002. Several papers have already been published utilizing the DC3000 draft genome sequence (13, 27, 36, 85). Thus, the likely impact of having the genome sequence for DC3000 will, no doubt, be quite significant. These first uses of the DC3000 genome sequence were largely focused on the Hrp system. Because Hrp promoters contain a *cis* element, the Hrp box (see above), it is possible to search for this sequence throughout the genome of DC3000. Fouts *et al.* (27) recognized that several known Hrp promoters contained atypical Hrp boxes. To allow for a more thorough search for additional Hrp promoters, a hidden Markov model (HMM) was used. This search revealed several

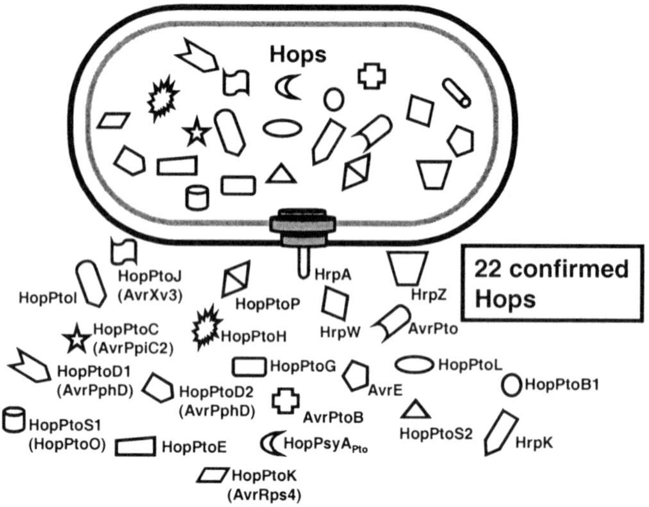

Figure 4. The confirmed inventory of Hop proteins from *P. s. tomato* DC3000. The bacterial cell is depicted as a rod that contains one Hrp apparatus that crosses the gram-negative bacterial periplasm. Inside and outside of the bacterial cell are objects that represent Hop proteins confirmed to be secreted by the DC3000 Hrp system in culture secretion assays, translocation assays, or on the basis of the secretion of a closely-related homolog (in the case of AvrE and HopPsyA$_{Pto}$). The total confirmed Hop inventory is presently 22. This does not include several good candidate Hops that have not as-of-yet been tested for secretion. The references for each Hop are noted in the text.

important aspects about the *P. syringae* Hrp system. First, some Hrp promoters express regulatory or toxin biosynthesis proteins instead of Hops. This is in some ways disappointing because it would have made identification of *hop* genes much easier if every Hrp promoter away from the Hrp pathogenicity island expressed a *hop* gene. Second, some Hrp boxes of known *avr* genes had relatively poor HMM values indicating that real Hrp-related genes await discovery within a relatively large pool of candidate genes. And third, perhaps most importantly, the research allowed the first glimpse of what known *avr/hop* genes are contained within DC3000.

An immediate goal of the DC3000 genome project is to determine which of the ORFs downstream of apparent Hrp promoters encode Hops. Two recent papers make significant progress in attaining this goal. Guttman *et al.* (36) used an AvrRtp2 transposon to identify 13 Hops from *P. s. maculicola* ES4326. Many of these are homologs of Avr proteins from other *P. syringae* pathovars and several are likely to represent helper proteins. While doing their Hop search in *P. s. maculicola* the researchers recognized that Hops have an exceptionally high serine content. This allowed for a screen of the draft genome of DC3000 for ORFs downstream of typical Hrp promoters for this characteristic and for them to make predictions about whether the ORF encoded a Hop. Two of these putative DC3000 Hops, named HopPtoO and HopPtoP, were confirmed to be translocated into plant cells when fused to the AvrRpt2 reporter (36).

In the second paper, Petnicki-Ocwieja *et al.* (85) describe a two-pronged genome-wide search for DC3000 Hops. In their first Hop search they screened ORFs downstream of Hrp promoters that had HMM *E* values <1e-3 (which included typical and moderately atypical Hrp boxes) for horizontal transfer indicators. Experimental testing confirmed 5 of these encoded novel proteins secreted via the Hrp system in culture and were given the following Hop names: HopPtoE, HopPtoG, HopPtoH, HopPtoI, and HopPtoS1. Interestingly, HopPtoS1 shares similarity with ADP-ribosyltransferases, enzymes that modify signal transduction pathways. Five different proteins that showed homology to Avr proteins from different *P. syringae* pathovars proved also to be secreted or translocated. Since the avirulence activity of the DC3000 Avr homologs was unknown they were renamed HopPtoC (AvrPpiC2 homolog), HopPtoD1 and HopPtoD2 (AvrPphD homologs), HopPtoJ (AvrXv3), and HopPtoK (AvrRps4 homolog). When all of the known Hop inventory of *P. syringae* was compared, shared characteristics within the amino termini were recognized (85). These Hop characteristics or "rules" allowed an algorithm to be written that was used to search the DC3000 draft genome sequence for ORFs that shared these characteristics. Importantly, this allowed for a Hop search independent of Hrp promoters and yielded a pool of 32 ORFs that were enriched for *hop* genes. Two of the highly-ranked candidate *hop* genes within this pool encoded proteins that were secreted in culture and were given the names HopPtoS2 and HopPtoL (85). HopPtoL shares similarity with SrfC, a candidate type III effector from *S. enterica*, which adds to the growing list of type III-secreted proteins shared between plant and animal pathogens. HopPtoS2 possesses significant similarity to ADP-ribosyltransferases as did two other ORFs identified in this genome-wide search. ADP-ribosyltransferases have been known for quite some time to be important in animal pathogens (26), but it now appears that these enzymes also play an important role in the bacterial pathogenesis of plants.

Because many new Hop proteins have recently been identified, a useful exercise is to tally all of the Hops confirmed to travel the Hrp pathway in DC3000 (Fig. 4 shows a summary of the DC3000 Hop inventory). The DC3000 Hrp system secretes the helper proteins HopPtoP (36), HrpA (91), HrpW (19), and HrpZ (40). In addition, the DC3000 genome is known to carry at least 12 *avr* homologs out of which the following have been demonstrated to encode a Hop: AvrPto (109), AvrPtoB (57), AvrE (31), HopPsyA$_{Pto}$ (109), HopPtoC (85), HopPtoD1 (85), HopPtoD2 (85), HopPtoJ (85), and HopPtoK (85). Several other novel Hops were identified because of their secretion or translocation phenotype. These include HopPtoB1 (Petnicki-Ocwieja and Alfano, manuscript submitted), HopPtoE (85), HopPtoG (85), HopPtoH (85), HopPtoI (85), HopPtoL (85), HopPtoS1/HopPtoO (36, 85), HopPtoS2 (85), and HrpK (van Dijk and Alfano, manuscript submitted). Adding all of these Hops together brings the current confirmed DC3000 Hop inventory to 22. To our knowledge this is the largest confirmed inventory of type III-secreted proteins from any type III system described. It will be interesting to see if this remains the case after researchers search other genomes for genes that encode type III-secreted proteins using genome-wide approaches.

It is worth noting that the DC3000 confirmed Hop inventory is likely to continue to enlarge because there are at least 7 additional Avr proteins, 5 other helper protein homologs, and several other putative Hops identified that need to be tested to determine their secretion status (27, 36, 85). A conservative estimate of the total Hops present in DC3000 is about 40. However, it would not be that surprising if the confirmed Hop inventory of DC3000 reached 50 or more. Clearly, we have much work ahead of us to assign roles for each of these proteins in Hrp secretion and/or pathogenesis.

Concluding Remarks

It is an exciting time to be studying the Hrp systems of *P. syringae*. We now have a large number of Hops with little known about what they do in bacterial-plant interactions. Perhaps, a reasonable analogy would be as if this was the first act of a play in which we have been introduced to a rogues' gallery of characters, and now we are eagerly waiting for the plot to thicken. To develop these characters (i.e., the Hops) we need to continue to take advantage of the new technologies available in cell and molecular biology. The continued development of additional cellular and molecular markers is extremely important in order to hone in on effector targets. Moreover, including intensive bioinformatic analyses and structure determination of Hops should facilitate plant target identification. In short, we have many challenges ahead of us. But, the anticipation of discovering what Hops do to the plant to favor parasitism and what hidden secrets their plant targets will reveal about plant biology should expedite this research.

Acknowledgements

We thank members of the Alfano laboratory and Karin van Dijk for reviewing this chapter before submission in June 2002. Work in our laboratory was supported in part by National Science Foundation Grants IBN-0096348 and DBI-0077622 and National Research Initiative Competitive Grants Program, US Department of Agriculture Grant 01-35319-10019.

Literature Cited

1. Aldon D, Brito B, Boucher C, Genin S (2000) A bacterial sensor of plant cell contact controls the transcriptional induction of *Ralstonia solanacearum* pathogenicity genes. EMBO 19:2304-2314.
2. Alfano J R, Bauer D W, Milos T M, Collmer A (1996) Analysis of the role of the *Pseudomonas syringae* pv. *syringae* HrpZ harpin in elicitation of the hypersensitive response in tobacco using functionally nonpolar *hrpZ* deletion mutants, truncated HrpZ fragments, and *hrmA* mutations. Mol. Microbiol. 19:715-728.
3. Alfano J R, Charkowski A O, Deng W -L, Badel J L, Petnicki-Ocwieja T, van Dijk K, Collmer A (2000) The *Pseudomonas syringae* Hrp pathogenicity island has a tripartite mosaic structure composed of a cluster of type III secretions genes bounded by exchangeable effector and conserved effector loci that contribute to parasitic fitness and pathogenicity in plants. Proc. Natl. Acad. Sci. USA 97:4856-4861.
4. Alfano J R, Collmer A (1996) Bacterial pathogens in plants: Life up against the wall. Plant Cell 8:1683-1698.
5. Alfano J R, Collmer A (1997) The type III (Hrp) secretion pathway of plant pathogenic bacteria: Trafficking harpins, Avr proteins, and death. J. Bacteriol. 179:5655-5662.
6. Alfano J R, Kim H -S, Delaney T P, Collmer A (1997) Evidence that the *Pseudomonas syringae* pv. *syringae hrp*-linked *hrmA* gene encodes an Avr-like protein that acts in an *hrp*-dependent manner within tobacco cells. Mol. Plant-Microbe Int. 10:580-588.
7. Anderson D M, Fouts D E, Collmer A, Schneewind O (1999) Reciprocal secretion of proteins by the bacterial type III machines of plant and animal pathogens suggests universal recognition of mRNA targeting signals. Proc. Natl. Acad. Sci. USA 96:12839-12843.

8. Anderson D M, Schneewind O (1997) A mRNA signal for the type III secretion of Yop proteins by *Yersinia enterocolitica*. Science 278:1140-1143.
9. Anderson D M, Schneewind O (1999) *Yersinia enterocolitica* type III secretion: an mRNA signal that couples translation and secretion of YopQ. Mol. Microbiol. 31:1139-1148.
10. Arnold D L, Jackson R W, Fillingham A J, Goss S C, Taylor J D, Mansfield J W, Vivian A (2001) Highly conserved sequences flank virulence genes: isolation of novel avirulence genes from *Pseudomonas syringae* pv. *pisi*. Microbiol. 147:1171-1182.
11. Bender C L, Alarcon-Chaidez F, Gross D. C (1999) *Pseudomonas syringae* phtotoxins: Mode of action, regulation, and biosynthesis by peptide and polyketide synthetases. Microbiol. Mol. Biol. Rev. 63:266-292.
12. Bennett J C, Hughes C (2000) From flagellum assembly to virulence: The extended family of type III export chaperones. Trends Microbiol. 8:202-204.
13. Boch J, Joardar V, Gao L, Robertson T L, Lim M, Kunkel B N (2002) Identification of *Pseudomonas syringae* pv. *tomato* genes induced during infection of *Arabidopsis thaliana*. Mol. Microbiol. 44:73-88.
14. Bogdanove A J, Bauer D W, Beer S V (1998) *Erwinia amylovora* secretes DspE, a pathogenicity factor and functional AvrE homolog, through the Hrp (type III Secretion) pathway. J. Bacteriol. 180:2244-2247.
15. Boyd A P, Lambermont I, Cornelis G (2000) Competition between the Yops of *Yersinia enterocolitica* for delivery in eukaryotic cells: Role of the SycE chaperone binding domain of YopE. J. Bacteriol. 182:4811-4821.
16. Boyes D C, Nam J, Dangl J L (1998) The *Arabidopsis thaliana* RPM1 disease resistance gene product is a peripheral plasma membrane protein that is degraded coincident with the hypersensitive response. Proc. Natl. Acad. Sci. USA 95.
17. Brown I R, Mansfield J W, Taira S, Roine E, Romanstuch M (2001) Immunocytochemical localization of the HrpA and HrpZ supports a role for the Hrp pilus in the transfer of effector proteins from *Pseudomonas syringae* pv. *tomato* across the host plant cell wall. Mol. Plant-Microbe Int. 3:394-404.
18. Casper-Lindley C, Dahlbeck D, Clark E T, Staskawicz B J (2002) Direct biochemical evidence for type III secretion-dependent translocation of the AvrBs2 effector protein into plant cells. Proc. Natl. Acad. Sci. USA 99:8336-8341.
19. Charkowski A O, Alfano J R, Preston G, Yuan J, He S Y, Collmer A (1998) The *Pseudomonas syringae* pv. *tomato* HrpW protein has domains similar to harpins and pectate lyases and can elicit

the plant hypersensitive response and bind to pectate. J. Bacteriol. 180:5211-5217.

20. Chen Z, Kloek A P, Boch J, Katagiri F, Kunkel B N (2000) The *Pseudomonas syringae avrRpt2* gene product promotes pathogen virulence from inside plant cells. Mol. Plant-Microbe Int. 13:1312-1321.

21. Cheng L W, Schneewind O (2000) Type III machines of gram-negative bacteria: delivering the goods. Trends Microbiol. 8:214-220.

22. Ciesiolka L D, Hwin T, Gearlds J D, Minsavage G V, Saenz R, Bravo M, Handley V, Conover S M, Zhang H, Caprogno J, Phengrasamy N B, Toms A O, Stall R E, Whalen M. C (1999) Regulation of expression of avirulence gene *avrRxv* and identification of a family of host interaction factors by sequence analysis of *avrBsT*. Mol. Plant -Microbe Int. 12:35-44.

23. Collmer A, Badel J L, Charkowski A O, Deng W L, Fouts D E, Ramos A R, Rehm A H, Anderson D M, Schneewind O, van Dijk K, Alfano J R (2000) *Pseduomonas syringae* Hrp type III secretion system and effector proteins. Proc. Natl. Acad. Sci. USA 97:8770-8777.

24. Darwin K H, Miller V L (2001) Type III secretion chaperone-dependent regulation: activation of virulence genes by SicA and InvF in *Salmonella typhimurium*. EMBO J. 20:1850-1862.

25. Ebel F, Podzadel T, Rohde M, Kresse A U, Kramer S, Deibel C, Guzman C A, Chakraborty T (1998) Initial binding of Shiga toxin-producing *Escherichia coli* to host cells and subsequent induction of actin rearrangements depend on filamentous EspA-containing surface appendages. Mol. Microbiol. 30:147-161.

26. Finlay B B, Falkow S (1997) Common themes in microbial pathogenicity revisited. Microbiol. Mol. Biol. Rev. 61:136-169.

27. Fouts D E, Abramovitch R B, Alfano J R, Baldo A M, Buell C R, Cartinhour S, Chatterjee A K, D'Ascenzo M, Gwinn M, Lazarowitz S G, Lin N -C, Martin G B, Rehm A H, Schneider D J, van Dijk K, Tang X, Collmer A (2002) Genomewide identification of *Pseudomonas syringae* pv. *tomato* DC3000 promoters controlled by the HrpL alternative sigma factor. Proc. Natl. Acad. Sci. USA 99:2275-2280.

28. Francis M S, Lloyd S A, Wolf-Watz H (2001) The type III secretion chaperone LcrH co-operates with YopD to establish a negative, regulatory loop for control of Yop synthesis in *Yersinia pseudotuberculosis*. Mol. Microbiol. 42:1075-1093.

29. Galán J E, Collmer A (1999) Type III secretion machines: Bacterial devices for protein delivery into host cells. Science 284:1322-1328.

30. Galán J E, Zhou D (2000) Striking a balance: modulation of the actin cytoskeleton by *Salmonella*. Proc. Natl. Acad. Sci. USA 97:8754-8761.

31. Gaudriault S, Malandrin L, Paulin J -P, Barny M -A (1997) DspA, an essential pathogenicity factor of *Erwinia amylovora* showing homology with AvrE of *Pseudomonas syringae*, is secreted via the Hrp secretion pathway in a DspB-dependent way. Mol. Microbiol. 26:1057-1069.

32. Ginocchio C C, Olmsted S B, Wells C L, Galán J E (1994) Contact with epithelial cells induces the formation of surface appendages on *Salmonella typhimurium*. Cell 76:717-724.

33. Gopalan S, Bauer D W, Alfano J R, Loniello A O, He S Y, Collmer A (1996). Expression of the *Pseudomonas syringae* avirulence protein AvrB in plant cells alleviates its dependence on the hypersensitive response and pathogenicity (Hrp) secretion system in eliciting genotype-specific hypersensitive cell death. Plant Cell 8:1095-1105.

34. Grimm C, Aufsatz W, Panopoulos N J (1995) The *hrpRS* locus of *Pseudomonas syringae* pv. *phaseolicola* constitutes a complex regulatory unit. Mol. Microbiol. 15:155-165.

35. Guttman D S, Greenberg J T (2001) Functional analysis of the type III effectors AvrRpt2 and AvrRpm1 of *Pseudomonas syringae* with the use of a single-copy genomic integration system. Mol. Plant-Microbe Int. 14:145-155.

36. Guttman D S, Vinatzer B A, Sarkar S F, Ranall M V, Kettler G, Greenberg J T (2002) A functional screen for the type III (Hrp) secretome of the plant pathogen *Pseudomonas syringae*. Science 295:1722-1726.

37. Hahn M G, Bucheli P, Cervone F, Doares S H, O'Neill R A, Darvill A, Albersheim P (1988) The roles of cell wall constituents in plant-pathogen interactions, p. 131-181. *In* E. W. Nester and T. Kosuge (ed.), Plant-microbe interactions: molecular and genetic perspectives, vol. 3. Macmillan, New York.

38. Ham J H, Bauer D W, Fouts D E, Collmer A (1998) A cloned *Erwinia chrysanthemi* Hrp (type III protein secretion) system functions in *Escherichia coli* to deliver *Pseudomonas syringae* Avr signals to plant cells and to secrete Avr proteins in culture. Proc. Natl. Acad. Sci. USA 95:10206-10211.

39. He S Y (1998) Type III protein secretion systems in plant and animal pathogenic bacteria. Annu. Rev. Phytopathol. 36:363-392.

40. He S Y, Huang H -C, Collmer A (1993) *Pseudomonas syringae* pv. *syringae* harpin$_{Pss}$: a protein that is secreted via the Hrp pathway and elicits the hypersensitive response in plants. Cell 73:1255-1266.

41. Hendrickson E I, Guevara P, Penaloza-Vazquez A, Shao J, Bender C L, Ausubel F M (2000) Virulence of the phytopathogen *Pseudomonas syringae* pv. *maculicola* is *rpoN* dependent. J. Bacteriol. 182:3498-3507.

42. Hendrickson E I, Guevera P, Ausubel F M (2000) The alternative sigma factor RpoN is required for *hrp* activity in *Pseudomonas syringae* pv. *maculicola* and acts at the level of *hrpL* transcription. J. Bacteriol. 182:3508-3516.

43. Hoiczyk E, Blobel G (2001) Polymerization of a single protein of the pathogen *Yersinia enterocolitica* into needles punctures eukaryotic cells. Proc. Natl. Acad. Sci. USA 98:4669-4674.

44. Hoyos M E, Stanley C M, He S Y, Pike S, Pu X -A, Novacky A (1996) The interaction of $Harpin_{Pss}$, with plant cell walls. Mol. Plant-Microbe Int. 9:608-616.

45. Hueck C J (1998) Type III protein secretion systems in bacterial pathogens of animals and plants. Microbiol. Mol. Biol. Rev. 62:379-433.

46. Hutcheson S W, Bretz J, Sussan T, Jin S, Pak K (2001) Enhancer-binding proteins HrpR and HrpS interact to regulate *hrp*-encoded type III protein secretion in *Pseudomonas syringae* strains. J. Bacteriol. 183:5589-5598.

47. Huynh T V, Dahlbeck D, Staskawicz B J (1989) Bacterial blight of soybean: Regulation of a pathogen gene determining host cultivar specificity. Science 245:1374-1377.

48. Innes R W (2001) Targeting the targets of type III effector proteins secreted by phytopathogenic bacteria. Mol. Plant Pathol. 2:109-115.

49. Innes R W, Bent A F, Kunkel B N, Bisgrove S R, Staskawicz B J (1993) Molecular analysis of avirulence gene *avrRpt2* and identification of a putative regulatory sequence common to all known *Pseudomonas syringae* avirulence genes. J. Bacteriol. 175:4859-4869.

50. Iriarte M, Cornelis G R (1998) YopT, a new *Yersinia* Yop effector protein, affects the cytoskeleton of host cells. Mol. Microbiol. 29:915-929.

51. Jackson R W, Athanassopoulos E, Tsiamis G, Mansfield J W, Sesma A, Arnold D L, Gibbon M J, Murillo J, Taylor J D, Vivian A (1999) Identification of a pathogenicity island, which contains genes for virulence and avirulence, on a large native plasmid in the bean pathogen *Pseudomonas syringae* pathovar *phaseolicola*. Proc. Natl. Acad. Sci. USA 96:10875-10880.

52. Jakobek J L, Smith J A, Lindgren P B (1993) Suppression of bean defense responses by *Pseudomonas syringae*. Plant Cell 5:57-63.

53. Jin Q, He S -Y (2001). Role of the Hrp pilus in type III protein secretion in *Pseudomonas syringae*. Science 294:2556-2558.

54. Jin Q, W Hu, Brown I R, McGhee G, Hart P, Jones A L, He S Y (2001). Visualization of secreted Hrp and Avr proteins along the Hrp pilus during type III secretion in *Erwinia amylovora* and *Pseudomonas syringae*. Mol. Microbiol. 40:1129-1139.
55. Keen N T (1990) Gene-for-gene complementarity in plant-pathogen interactions. Annu. Rev. Genet. 24:447-463.
56. Kim J F, Alfano J R (2002) Pathogenicity islands and virulence plasmids of bacterial plant pathogens. Pages 127-147 in: Curr. Top. Microbiol. Immunol., vol. 264/2. J. Hacker (ed.), Springer-Verlag, Berlin.
57. Kim Y J, Lin N -C, Martin G B (2002) Two distinct *Pseudomonas* effector proteins interact with the Pto kinase and activate plant immunity. Cell 109:589-598.
58. Kjemtrup S, Nimchuk Z, Dangl J L (2000) Effector proteins of phytopathogenic bacteria: Bifunctional signals in virulence and host recognition. Curr. Opin. Microbiol. 3:73-78.
59. Kubori T, Matsushima Y, Nakamura D, Uralil J, Lara-Tejero M, Sukhan A., Galán J E, Aizawa S -I (1998) Supramolecular structure of the *Salmonella typimurium* type III protein secretion system. Science 280:602-605.
60. Lahaye T, Bonas U (2001) Molecular secrets of bacterial type III effector proteins. Trends Plant Sci. 6:1360-1385.
61. Leach J E White F F (1996) Bacterial avirulence genes. Annu. Rev. Phytopathol. 34:153-179.
62. Lee J, Klessig D F, Nurnberger T (2001) A harpin binding site in tobacco plasma membranes mediates activation of the pathogenesis-related gene *HIN1* independent of extracellular calcium but dependent on mitogen-activated protein kinase activity. Plant Cell 13:1079-1093.
63. Lee J, Klusener B, Tsiamis G, Stevens C, Neyt C, Tampakaki A P, Panopoulos N J, Noller J, Weiler E W, Cornelis G R, Mansfield J W (2001) $HrpZ_{Psph}$ from the plant pathogen *Pseudomonas syringae* pv. *phaseolicola* binds to lipid bilayers and forms an ion-conducting pore *in vitro*. Proc. Natl. Acad. Sci. USA 98:289-294.
64. Leister R T, Ausubel F M, Katagiri F (1996) Molecular recognition of pathogen attack occurs inside of plant cells in plant disease resistance specified by *Arabidopsis* genes *RPS2* and *RPM1*. Proc. Natl. Acad. Sci. U.S.A 93:15497-15502.
65. Li C -M, Brown I, Mansfield J, Stevens C, Boureau T, Romantschuk M, Taira S (2002) The Hrp pilus of *Pseudomonas syringae* elongates from its tip and acts as a conduit for translocation of the effector protein HrpZ. EMBO J 21:1909-1915.

66. Lloyd S A, Forsberg A, Wolf-Watz H, Francis M S (2001) Targeting exported substrates to the *Yersinia* TTSS: different functions for different signals? Trends Microbiol. 9:367-371.
67. Lloyd S A, Norman M, Rosqvist R, Wolf-Watz H (2001) *Yersinia* YopE is targeted for type III secretion by N-terminal, not mRNA, signals. Mol. Microbiol. 39:520-531.
68. Lloyd S A, Sjostrom M, Andersson S, Wolf-Watz H (2002) Molecular characterization of type III secretion signals via analysis of synthetic N-terminal amino acid sequences. Mol. Microbiol. 43:51-59.
69. Lonetto M A, Brown K L, Rudd K E, Buttner M J (1994) Analysis of the *Streptomyces coelicolor sigE* gene reveals the existence of a subfamily of eubacterial RNA polymerase s factors involved in the regulation of extracytoplasmic functions. Proc. Natl. Acad. Sci. U.S.A 91:7573-7577.
70. Lorang J M, Keen N T (1995) Characterization of *avr*E from *Pseudomonas syringae* pv. *tomato*: A *hrp*-linked avirulence locus consisting of at least two transcriptional units. Mol. Plant-Microbe Int. 8:49-57.
71. Mackey D, Holt B. F, III, Wiig A, Dangl J L (2002) RIN4 interacts with *Pseudomonas syringae* type III effector molecules and is required for RPM1-mediated resistance in *Arabidopsis*. Cell 108:743-754.
72. Macnab R M (1999) The bacterial flagellum: reversible rotary propeller and type III export apparatus. J. Bacteriol. 181:7149-7153.
73. Mansfield J, Jenner C, Hockenhull R, Bennett M A, Stewart R (1994) Characterization of *avrPphE*, a gene for cultivar-specific avirulence from *Pseudomonas syringae* pv. *phaseolicola* which is physically linked to *hrpY*, a new *hrp* gene identified in the halo-blight bacterium. Mol. Plant-Microbe Int. 7:726-739.
74. Marenda M, Brito B, Callard D, Genin S, Barberis P, Boucher C, Arlat M (1998) PrhA controls a novel regulatory pathway required for the specific induction of *Ralstonia solanacearum hrp* genes in the presence of plant cells. Mol. Microbiol. 27:437-453.
75. Ménard R, Sansonetti P, Parsot C, Vasselon T (1994) Extracellular association and cytoplasmic partitioning of the IpaB and IpaC invasins of *S. flexneri*. Cell 79:515-525.
76. Mudgett M B, Chesnikova O, Dahlbeck D, Clark E T, Rossier O, Bonas U, Staskawicz B J (2000) Molecular signals required for type III secretion and translocation of the *Xanthomonas campestris* AvrBs2 protein to pepper plants. Proc. Natl. Acad. Sci. USA 97:13324-13329.
77. Mudgett M B, Staskawicz B J (1999) Characterization of the *Pseudomonas syringae* pv. *tomato* AvrRpt2 protein:

demonstration of secretion and processing during bacterial pathogenesis. Mol. Microbiol. 32:927-941.

78. Mudgett M B, Staskawicz B J (1998) Protein signaling via type III secretion pathways in phytopatogenic bacteria. Curr. Opin. Microbiol. 1:109-114.

79. Neyt C, Cornelis G R (1999) Insertion of a Yop translocation pore into the macrophage plasma membrane by *Yersinia enterocolitica*: requirement for translocators YopB and YopD, but not LcrG. Mol. Microbiol. 33:971-981.

80. Nimchuk Z, Marois E, Kjemtrup S, Leister R T, Katagiri F, Dangl J L (2000) Eukaryotic fatty acylation drives plasma membrane targeting and enhances function of several type III effector proteins from *Pseudomonas syringae*. Cell 101:353-363.

81. Nimchuk Z, Rohmer L, Chang J H, Dangl J L (2001) Knowing the dancer from the dance: *R*-gene products and their interactions with other proteins from host and pathogen. Curr. Opin. Plant Biol. 4:288-294.

82. Orth, K (2002) Function of the *Yersinia* effector YopJ. Curr. Opin. Microbiol. 5:48-53.

83. Orth, K, Palmer L E, Bao Z Q, Stewart S, Rudolph A E, Bliska J B, Dixon J E (1999) Inhibition of the mitogen-activated protein kinase kinase superfamily by a *Yersinia* effector. Science 285:1920-1923.

84. Orth K, Xu Z, Mudgett M B, Bao Z Q, Palmer L E, Bliska J B, Mangel W F, Staskawicz B, Dixon J E (2000) Disruption of Signaling by *Yersinia* effector YopJ, a Ubiquitin-like protein protease. Science 290:1594-1597.

85. Petnicki-Ocwieja T, Schneider D J, Tam V C, Chancey S T, Shan L, Jamir Y, Schechter L M, Janes M D, Buell C R, Tang X, Collmer A, Alfano J R (2002) Genomewide identification of proteins secreted by the Hrp type III protein secretion system of *Pseudomonas syringae* pv. *tomato* DC3000. Proc. Natl. Acad. Sci. USA 99:7652-7657.

86. Plano G V, Day J B, Ferracci F (2001) Type III export: new users for an old pathway. Mol. Microbiol. 40:284-293.

87. Preston G, Deng W -L, Huang H -C, Collmer A (1998) Negative regulation of *hrp* genes in *Pseudomonas syringae* by HrpV. J. Bacteriol. 180:4532-4537.

88. Preston G, Huang H -C, He S Y, Collmer A (1995) The HrpZ proteins of *Pseudomonas syringae* pvs. *syringae, glycinea,* and *tomato* are encoded by an operon containing *Yersinia ysc* homologs and elicit the hypersensitive response in tomato but not soybean. Mol. Plant-Microbe Interact. 8:717-732.

89. Puri N, Jenner C, Bennett M, Stewart R, Mansfield J, Lyons N, Taylor J (1997) Expression of *avrPphB*, an avirulence gene from

Pseudomonas syringae pv. *phaseolicola*, and the delivery of signals causing the hypersensitive reaction in bean. Mol. Plant-Microbe Int. 10:247-256.

90. Ramamurthi K S, Schneewind O (2002) *Yersinia enterocolitica* type III secretion: Mutational analysis of the *yopQ* secretion signal. J. Bacteriol. 184:3321-3328.

91. Roine E, Wei W, Yuan J, Nurmiaho-Lassila E -L, Kalkkinen N, Romantschuk M, He S Y (1997) Hrp pilus: An *hrp*-dependent bacterial surface appendage produced by *Pseudomonas syringae* pv. *tomato* DC3000. Proc. Natl. Acad. Sci. U.S.A 94:3459-3464.

92. Salmeron J M, Staskawicz B J (1993) Molecular characterization and *hrp* dependence of the avirulence gene *avrPto* from *Pseudomonas syringae* pv. *tomato*. Mol. Gen. Genet. 239:6-16.

93. Schesser K, Frithz-Lindsten E, Wolf-Watz H (1996) Delineation and mutational analysis of the *Yersinia pseudotuberculosis* YopE domains which mediate translocation across bacterial and eukaryotic cellular membranes. J. Bacteriol. 178:7227-7233.

94. Scofield S R, Tobias C M, Rathjen J P, Chang J H, Lavelle D T, R. W. Michelmore, Staskawicz B J (1996) Molecular basis of gene-for-gene specificity in bacterial speck disease of tomato. Science 274:2063-2065.

95. Sekiya K, Ohishi M, Ogino T, Tamano K, Sasakawa C, Abe A (2001) Supermolecular structure of the enteropathogenic *Escherichia coli* type III secretion system and its direct interaction with the EspA sheath-like structure. Proc. Natl. Acad. Sci. USA 98:11638-11643.

96. Shan L, Thara V K, Martin G B, Zhou J, Tang X (2000) The *Pseudomonas* AvrPto protein is differentially recognized by tomato and tobacco and is localized to the plant plasma membrane. Plant Cell 12:2323-2337.

97. Shao F, Merritt P M, Bao Z, Innes R W, Dixon J E (2002) A *Yersinia* effector and a *Pseudomonas* avirulence protein define a family of cysteine proteases functioning in bacterial pathogenesis. Cell 109:575-588.

98. Shen H, Keen N T (1993) Characterization of the promoter of avirulence gene D from *Pseudomonas syringae* pv. *tomato*. J. Bacteriol. 175:5916-5924.

99. Simonich M T, Innes R W (1995) A disease resistance gene in *Arabidopsis* with specificity for the *avrPph3* gene of *Pseudomonas syringae* pv. phaseolicola. Mol. Plant-Microbe Int. 8:637-640.

100. Sory M -P, Boland A, Lambermont I, Cornelis G R (1995) Identification of the YopE and YopH domains required for secretion and internalization into the cytosol of macrophages,

using the *cyaA* gene fusion approach. Proc. Natl. Acad. Sci. U.S.A 92:11998-12002.

101. Staskawicz B J, Mudgett M B, Dangl J L, Galán J E (2001) Common and contrasting themes of plant and animal diseases. Science 292:2285-2289.

102. Stebbins C E, Galán J E (2001) Maintenance of an unfolded polypeptide by a cognate chaperone in bacterial type III secretion. Nature 414:77-81.

103. Stevens C, Bennett M A, Athanassopoulos E, Tsiamis G, Taylor J D, Mansfield J W (1998) Sequence variations in alleles of the avirulence gene *avrPphE.R2* from *Pseudomonas syringae* pv. *phaseolicola* lead to loss of recognition of the AvrPphE protein within bean cells and a gain in cultivar-specific virulence. Mol. Microbiol. 29:165-177.

104. Swords K M M, Dahlbeck D, Kearney B, Roy M, Staskawicz B J (1996) Spontaneous and induced mutations in a single open reading frame alters both virulence and avirulence in *Xanthomonas campestris* pv. *vesicatoria avrBs2*. J. Bacteriol. in press.

105. Tampakaki A P, Panopoulos N J (2000) Elicitation of hypersensitive cell death by extracellularly targeted HrpZ $_{Psph}$ produced in planta. Mol. Plant-Microbe Int. 13:1366-1374.

106. Tang X, Frederick R D, Zhou J, Halterman D A, Jia Y, Martin G B (1996) Physical interaction of AvrPto and the Pto kinase defines a recognition event involved in plant disease resistance. Science 274:2060-2063.

107. Tsiamis G, Mansfield J W, Hockenhull R, Jackson R W, Sesma A, Athanassopoulos E, Bennett M A, Stevens C, Vivian A, Taylor J D, Murillo J (2000) Cultivar-specific avirulence and virulence functions assigned to *avrPphF* in *Pseudomonas syringae* pv. *phaseolicola*, the cause of bean halo-blight disease. EMBO J. 19:3204-3214.

108. Tucker S C, Galán J E (2000) Complex function for SicA, a *Salmonella enterica* serovar *typhimurium* type III associated chaperone. J. Bacteriol. 182:2262-2268.

109. van Dijk K, Fouts D E, Rehm A H, Hill A R, Collmer A, Alfano J R (1999) The Avr (effector) proteins HrmA (HopPsyA) and AvrPto are secreted in culture from *Pseudomonas syringae* pathovars via the Hrp (type III) protein secretion system in a temperature and pH sensitive manner. J. Bacteriol. 181:4790-4797.

110. van Dijk K, Tam V C, Records A R, Petnicki-Ocwieja T, Alfano J R (2002) The ShcA protein is a molecular chaperone that assists in the secretion of the HopPsyA effector from the type III (Hrp)

protein secretion system of *Pseudomonas syringae*. Mol. Microbiol. 44:1469-1481.

111. Van Gijsegem F, Vasse J, Camus J C, Marenda M, Boucher C (2000) *Ralstonia solanacearum* produces Hrp-dependent pili that are required for PopA secretion but not for attachment of bacteria to plant cells. Mol. Microbiol. 36:249-260.

112. Vivian A, Arnold D L (2000) Bacterial effector genes and their role in host-pathogen interactions. J. Plant Pathol. 82:163-178.

113. Vivian A, Gibbon M J (1997) Avirulence genes in plant-pathogenic bacteria: signals or weapons. Microbiol. 143:693-704.

114. Voisey C R, Slusarenko A J (1989) Chitinase mRNA and enzyme activity in *Phaseolus vulgaris* (L.) increase more rapidly in response to avirulent than to virulent cells of *Pseudomonas syringae* pv. *phaseolicola*. Physiol. Mol. Plant Pathol. 35:403-412.

115. Wattiau P, Bernier B, Deslee P, Michiels T, Cornelis G R (1994) Individual chaperones required for Yop secretion by *Yersinia*. Proc. Natl. Acad. Sci. U.S.A 91:10493-10497.

116. Wattiau P, Woestyn S, Cornelis G R (1996) Customized secretion chaperones in pathogenic bacteria. Mol. Microbiol. 20:255-262.

117 Wei W, Plovanich-Jones A, Deng W -L, Jin Q -L, Collmer A, Huang H -C, He S -Y (2000) The gene coding for the Hrp pilus structural protein is required for type III secretion of Hrp and Avr proteins in *Pseudomonas syringae* pv. *tomato*. Proc. Natl. Acad. Sci. USA 97:2247-2252.

118. Whalen M, Wang J F, Carland F M, Heiskell M E, Dahlbeck D, Minsavage G V, Jones J B J, Scott J W, Stall R E, Staskawicz B (1993) Avirulence gene *avrRxv* from *Xanthomonas campestris* pv. *vesicatoria* specifies resistance on tomato line Hawaii 7998. Mol. Plant-Microbe Int. 6:616-627.

119. Xiao Y, Heu S, Yi J, Lu Y, Hutcheson S W (1994) Identification of a putative alternate sigma factor and characterization of a multicomponent regulatory cascade controlling the expression of *Pseudomonas syringae* pv. *syringae* Pss61 *hrp* and *hrmA* genes. J. Bacteriol. 176:1025-1036.

120. Xiao Y, Lu Y, Heu S, Hutcheson S W (1992) Organization and environmental regulation of the *Pseudomonas syringae* pv. *syringae* 61 *hrp* cluster. J. Bacteriol. 174:1734-1741.

121. Yang K -Y, Liu Y, Zhang S (2001) Activation of a mitogen-activated protein kinase pathway is involved in disease resistance in tobacco. Proc. Natl. Acad. Sci. USA 98:741-746.

122. Yuan J, He S Y (1996) The *Pseudomonas syringae* Hrp regulation and secretion system controls the production and secretion of multiple extracellular proteins. J. Bacteriol. 178:6399-6402.

123. Zhang S, Klessig D F (2001) MAPK cascades in plant defense signaling. Trends Plant Sci. 6:520-527.

Dissecting the Avirulence and Resistance Components that Comprise the Hypersensitive Response to *Cauliflower mosaic virus* in *Nicotiana*

James E. Schoelz, Karuppaiah Palanichelvam, Anthony B. Cole, Loránt Király, and John Cawly

Introduction

The hypersensitive response (HR) is an active defense response that is triggered in plants when a plant resistance (*R*) gene product recognizes a specific pathogen gene product called an avirulence (*Avr*) gene (5, 40, 51). The outcome of this recognition event is a cascade of plant defense responses which includes the production of reactive oxygen species, pathogenesis-related (PR) proteins, systemic acquired resistance and localized cell death at the initial infection site (24, 36, 47, 77). These defense responses have been the object of intense study for over thirty years, as researchers have tried to elucidate the contribution of each component to the resistance response. For example, it has been recently suggested that the cell death component of HR is an example of programmed cell death in plants (24, 25, 45).

Although cell death has been considered to be an integral part of HR, through the years there has been speculation about whether cell death is an absolute requirement for resistance conditioned by HR. As early as 1972, Király and coworkers suggested that the hypersensitive response elicited by *Phytophthora infestans* was incidental to disease resistance (58). Studies of viral *Avr* genes have shown that elicitation of the resistance response can become uncoupled from the elicitation of cell death. For example, the coat protein gene of *Tobacco mosaic virus* (TMV) elicits HR in tobacco that carry the *N'* gene. Mutations within the coat protein will alter this *Avr* gene product such that the virus will elicit a systemic HR (22). Similarly, a single amino acid change within the *Cucumber mosaic virus* (CMV) 2a polymerase results in a systemic HR in cowpea, whereas the wild type virus elicits a HR that restricts the movement of the virus to the inoculated leaf (57). These mutagenesis studies of viral *Avr* genes have led to the suggestion that different plant genes might be involved in eliciting the HR and the localization response (57).

On the host side, evidence has accumulated that resistance and cell death can be genetically separated. For example, the potato *Rx* gene conditions an extreme form of resistance to *Potato virus X* (PVX) (3, 61).

At first, this resistance was not considered to be related to the HR induced by other *R* gene products. However, the basic structure of the *Rx* gene product is similar to those of other *R* gene products that do elicit HR . Furthermore, it has been shown that if the PVX coat protein, the viral avirulence gene product, is expressed in *Rx* plants in a transient transformation assay, then the coat protein will elicit HR (6). Thus, it is thought that the resistance conditioned by *Rx* to PVX occurs so rapidly that the PVX coat protein cannot attain a concentration sufficient to trigger a visible HR. A similar model has been proposed to explain the resistance conferred by the *HRT* gene in *Arabidopsis thaliana* to *Turnip crinkle virus* (TCV). In this case, the *A. thaliana* ecotype that carries the *HRT* gene does respond to TCV with an HR (20). However, transgenic plants that overexpress *HRT* exhibit a micro HR or no HR, and are thought to be resistant to TCV because the plants respond rapidly to the infection (20). Interestingly, transgenic plants that express lower levels of *HRT* respond to TCV with systemic HR; a second recessive gene, designated *rrt,* has been found to be required for resistance (55). It is also possible to knock out the cell death pathway, and retain resistance. Yu and coworkers (96) isolated an *A. thaliana* mutant, *dnd1*, that lost the capacity to respond to *Pseudomonas syringae* pv. *glycinea* Race 4 with HR, yet still exhibited resistance to Race 4. Finally, there are many examples of resistance that are not associated with HR (11, 63, 65).

In this chapter, we describe a hypersensitive response of *Nicotiana* to *Cauliflower mosaic virus* that has proven amenable for uncoupling cell death from resistance. In the first section, we describe the genetic variation that occurs in the CaMV/*Nicotiana* pathosystem. This degree of variation in both the host and pathogen dictates the type of questions that can be addressed. In the next section, we discuss what is known about the nature of the CaMV *Avr* gene. In the last section, we describe the evidence that two plant gene products are able to recognize this CaMV *Avr* gene protein to trigger separate resistance and cell death pathways. If both plant genes are present in a single host, then the outcome is a necrotic local lesion and the limitation of viral movement - i.e. HR.

Genetic Variation in the Response of *Nicotiana* Species to CaMV Infection

There are two general approaches that can be taken to demonstrate that the hypersensitive response of the host can be genetically dissected into separate cell death and resistance components. One approach has been to mutagenize plants that respond to pathogens with HR in an attempt to knock out either the cell death pathway or the resistance pathway. Yu and coworkers (96, 97) used this strategy to isolate the *Arabidopsis* mutant, *dnd1*, which lost the capacity to respond with HR

Table 1. Response of *Nicotiana* species to infection by CaMV strains W260 and D4.

	Host			
CaMV strain	*N. edwardsonii*	*N. glutinosa*	*N. clevelandii*	*N. bigelovii*
W260	HR[a]	CLL[b] Resistant	Systemic Cell Death	Systemic Mosaic
D4	Systemic Mosaic	Systemic Mosaic	Systemic Mosaic	Systemic Mosaic

[a]HR = Hypersensitive Response; [b]CLL = Chlorotic Local Lesions

to *Pseudomonas syringae* pv. *glycinea* Race 4, but retained resistance to this pathogen. The alternative strategy would be to screen for natural variants that exist within a genus or species, which is the approach that has been taken with CaMV.

It turns out that a significant amount of natural genetic variation exists in the response of *Nicotiana* species to CaMV. Consequently, it is important at the outset of this chapter to describe the variation that occurs on both the host and pathogen sides of the interaction. The CaMV/*Nicotiana* pathosystem we use consists of two strains of CaMV and four *Nicotiana* species (Table 1). The eight interactions illustrated in Table 1 have allowed a characterization of both virus and host determinants for HR, local and systemic cell death, and suppression of cell death.

The most important requirement in this system was to find a *Nicotiana* species that responded with HR to one or more CaMV strains. The species that we settled on was *N. edwardsonii*, which develops necrotic local lesions approximately 8 to 10 days post inoculation (dpi) with CaMV strain W260 (80). Under most environmental conditions, the W260 virus infection remains limited to the inoculated leaf. W260 virions can be readily detected in the inoculated leaf, but their movement into the upper, noninoculated leaves is restricted.

One interesting feature about *N. edwardsonii* is that it is not found in nature; it is a species hybrid that originated from a cross between *N. glutinosa* and *N. clevelandii* (13, 14). Interestingly, when these two parent species were evaluated for their response to W260 infection, neither responded with development of an HR. *N. clevelandii* responded to W260 infection with local and systemic cell death (Table 1). In contrast, *N. glutinosa* was resistant to W260, but inoculated leaves developed local chlorotic lesions rather than the necrotic local lesions typically associated with HR (Table 1). W260 did not induce any symptoms in upper noninoculated portions of the plant, and although virion particles could be detected in the inoculated leaves, they were not found in upper leaves (18). The reactions of the progenitors of *N. edwardsonii* to W260 suggested that its hypersensitive response to W260 infection might be conditioned by two separate plant genes; resistance to W260 is derived from *N. glutinosa*, whereas cell death is derived from *N. clevelandii*.

The fourth *Nicotiana* species that was used in this system was *N. bigelovii*. Unlike *N. clevelandii*, this host responds to W260 infection with a system mosaic (Table 1). Interestingly, the W260 titers found in systemically infected *N. bigelovii* and *N. clevelandii* leaves are comparable (59), so cell death does not appear to be triggered by differences in viral titer. By making crosses between *N. bigelovii* and *N. clevelandii*, it was possible to characterize the inheritance of the systemic cell death trait (59).

The other key component in this system was the D4 strain of CaMV. In contrast to W260, the D4 strain of CaMV did not elicit a resistance response or cell death in any of the four *Nicotiana* species. D4 induced chlorotic primary lesions on the inoculated leaves 8 – 10 dpi and a chlorotic mosaic on the upper portions of the plant at 18 – 22 dpi (Table 1)(18, 79). Furthermore, D4 virions could be readily detected in both inoculated and systemically infected leaves (Table 1). With the inclusion of the D4 virus in this system, it was possible to make chimeras with W260 to identify the viral gene responsible for avirulence.

CaMV Gene VI is an Avirulence Gene; it Elicits HR in *N. edwardsonii* and Systemic Cell Death in *N. clevelandii*

Studies with Chimeric Viruses

Early experiments with CaMV and *Nicotiana* focused exclusively on the pathogen side of the interaction. Whereas the genetic analysis of *Nicotiana* initially posed some challenges, the manipulation of the CaMV genome has been quite simple. CaMV is the type member of the caulimovirus group. Its genome consists of circular, double-stranded (ds) DNA approximately 8000 bp in length. It was the first plant virus genome to be completely sequenced (41, 43), and the first plant virus to be cloned in infectious form (53, 62). The genome of CaMV, illustrated in Figure 1, has been found to encode six proteins (52, 67). The primary question that interested us was, "which viral genes are responsible for eliciting HR in *N. edwardsonii* and systemic cell death in *N. clevelandii*?" To answer this question, chimeric viruses were constructed between the D4 and W260 strains of CaMV and then tested for their ability to trigger cell death or HR.

The requirements of a complete genome sequence and infectious clone are now considered prerequisites for any molecular study of plant viruses, and are certainly the starting point for identifying viral *Avr* genes. CaMV is arguably the easiest of all plant viruses to clone, given that its

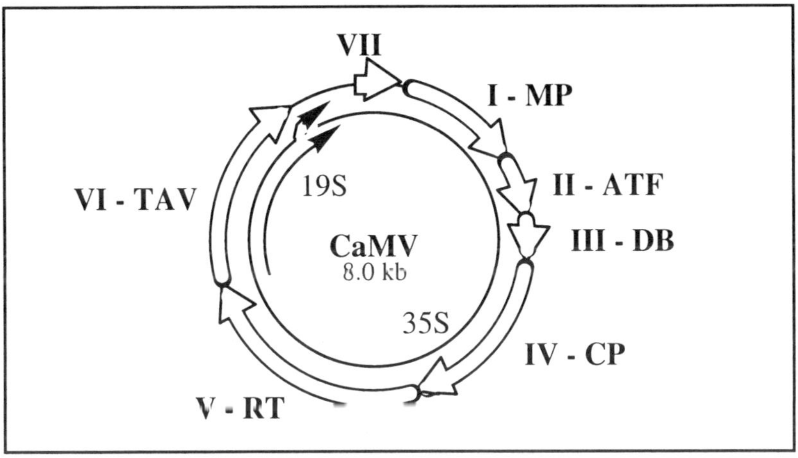

Figure 1. Genome structure of CaMV. The viral nucleic acid is composed of circular, double-stranded DNA. The positions of the six major genes of CaMV that comprise the viral genome are indicated by the outer arrows. No protein product has yet been found for gene VII. The functions of the six gene products are: MP, movement protein; ATF, aphid transmission factor; DB, DNA binding protein; CP, coat protein; RT, reverse transcriptase; and TAV, translational transactivator. The two curved arrows inside of the genome map indicate the positions of the two CaMV RNA transcripts, the 19S and 35S RNAs.

genome consists of circular dsDNA. Several restriction enzymes have been identified that cleave the viral DNA only once, which further facilitates the cloning of the viral DNA into bacterial plasmid vectors. It is also fairly simple to initiate infections in turnip leaves from cloned, viral DNA. To initiate an infection, the viral DNA is released from the plasmid vector through digestion with the appropriate restriction enzyme. This mixture is applied to a glass rod and then gently rubbed onto turnip leaves to introduce the viral DNA into the plant cell (53, 62). Once inside a plant cell, the viral DNA is re-circularized by plant DNA ligases, and the infection ensues. It is not uncommon to initiate infections in 100% of the turnips inoculated with cloned DNA. Turnips are always the first host to be inoculated with cloned CaMV DNA because they are universally susceptible to CaMV strains and infections are initiated at a much higher rate than in *Nicotiana*. Once the virus has been established in turnips, these plants then serve as the inoculum source for host range and symptom studies in *Nicotiana* species.

Chimeric viruses could be constructed between D4 and W260 because the restriction enzyme maps of these two strains of CaMV are quite similar; consequently, it was possible to swap DNA segments delimited by common restriction enzyme sites to construct a series of reciprocal chimeric viruses. Using this approach, it was shown that W260 gene VI was responsible for eliciting both HR in *N. edwardsonii* and systemic cell death *in N. clevelandii* (59, 94). In contrast, a chimeric virus that contained gene VI of D4 induced a systemic mosaic in both hosts. A further series of chimeric viruses showed that both the cell death and HR elicitors could be mapped to the 5'-proximal third of gene VI (59). Interestingly, the same region of gene VI has recently been shown to overcome resistance in *Arabidopsis thaliana* (4). The experiments in the next section provided the conclusive proof that W260 gene VI was an *Avr* gene and that its protein product (P6) was responsible for triggering HR and cell death.

Uncoupling the Translational Transactivator Function of CaMV P6 from its Function as an *Avr* Gene Product

Unlike the *Avr* genes of bacteria and fungi, a considerable amount is known about the functions of the viral *Avr* genes. Most plant viruses have very small genome sizes; they have the capacity to encode anywhere from three to ten proteins to fulfill the requirements for replication, gene expression, cell-to-cell movement and encapsidation. To date, every viral gene that has been shown to be an *Avr* gene has always had an essential role in the viral disease cycle. Table 2 lists some well-characterized viral *Avr* genes, as well as the hosts in which they elicit an HR. Although in many cases, the viral coat protein has been found to elicit HR, it is generally accepted that virtually any viral gene product may serve as a target for triggering HR in plants (21). This observation is underscored in Table 2, as viral proteins involved in genome expression, replication, movement and encapsidation have all been identified as Avr proteins. In the case of CaMV, evidence has existed as early as 1984 that CaMV gene VI can act as an *Avr* gene (28, 79). Sometimes, however, the increased knowledge concerning the multiple functions of viral *Avr* gene products can create problems, and in fact, this has been the case with the CaMV P6 protein .

The primary role identified for P6 in the CaMV infection cycle is to modify the host translation machinery to facilitate the translation of the polycistronic CaMV 35S RNA. This function for P6, has been designated as the translational transactivator (TAV) function (9, 42, 49, 81). The basic assay for TAV function is illustrated in Figure 2. The bicistronic constuct used most frequently in the TAV assay consists of CaMV ORF VII, followed by a CaMV ORF I fused to GUS or CAT (Fig. 2A). When this bicistronic mRNA is introduced into a plant cell, host ribosomes will scan the mRNA sequence starting from the 5' end until the AUG for gene VII is encountered, then read through this cistron and drop off the mRNA. Eukaryotic ribosomes are unable to efficiently initiate translation of the second cistron. However, if CaMV P6 gene is co-introduced into the plant

Table 2 - Representative Virus Gene Products that Trigger a Hypersensitive Response[a]

Barley stripe mosaic virus	gamma b	*Chenopodium amaranticolor*	?[b]	75
Bean dwarf mosaic virus	BV1[c]	*P. vulgaris* cv. Othello	?	44
Cauliflower mosaic virus	P6[d]	*N. edwardsonii*	This Chapter	94
	P6	*D. stramonium*	?	28, 79
Cucumber mosaic virus	2a[e]	Cowpea	?	57
Pepper mild mottle virus	Coat Protein	Pepper	L^3	7
Potato virus X	Coat protein	Potato	*Nx*	56
	25kDa[f]	Potato	*Nb*	66
Tobacco mosaic virus	Coat Protein	*N. sylvestris*	*N'*	60, 78
	Coat Protein	Eggplant	?	26
	Coat Protein	Pepper	L^3	27
	30 kDa[f]	Tomato	*Tm-2*	10, 68
	Replicase[e]	*N. glutinosa*	*N*	71
Tomato bushy stunt virus	P19[g]	*N. tabacum*	?	82
	P22[f]	*N. edwardsonii*	?	82
Turnip crinkle virus	Coat protein	*A. thaliana* ecotype Di-0	*HRT*	30, 85

[a]Adapted from Table 10.2 of Hull (54), with kind permission of the author and the copyright holder © Academic Press.
[b]Host *R* genes that recognize viral *Avr* genes, if known.
[c]a viral protein that shuttles ss- and dsDNA from the nucleus to the cytoplasm.
[d]a viral gene product that facilitates expression of other viral genes.
[e]a viral component of the RNA-dependent RNA polymerase.
[f]a viral protein required for cell-to-cell movement.
[g]a viral protein required for host-dependent systemic infection.

cell along with the bicistronic reporter mRNA, then the TAV function of P6 will alter the host translational machinery to facilitate translation of the GUS gene in the second cistron (Fig. 2B).

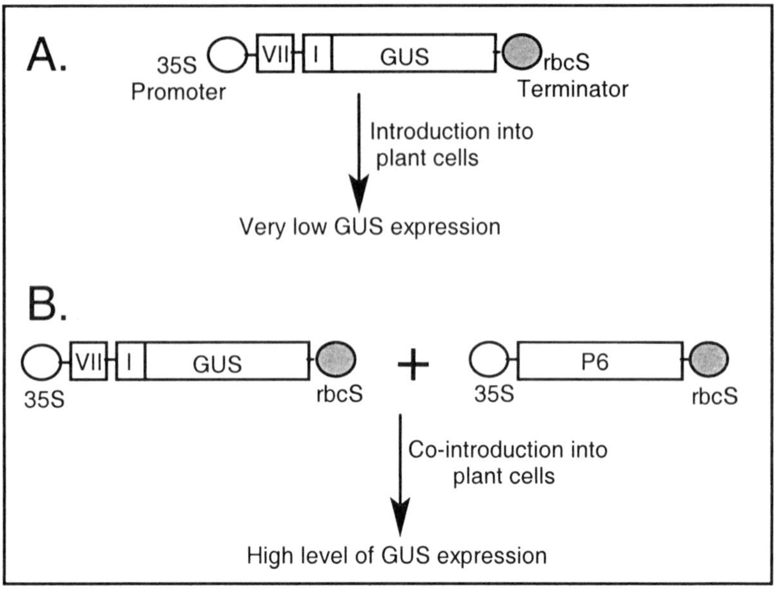

Figure 2. The assay for TAV function associated with CaMV P6. A. The bicistronic reporter cassette consists of gene VII, followed by a gene I-GUS fusion in the second cistron. The transcription of this mRNA is driven by the CaMV 35S promoter and the rbcS termination signal. B. GUS expression from the bicistronic plasmid is greatly enhanced when CaMV gene VI is co-introduced with the reporter plasmid into plant cells. TAV function is evaluated in one of three ways. In the original method, the reporter cassette and gene VI expression plasmids were electroporated separately or together into plant protoplasts (9, 49). In subsequent methods the two constructs were incorporated into the T DNA of an *Agrobacterium* binary vector, and then transiently expressed by agroinfiltration of plant tissues (73) or used for stable transformation of plants (98).

It is not known exactly how P6 facilitates translation of bicistronic mRNAs, although recent evidence indicates that it interacts with polysomes to allow reinitiation of translation of polycistronic messages (74). The discovery of the TAV function of P6 has been useful for understanding how a complex, polycistronic mRNA such as the CaMV 35S RNA could be translated after it is transcribed in its plant cells. CaMV P6 has been shown to transactivate the expression of reporter genes in plant protoplasts derived from host and non-host plants (9, 49), in transgenic plants (98) in the yeast, *Saccharomyces cerevisiae* (84) and in *in vitro* systems (76).

The observation that P6 can transactivate the expression of reporter genes has created some problems towards understanding its role as an elicitor of HR. For example, there is a possibility that P6 could indirectly elicit HR by modifying the expression of other host or virus genes (98). Until recently this potential problem has limited the acceptance of CaMV gene VI as a legitimate *Avr* gene.

To prove that gene VI of CaMV strain W260 is responsible for eliciting HR in *N. edwardsonii* and cell death in *N. clevelandii*, we adopted a technique called agroinfiltration (38). Briefly, a putative *Avr* gene (or other gene) is placed under the control of a constitutive promoter and into the T-DNA of a binary vector of *Agrobacterium tumefaciens*. Expression of this gene is achieved when *Agrobacterium* containing this binary vector is treated with acetosyringone and infiltrated into the leaf. Agroinfiltration had previously been used successfully to illustrate the function of *Avr* genes from several organisms, including TMV (1, 39), PVX (6), *Cladosporium fulvum* (89, 91), *Pseudomonas syringae* pv. *tomato* (83, 88), and *Xanthomonas campestris* pv. *vesicatoria* (90).

We found that gene VI of W260 elicited HR in *N. edwardsonii* approximately four days after agroinfiltration, whereas gene VI of D4 did not elicit HR even after three weeks (72). In addition, W260 gene VI elicited cell death in *N. clevelandii* approximately two weeks after infiltration, whereas D4 did not elicit cell death. Thus, by using this agroinfiltration technique, it could be shown that gene VI was responsible for eliciting HR rather than one of the other CaMV genes, a confirmation of the results obtained with chimeric viruses (28, 59, 79). A further experiment showed that the protein product of W260 gene VI, rather than the DNA or RNA, was responsible for eliciting HR (72).

The agroinfiltration assay was then adapted to evaluate the TAV function of the CaMV P6. TAV function could be measured by inserting the bicistronic reporter construct in Fig. 2A into the T- region of the *A. tumefaciens* binary vector. A significantly higher level of GUS activity was detected in plant tissues when the bicistronic reporter was co-agroinfiltrated with CaMV gene VI than when the reporter was infiltrated by itself (73). Thus, a single agroinfiltration bioassay could be used to investigate the relationship between the sequences of P6 required for translational transactivation and elicitation of HR. The key to this dual assay was that TAV function could be assessed before the onset of HR that would be triggered by W260 P6.

We found that the TAV function of D4 could not be distinguished from that of W260, even though P6 of W260 elicited HR in *N. edwardsonii* while P6 of D4 did not elicit any response (73). The same amount of GUS protein was expressed in plant tissues regardless of whether P6 was derived from W260 or D4. Consequently, differences in

TAV function did not account for the *Avr* function of W260 P6; this study provided the final conclusive proof that W260 P6 is a true *Avr* gene product. Furthermore, it showed that the *Avr* function of P6 is likely unrelated to its TAV function.

STRUCTURAL CHARACTERIZATION OF THE CAMV AVIRULENCE GENE

So, what is the difference between the two versions of CaMV P6 such that the version synthesized by strain W260 triggers HR or systemic cell death, whereas the version synthesized by strain D4 does not elicit any apparent host defense response? Studies with chimeric viruses have shown that the amino-terminal third of gene VI is responsible for eliciting HR (59, 94). Within this 182 amino acid stretch, there are 21 amino acid differences between D4 and W260. Presumably, one or more of these amino acid substitutions in the P6 sequence are responsible for triggering HR in a viral infection. Studies are underway to identify specifically which amino acids within P6 contribute to the HR phenotype.

The agroinfiltration studies have revealed a surprisingly different perspective on the structural requirements for elicitation of HR by W260 P6. It turns out that in this type of assay, the avirulence function of W260 gene VI is very sensitive to any perturbations in sequence. A deletion of only 10 amino acids on the amino-terminus, or 39 amino acids on the carboxy-terminus, completely abolished the avirulence function of W260 P6 (73). Interestingly, both of these deletion mutants had full TAV activity, which proved that the respective P6 proteins were expressed. Furthermore an insertion of just two codons into the N-terminal third of the W260 P6 protein abolished HR, but had no effect on TAV function. Consequently, although it is likely that individual amino acids within P6 can be identified that are involved in elicitation of HR, it is apparent that the three dimensional structure of the protein must also be retained.

The stringent requirements associated with the avirulence function of W260 P6 differ from that reported for the replicase of TMV, which elicits HR in *N*-gene tobacco. It has been shown that large portions of the TMV replicase can be eliminated, and that the helicase domain is sufficient to elicit HR (1, 2, 39). In any case, it is apparent that the three-dimensional structure of either an isolated domain or the entire Avr protein is necessary for recognition by a resistance gene product. For example, an analysis of the three dimensional structure of the TMV coat protein has revealed a central hydrophobic cavity in the coat protein is required for *N'* gene recognition (86, 87).

The evidence to date suggests that the recognition of viral *Avr* gene products by its cognate resistance gene product may be unrelated to the function of the virus protein in the infection cycle. For example, it has been shown that the cell-to-cell movement function of *Tomato bushy stunt virus* (TBSV) P22 can be inactivated by site-directed mutations, but these

P22 mutants still retain the capacity to elicit HR in *N. edwardsonii* (15). Conversely, other point mutations in P22 knocked out the HR function, but the mutant virus could still move from cell-to-cell and systemically. Similarly, the *N* gene product in tobacco recognizes the helicase portion of the TMV replicase (1, 39), but ATPase function associated with the helicase does not appear to be related to elicitation of HR (39). In the case of CaMV, it has been shown the inactivation of the Avr function of P6 has no effect on its TAV function. It remains to be seen if P6 mutants can be found that have no TAV activity, but can still elicit HR.

Evidence that the Hypersensitive Response of *N. edwardsonii* can be Genetically Dissected into Resistance and Cell Death Components

It is generally accepted that the hypersensitive response to pathogen attack is conditioned by single, dominant genes. It has been demonstrated empirically that cell death and resistance in most cases are intertwined. However, there is a growing body of evidence to show that cell death and resistance can become unlinked. For example, the *N* gene can be debilitated *in vitro* and then introduced back into *Nicotiana* such that TMV triggers cell death, but resistance has been compromised (35). The net result of this type of host/pathogen interaction is systemic cell death. There is also evidence of that cell death in *Arabidopsis* to *P. syringae* can be knocked out, but resistance retained (96, 97). Perhaps the best system to date for illustrating the uncoupling of cell death from resistance is the CaMV/*Nicotiana* pathosystem. In this system, it has been possible to combine a systemic cell death trait with a nonnecrotic resistance to create a hybrid that responds with HR. More importantly, the segregation of cell death and resistance from each other can be traced in subsequent crosses.

The central hypothesis of this work is that the HR of *N. edwardsonii* to W260 infection is conditioned by an interaction between two genes in the host and a single gene in the virus. *N. edwardsonii* is an amphidiploid that was synthesized from *N. glutinosa* and *N. clevelandii* by Christie in the late sixties (13). The evidence indicates that both parental species contribute traits that condition the HR of *N. edwardsonii* to W260 infection. One host gene, derived from *N. glutinosa*, interacts with W260 gene VI to condition resistance, whereas a second gene, derived from *N. clevelandii*, interacts with W260 gene VI to condition the cell death response. Further evidence that cell death can be uncoupled from resistance can be seen in a cross between *N. edwardsonii* and *N. bigelovii*. The hybrid plants that result from this cross are resistant to W260 infection, but the cell death reaction is suppressed. The evidence for each of these assertions is described in the following sections.

A SYSTEMIC CELL DEATH SYMPTOM TRIGGERED BY CAMV W260 GENE VI IN *N. CLEVELANDII* IS CONDITIONED BY A SINGLE HOST GENE

There are many examples in the literature in which it has been shown that plant viruses will elicit a systemic cell death symptom in their hosts. For example, TBSV elicits systemic cell death in several hosts, including *N. clevelandii*, spinach, and *N. benthamiana* (15, 82). In the case of a satellite virus of CMV, this reaction has been considered a form of programmed cell death (95). Given the small genome size of plant viruses, it also has not been difficult to identify the viral gene product that triggers systemic cell death. In addition to CaMV P6, the P19 protein of TBSV will elicit systemic cell death in *N. clevelandii* (82). There are, however, few host-virus systems in which it has been possible to examine the inheritance of the systemic cell death trait in the host. The interaction of CaMV with its *Nicotiana* hosts is one system where this has been accomplished.

The inheritance of a systemic cell death trait was characterized by taking advantage of the difference in symptoms induced by CaMV strain W260 in *N. bigelovii* and *N. clevelandii* (Table 1). W260 elicits systemic cell death in *N. clevelandii* and only a mosaic in *N. bigelovii*. We found that we could make an interspecific cross between these two species and that their progeny would be fertile. The two species have the same chromosome number (n=24) and are considered to be closely related to each other (48). In our crosses, all F1 plants displayed a systemic mosaic when inoculated with W260. In the F2 generation, infected plants revealed a 3:1 segregation for systemic mosaic vs. necrosis. This analysis indicated that a single locus, designated *ccd1* (for CaMV cell death), determined whether *Nicotiana* species responded with systemic cell death or mosaic (59). The *ccd1* locus from *N. clevelandii* might specify a protein that recognizes P6 of W260 to trigger systemic cell death. Alternatively, *N. bigelovii* might be considered to contain a dominant suppressor of cell death. Further evidence for this cell death suppressor is presented in later sections.

THE NONNECROTIC RESISTANCE OF *N. GLUTINOSA* TO W260 INFECTION CAN BE CONVERTED TO AN HR THROUGH A SIMPLE CROSS WITH *N. CLEVELANDII*

There are several examples in the literature in which the outcome of resistance to plant viruses does not result in HR. One such case concerns the resistant response of *N.glutinosa* to W260 infection. Under most environmental conditions, *N. glutinosa* responds to W260 with chlorotic local lesions. This is considered a resistance response because the W260 virus remains localized within these inoculated leaves. Interestingly, when *N. glutinosa* is crossed with *N. clevelandii*, then the hybrid plants respond to CaMV strain W260 with HR (18). Inoculated leaves develop necrotic lesions and the plants remain resistant to W260 infection. The development of HR in these hybrid plants is a specific response to this CaMV strain, as the virulent CaMV isolate D4 elicits chlorotic lesions and a systemic infection (18). The implication of this study is that *N. clevelandii* contributes a genetic factor to the hybrid, the *ccd1* gene, which triggers cell death upon recognition of W260 P6. Since the W260 virus remains localized to the inoculated leaf in these plants, the visible response of the hybrid to W260 infection is a necrotic lesion.

THE HOST RESISTANCE AND CELL DEATH THAT COMPRISE THE HR OF *N. EDWARDSONII* CV. COLUMBIA TO CAMV STRAIN W260 CAN BE GENETICALLY SEPARATED

The strategy that has been used to characterize the segregation of host resistance from cell death elicited by CaMV is similar to that used 75 years ago for the genetic analysis of the *N* gene, a resistance gene that was recently cloned and that conditions resistance to TMV (93). Clausen and Goodspeed (16) introduced the *N* gene from *N. glutinosa* to *N. tabacum* var. Purpurea by creating the interspecific hybrid, *N. digluta*. *N. digluta* (n = 36) consisted of the full genomes of *N. glutinosa* (n = 12) and *N. tabacum* (n = 24). These plants were then crossed with *N. tabacum*, and all responded with HR. To prove that resistance to TMV was conditioned by a single, dominant gene, the F1 plants were selfed and also backcrossed to *N. tabacum* (reviewed in 37). The N gene was eventually introgressed into the *N. tabacum* genome by continually selecting plants that exhibited N-gene resistance and backcrossing them with *N. tabacum*.

Interestingly, the resistance to CaMV is also derived from *N. glutinosa*. To characterize this resistance, *N. edwardsonii* (n = 36) was resynthesized from a cross between *N. glutinosa* (n = 12) and *N. clevelandii* (n = 24)(18, 46). The resynthesized plants were named *N. edwardsonii* cv. Columbia because although they had the same parents as the original *N. edwardsonii*, they exhibited differences in growth habit from the original (18). The *N. edwardsonii* cv. Columbia plants were subsequently crossed with *N. clevelandii*, which is susceptible to CaMV strain W260, and nearly all responded with resistance and local cell death. The inheritance of resistance to CaMV was then characterized in both the F2 population and in a backcross population to *N. clevelandii*. One important aspect of this work was that the F2 progeny were also examined for the inheritance of the *N* gene. Thus it was possible to use the *N* gene to confirm that single genes would segregate properly in the cross between *N. edwardsonii* cv. Columbia and *N. clevelandii* (18).

F1 plants derived from a cross between the *N. edwardsonii* cv. Columbia and *N. clevelandii* respond primarily to inoculation of W260 with HR: necrotic lesions and resistance. When these plants are selfed, resistance segregated independently of cell death in the F2 generation.

Four different classes of plants could be unambiguously identified: resistant with necrotic lesions (HR), susceptible with systemic mosaic, resistant with chlorotic lesions, and susceptible with systemic cell death (18). Only the first two of these classes would be expected if cell death consistently segregated with resistance. The two additional categories provided evidence that cell death and resistance had become uncoupled. In one category, a significant number of F2 plants developed a systemic cell death symptom. The second category consisted of plants that were resistant to W260, but developed chlorotic lesions rather than necrotic lesions. This evidence indicates that resistance to CaMV strain W260 is conditioned by a gene derived from *N. glutinosa*, whereas a second gene, derived from *N. clevelandii*, triggers cell death. Further backcrosses with *N. clevelandii* are underway to introgress the CaMV resistance gene into *N. clevelandii*.

Induction of PR Proteins by CaMV is Associated with Resistance rather than Cell Death

One of the hallmarks of the hypersensitive response to plant pathogens is the production of pathogenesis-related (PR) proteins (8). Interestingly, several studies have shown that PR proteins are not responsible for virus resistance. For example, transgenic plants that constitutively express PR-1 do not exhibit resistance to viruses (23, 64). The induction of PR proteins, however, is dependent upon an increase in salicylic acid (SA), and several studies have shown that SA is a component in the defense response to viruses (31). For example, resistance to TMV is mediated by an SA-dependent pathway that diverges from the pathway required for PR protein induction (12, 70). The analysis of PR protein expression is useful, though, because it is indicative of which defense pathways are activated in response to CaMV.

To determine if CaMV could induce PR proteins in *Nicotiana*, we initially characterized the response of *N. edwardsonii* to the avirulent W260 strain and the virulent D4 strain. As expected, both PR-1 and PR-5 proteins were elicited by W260, whereas the PR proteins were either mildly elicited, or not elicited at all, by the virulent D4 strain (18). The analysis of the parents of *N. edwardsonii*, *N. glutinosa* and *N. clevelandii*, indicated that induction of PR proteins by W260 was associated with resistance rather than cell death (18). Other studies have used biochemical approaches to show that induction of PR proteins can be uncoupled from cell death. For example, peptides that inhibit the function of caspases, a key component in programmed cell death in animals, can block HR-induced cell death in plants (29). However, the caspase inhibitors have no effect on the induction of defense genes that are associated with HR. Furthermore, it has been shown that HR-induced cell death is inhibited at low oxygen pressure, but plants are still resistant to TMV (69). Thus, the genetic approach taken with CaMV complements biochemical studies that show that PR protein production may be associated with the resistance response rather than with cell death.

LOCAL CELL DEATH IN *N. EDWARDSONII* IS SUPPRESSED IN A CROSS WITH *NICOTIANA BIGELOVII*

Our evidence indicated that the cell death component in the HR of *N. edwardsonii* to CaMV is derived from *N. clevelandii*. It had previously been shown that the systemic cell death response of *N. clevelandii* to CaMV strain W260 could be suppressed in a cross with *N. bigelovii*. Furthermore, the suppression contributed by *N. bigelovii* was conditioned by a single, dominant gene (59). Consequently, we reasoned that it might be possible to suppress the cell death trait associated with the HR of *N. edwardsonii* through a simple cross with *N. bigelovii*.

In fact, F1 plants derived from a cross between *N. edwardsonii* and *N. bigelovii* developed local chlorotic lesions in response to W260, yet the plants remained resistant to systemic infection by W260. The suppression of cell death was also evident at the microscopic level, as the chlorotic lesions did not retain Evan's blue stain (17). Evan's blue can be used to assess the vitality of cells; living cells do not take up the stain, whereas dead cells stain a deep blue. In contrast to the *N. edwardsonii* x *N. bigelovii* cross, F1 plants derived from an *N. edwardsonii* X *N. clevelandii* cross reacted with HR upon inoculation with W260 and these lesions stained blue upon treatment with Evan's blue. This test showed that a factor from *N. bigelovii* suppressed the development of local cell death in *N. edwardsonii* (17) as well as systemic cell death in *N. clevelandii* (59). Since *N. edwardsonii* is derived from *N. clevelandii* (13), it has been speculated that the suppressor has targeted the cell death factor derived from *N. clevelandii* (17).

The *N. edwardsonii* genome also contains the *N* gene, which conditions HR against TMV (13). Consequently, it was possible to determine if the cell death suppressor would be active against HR induced by a virus unrelated to CaMV. Interestingly, TMV elicited HR in both *N. edwardsonii* and the *N. edwardsonii* X *N. bigelovii* hybrid (17). Thus, the suppression of cell death appears to be specific to CaMV. This specificity of suppression may be an important clue as to where in the pathway cell death is halted. The suppression must act near the recognition event between host and pathogen, perhaps even disrupting recognition in some manner. Otherwise it would be expected that cell death induced by TMV would be suppressed as it is with CaMV infection.

It is generally thought that the cell death triggered during HR may be a form of programmed cell death, and that there may be similarities to animal apoptosis (24, 25, 45, 92). As comparisons are made between cell death mechanisms in plants and animals, one question to be considered is,

"Are there suppressors of cell death in plants?" The speculation associated with this question has taken two paths. One direction has led into the study of disease lesion mimics. Some lesion mimic mutants, such as the *Arabidopsis lsd1* and maize *Lls1* mutants, are thought to represent knockouts of genes that repress cell death (33, 50). It is considered that plants that have sustained mutations in these regulatory genes are unable to control the initiation of cell death, and so lesions appear on leaves of these plants in response to developmental programs or the environment (25). A second research direction has led to the introduction and study of animal antiapoptosis genes in plants. The expression of animal antiapoptosis genes such as human *Bcl-2* and *Bcl-xl* in transgenic plants actually blocked the development of disease induced by necrogenic plant pathogens (32). The interaction of CaMV with its *Nicotiana* hosts may add a new dimension to this research area; this interaction demonstrates the existence of a plant gene that blocks the development of cell death in a plant-microbe interaction.

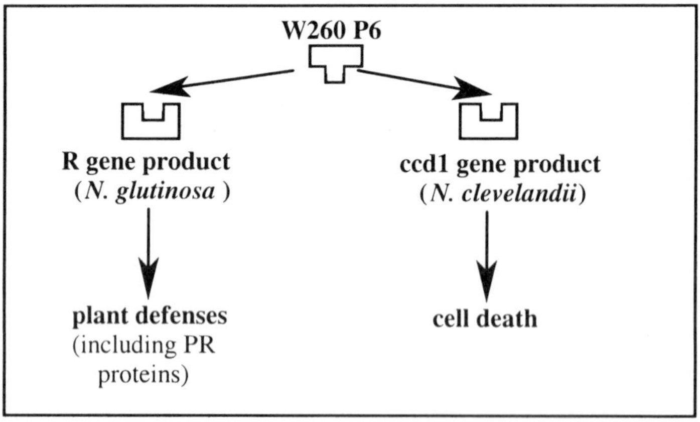

Figure 3. Model that illustrates the elicitation of HR in *N. edwardsonii* by CaMV strain W260. The hypersensitive response of *N. edwardsonii* to CaMV is determined by the interaction of CaMV gene VI with two plant genes. CaMV gene VI interacts with a resistance gene that is derived from *N. glutinosa*, and triggers a plant defense response, including the production of PR-proteins. CaMV gene VI interacts with a cell death gene, designated *ccd*1, that is derived from *N. clevelandii* and triggers a cell death pathway.

Concluding Remarks : Towards A Model for the Elicitation of HR and Plant Defenses by CaMV

The interaction between CaMV and *Nicotiana* species may represent an example of a unique gene-for-gene system, as illustrated in Figure 3. In this example, HR is conditioned by the interaction of a single viral avirulence gene, CaMV gene VI, with two host genes; one host gene triggers cell death and a second host gene triggers resistance. If the cell death gene is present and the resistance gene is absent, as with *N. clevelandii*, then the outcome is systemic cell death. The end result of the resistance cascade is the induction of PR proteins. These proteins are not induced by the cell death pathway.

The model for induction of resistance to CaMV differs from models proposed for the function of the virus resistance genes *Rx* and *HRT*. These models describe a continuum from extreme resistance, through micro HR, to HR (6, 20). Extreme resistance occurs in the absence of HR through the normal function of the *Rx* gene or through overexpression of *HRT* in transgenic plants. In essence, no HR develops because the plant responds too rapidly for the virus to elicit HR. Micro HR develops through moderate expression of *HRT* in transgenic plants, whereas a systemic HR develops in transgenic plants that express a low level of *HRT* (20, 55). In the case of extreme resistance against TCV, the plant defense response occurred so rapidly that an insufficient signal was produced for PR protein expression. In addition, PR proteins were only weakly induced in transgenic *HRT* plants that exhibited micro HR (20).

The non-necrotic resistance against CaMV exhibited by *N. glutinosa* and within the F2 population does not have characteristics of extreme resistance. Plants that displayed non-necrotic resistance to CaMV had prominent chlorotic lesions and PR proteins were strongly elicited in *N. glutinosa* by CaMV strain W260. This differs from extreme resistance and micro HR because no visible symptoms are associated with these two forms of resistance, and PR proteins are either not expressed or expressed very weakly. Furthermore, we found that non-necrotic resistance could be combined genetically with a cell death gene and the outcome of this cross was an HR. Consequently, the form of resistance to CaMV that we have described may extend the continuum from extreme resistance through HR to the non-necrotic CaMV resistance. This continuum has also been noted in describing the response of bean cultivars to *Bean common mosaic virus* (19).

In addition to differences in the resistance response, the systemic cell death elicited by CaMV differs from the systemic cell death induced by TCV. The systemic cell death caused by TCV occurred in transgenic *A. thaliana* plants that expressed relatively low levels of *HRT* and lacked the recessive *rrt* gene. This recognition event resulted in a high level of PR-1 protein. In contrast, neither PR-1 nor PR 5 proteins were elicited in *N. clevelandii* plants that displayed prominent systemic cell death symptoms in response to an interaction between CaMV gene VI and *ccd1*.

Consequently, it appears that a narrower subset of defense genes are activated by the interaction between CaMV gene VI and *ccd1* than between the TCV coat protein and the *HRT* gene product. The subset of genes activated by the CaMV/*ccd1* interaction may be valuable because it isolates the cell death pathway from defense pathways.

The role of *ccd1* in activation of cell death may be more related to the *N* gene than to *HRT*. It has recently been found that two transcripts, N_S and N_L, are produced from the *N* gene (34). Both transcripts, and their protein products, appear to be required for resistance to TMV. Interestingly, transgenic plants that expressed only the N_S transcript developed a systemic HR upon inoculation with TMV. Consequently, *ccd1* may be a flawed form of the CaMV resistance gene that is present in *N. glutinosa*.

References

1. Abbink T E M, Tjernberg P A, Bol J F, Linthorst H J M (1998) Tobacco mosaic virus helicase domain induces necrosis in *N* gene-carrying tobacco in the absence of virus replication. Mol. Plant-Microbe Interact. 11:1242-1246.
2. Abbink T E M, de Vogel J, Bol J F, Linthorst H J M (2001) Induction of a hypersensitive response by chimeric helicase sequences of tobamoviruses U1 and Ob in *N*-carrying tobacco. Mol. Plant-Microbe Interact. 14:1086-1095.
3. Adams S E, Jones R A C, Coutts R H A (1986) Expression of *Potato virus X* resistance gene *Rx* in potato leaf protoplasts. J. Gen. Virol. 67:2341-2345.
4. Agama, K, Beach, S, Schoelz, J, Leisner, S M (2002) The 5' third of Cauliflower mosaic virus gene VI conditions resistance breakage in *Arabidopsis* ecotype Tsu-0. Phytopathology 92: 190-196.
5. Baker B, Zambryski P, Staskawicz B, Dinesh-Kumar S P (1997) Signaling in plant-microbe interactions. Science 276:726-733.
6. Bendahmane A, Kanyuka K, Baulcombe DC (1999) The *Rx* gene from potato controls separate virus resistance and cell death responses. Plant Cell 11:781-791.
7. Berzal-Herranz A, de la Cruz A, Tenllado F, Díaz-Ruíz L, López L, Sanz, A I, Vaquero C, Serra, M T, and García-Luque, I (1995) The *Capsicum* L3 gene-mediated resistance against the tobamoviruses is elicited by the coat protein. Virology 209:498-505.
8. Bol J F, Linthorst H J M, Cornelissen B J C (1990). Plant pathogenesis-related proteins induced by virus infection. Annu. Rev. Phytopathol. 28:113-138.
9. Bonneville J M, Sanfacon H, Fütterer J, Hohn T (1989)

Posttranscriptional trans-activation in cauliflower mosaic virus. Cell 59:1135-1143.

10. Calder V L, Palukaitis, P (1992) Nucleotide sequence analysis of the movement genes of resistance breaking strains of tomato mosaic virus. J. Gen. Virol. 73:165-168.
11. Callaway A, Liu W, Andrianov V, Stenzler L, Zhao J, Wettlaufer S, Jayakumar P, Howell S H (1996) Characterization of cauliflower mosaic virus (CaMV) resistance in virus-resistant ecotypes of *Arabidopsis*. Mol. Plant-Microbe Interact. 9:810-818.
12. Chivasa S, Murphy A M, Naylor M, Carr J P (1997) Salicylic acid interferes with Tobacco mosaic virus replication via a novel salicylhydroxamic acid-sensitive mechanism. Plant Cell 9:547-557.
13. Christie, S R (1969) *Nicotiana* hybrid developed as a host for plant viruses. Plant Disease Reporter 53:939-941.
14. Christie S R, Hall D W (1979). A new hybrid species of *Nicotiana* (Solanaceae). Baileya 20:133-136.
15. Chu M, Park J-W, and Scholthof H B (1999) Separate regions on the tomato bushy stunt virus p22-protein mediate cell-to-cell movement versus elicitation of resistance responses. Mol. Plant-Microbe Interact. 12:285-292.
16. Clausen R E, Goodspeed T H (1925) Interspecific hybridization in *Nicotiana*. II. A tetraploid *glutinosa-tabacum* hybrid, an experimental verification of Winge's hypothesis. Genetics 10:278-284.
17. Cole, A B (2001) Investigations into the hypersensitive response of *Nicotiana* species to virus infections. Ph.D dissertation, University of Missouri, Coumbia MO, 185 pp.
18. Cole A B, Király L, Ross K., Schoelz J E (2001). Uncoupling resistance from cell death in the hypersensitive response of *Nicotiana* species to Cauliflower mosaic virus infection. Mol. Plant-Microbe. Interact. 14:31-41.
19. Collmer C W, Marston M F, Taylor J C, Jahn M (2000) The *I* gene of bean: a dosage-dependent allele conferring extreme resistance, hypersensitive resistance, or spreading vascular necrosis in response to the potyvirus *Bean common mosaic virus*. Mol. Plant-Microbe Interact. 13:1266-1270.
20. Cooley M B, Pathirana S, Wu H-J, Kachroo P, Klessig D F (2000) Members of the *Arabidopsis HRT/RPP8* family of resistance genes confer resistance to both viral and oomycete pathogens. Plant Cell 12:663-676.
21. Culver, J N (1997) Viral avirulence genes. Pages 196-219 in: Plant-Microbe Interactions, vol 2. Chapman & Hall, New York.

22. Culver J N, Dawson W O (1989) Point mutations in the coat protein gene of tobacco mosaic virus induce hypersensitivity in *Nicotiana sylvestris*. Mol. Plant-Microbe Interact. 2:209-213.
23. Cutt J R, Harpster M H, Dixon D C, Carr J P, Dunsmuire P, Klessig D F (1989) Disease response to tobacco mosaic virus in transgenic tobacco plants that constitutively express the pathogenesis-related PR-1b gene. Virology 173:89-97.
24. Dangl J L, Dietrich R A, Richberg M H (1996) Death don't have no mercy: Cell death programs in plant-microbe interactions. Plant Cell 8:1793-1807.
25. Dangl J L, Dietrich, R A, Thomas H (2000) Senescence and programmed cell death. In "Biochemistry and Molecular biology of Plants" (Buchanan B, Gruissem W, Jones R, eds.) American Society of Plant Physiologists, pgs 1044 - 1100.
26. Dardick C D, Culver J N (1997) Tobamovirus coat proteins: elicitors of the hypersensitive response in *Solanum melongena* (eggplant). Mol. Plant -Microbe Interact. 10:776-778.
27. Dardick C. D, Taraporewala Z, Lu B, Culver J N (1999) Comparison of tobamovirus coat protein structural features that affect elicitor activity in pepper, eggplant and tobacco. Mol. Plant-Microbe Interact. 12:247-251.
28. Daubert S, Schoelz J, Debao L, Shepherd R J (1984) Expression of disease symptoms in cauliflower mosaic virus genomic hybrids. J. Mol. Appl. Genet. 2:537-547.
29. del Pozo O, Lam E. (1998) Caspases and programmed cell death in the hypersensitive response of plants to pathogens. Current Biology 8:1129-1132.
30. Dempsey, D A, Wobbe, K K, Klessig, D F (1993) Resistance and susceptible responses of *Arabidopsis thaliana* to turnip crinkle virus. Phytopathology 83:1021-1029.
31. Dempsey D, Shah J, Klessig D F (1999) Salicylic acid and disease resistance in plants. Crit. Rev. Plant Sci. 18:547-575.
32. Dickman, M B, Park Y K, Oltersdorf T, Li W, Clemente T, and French R (2001) Abrogation of disease development in plants expressing animal antiapoptotic genes. Proc. Natl. Acad. Sci. USA 98:6957-6962.
33. Dietrich, R A, Richberg M H, Schmidt R, Dean C, and Dangl J L (1997) A novel zinc finger protein is encoded by the *Arabidopsis LSD1* gene and functions as a negative regulator of plant death.
34. Dinesh-Kumar S P, Baker B J (2000) Alternatively spliced *N* resistance gene transcripts: Their possible role in *Tobacco mosaic virus* resistance. Proc. Natl. Acad. Sci. USA 97:1908-1913.
35. Dinesh-Kumar S P, Tham W-H, Baker, B J (2000) Structure function analysis of the tobacco mosaic virus resistance gene *N*. Proc. Natl. Acad. Sci. USA 97:14789-14794.

36. Dixon R A, Harrison M J, Lamb C J (1994) Early events in the activation of plant defense responses. Annu. Rev. Phytopathol. 32:479-501.
37. Dunigan D D, Golemboski D B, Zaitlin, M (1987) Analysis of the *N* gene of *Nicotiana*. In "Plant Resistance to Viruses"(Chichester: Wiley) p 120-135.
38. English J J, Davenport G F, Elmayan T, Vaucheret H, Baulcombe D C (1997) Requirement of sense transcription for homology-dependent virus resistance and trans-activation. Plant J. 12:597-603.
39. Erickson F, Holzberg S, Calderon-Urrea A, Handley V, Axtell M, Corr C, Baker, B (1999) The helicase domain of the TMV replicase proteins induces the *N*-mediated defense response in tobacco. Plant J. 18:67-75.
40. Flor H H (1971) Current status of the gene-for-gene concept. Annu. Rev. Phytopathol. 9:275-296.
41. Franck A, Guilley H, Jonard G, Richards K, Hirth L (1980) Nucleotide sequence of cauliflower mosaic virus DNA. Cell 21, 285-294.
42. Fütterer J, Hohn T (1991) Translation of a polycistronic mRNA in the presence of the cauliflower mosaic virus transactivator protein. EMBO J. 10:3887-3896.
43. Gardner R C, Howarth A, Hahn P, Brown-Leudi M, Shepherd R J, Messing J. (1981). The complete nucleotide sequence of an infectious clone of cauliflower mosaic virus by M13mp7 shotgun sequencing. Nucleic Acids Res. 9:2871-2888.
44. Garrido-Ramirez E R, Sudarshana M R, Lucas W J, Gilbertson R L (2000) Bean dwarf mosaic virus BV1 protein is a determinant of the hypersensitive response and avirulence in *Phaseolus vulgaris*. Mol. Plant-Microbe Interact. 13:1184-1194.
45. Gilchrist, D G (1998) Programmed cell death in plant disease: the purpose and promise of cellular suicide. Annu. Rev. Phytopathol. 36:393-414.
46. Gland A (1981) Doubling chromosomes in interspecific hybrids by colchicine treatment. Cruciferae Newsletter 6:20-22.
47. Goodman R N, Novacky A J (1994) The Hypersensitive Reaction in Plants to Pathogens. American Phytopathological Society, St. Paul.
48. Goodspeed T H (1954) The genus *Nicotiana*. Chronica Botanic Company (Waltham MA) 536 pp.
49. Gowda S, Wu F C, Scholthof H B, Shepherd R J (1989) Gene VI of figwort mosaic virus (caulimovirus group) functions in posttranscriptional expression of genes on the full-length RNA transcript. Proc. Natl. Acad. Sci. USA 86:9203-9207.

50. Gray, J, Close P S, Briggs S P, Johal G S (1997) A novel suppressor of cell death in plants encoded by the *Lls1* gene of maize. Cell 89:25-31.
51. Hammond-Kosack K E, Jones J D G (1996) Resistance gene-dependent plant defense responses. Plant Cell 8:1773-1791.
52. Hohn T, Fütterer J (1997) The proteins and functions of plant pararetroviruses: knowns and unknowns. Crit. Rev. Plant Sci. 16:133-161.
53. Howell S H, Walker L L, Dudley, R K (1980) Cloned cauliflower mosaic virus DNA infects turnips (*Brassica rapa*). Science 208:1255-1267.
54. Hull, R (2001) Matthews' Plant Virology. Academic Press, San Diego.
55. Kachroo P, Yoshioka K, Shah J, Dooner H K, Klessig D F (2000) Resistance to turnip crinkle virus in *Arabidopsis* is regulated by two host genes and is salicylic acid dependent but *NPR1*, ethylene and jasmonate independent. Plant Cell 12:677-690.
56. Kavanagh T, Goulden M, Santa Cruz S, Chapman S, Barker I, Baulcombe D (1992) Molecular analysis of a resistance-breaking strain of potato virus X. Virology 189:609-617.
57. Kim C-H, Palukaitis, P (1997) The plant defense response to cucumber mosaic virus in cowpea is elicited by the viral polymerase gene and affects virus accumulation in single cells. EMBO J. 16:4060-4068.
58. Király Z, Barna B, Ersek T (1972) Hypersensitivity as a consequence, not the cause of plant resistance to infection. Nature 239:456-458.
59. Király L, Cole A B, Bourque J E, Schoelz J E (1999) Systemic cell death is elicited by the interaction of a single gene in *Nicotiana clevelandii* and gene VI of cauliflower mosaic virus. Mol. Plant-Microbe Interact. 12:919-925.
60. Knorr, D A, Dawson, W O (1988) A point mutation in the tobacco mosaic virus capsid protein gene induces hypersensitivity in *Nicotiana sylvestris*. Proc. Natl. Acad. Sci. USA 85:170-174.
61. Köhm B A, Goulden M G, Gilbert J E, Kanavaugh T A, Baulcombe D C (1993) A *Potato virus X* resistance gene mediates an induced, nonspecific resistance in protoplasts. Plant Cell 5:913-920.
62. Lebeurier G L, Hirth L, Hohn B, Hohn T (1980) Infectivities of native and cloned DNA of cauliflower mosaic virus. Gene 12:139-146.
63. Leisner S M, Turgeon R, Howell S H (1993) Effects of host plant development and genetic determinants on the long-distance movement of cauliflower mosaic virus in *Arabidopsis*. Plant Cell 5:191-202.

64. Linthorst H J M, Meuwissen R L J, Kaufman S, Bol J F (1989) Constitutive expression of pathogenesis-related proteins PR-1, GRP, and PRS in tobacco has no effect on virus infection. Plant Cell 1:285-291.

65. Majahan S K, Chishom S T, Whitham S A, Carrington J C (1998) Identification and characterization of a locus (*RTM1*) that restricts long-distance movement of tobacco etch virus in *Arabidopsis* thaliana. Plant J. 14:177-186.

66. Malcuit I, Marano M R, Kavanaugh T A, de Jong W, Forsyth A, Baulcombe D C, Shields D C, Kavanagh T A (1999) The 25-kDa movement protein of PVX elicits *Nb*-mediated hypersensitive cell death in potato. Mol. Plant-Microbe Interact. 12:536-543.

67. Mason W S, Taylor J M, Hull R (1987) Retroid virus genome replication. Adv. Virus. Res. 32:35-96.

68. Meshi T, Motoyoshi F, Maeda T, Yoshiwoka S, Watanabe H, Okada Y (1989) Mutations in the tobacco mosaic virus 30-kD protein gene overcome Tm-2 resistance in tomato. Plant Cell 1:515-522.

69. Mittler R, Shulaev V, Seskar M, Lam E (1996) Inhibition of programmed cell death in tobacco plants during pathogen-induced hypersensitive response at low oxygen pressure. Plant Cell 8:1991-2001.

70. Murphy A M, Chivasa S, Singh D P, Carr J P (1999) Salicylic acid-induced resistance to viruses and other pathogens: a parting of the ways? Trends in Plant Science 4:155-160.

71. Padgett H S, Beachy, R N (1993) Analysis of a tobacco mosaic virus strain capable of overcoming *N* gene-mediated resistance. Plant Cell 5:577-586.

72. Palanichlevam K, Cole A B, Shababi M, Schoelz J E (2000) Agroinfiltration of cauliflower mosaic virus gene VI elicits a hypersensitive response in *Nicotiana* species. Mol. Plant-Microbe Interact. 13:1275-1279.

73. Palanichlevam K, Schoelz J E (2002) A comparative analysis of the avirulence and translational transactivator functions of gene VI of *Cauliflower mosaic virus*. Virology 293:225-233.

74. Park H-S, Himmelbach A, Browning K S, Hohn, T, and Ryabova L A (2001) A plant viral "reinitiation" factor interacts with the host translational machinery. Cell 106:723-733.

75. Petty, I T D, Donald, R G K, Jackson, A O (1994) Multiple genetic determinants of barley stripe mosaic virus influence lesion phenotype on *Chenopodium amaranticolor*. Virology 198:218-226.

76. Ranu R S, Gowda S, Scholthof H, Wu F C, Shepherd R J (1996). *In vitro* translation of the full-length RNA transcript of figwort mosaic virus (Caulimovirus). Gene Expression 5:143-153.

77. Ryals J A, Neuenschwander U H, Willits M G, Molina A, Steiner H-Y, Hunt, M D (1996) Systemic acquired resistance. Plant Cell 8:1809-1819.
78. Saito T, Meshi T, Takamatsu N, Okada Y (1987) Coat protein gene sequence of tobacco mosaic virus encodes a host response determinant. Proc. Natl. Acad. Sci. USA 84:6074-6077.
79. Schoelz J E, Shepherd R J, Daubert S. (1986) Region VI of cauliflower mosaic virus encodes a host range determinant. Mol. Cell Biol. 6:2632-2637.
80. Schoelz J E, Shepherd R J (1988) Host range control of cauliflower mosaic virus. Virology 162:30-37.
81. Scholthof H B, Gowda S, Wu F C, Shepherd R J (1992). The full-length transcript of a caulimovirus is a polycistronic mRNA whose genes are trans-activated by the product of gene VI. J. Virol. 66:3131-3139.
82. Scholthof H B, Scholthof K-B G, Jackson A O (1995) Identification of tomato bushy stunt virus host-specific symptom determinants by expression of individual genes from a potato virus X vector. Plant Cell 7:1157-1172.
83. Scofield S R, Tobias C M, Rathjen J P, Chang, J H, Lavell D T, Michelmore R W, Staskawicz B J (1996) Molecular basis of gene-for-gene specificity in bacterial speck disease of tomato. Science 274:2063-2065.
84. Sha Y, Broglio E P, Cannon J F, Schoelz J E (1995) Expression of a plant viral polycistronic mRNA in yeast, *Saccharomyces cerevisiae*, mediated by a plant virus translational transactivator. Proc. Natl. Acad. Sci. USA 92:8911-8915.
85. Simon A E, Li X H, Lew J E, Strange R, Zhang C, Polacco M, Carpenter C D (1992) Susceptibility and resistance of *Arabidopsis thaliana* to turnip crinkle virus. Mol. Plant-Microbe Interact. 5:496-503.
86. Taraporewala Z F, Culver J N (1996) Identification of an elicitor active site within the three-dimensional structure of the tobacco mosaic tobamovirus coat protein. Plant Cell 8:169-178.
87. Taraporewala Z F, Culver J N (1997) Structural and functional conservation of the tobamovirus coat protein elicitor active site. Mol. Plant-Microbe Interact. 10:597-604.
88. Tang X, Frederick R D, Zhou J, Halterman D A, Jia Y, Martin G B (1996) Initiation of plant disease resistance by physical interaction of *AvrPto* and *Pto* kinase. Science 274:2060-2063.
89. Thomas C M, Tang S, Hammond-Kosack K, Jones J D G (2000) Comparison of the hypersensitive response induced by the tomato *Cf-4* and *Cf-9* genes in *Nicotiana* spp. Mol. Plant-Microbe Interact. 13:465-469.

90. Van den Ackerveken G, Marois E, Bonas U (1996) Recognition of the bacterial avirulence protein *AvrBs3* occurs inside the host plant cell. Cell 87:1307-1316.
91. Van der Hoorn R A L, Laurent F, Roth R, De Wit P J G M (2000) Agroinfiltration is a versatile tool that facilitates comparative analyses of *Avr9/Cf-9*-induced and *Avr4/Cf-4*-induced necrosis. Mol. Plant-Microbe Interact. 13:439-446.
92. Wang H, Li J, Bostock R M, Gilchrist D G (1996) Apoptosis: a functional paradigm for programmed plant cell death induced by a host-selective phytotoxin and invoked during development. Plant Cell 8:375-391.
93. Whitham S, Dinesh-Kumar S P, Choi D, Heyl R, Corr C, Baker B (1994) The product of the *Tobacco mosaic virus* resistance gene *N*: similarity to Toll and the interleukin-1 receptor. Cell 78:1101-1115.
94. Wintermantel W M, Anderson E J, Schoelz J E (1993) identification of domains within gene VI of cauliflower mosaic virus that influence systemic infection of *Nicotiana bigelovii* in a light-dependent manner. Virology 196:789-798.
95. Xu P, Roossinck M J (2000) Cucumber mosaic virus D satellite RNA-induced programmed cell death in tomato. Plant Cell 12, 1079-1092.
96. Yu I-C, Parker J, Bent, A F (1998) Gene-for-gene resistance without the hypersensitive response in *Arabidopsis dnd1* mutant. Proc. Natl. Acad. Sci. USA 95:7819-7824.
97. Yu I-C, Fengler K A, Clough S J, Bent A F (2000) Identification of *Arabidopsis* mutants exhibiting an altered hypersensitive response in gene-for-gene disease resistance. Mol. Plant-Microbe Interact. 13:277-286.
98. Zijlstra C, Hohn T (1992) Cauliflower mosaic virus gene VI controls translation from dicistronic expression units in transgenic *Arabidopsis* plants. Plant Cell 4:1471-1484.

Gene Discovery in Sedentary Plant-Parasitic Nematodes

Geert Smant, Ling Qin, Aska Goverse, Arjen Schots, Johannes Helder and Jaap Bakker

Plant-Microbe Interactions

Evolution of communities of organisms has resulted in many kinds of interactions varying from peaceful, separate co-existence (= non-interaction) to symbiotic or parasitic relationships. Some pathogens have developed sophisticated mechanisms to interact with their hosts and start a durable relationship. Durable parasitic relationships are fascinating and scientifically interesting as they illustrate the maximal impact of co-evolution. Often these parasites have evolved the ability to recognize individual compounds unintentionally produced by their hosts. These signals will then trigger the release of an array of pathogenicity factors from the parasites. Comprehension of the molecular events underlying the resulting intimate interactions will lead to a better understanding of fundamental biological processes as well as the development of new approaches to elegantly and specifically control harmful pests.

Plant-Parasitic Nematodes

Nematodes, members of the phylum Nematoda, are present in almost all the imaginable habitats on earth. Most nematodes are bacteriophagous, mycetophagous, or live as saprophytes on organic material. Relatively few nematode species evolved into parasites of plants or animals. Plant-parasitic nematodes have various feeding strategies. Most of them are either ectoparasitic or migratory endoparasitic, which means they use their stylet to remove the cell content from individual root cells. The contact time is highly variable ranging from 5-10 s to several days. Subsequently, the nematode will move on, and feed on another root segment, not necessarily from the same plant. By contrast, sedentary endoparasitic nematodes have evolved complex relationships with their host plants and they complete the whole life cycle by withdrawing nutrients solely from a fixed feeding site inside the host plant root. The family *Heteroderidae* (order *Tylenchida*) includes cyst (*Heterodera* and *Globodera* spp.) and root-knot (*Meloidogyne* spp.) nematodes. Because of the damage these nematodes cause to a wide range of crops, this family of sedentary endoparasitic nematodes is highly relevant and will be the main focus of this chapter (37, 73).

PLANT-NEMATODE INTERACTIONS

Root-knot and cyst nematodes have five different developmental stages and – without the adult stage – the end of each of these stages is marked by a molt. The embryonic first-stage juvenile (J1) molts within the egg resulting in a second-stage juvenile (J2). In some cyst nematode species, this J2 is in diapause, and the dormant J2 will respond to hatching stimuli only after 8-12 months incubation at relatively low temperatures ($\approx$ 4°C) (60). After diapause, hatching of J2 is greatly stimulated by root exudates from host plants. These exudates (or diffusates) are complex mixtures of compounds released by host plant roots including so-called eclepins. In case of the soybean cyst nematode, these eclepins stimulate at low concentrations, 10^{-11} to 10^{-12} g ml^{-1}, the hatching of J2 from the eggs (51).

The infective juveniles (J2s) invade the root of a host plant just behind the apex, in the elongation or the differentiation zone. After root penetration, the J2s migrate intracellularly (cyst nematodes) or intercellularly (root-knot nematodes) through the cortex. Cyst nematodes migrate in the direction of the vascular cylinder, whereas the root-knot nematodes orient themselves to the root tip. Juveniles of the latter genus continue their intercellular migration to the meristematic zone. In the translucent roots of *Arabidopsis thaliana* it is observed that the juveniles of *Meloidogyne incognita* continue migration by making a U-turn into the vascular cylinder and proceed until they reach the differentiated vascular tissue at the level of their entry in the root. Parasitic J2s possess a protrusible, hollow spear called a stylet with which the nematode pierces cell walls. The migration is not only facilitated by physical impact of the stylet thrusts but also by cell wall-degrading enzymes that are secreted by the invading nematode (81). Upon arrival at the appropriate cell type the nematode induces the formation of a feeding site. The feeding site is the sole source of plant nutrients for the sedentary nematodes and constitutes a crucial aspect of the parasitic cycle (37, 83, 84).

The feeding site of root-knot nematodes arises from 2-12 parenchymatic xylem cells in the differentiation zone of the root (32, 42). These cells are redifferentiated into large hypertrophied multinucleate giant-cells. The multinucleate state of the giant cells is caused by acytokinetic mitosis in the feeding site initials. The giant cells are metabolically highly active, which is deduced from the high accumulation of subcellular organelles in the cytoplasm (*e.g.* rough endoplasmic reticulum, plastids, mitochondria, and nuclei). For cyst nematodes, feeding site formation starts with the fusion of the initial syncytial cell with an adjacent cell by a (partial) cell wall breakdown. Subsequently, more neighboring cells are incorporated and the process of cell fusion progresses for a few weeks. Finally, the resulting syncytium (mainly localized within the stele) may include of up to several hundreds of cells (42). In contrast to giant-cells no acytokinetic mitosis is observed in syncytial cells. Instead, the high DNA content in syncytial nuclei is the outcome of repeated cycles of endoreduplication (29). The DNA multiplication in nuclei of feeding sites implies a high gene dosage, which is able to support hypertrophy in feeding sites. Nematode growth and development demands a steady increase in the quantity of nutrients that is removed from the syncytium. This nematode-induced metabolic sink is maintained by intensive phloem unloading (6).

As a result of feeding, the nematode changes. Its body wall muscles degenerate, the body enlarges, and the nematode becomes sedentary. After several weeks obligatory sexual reproduction takes place in most cyst nematode species. For the majority of cyst nematode species, sex is determined epigenetically. Poor nutrition will result in the development of males whereas favorable nutritional conditions will lead to the development of females (55). Reproduction of root-knot nematodes, on the other hand, is almost exclusively parthenogenetic; in spite of the absence of mating, males occur regularly under unfavorable conditions (77).

Secretions from Sedentary Plant-Parasitic Nematodes

Nematode secretions have been implicated with many aspects of the nematode-plant interaction (35). They are presumed to be involved in hatching, in self-defense, in migration through plant tissue, and the induction and maintenance of the feeding site. Nematode secretions originate from a range of body structures including the cuticle, the amphids, and esophageal gland cells. In the paragraphs below we give an overview of the genes that encode secretory proteins and that are specifically expressed in these body structures.

Cuticle

For most of their active life the sedentary endoparasitic nematodes lay embedded in plant tissue where they are constantly exposed to a wide range of defense mechanisms of the plant (80). The cuticle that covers the nematode completely is the first protective layer against the chemical and physical impact of the plant's defenses (40). The recent identification of a retinol- and fatty acid binding protein in the potato cyst nematode *Globodera pallida* illustrates the chemical warfare at the interface of nematode and host plant (64). This protein, which binds to linolenic and linoleic acids and inhibits the lipoxygenase-mediated modification of these compounds, is localized to the cuticular surface of the infective juvenile. Peroxidation of linolenic acid by lipoxygenase is an early step in synthesis of jasmonic acid – a recognized systemic plant defense signal transducer. Furthermore, lipoxygenase mediated peroxidation of lipids effectively generates reactive oxygen species in plants. By producing a potent inhibitor at its surface the nematode may be able to down-regulate a major first line defense mechanism in plants.

Reactive oxygen species are pivotal in self-defense throughout the animal and plant kingdom. To some extent, endoparasites of animals and plants have to deal with a chemically similar hostile environment in spite of principal differences in their hosts. Direct comparison of expressed sequence tag (EST) databases of plant and animal parasites provides evidence for existence of homologous anti-oxidant genes. For instance, the retinol- and fatty acid binding protein has a conserved counterpart in animal parasites. The same holds true for peroxiredoxin, which is also found at the surface of the cuticle of *Globodera rostochiensis* (69). Peroxiredoxins are a family of peroxidases that are able to remove hydrogen peroxide, which is produced at the nematode-plant interface (80). Similarly, the activity of superoxide dismutase, a scavenger enzyme of free radicals, is detected in collected secretions of the *G. rostochiensis* (68). Genes encoding extracellular superoxide dismutase have already been cloned from animal parasites (*e.g. Haemonchus contortus*[1]) and considerable effort is undertaken to identify homologues in plant-parasitic nematodes. In summary, evidence is accumulating that parasitic nematodes of plant and animals have evolved a similar system associated with the cuticle to protect themselves against host defenses.

AMPHIDS

The function of the two small structures on either side of the mouth of plant-parasitic nematodes – the amphids – is still unclear. Electron micrographs of the amphids reveal similarities to chemosensory organs in other animal species. Because of their position at the head they are in close proximity of the feeding site and it is speculated that they play a role during feeding site formation and maintenance. Microscopic observations of amphidial secretions show that they are in direct contact with a so-called feeding plug in the cell walls of feeding site initials.

To date, only two amphid specific genes have been cloned from plant-parasitic nematodes. The first one, *Gr-ams-1*, was cloned from *G. rostochiensis* (41) and is similar to a group of SXP proteins and *RAL-2* homologues. The SXP/*RAL-2* homologues constitute a family of small proteins (molecular mass of 17-20 kDa) with a high immunodiagnostic potential for lymphatic filariasis in humans (67). Homologues of the SXP/*RAL-2* protein family have only been found within the phylum Nematoda. Unfortunately there is no information available on the

---

[1] SWISS-PROT accession P51547

functional role of the SXP/*RAL-2* protein family in animal parasites. Indirect evidence suggests that the SXP/*RAL-2* homologues are secreted from the hypodermis of animal parasitic nematodes. *In situ* hybridization experiments with *Gr-ams-1* localized transcription of this gene in the gland cells aligning the amphids. The protein predicted from *Gr-ams-1* harbors a signal peptide for secretion.

The second known amphid specific gene, *Mi-map-1,* was found as a putative avirulence gene in an AFLP-based strategy comparing near-isogenic lines of *M. incognita* that have a differential response to the *Mi-1* resistance gene in tomato (72). Immunofluorescence microscopy with antisera raised against a synthetic peptide of 15 amino acids designed from *Mi-map-1* localized the protein in amphidial secretions. The *Mi-map-1* is a pioneering sequence in the database. Until more functional data on *Gr-ams-1* and *Mi-map-1* becomes available or the identity of other proteins in amphidial secretions is resolved it remains unclear how they contribute to the nematode-plant interaction.

Esophageal Glands

Compared to nematodes that feed on bacteria, plant-parasitic nematodes have large esophageal glands. Nematodes of the order Tylenchida to which the sedentary endoparasites belong, have one dorsal and two subventral esophageal glands. The cellular architecture of an esophageal gland in nematodes is completely dedicated to its secretory function. Each gland is a single cell with a cytoplasmic extension that terminates in an ampulla, which serves as a reservoir for secretory granules. The ampullae are connected to the lumen of the esophagus; in this way the gland secretions can be released into the esophageal lumen. The dorsal gland ends just behind the stylet whereas the subventral gland cells are connected to the lumen of the esophagus in the metacorpus just behind the pump chamber. The secretions are eventually injected into plant tissue through the stylet. The stylet, the muscular metacorpus and the large single-celled esophageal glands are considered as specialized adaptations to plant parasitism (21, 36).

For decades the esophageal glands in nematodes have been recognized as a major source of proteins involved in parasitism. However, many standard molecular procedures proved to be ineffective in identifying parasitism genes from sedentary parasitic nematodes. The seemingly impenetrable molecular interaction between obligate parasitic nematodes and host plants caused nematology to lag behind other fields in plant pathology. The first parasitism gene that encodes a secretory protein from an esophageal gland was cloned in (1998) (75). The last few years several novel molecular techniques have successfully been applied to plant-parasitic nematodes, which led to rapid developments in gene discovery in these parasites. The second part of this chapter will highlight these developments as well as their significance for our understanding of plant-nematode interactions.

Methods for Identifying Nematode Parasitism Genes

COLLECTION OF CHEMICALLY INDUCED NEMATODES SECRETIONS

The most direct way to identify the nature of nematodes esophageal gland secretions is to collect the proteins emanating from the stylet orifice for analysis. Individual juveniles contain only nanogram quantities of total extractable protein (17). The quantity of naturally secreted proteins is at most in the range of picograms. In order to collect sufficient material to perform a protein analysis one needs to handle huge numbers of individuals. To further promote the release of stylet secretions, a range of chemical compounds have been applied to suspensions of juveniles.

Two chemical reagents are now commonly used to collect secretions from pre-parasitic juveniles *in vitro*: a serotonin (5-hydroxytryptamine) analogue called 5-methyoxy-N, N-dimethyltryptamine-hydrogen-oxalate (DMT) and resorcinol (53). The former is used for cyst nematodes, the latter for root-knot nematodes. For DMT it was shown that it modulates feeding activity in the nematodes *Caenorhaditis elegans* and *Ascaris suum* (70, 78). Binding of serotonin to its receptor in esophageal muscles results in a dramatic increase in esophageal pumping. A similar effect is observed in plant-parasitic nematodes with the convenient side effect of enhanced salivation of stylet secretions (28, 68). The mode of action of resorcinol, which presumably also interferes neurotransmission in nematodes, is unknown.

The biological relevance of secretions produced upon exposure to these chemicals is difficult to assess. The production of stylet secretions *in vitro* may not represent the secretions produced *in planta*. If available, a natural secretion-inducing substance would be preferred. Potato root diffusate has long been used as the hatching stimulus of the potato cyst nematode (60). Recently, it was shown that exposure to root diffusate induced the release of secretory proteins by freshly hatched J2 (74). Potato root diffusate-induced secretions probably closely resemble the set of proteins that is released during the onset of plant parasitism.

A formidable hurdle that has to be taken prior to any analysis of collected stylet secretions is to secure that they are essentially free from microbial contaminants. Continuous monoxenic cultures of obligatory plant parasites often suffer from severe population depression after a few successive generations *in vitro*. Given this biological phenomenon combined with the long generation time it is difficult to rear sedentary nematodes on a large scale in monoxenic cultures. Hence, juveniles are often taken from greenhouse cultures and treated with antibiotics (*e.g.*

streptomycine, penicilline, and chlorhexidine) prior to collection of the stylet secretions (31). Surface sterilization, however, can only be applied at a cost, namely a reduced viability of the juveniles.

IMMUNOPURIFICATION

The inability to collect sufficient nematode secretions for direct protein analysis prompted a number of groups to raise monoclonal antibodies (mAbs) against these secretions (34). Actually, this approach resulted in the identification of the first nematode gene for parasitism. MAbs were used to immunopurify proteins for sequence analysis and the first subventral gland secretory proteins, β-1,4-endoglucanases, were identified by using degenerate oligonucleotides and PCR based cloning (75). In attempts to identify dorsal gland proteins from cyst or root-knot nematodes, several mAbs have been raised that specifically recognized the dorsal glands of cyst and root-knot nematodes. In 1988, a mAb specific to the dorsal gland and its extension in second stage juveniles from the soybean cyst nematode *H. glycines* was identified (2). Later, mAbs specific for the dorsal glands of *H. glycines* and *M. incognita* were used for immunological screening of expression libraries and yielded cDNA clones that are still being characterized (13, 14, 28). In summary, the mAb-based approach is time-consuming, appears to be biased towards immunodominant proteins and is only moderately effective.

EXPRESSED SEQUENCE TAGS

Expressed sequence tags are single pass sequences of cDNA clones selected randomly from a library (1). In (1999) the Parasitic Nematode EST Sequencing project (see Nematode Net[2]) took off and is now the main producer of ESTs from parasitic nematode species (51). The target of this initiative is ~300,000 ESTs in 2003 of which a substantial proportion will be from plant parasites.

The representation of the genes in a cDNA library depends on the physiological and developmental stage of an organism and the tissue from which the messenger RNA is isolated. The most commonly practiced methods use whole plant-parasitic nematodes as a source to prepare the library (11, 52, 63). The minimal number of juveniles that are required to achieve a representative cDNA library add up to at least one hundred thousand. This threshold has been the reason that so far cDNA libraries are predominantly made from pre-parasitic juveniles and adult females. To extract these numbers of individuals from plants during the formation of the feeding sites is not feasible.

---

[2] at http://www.nematode.net

The majority of the ESTs of plant-parasitic nematodes that are currently available in GenBank (~36,000 in dbEST release 051002) are from libraries of pre-parasitic juvenile stages. None of the cDNA libraries in these projects were normalized or subtracted which means that the majority of these ESTs reflect the abundantly transcribed genes. Moreover, ESTs from these pre-parasitic stages are likely to reveal genes up-regulated just prior to plant invasion as well as genes that are constitutively expressed at a high level. The subventral esophageal glands are actively producing secretory proteins in pre-parasitic juveniles (5). Hence, many subventral esophageal gland genes were tagged using ESTs from pre-parasitic juveniles. The nature of these genes (*e.g.* cellulase (27, 71, 75, 79), pectate lyase (62), polygalacturonase (39), xylanase (12), and cellulose binding proteins (19)) and their temporal expression patterns suggest that the primary function of the subventral glands is to facilitate cell wall degradation during plant invasion and intra- or intercellular migration.

In order to decrease the amount of template for the preparation of libraries some groups have used cDNA amplification based on the spliced-leader sequence (47). This leader sequence of 22 nucleotides is *trans*-spliced from a separate locus in the genome to the 5'-end of the messenger RNAs (57, 58). *Trans*-splicing is observed for a large proportion of the genes in the phylum Nematoda. Obviously, the advantage of such amplification is that only full-length transcripts will be represented in the library. The disadvantage of using the spliced-leader sequence lies in the lack of knowledge on the prevalence of this leader sequence in other nematode species than *C. elegans* and *Ascaris lumbricoides* (70-90% of the genes) (50). Furthermore, it is also not known whether the presence of the spliced-leader is biased towards certain functional classes of genes. From our preliminary studies using an adapted cDNA-AFLP protocol and the spliced-leader (SL-1) sequence as one of the primers, we find that approximately 50% of the genes are *trans*-spliced in the *G. rostochiensis* (L. Qin, unpublished result).

TISSUE SPECIFIC LIBRARIES

If the objective of an EST project is aimed at tagging genes involved in parasitism, then the bulk of the ESTs derived from whole nematodes will be discarded as irrelevant. The selection criteria for relevance are homology with accessions in sequence databases, *in situ* hybridization to the esophageal glands and the predicted extracellular destiny of the encoded protein (*e.g.* Signal P and PSORT computer programs). Since a large proportion of the ESTs (>40 %) produced from plant-parasites are novel sequences, homology searches are only moderately effective. In addition, whole mount *in situ* hybridization with plant-parasitic nematodes is time-consuming, expensive and moderately successful. On average 50% of the probes used for *in situ* hybridizations produce a reliable signal. Hence, several groups have devised refined methods to make a robust first selection in the transcriptome of the nematodes.

A powerful improvement in the efficiency of EST projects can be achieved by using tissue specific cDNA libraries. The infective juveniles of sedentary plant-parasitic nematodes measure approximately 500 microns in length and 25 microns in diameter, which makes micro-dissection of the esophageal glands for template isolation a formidable task. The first attempt to prepare an esophageal gland region specific cDNA library was made by Lambert and coworkers (46). They removed the parts of the parasitic juveniles of *Meloidogyne javanica* anterior and posterior to the esophageal gland region. The primary template of the remaining gland region of three individual nematodes was amplified using the spliced-leader sequence and cloned into a plasmid vector. This library was subsequently screened with radiolabeled cDNAs from both the gland region and the tail region, and colonies that exclusively hybridized with cDNAs from the gland region were considered good candidates for parasitism genes.

Lambert *et al.* (46) pursued one particular clone that showed a weak homology to a bacterial chorismate mutase. Probes made from this gene, *Mj-cm-1*, hybridized specifically to both types of esophageal gland cells. Lambert *et al.* were the first to provide evidence for the presence of chorismate mutase in animals. The protein encoded by *Mj-cm-1*, which is predicted to be extracellular, was able to functionally complement a chorismate mutase deficient strain of *Escherichia coli*. Chorismate mutase converts chorismate, the end product of the Shikimate pathway in many organisms, to the precursor of the aromatic amino acids. While it is reasonable to assume that this enzyme is injected from the gland cells into the plant, at present it remains unclear how this enzyme contributes to the parasitic strategy of nematodes.

In an elegant procedure Wang *et al.* (82) have successfully used a micro-aspirator to isolate sufficient messenger RNA to make a cDNA library from the gland region of a small number of individuals of the parasitic stages of *H. glycines*. In theory, these gland libraries are the most direct and efficient means to identify parasitism genes that encode esophageal gland secretory proteins. A drawback of these methods is the risk of the so-called Monte Carlo effect, which refers to an inherent limitation of the PCR amplification of small amounts of complex templates (43). Below a certain threshold copy number of cDNA templates, stochastic variations in amplification occur that undermine the reproducibility and increase the redundancy of PCR amplified cDNA libraries. However, highly and moderately expressing genes, which will presumably constitute the majority of the parasitism genes in the esophageal glands, are less affected by these types of variations. Furthermore, Wang and coworkers (82) experienced considerable contamination from bacterial genes in their libraries, which is an intrinsic risk of working with minute amounts of starting material.

YEAST SIGNAL PEPTIDE SELECTION AND SUPPRESSIVE SUBTRACTIVE HYBRIDIZATION

Thousands of genes involved in the secretory function and the metabolism of the esophageal gland cell are abundantly represented among the ESTs obtained from the gland specific libraries. To eliminate these housekeeping genes from the gland specific libraries Wang *et al.* (82) have subcloned a gland library in a yeast expression vector that allows for a positive selection of those genes that encode a signal peptide for secretion (44). Proteins encoded by parasitism genes are most likely to be secreted outside the nematode by means of a signal peptide. Genes (or 5'-end fragments thereof) subcloned in-frame with a modified invertase gene, which lacks a start codon and a signal peptide, initiated the translocation of the nascent fusion protein to the extracellular space of the yeast *Saccharomyces cerevisiae*. Only yeast transformants that harbor a properly secreted invertase fusion protein are able to grow on a sucrose medium.

At present several hundred yeast colonies, representing fourteen cDNA clusters, have been selected on sucrose medium with the signal peptide selection procedure (82). Nine of these clusters are predicted to encode extracellular proteins. Three of them are specifically expressed in the dorsal esophageal gland cell in parasitic stages of *H. glycines*. For the other clusters no hybridization signal was detected in parasitic juveniles. Remarkably, all three putative parasitism genes encode novel protein sequences.

Gao *et al.* (25) have combined tissue specific libraries and PCR mediated subtractive hybridization in order to eliminate the housekeeping genes from the gland enriched cDNA libraries of *H. glycines*. They micro-aspirated the contents of both the esophageal gland region and the intestinal region of parasitic stages to produce cDNA templates. The template of the intestinal region was then subtracted from the gland cDNA using suppressive subtractive hybridization. The remaining template was cloned into a library plasmid, and further analyzed by DNA sequencing and *in situ* hybridization. This procedure resulted in cDNA clones representing 23 genes of which 8 were predicted to encode extracellular proteins. Three genes were exclusively expressed in the dorsal esophageal gland whereas one gene expressed specifically in the subventral esophageal gland cells of parasitic juveniles.

The only subventral gland specific clone isolated by Gao and co-workers is a homologue of the venom allergen antigen 5 family secreted by hymenopteran insects (23). Other homologues of this protein family have been found in the *C. elegans* genome, in animal parasitic nematodes (33) and in other plant-parasitic nematode species *M. incognita* (20) and *G.*

rostochiensis (L. Qin, unpublished results). The biological role of these homologues in nematodes is obscure. One of the dorsal gland specific transcripts found in this study is similar to a proline-rich glycoprotein with an unknown function in saliva from rat (54). The other dorsal gland specific transcripts are pioneering sequences of which one was found in the yeast signal peptide system too (82).

RNA FINGERPRINTING-THE CLASSICAL WAY

Biological responses and developmental processes are precisely controlled at the level of gene expression. Information on the temporal and spatial regulation of gene expression often sheds light on the potential function of a particular gene. Powerful techniques capable to reveal differential expression patterns of a large number of genes should enable the identification of parasitism genes.

With this in mind Ding *et al.* (19, 20) compared transcription patterns in pre-parasitic and parasitic second stage juveniles of *M. incognita*. cDNA fragments up-regulated in parasitic juveniles 48 h post-inoculation were displayed on gels following amplification of the templates with random oligonucleotide primers. Using this procedure the authors isolated two genes, *Mi-msp-1* and *Mi-cbp-1*, specifically expressed in the two subventral esophageal gland cells. *Mi-msp-1* was the first homologue of the hymenopteran venom allergen AG5-protein family cloned from a plant-parasitic nematode (see above). *Mi-cbp-1* is characterized by a cellulose-binding domain linked to a second domain with unknown function. The cellulose-binding domain in *Mi-cbp-1* has the highest similarity with its counterparts in nematode cellulases, which are linked to a catalytic domain (14). No catalytic activity was found for the second domain in *Mi-cbp-1*. Both *Mi-msp-1* and *Mi-cbp-1* are predicted to encode extracellular proteins. Antisera raised against recombinant *Mi-cbp-1* labeled the resorcinol induced stylet secretions from pre-parasitic juveniles confirming the predicted extracellular destiny of the protein. The presence of a cellulose-binding domain of *Mi-cbp-1* suggests that it may interact with plant cell walls during penetration and feeding site initiation. The finding that recombinant *Mi-cbp-1* binds to the cell walls of tobacco cell suspension culture supports this hypothesis.

RNA FINGER PRINTING – cDNA-AFLP

cDNA-AFLP is a novel RNA fingerprinting technique to identify differentially expressed genes (3). cDNAs are digested by two restriction enzymes and oligonucleotide adapters are ligated to the resulting restriction fragments to generate template DNA for PCR. PCR primers complementary to the adapter sequences with additional selective nucleotides at the 3' end enable the amplification of a manageable number of cDNA fragments. Unlike classical differential display methods that make use of small random oligomer primers (48), relatively high annealing temperatures can be used and, hence, cDNA-AFLP is more stringent and reproducible. Furthermore, because only perfectly matching templates are amplified highly homologous genes can be distinguished.

In our laboratory we have exploited the biology of the potato cyst nematode *G. rostochiensis* using cDNA-AFLP to identify parasitism genes expressed in the esophageal glands (66). The experimental set-up is founded on an observed response of the esophageal gland cells in pre-parasitic juveniles to root diffusates. Prior to plant invasion pre-parasitic infective juveniles of the potato cyst nematode undergo an obligatory dormancy. The fully developed second stage juveniles can endure this diapause in a desiccated state. After a cold period the juveniles end their dormancy and rehydrate while soaking in water. Remarkably, the most prominent change in the structure of the juvenile during rehydration is the activation of the subventral esophageal glands. The dorsal gland is activated too but only after exposure to root diffusates of a host plant and subsequent hatching (61). Taking samples during this sequence of events yields highly similar stages that differ primarily in the transcriptional activity of the esophageal glands.

In this experimental set up it is assumed that the majority of dorsal gland specific parasitism genes in pre-parasitic juveniles of *G. rostochiensis* are up-regulated following exposure to root diffusates. Template preparation for cDNA-AFLP requires large numbers of nematodes, which confines the use of the technique to developmental stages that are easily isolated - pre-parasitic juveniles and adult females. Therefore, changes in transcription of parasitism genes that occur in between these stages will be missed, which is an evident weakness.

Approximately 16,000 AFLP generated cDNA fragments of three pre-parasitic juvenile stages were displayed on gel, which covers about 70% of the genome of *G. rostochiensis* (L. Qin, unpublished results). About 400 fragments were up-regulated either in the stage with subventral gland activity or in the hatched juveniles in which both subventral and dorsal esophageal glands are active. These fragments were excised from the gel and subjected to DNA sequencing. To date, about 30 esophageal gland specific genes have been identified (L. Qin, unpublished result). Two of the dorsal esophageal gland specific, *Gr-dgl-1* and *Gr-dgl-3*, encode small extracellular proteins that have no match in sequence databases. The predicted molecular weight of the *Gr-dgl-1* and *Gr-dgl-3* is smaller than 7 kDa. Previously, Goverse *et al.* (31) indirectly showed the presence of small proteins in secretions of *G. rostochiensis* that were able to stimulate cell proliferation in tobacco protoplasts. We are currently investigating a possible link between *Gr-dgl-1* and/or *Gr-dgl-3* and the mitogenic activity in stylet secretions.

We have also identified a multiple gene family named *Gr-dgl-2x*, which shares significant homology with RanBPMs (Ran-Binding Protein in Microtubule organizing center) from various organisms (56, 59). These genes are up-regulated in the infective second-stage juvenile and specifically expressed in the dorsal esophageal gland. The predicted RanBPM proteins are preceded by a signal-peptide for secretion. The *Gr-dgl-2x* family was shown to be homologous to the N-terminal parts of a number of RanBPMs from *Xenopus laevis*, from fission yeast (*Schizosaccharomyces pombe*), from *C. elegans* and from *Homo sapiens*. Only the function of the *H. sapiens* RanBPM protein has been studied in some more detail (56). Currently, we are investigating the possible roles of these RanBPM-like proteins in feeding site induction.

FUNCTIONAL GENOMICS *CONTINUED*

The limitation of the EST approach is that it will not reveal the potential functions of the genes if they do not share homologies with functionally annotated genes in the database. It is therefore necessary to link ESTs with functional genomics techniques. Qin *et al.* have developed the computer program GenEST to link ESTs with cDNA-AFLP expression profiles *in silico* (65). In GenEST a catalogue is built of the cDNA-AFLP fragments of all expressed genes using fragment length and the sequences of the extended endonuclease recognition sites as unique identifiers. From the catalogue, ESTs, which are predicted by the program to have interesting expression patterns, can be quickly identified. *Vice versa*, using the identifiers of a band displayed on a cDNA-AFLP gel, the cDNA sequence(s) corresponding to this band can be obtained.

Alternatively, the expression pattern of ESTs can also be analyzed using cDNA microarray technique. De Boer *et al.* (18) have spotted a gland specific library of *H. glycines* (see above) on a glass-slide and probed it with fluorescent cDNA of various developmental stages. They were able to display expression patterns of ~1,350 cDNA clones from a gland library of parasitic juveniles.

PROTEOMICS

In (1992) a first attempt was made to identify proteins of plant-parasitic nematodes directly from two dimensional electrophoresis gels. To this purpose De Boer *et al.* (16) made protein extracts from 3,300 anterior and posterior parts of the pre-parasitic juveniles of *G. rostochiensis*. The aim of this daunting effort was to isolate esophageal gland specific proteins. At that time routine peptide sequencing using mass-spectrometry was not available for such low concentrations of proteins. Therefore, one protein spot was excised from the gel and injected into a mouse for monoclonal antibody production. Immunopurification with a specific mAb should have provided sufficient material for amino terminal protein sequencing using Edman chemistry (76). Unfortunately, the immunization did not produce antibodies that reacted with the esophageal glands. Beyond any doubt with the current developments in protein sequencing by mass spectrometry similar efforts in the future will be more fruitful (49).

Parasitism Genes *anno* 2002

The new millennium marks the end of a period of decades that is best characterized as a struggle to identify nematode genes involved in plant parasitism. In the last five years several adaptations have been made to molecular techniques to make them suitable for plant-nematode interactions. These developments allowed this field of biology to finally enter the era of genomics. At present practically all limitations to gene discovery are lifted and the number of identified candidate parasitism genes from plant-parasitic nematodes extends exponentially.

The sequencing of the genome of the bacteriophagous nematode *C. elegans* was completed in (1999) (8). It was expected that genome projects with plant-parasites would greatly benefit from the annotated sequences of *C. elegans*. This holds true for genes involved in general processes, however, as a consequence of the adaptations to parasitism, plant parasites have evolved a set of unique parasitism genes that have no counter parts in other nematodes.

For many of these genes their function can be deduced from homologues in protein databases from other plant pathogens. The identity of the cell wall degrading enzymes released from the subventral esophageal glands was resolved this way. Based on these findings the two subventral esophageal gland cells are now recognized as organs that facilitate the migration of infective juveniles and adult males in plants. This doesn't necessarily mean that these subventral glands are exclusively dedicated to this function. The expression of homologues of the hymenopteran venom allergen protein family and chorismate mutase suggests that the subventral esophageal glands may be involved in other functions as well.

Based on changes in the ultrastructure of the dorsal esophageal gland during the parasitic cycle its function is implicated in feeding site induction and maintenance, and feeding tube formation. An essential element in the induction of feeding sites is genome multiplication. Knowledge of the parasitism genes expressed in the dorsal esophageal gland could provide us with clues how this process is initiated. However, the majority of the candidate parasitism genes in the dorsal esophageal gland cell fit into the category of pioneers. This leaves us at the brink of a new challenging period in which we will have to devise novel functional assays for parasitism genes.

Functional Assays and Future Prospects

The key test to establish whether candidate parasitism genes are of any importance to the plant-nematode interaction is to eliminate their effect by gene-inactivation. In *C. elegans* gene-inactivation is routinely done by genetic transformation via microinjection of DNA into the gonads of hermaphrodites (22). *C. elegans* is such a good genetic model for its short generation time (~3 days), its ability to reproduce on petri-dishes seeded with bacteria, and the presence of self-fertilizing hermaphrodites. In contrast, sedentary plant-parasitic nematodes have a generation time of at least several weeks, engage in a biotrophic interaction with host plants, and have complex modes of reproduction. As compared to *C. elegans* the thick and non-transparent cuticle of adult female plant-parasites makes it difficult to inject the gonads. Moreover, there is no selective marker available for easy identification of transformed plant-parasites. In short, currently no routine transformation system with significant efficiency is available for plant-parasitic nematodes.

Introduction of double-stranded RNA (dsRNA) is able to specifically disrupt the activity of genes containing homologous sequences in *C. elegans* (4, 9, 24). dsRNA can be delivered in several ways to achieve this gene silencing effect: (a) it can be micro-injected into the body cavity of the nematode; (b) bacteria transformed with a dsRNA-encoding construct can be fed to the nematode; (c) the nematode can be soaked in solutions containing dsRNA. Because of the difficulties in microinjecting plant-parasitic nematodes *in situ*, the first method is obviously not suitable. The second option is also not feasible because obligate plant-parasitic nematodes do not feed on bacteria. To overcome these difficulties, host plants could be transformed with constructs encoding short complementary RNA molecules that produce dsRNA with a hairpin (7). When nematodes are feeding on the transgenic plants, they may automatically take up dsRNA. It was shown that the 21-23 nucleotide fragments of dsRNA are guiding targeted mRNA degradation (85). Such small dsRNA molecules should easily pass the narrow stylet opening of the nematode. A major advantage of the use of transgenic plants is that as long as the nematode feeds from the plant it will be exposed to fresh dsRNA molecules, which could ensure a more significant effect. However, the time that it takes to produce and select transgenic plants harbouring the dsRNA constructs makes this procedure less suitable for large-scale studies. It is also worthwhile testing whether soaking the plant-parasitic nematodes in dsRNA solution will have the same effect as for *C. elegans*.

The second crucial step to the understanding of the function of parasitism genes in the nematode-plant interaction is to study their effect on the structure and physiology of plant cells. For example, the heterologous expression of a cellulose binding protein from *G. rostochiensis* using a Cauliflower Mosaic Virus 35S promoter in tobacco produced a stunted phenotype (L. Qin & A. Goverse, unpublished results). Time considerations have prompted some laboratories to use plant viruses (*e.g.* Potato Virus X) for heterologous expression in host plants. In some cases, the Potato Virus X-infected plants displayed unusual phenotypes (L. Qin & A. Goverse, unpublished results). However, these observations were complicated by the fact that expression of non-parasitism related genes often inflicted similar symptoms. Experiments like these are a fairly crude way to examine a potential role of parasitism genes. A more subtle and localized expression confined to certain cell types (*e.g.* procambial cells) may produce more informative phenotypes. Alternatively, the effect of parasitism genes can be investigated using transient expression in plant protoplast transfections (45) or cell suspension assays (10).

To assign a function in parasitism to pioneering sequences will constitute the biggest challenge for the coming 10 years. Future developments in bio-informatics may provide more clues for the function of some of the pioneers. Resolving the biological functions of the other putative parasitism genes will rely on the design of 'smart' functional assays. Rate limiting to the development of these functional assays is the availability of molecular markers that are indicative for fundamental processes such as cell cycle regulation and cell division, accumulation of plant hormones, and rearrangements of the cytoskeleton. Significant progress has recently been made in identifying markers for cell cycle regulation (15) and hormone accumulation (30, 38), which may prove to be excellent tools for functional assays in the near future.

References

1. Adams, M D , Kelley, J M , Gocayne, J D , Dubnick, M , Polymeropoulos, M H , Xiao, H , Merril, C R , Wu, A , Olde, B , Moreno, R F , et al (1991) Complementary DNA sequencing: expressed sequence tags human genome project Science 252:1651-1656
2. Atkinson, H J , Harris, P D , Halk, E J , Novitski, C E , Leighton-Sands, J , Nolan, P , Fox, P C , Sands, J L (1988) Monoclonal antibodies to the soybean cyst nematode, *Heterodera glycines* Ann Appl Biol 112:459-469
3. Bachem, C W B , Van der Hoeven, R S , De Bruijn, S M , Vreugdenhil, D , Zabeau, M , Visser, R G (1996) Visualization of differential gene expression using a novel method of RNA

fingerprinting based on AFLP: Analysis of gene expression during potato tuber development Plant J 9:745-753
4. Barstead, R (2001) Genome-wide RNAi Curr Opin Chem Biol 5:63-66
5. Blair, L , Perry, R N , Oparka, K , Jones, J T (1999) Activation of transcription during the hatching process of the potato cyst nematode *Globodera rostochiensis* Nematology 1:103-111
6. Bockenhoff, A , Prior, D A M , Grundler, F M W , Oparka, K J (1996) Induction of phloem unloading in *Arabidopsis thaliana* roots by the parasitic nematode *Heterodera schachtii* Plant J 112:1421-1427
7. Bosher, J M , Labouesse, M (2000) RNA interference: genetic wand and genetic watchdog Nature Cell Biol 2:E31-E36
8. *Caenorhabditis-elegans*-Sequencing-Consortium (1998) Genome sequence of the nematode *C elegans*: A platform for investigating biology Science 282:2012-2018
9. Carthew, R W (2001) Gene silencing by double-stranded RNA Curr Opin Cell Biol 13:244-248
10. Crespi, M , Galvez, S (2000) Molecular mechanisms in root nodule development J Plant Growth Regul 19:155-166
11. Dautova, M , Rosso, M N , Abad, P , Gommers, F J , Bakker, J , Smant, G (2001) Single pass cDNA sequencing - a powerful tool to analyse gene expression in pre-parasitic juveniles of the southern root-knot nematode *Meloidogyne incognita* Nematology 3:129-139
12. Dautova, M , Overmars, H A , Schots, A , Gommers, F J , Bakker, J , Smant, G (2001) A novel cell degrading enzyme in the plant-parasitic nematode *Meloidogyne incognita* Phytopathology 91:S21 (Abstr)
13. Davis, E L , Allen, R , Hussey, R S (1994) Developmental expression of esophageal gl antigens their detection in stylet secretions of *Meloidogyne incognita* Fund. Appl. Nematol. 17:255-262
14. Davis, E L , Hussey, R S , Baum, T J , Bakker, J , Schots, A (2000) Nematode parasitism genes Ann Rev Phytopathol 38:365-396
15. de Almeida Engler, J D , De Vleesschauwer, V , Burssens, S , Celenza, J L , Inze, D , Van Montagu, M , Engler, G , Gheysen, G (1999) Molecular markers and cell cycle inhibitors show the importance of cell cycle progression in nematode-induced galls syncytia Plant Cell 11:793-807
16. De Boer, J M (1996) Towards identification of oesophageal gl proteins in *Globodera rostochiensis* PhD thesis, Wageningen Agricultural University, Wageningen 144 pp

17. De Boer, J M , Overmars, H A , Bakker, J , Gommers, F J (1992) Analysis of two-dimensional protein patterns from developmental stages of the potato cyst nematode, *Globodera rostochiensis* Parasitology 105:461-474
18. De Boer, J M , Wang, X , Allen, R , Hussey, R S , Davis, E L , Baum, T J (2001) Microarray screening of a cDNA library from the esophageal gl s of the soybean cyst nematode Proceedings of 10th International Congress on Molecular Plant-Microbe Interactions, Madison, Winsconsin:P461 (Abstr)
19. Ding, X , Shields, J , Allen, R , Hussey, R S (1998) A secretory cellulose-binding protein cDNA cloned from the root-knot nematode (*Meloidogyne incognita*) Mol Plant-Microbe Interact 11:952-959
20. Ding, X , Shields, J , Allen, R , Hussey, R S (2000) Molecular cloning characterisation of a venom allergen AG5-like cDNA from *Meloidogyne incognita* Int J Parasitol 30:77-81
21. Endo, B Y (1984) Ultrastructure of the esophagus of larvae of the soybean cyst nematode, *Heterodera glycines* Proc Heminth Soc Wash 51:1-24
22. Epstein, H F , Shakes, D C (1995) *Caenorhabiditis elegans*: Modern Biological Analysis of an Organism Academic Press, San Diego 658 pp
23. Fang, K S , Vitale, M , Fehlner, P , King, T P (1988) cDNA cloning primary structure of a white-face hornet venom allergen, antigen 5 Proc Natl Acad Sci U S A 85:895-899
24. Fire, A , Xu, S Q , Montgomery, M K , Kostas, S A , Driver, S E, Mello, C C (1998) Potent specific genetic interference by double-str ed RNA in *Caenorhabditis elegans* Nature 391:806-811
25. Gao, B L , Allen, R , Maier, T , Davis, E L , Baum, T J , Hussey, R S (2001) Identification of putative parasitism genes expressed in the esophageal gl cells of the soybean cyst nematode *Heterodera glycines* Mol Plant-Microbe Interact 14:1247-1254
26. Gao, B L , Allen, R, Maier, T , Davis, E L Baum, T J , Hussey, R S (2001) Molecular characterisation expression of two venom allergen-like protein genes in *Heterodera glycines* Int J Parasitol 31:1617-1625
27. Goellner, M , Smant, G , De Boer, J M , Baum, T J , Davis, E L (2000) Isolation of beta-1,4-endoglucanase genes from *Globodera tabacum* their expression during parasitism J Nematol 32:154-165
28. Goverse, A , Davis, E L , Hussey, R S (1994) Monoclonal antibodies to the esophageal glands and stylet secretions of *Heterodera glycines* J Nematol 26:251-259

29. Goverse, A , Engler, J D , Verhees, J , van der Krol, S , Helder, J , Gheysen, G (2000) Cell cycle activation by plant parasitic nematodes Plant Mol Biol 43:747-761
30. Goverse, A , Overmars, H , Engelbertink, J , Schots, A , Bakker, J , Helder, J (2000) Both inductionand morphogenesis of cyst nematode feeding cells are mediated by auxin Mol Plant-Microbe Interact 13:1121-1129
31. Goverse, A , van der Voort, J R , van der Voort, C R , Kavelaars, A , Smant, G , Schots, A , Bakker, J , Helder, J (1999) Naturally induced secretions of the potato cyst nematode co-stimulate the proliferation of both tobacco leaf protoplasts and human peripheral blood mononuclear cells Mol Plant-Microbe Interact 12:872-881
32. Guida, P , Bleve-Zacheo, T , Zacheo, G (1991) Galls induced by nematodes on tomato roots *in vitro and in vivo* Giorn Bot Ital 125:968-969
33. Hawdon, J M , Narasimhan, S , Hotez, P J (1999) *Ancylostoma* secreted protein 2: cloning and characterization of a second member of a family of nematode secreted proteins from *Ancylostoma caninum* Mol Biochem Parasitol 99:149-165
34. Hussey, R S (1989) Monoclonal antibodies to secretory granules in esophageal gl s of *Meloidogyne* species J Nematol 21:392-398
35. Hussey, R S (1989) Disease-inducing secretions of plant-parasitic nematodes Ann Rev Phytopathol 27:123-141
36. Hussey, R S , Mims, C W (1990) Ultrastructure of esophageal glands and their secretory granules in the root-knot nematode *Meloidogyne incognita* Protoplasma 156:9-18
37. Hussey, R S , Grundler, F M W (1998) Nematode parasitism of plants pp 213-243 in: Physiology and Biochemistry of Free Living Plant Parasitic Nematodes R N Perry, D J Wright, eds CAB International, Oxon, UK
38. Hutangura, P , Mathesius, U , Jones, M G K , Rolfe, B G (1999) Auxin induction is a trigger for root gall formation caused by root-knot nematodes in white clover is associated with the activation of the flavonoid pathway Austr J Plant Physiol 26:221-231
39. Jaubert, S , Laffaire, J -B , Abad, P , Rosso, M N (2001) Cloning of two pectinolytic enzymes transcribed in the esophageal gl s of the root-knot nematode *Meloidogyne incognita* Proceedings of 10th International Congress on Molecular Plant-Microbe Interactions, Madison, Winsconsin:P469 (Abstr)
40. Jones, J T , Perry, R N , Johnston, M R L (1993) Changes in the ultrastructure of the cuticle of the potato cyst nematode, *Globodera rostochiensis*, during development and infection Fundam Appl Nematol 16:433-445

41. Jones, J T , Smant, G , Blok, V C (2000) SXP/RAL-2 proteins of the potato cyst nematode *Globodera rostochiensis*: secreted proteins of the hypodermis and amphids Nematology 2:887-893
42. Jones, M G K (1981) Host cell responses to endoparasitic nematode attack: structure and function of giant cells and syncytia Ann Appl Biol 97:353-372
43. Karrer, E E , Lincoln, J E , Hogenhout, S , Bennett, A B , Bostock, R M , Martineau, B , Lucas, W J , Gilchrist, D G , Alexander, D (1995) *In situ* isolation of mRNA from individual plant cells: Creation of cell-specific cDNA libraries Proc Natl Acad Sci U S A 92:3814-3818
44. Klein, R D , Gu, Q , Goddard, A , Rosenthal, A (1996) Selection for genes encoding secreted proteins and receptors Proc Natl Acad Sci U S A 93:7108-7113
45. Kovtun, Y , Chiu, W L , Tena, G , Sheen, J (2000) Functional analysis of oxidative stress-activated mitogen-activated protein kinase cascade in plants Proc Natl Acad Sci U S A 97:2940-2945
46. Lambert, K N , Allen, K D , Sussex, I M (1999) Cloning and characterization of an esophageal-gl -specific chorismate mutase from the phytoparasitic nematode *Meloidogyne javanica* Mol Plant-Microbe Interact 12:328-336
47. Latteman, C T , Apfel, H (1997) Pcr based amplification of total cdna with high fidelity and high yield from minute amounts of parasite RNA Int J Parasitol 27:955-958
48. Liang, P , Pardee, A B (1992) Differential display of eukaryotic messenger RNA by means of the polymerase chain reaction Science 257:967-971
49. Mann, M , Hendrickson, R C , Pandey, A (2001) Analysis of proteins and proteomes by mass spectrometry Ann Rev Biochem 70:437-473
50. Maroney, P A , Denker, J A , Darzynkiewicz, E , Laneve, R , Nilsen, T W (1995) Most mRNAs in the nematode *Ascaris lumbricoides* are trans-spliced: A role for spliced leader addition in translational efficiency RNA 1:714-723
51. Masamune, T , Anetai, M , Takasugi, M , Katsui, N (1982) Isolation of a natural hatching stimulus, glycinoeclepin A, for the soybean cyst nematode Nature 297:495-496
52. McCarter, J , Abad, P , Jones, J T , Bird, D (2000) Rapid gene discovery in plant parasitic nematodes via Expressed Sequence Tags Nematology 2:719-731
53. McClure, M A , Von-Mende, N (1987) Induced salivation in plant-parasitic nematodes Phytopathology 77:1463-1469
54. Miao, Y J , Subramaniam, N , Carlson, D M (1995) cDNA cloning and characterization of rat salivary glycoproteins Novel

members of the proline-rich-protein multigene families Eur J Biochem 228:343-350
55. Mugniery, D , Fayet, G (1984) Sex determination in *Globodera rostochiensis* Woll and influence of infestation levels on the penetration, developpment and sex of the nematode Rev Nematol 7:223-238
56. Nakamura, M , Masuda, H , Horii, J , Kuma, K , Yokoyama, N , Ohba, T , Nishitani, H , Miyata, T , Tanaka, M , Nishimoto, T (1998) When overexpressed, a novel centrosomal protein, RanBPM, causes ectopic microtubule nucleation similar to gamma-tubulin J Cell Biol 143:1041-1052
57. Nilsen, T W (1997) *Trans*-splicing Page 310-334 in: Frontiers in Molecular Biology: Eukaryotic mRNA Processing A R Krainer ed IRL Press, Oxford
58. Nilsen, T W (2001) Evolutionary origin of SL-addition trans-splicing: still an enigma Trends Genet 17:678-680
59. Nishitani, H , Hirose, E , Uchimura, Y , Nakamura, M , Umeda, M, Nishii, K , Mori, N , Nishimoto, T (2001) Full-sized RanBPM cDNA encodes a protein possessing a long stretch of proline and glutamine within the N-terminal region, comprising a large protein complex Gene 272:25-33
60. Perry, R N (1989) Dormancy and hatching of nematode eggs Parasitol Today 5:377-383
61. Perry, R N , Zunke, U , Wyss, U (1989) Observations on the response of the dorsal and subventral oesophageal gl s of *Globodera rostochiensis* to hatching stimulation Rev Nematol 12:91-96
62. Popeijus, H , Overmars, H , Jones, J , Blok, V , Goverse, A , Helder, J , Schots, A , Bakker, J , Smant, G (2000) Enzymology - Degradation of plant cell walls by a nematode Nature 406:36-37
63. Popeijus, M , Blok, V C , Cardle, L , Bakker, E , Phillips, M S , Helder, J , Smant, G , Jones, J T (2000) Analysis of genes expressed in second stage juveniles of the potato cyst nematodes *Globodera rostochiensis* and *G pallida* using the expressed sequence tag approach Nematology 2:567-574
64. Prior, A , Jones, J T , Blok, V C , Beauchamp, J , McDermott, L , Cooper, A , Kennedy, M W (2001) A surface-associated retinol- and fatty acid-binding protein (Gp-FAR-1) from the potato cyst nematode *Globodera pallida*: lipid binding activities, structural analysis and expression pattern Biochemical J 356:387-394
65. Qin, L , Prins, P , Jones, J T , Popeijus, H , Smant, G , Bakker, J , Helder, J (2001) GenEST, a powerful bidirectional link between cDNA sequence data and gene expression profiles generated by cDNA-AFLP Nucl Acids Res 29:1616-1622

66. Qin, L , Overmars, H , Helder, J , Popeijus, H , van der Voort, J R Groenink, W , van Koert, P , Schots, A , Bakker, J , Smant, G (2000) An efficient cDNA-AFLP-based strategy for the identification of putative pathogenicity factors from the potato cyst nematode *Globodera rostochiensis* Mol Plant-Microbe Interact 13:830-836

67. Rao, K V N , Eswaran, M , Ravi, V , Gnanasekhar, B , Narayanan, R B , Kaliraj, P , Jayaraman, K , Marson, A , Raghavan, N , Scott, A L (2000) The *Wuchereria bancrofti* orthologue of *Brugia malayi* SXP1 and the diagnosis of bancroftian filariasis Mol Biochem Parasitol 107:71-80

68. Robertson, L , Robertson, W M , Jones, J T (1999) Direct analysis of the secretions of the potato cyst nematode *Globodera rostochiensis* Parasitology 119:167-176

69. Robertson, L , Robertson, W M , Sobczak, M , Helder, J , Tetaud, E , Ariyanayagam, M R , Ferguson, M A J , Fairlamb, A , Jones, J T (2000) Cloning, expression and functional characterisation of a peroxiredoxin from the potato cyst nematode *Globodera rostochiensis* Mol Biochem Parasitol 111:41-49

70. Rogers, C M , Franks, C J , Walker, R J , Burke, J F , Holden Dye, L (2001) Regulation of the pharynx of *Caenorhabditis elegans* by 5-HT, octopamine, and FMRFamide-like neuropeptides J Neurobiol 49:235-244

71. Rosso, M N , Favery, B , Piotte, C , Arthaud, L , De, B J M , Hussey, R S , Bakker, J , Baum, T J , Abad, P (1999) Isolation of a cDNA encoding a beta-1,4-endoglucanase in the root-knot nematode *Meloidogyne incognita* and expression analysis during plant parasitism Mol Plant-Microbe Interact 12:585-591

72. Semblat, J P , Rosso, M N , Hussey, R S , Abad, P , Castagnone, S P (2001) Molecular cloning of a cDNA encoding an amphid-secreted putative avirulence protein from the root-knot nematode *Meloidogyne incognita* Mol Plant-Microbe Interact 14:72-79

73. Sijmons, P C , Atkinson, H J , Wyss, U (1994) Parasitic strategies of root nematodes and associated host cell responses Ann Rev Phytopathol 32:235-259

74. Smant, G , Goverse, A , Stokkermans, J P W G , De Boer, J M , Pomp, H , Zilverentant, J F , Overmars, H A , Helder, J , Schots, A , Bakker, J (1997) Potato root diffusate induced secretion of soluble, basic proteins originating from the subventral esophageal glandsf potato cyst nematodes Phytopathology 87:839-845

75. Smant, G , Stokkermans, J P W G , Yan, Y , De Boer, J M , Baum, T J , Wang, X , Hussey, R S , Gommers, F J , Henrissat, B, Davis, E L , Helder, J , Schots, A , Bakker, J (1998) Endogenous cellulases in animals: Isolation of b-1,4-

endoglucanase genes from two species of plant-parasitic cyst nematodes Proc Natl Acad Sci U S A 95:4906-4911

76. Speicher, D W (1989) Microsequencing with PVDF membranes: Efficient electroblotting direct protein adsoprtion and sequencer program modifications Pages 24-35 in: Techniques in Protein Chemistry T E Hugli, ed Academic Press, San Diego, CA

77. Triantaphyllou, A C (1985) Cytogenetics, cytotaxonomy phylogeny of root-knot nematodes Pages 113-133 in: An advance treatise on *Meloidogyne* J N Sasser, C C Carter, eds North Carolina State University Graphics, Raleigh, NC

78. Trim, J E , Holden Dye, L , Willson, J , Lockyer, M , Walker, R J (2001) Characterization of 5-HT receptors in the parasitic nematode, *Ascaris suum* Parasitology 122:207-217

79. Uehara, T , Kushida, A , Momota, Y (2001) PCR-based cloning of two beta-1,4-endoglucanases from the root-lesion nematode *Pratylenchus penetrans* Nematology 3:335 341

80. Waetzig, G H , Sobczak, M , Grundler, F M W (1999) Localization of hydrogen peroxide during the defence response of *Arabidopsis thaliana* against the plant-parasitic nematode *Heterodera glycines* Nematology 1:681-686

81. Wang, X , Meyers, D , Yan, Y , Baum, T J , Smant, G , Hussey, R S , Davis, E L (1999) In planta localization of a beta-1,4-endoglucanase secreted by *Heterodera glycines* Mol Plant-Microbe Interact 12:64-67

82. Wang, X , Allen, R , Ding, X , Goellner, M , Maier, T , de, B J M , Baum, T J , Hussey, R S , Davis, E L (2001) Signal peptide-selection of cDNA cloned directly from the esophageal gl cells of the soybean cyst nematode *Heterodera glycines* Mol Plant-Microbe Interact 14:536-544

83. Williamson, V M , Hussey, R S (1996) Nematode pathogenesis and resistance in plants Plant Cell 8:1735-1745

84. Wyss, U , Grundler, F M W (1992) Feeding behaviour of sedentary plant parasitic nematodes Neth J Plant Pathol 98, Suppl 2:165-173

85. Zamore, P D , Tueschl, T , Sharp, P A , Bartel, D P (2000) RNAi: double-str ed RNA directs the ATP-dependent cleavage of mRNA at 21 to 23 nucleotide intervals Cell 101:25-33

Diseases of Unknown Etiology[3]

L. W. Timmer and Alka Bhatia

Plant diseases have been described that are caused by viroids, viruses, phytoplasmas, spiroplasmas, protozoa, bacteria, algae, fungi, nematodes, and higher plants (1). No plant disease has been described that is caused by a prion. With that exception, all of the organisms known to cause disease in mammals and other organisms also cause disease in plants. Are there agents which cause plant diseases which are currently unknown? Probably, but it is not immediately obvious what those might be. Are there many diseases whose cause is presently unknown? Yes, there are many unknown diseases of widely grown crop plants and certainly many more of minor crops and non-cultivated plants.

Nevertheless, Agrios (1) in his plant pathology text devotes only a single paragraph to the subject. The diseases mentioned are waldsterben (forest decline), spear rot of oil palm, mango malformation, and citrus blight. A review of the lists of diseases of crop plants maintained on the American Phytopathological Society (APS) website reveals numerous diseases of which the cause has not been clearly identified (http://www.scisoc.org/online/common). Many of these diseases are listed as caused by graft-transmissible pathogens (GTPs) The majority of these diseases are of minor importance and have not been extensively studied. Another group of diseases is apparently the result of a complex of weak pathogens and stress from climate, pollution, or edaphic factors. Molecular techniques often allow rapid identification of a causal agent if it is related to some known organism. Nevertheless, there are a few diseases that have been extensively studied whose cause remains unknown (28).

We will first review the history of etiological studies and the discovery of various organisms as the cause of disease in plants. Then, those diseases of unknown etiology that appear to have a single causal agent will be covered. Most of these are graft-transmissible diseases of woody plants. Many have not been extensively studied but are probably caused by viruses, phytoplasmas, or systemic bacteria. Most could be elucidated by more intense investigation. We will then cover some examples of diseases of complex etiology. These diseases are often the result of a combination of micro-organisms, weather and edaphic factors,

---

[3]This research was supported by the Florida Agricultural Experiment Station, and approved for publication as Journal Series No. N-02160.

and man's activity. Proof of a causal role for each factor and the precise causes of some of these diseases may never be completely understood. Lastly, we will cover citrus blight, a disease which has been extensively investigated, but whose cause remains unknown. Finally, we will address the possibility that new diseases can arise and cause serious economic consequences. Our background is in citrus, and we draw most of our examples from that crop. However, a similar array of diseases of unknown etiology exist on many crops, especially woody perennials.

The History of Etiology of Plant Diseases

It is often quite straightforward to visually distinguish a healthy plant from a diseased plant based on symptoms or vigor of the plant. The question that would then arise would be what is causing a plant to be in an unhealthy condition? It is from this idea that the science of plant pathology developed–the need to prevent diseases in plants. For this feat to be accomplished, it was necessary to identify and control the causal factor and it was during such processes that the various groups of plant pathogens were discovered.

Besides parasitic plants, algae, and fungi, all the other groups of plant pathogens are invisible. A few fungi are easily seen without the aid of magnification. Therefore, it is logical that after parasitic plants, fungi were the first group to be 'discovered' as causing plant disease.

We can trace the discovery of plant pathogens over time which was a function of the seriousness of the disease outbreak and its inevitable effect on man (60). Many texts agree that occurrences of plant diseases were recorded as early as ca. 750 B.C., in the Old Testament. At that time, they were considered to be brought upon by God, and no one ventured to think otherwise. There are many records which show that the pathogens (fungi) observed on the diseased plants were thought to have developed from the plant and so they were seen as either arising from the plant itself or from the surrounding environment. This era exemplified the observe–deduce–speculate mode of thought.

It was not until the 17th century that certain fungi were actually shown to be the cause of the disease rather than the outcome. About this time, scientists and philosophers broadened their intellectual boundaries and dared to think differently from the dogma of society. The discovery of many plant pathogens was facilitated by the development and improvement of the compound microscope. The first fungal spores were observed under the microscope. Through keen observation and experimentation, it was found that the spores were often airborne and could grow on healthy plants or plant parts. The well-known bunt of wheat, caused by the fungus *Tilletia caries*, was shown by Tillet in 1755 to be spread to healthy plants just by dusting the plants with the dark powdery spores obtained from diseased plants. Despite this initial 'experiment', the idea that it was the spores themselves that were causing the disease did not take form until Prevost, in 1807, conducted a series of field experiments and concluded that it was the *Tilletia* spores that actually caused the disease. Then occurred the famous outbreak of late blight of potato in the mid-1800s. Many, including Berkeley (2), suspected a fungus to be the culprit, and this was later proved and confirmed in the early 1860s by Speerschneider and de Bary. These findings opened the door to the discovery of numerous other plant pathogenic fungi.

What about the diseased plants on which no organism was visible? Only signs and symptoms were seen on the plant. It was naturally much more challenging to find the causal organism when there was no way to see it! Thus, other groups of pathogens took a longer time to be discovered and for causality to be established. The initial process involved observation and characterization of symptoms, studies of the spread of diseased plants in the field, and their association with prevailing weather conditions. The advent of the light microscope permitted the constant association of a particular organism with particular diseases and their relationship to control measures that ameliorated a particular set of symptoms. Novel plant pathogens were discovered when none of the known pathogens was found to be the cause of the disease. Therefore, one had to conclude that there was something else causing the disease–something new or undiscovered.

BACTERIA

The compound microscope enabled the discovery of unique structures inside plant cells. These microscopic bodies were later classified as a new group of organisms called bacteria. Bacteria were first found to cause fire blight of pear and apple by Burrill in 1878 (1), and many other diseases such as crown gall. Even until 30 years ago, Pierce's disease of grapevines was thought to be caused by a virus because the disease could be transmitted by grafting and was known to be spread by leafhoppers–typical characteristics of viral diseases (46,47). Only in 1973, when by electron microscopy, a bacterium was found to be constantly associated with diseased plants and antibiotics were shown to control the disease, did it become apparent that it was a bacterium, a *Xyllella*, causing the disease and not a virus (23,42,51).

NEMATODES

Nematodes were discovered through constant association with diseased plants and morphological studies using the light microscope. It was often difficult to relate diseased/unhealthy plants with presence of nematodes. They were first reported to be present in wheat galls but were not suspected as the cause. From 1855 to 1859, the root knot nematode, bulb and stem nematode, and the sugarbeet cyst nematode were isolated from infected plant parts, and shown to reproduce the symptoms (55).

VIRUSES AND VIROIDS

Although viruses were not discovered till much later than fungi and bacteria (end of the 19th century), viral diseases were noted as far back as the early 18th century. Tobacco mosaic virus (TMV) was the first virus to be discovered in 1898 by Beijerinck, who termed it a "contagious living fluid." No organism could be associated with or seen in the diseased tissue, but the disease was transmitted from plant to plant by insects. So the possibility of it being a fungus, nematode, or bacterium was almost excluded. In an effort to isolate the causal organism, Beijerinck filtered the juice from infected plants through a filter designed to trap bacteria. The filtrate was still able to cause tobacco mosaic disease on healthy plants. Further experiments showed the causal organism to multiply within the plant and to pass through a layer of agar. It was at this point that a novel organism was suspected even though it could not be seen even with the compound microscope (1). Only when the electron microscope was developed was it found that this infectious particle was actually self-replicating in nature and was enclosed in a proteinaceous coat. With new techniques such as density gradient sedimentation, molecular techniques, and x-ray crystallography, many new viruses were discovered (1).

Viroids were discovered because they did not behave like typical nucleoproteins in density gradient centrifugation. They are extremely heat stable which was also not characteristic of viruses. When these infectious agents were purified, they were found to lack protein and found to consist of RNA. The infectious agents of diseases like potato spindle tuber and exocortis were found to be self-replicating nucleic acids which had properties and means of transmission distinct from most viruses (29,30).

PROTOZOA

A plant pathogenic protozoan was first observed in 1878 in cabbage affected by club-root, but at that time, *Plasmodiophora brassicae*, the organism causing the disease was classified as a fungus. In the early 20th century, flagellate protozoa referred to as *Phytomonas* were found to occur in the latex cells of *Euphorbia* plants, and it was thought that they fed on the sap but were not suspected to be the disease-causing agents (32). Stahel in 1931 correlated presence of protozoa in phloem cells of coffee trees with abnormal phloem formation and wilting of coffee bushes, but it was not until about 30 years later that the protozoan was actually proved to be the disease-causing agent (89). Since then, many other flagellate protozoa have been implicated in diseases such as coconut hartrot (71).

ALGAE

Algae have not traditionally been considered plant pathogens. A few grew on plant surfaces and could be detrimental but they were not parasitic. However, with closer study of cell wall chemistry and the molecular relationships between organisms, it was found that many of the organisms previously considered to be fungi were really achlorophyllous algae (16). Thus, many of the early studies which provided conclusive proof that fungi were the cause of plant diseases were conducted with algae. Phytophthora late blight of potato, Pythium root rots, and downy mildews are now known to be caused by organisms related to algae.

MOLLICUTES

This group of organisms was the last to be discovered because the symptoms they cause closely resemble those of virus infection. Their trademark symptoms include general reddening or yellowing of the plant and/or formation of witches' brooms. Electron microscopy and molecular techniques played a vital role in their discovery. Doi et al. (31) first described a mycoplasma-like organism in the phloem of infected mulberry plants and found it to be constantly present in diseased plants and absent in healthy plants. The disease could also be controlled using antibiotics; thus, a mycoplasma-like organism was suspected (57). They were pleomorphic and had no cell wall. For many years, these organisms were referred to as mycoplasma-like organisms due to their similarity to animal parasitic or saprophytic mollicutes. They are now referred to as phytoplasmas. These organisms have still not been cultured. However, a related group, the spiroplasmas, have been cultured. Numerous diseases of a wide range of plants are now known to be caused by mollicutes.

Etiology of Graft-Transmissible Pathogens of Citrus

The history of etiological studies of the systemic, graft-transmissible diseases of citrus is informative and, in great part, similar to that of other major perennial crops such as apples, grapes, and peaches. Studies of some citrus diseases have played a major role in the discovery of new groups of pathogens such as viroids and spiroplasmas. A common thread that runs through most of the discoveries of these pathogens is the development of means to transmit the diseases efficiently and of methods to detect the pathogen by bioassays, microscopy, serology, and molecular techniques (65).

By about 1960, most of the major systemic diseases of citrus had been well-described and most had been graft-transmitted (65). The major worldwide diseases at that time were tristeza, psorosis, exocortis, and cachexia. Stubborn disease was a problem in many arid citrus areas and greening disease (now huanglongbing) was a major problem in Asia and Africa.

Discovery of the causal agents of these diseases often required extended periods of research because symptoms are slow to appear in perennial plants and rapid assays had to be developed. Tristeza is aphid-transmitted and was eventually demonstrated to be caused by a closterovirus. Initial evidence came from the detection of the long, flexuous rods of the virus by electron microscopy (61). However, it was not until the transmissibility of the virus by mechanical means was achieved that the infectivity of the purified particles could be unequivocally demonstrated (39,43). Psorosis appeared to be a virus disease but the nature of the causal agent baffled investigators for many years. Eventually, the agent was mechanically transmitted and *Chenopodium quinoa* was found to be a local lesion host (41). Even then characterization proved difficult because the virus has two particles, both of which are needed for infectivity (26). The causal agent was finally found to represent a new group of viruses originally described as spiroviruses and now designated as ophioviruses (24).

Work with exocortis and cachexia was difficult because symptoms only appeared in many hosts after several years (33,34). Research proceeded more rapidly after mechanical transmissibility was demonstrated (40) and sensitive hosts such as citron, gynura, and other herbaceous plants were found (33,34). The pathogens involved were insensitive to heat (76) and subsequently, these diseases were shown to be caused by viroids. Exocortis was one of the first diseases proved to be caused by this agent. Even then, it took several more years to prove that cachexia was also caused by a viroid.

Stubborn disease is graft-transmissible but symptoms develop only slowly (10). No exceptionally sensitive host has been found. However, electron microscopic studies revealed "mycoplasma-like" bodies in phloem tissues (56). Subsequently, this agent was cultured (35) and described as *Spiroplasma citri*. Along with corn stunt, it was one of the first diseases found to be caused by a spiroplasma and was the first spiroplasma to be cultured (64).

Studies of greening disease (huanglongbing) were also complicated by slow assay procedures, even after psyllids were well established as vectors (36). Again, electron microscopic studies revealed the presence of a bacteria-like organism in phloem tissues. This bacterium has never been cultured so Koch's postulates have not been completed, but there is a constant association between the bacterium and disease symptoms. Modern molecular techniques have allowed characterization of the organism. The bacteria from Asian and African greening have been designated *Candidatus* Liberibacter asiaticus and *Candidatus* L. africanus, respectively (48).

Several important diseases have been discovered since the 1960s whose causal agents had to be determined. Citrus variegated chlorosis was described in Brazil in the early 1990s and has caused extensive losses in that country (18). Again, electron microscopy played a key role in identification of the pathogen as a xylem-limited bacterium. Because of the extensive work conducted in the 1970s and 80s on diseases like Pierce's disease of grape, plum leaf scald, and phony peach, it was a comparatively simple matter to identify the cause of CVC as *Xylella fastidiosa* (7).

Witches' broom of lime appeared in the 1970s in Oman but was not extensively studied until much later (11). Electron microscopy of diseased tissues revealed the presence of phytoplasma-like bodies in plant tissues. Again, the organism has not been cultured and Koch's postulates have not been completed, but there is a good association of the pathogen with the disease. Modern molecular techniques have allowed characterization of the organism and it has been designated as *Candidatus* Phytoplasma aurantifolia. It is the first citrus disease found to be caused by a phytoplasma (95).

Another new disease called citrus chlorotic dwarf was discovered in Turkey in the mid-1980s (62). It was found to be readily transmissible by grafting and by the bayberry whitefly and assumed to be a virus. A phloem-limited isometric virus particle is associated with the disease, but Koch's postulates have not been fulfilled and the virus at present has not been characterized or assigned to a virus group.

Thus, it would appear that the etiology of most of the important systemic citrus diseases is well-established and that the causes of significant new diseases are determined within a few years. However, there are still numerous graft-transmissible diseases for which the causal agents are not known. Admittedly, most of these diseases of unknown etiology are of minor economic importance. However, in citrus there are diseases like concave gum, cristacortis, and impietratura which cause distortion of trunk wood as well as foliar and occasional fruit symptoms (67). When they were widespread, they caused significant damage and loss of productivity of the trees. These diseases are graft-transmissible and readily detectable by foliar symptoms in inoculated seedlings. They do not appear to spread naturally in the field and have been largely eliminated in most citrus areas by budwood certification programs. They are probably caused by viruses. Given the lack of economic incentive, etiological studies of these diseases will probably not be actively pursued.

There are also a number of budunion creases (38) and other problems whose causes have not been identified. Some problems such as those caused by tristeza virus with sweet orange on sour orange rootstock and by tatterleaf virus with trees on trifoliate orange rootstock are well-characterized. Others such as the budunion problems between Pera sweet orange and Swingle citrumelo rootstock appear to be genetic in nature.

However, many others such as those affecting rough lemon rootstock and the Nagami kumquat disease appear to be due to transmissible agents. Until such diseases have more economic impact, they are unlikely to be investigated thoroughly.

There are various other diseases such as rubbery wood, citrus yellow mosaic, and leathery leaf which have been reported (37). Most have been demonstrated to be graft-transmissible. However, no further studies have been conducted and most are very localized. The grand enigma in the etiology of citrus diseases is blight. This disease is covered in a later section.

With the discovery of viroids, phytoplasmas, spiroplasmas, and systemic bacteria, many of the etiological problems of perennial crops have now been resolved. Apple scar skin and peach latent mosaic are now known to be caused by viroids. Rubbery wood of apple and peach yellows are known to be caused by phytoplasmas. Advances in virology have allowed identification of the causal agents of many diseases. Most of the diseases of this nature, which remain to be identified, are relatively unimportant economically.

Diseases of Complex Etiology

There are many diseases of plants, especially of trees and shrubs, which appear to be caused by several factors, but whose exact cause has not been ascertained. Pathogens are often implicated in these diseases, but environmental or edaphic factors and pollutants of various types may also be involved. Plants which have been subjected to stresses of heat, drought, freezes, or that have been weakened by attacks of insects or pathogens are often more susceptible to damage by weak pathogens. In many cases, genetic sensitivities to these types of diseases are also observed. The etiology of these diseases is usually uncertain because many factors are involved and it is difficult to reproduce the disease syndrome completely. In some cases, a different combination of the factors may result in the same disease syndrome.

CITRUS DECLINES

A disease referred to as Murcott or tangerine collapse often results in dieback of trees or even death (45). It usually occurs after trees bear an exceptionally large crop, which can severely drain carbohydrate reserves and make them susceptible to secondary pathogens. It occurs only on varieties which are alternate bearers and is often associated with environmental stress such as drought or cold damage. Trees on rootstocks which promote vigorous growth and large crops are more susceptible than trees on other stocks.

A distinct branch die-back disease occurs on Robinson and Fallglo tangerines. In this case, small branches or even entire limbs die with some gummosis at the point of contact with healthy wood. Applications of the fungicide benomyl ameliorate disease severity implying that fungal pathogens may be involved. *Lasiodiplodia theobromae* is frequently isolated from affected tissues. Inoculation with this fungus usually produces some necrosis but does not reproduce the disease syndrome. The disease appears to be caused by a complex of environmental stress, secondary pathogens, and genetic susceptibility.

Similar types of diseases are observed in the underground portion of citrus trees (15). Sudden death or dry root rot can result in total tree collapse and death of citrus trees. This disease is associated with fine-textured, water-logged soils. In some cases, clay pans which restrict drainage are associated with the problem. Overfertilization and excess nitrogen may also be a factor in the disease. Trees on trifoliate orange rootstock or hybrids of trifoliate seem to be more susceptible to this type of decline. The fungus most commonly isolated from affected roots is *Fusarium solani*. Inoculation of healthy roots with these isolates produces no symptoms. However, if carbohydrate reserves are reduced, for example, by severe pruning, this fungus can cause root necrosis (44). The decline appears to be a combination of infection of roots by weak pathogens following damage by anaerobic conditions or other environmental stresses.

MANGO DECLINE

Another decline and dieback disease occurs on mango trees (72,77). The disease is characterized by tip necrosis followed by twig dieback. The vascular system becomes discolored and trees may eventually die. The disease often occurs on highly calcareous soils where nutritional deficiencies are a problem. Many fungi such as *Alternaria*, *Cladosporium*, *Colletotrichum*, *Dothiorella*, and *Lasiodiplodia* can be isolated from the necrotic twigs (72). Inoculation of twigs with this fungus produces some symptoms, but does not reproduce the tree decline. Mango decline is also more common in orchards heavily infested with plant parasitic nematodes. As often occurs with these types of diseases, some cultivars are more seriously affected than others (74).

DECLINES OF ORNAMENTAL FRUIT AND SHADE TREES

Decline diseases are common on a wide variety of ornamental fruit and shade trees in urban and suburban settings (78). Trees in these situations often show dieback, poor growth, and even may die from unknown causes. Ornamental trees may be subject to stresses which are infrequent in forests or agricultural settings. Root systems may be confined by streets, sidewalks, and buildings. Canopies may be heavily pruned to avoid interference with powerlines. Soils may not have their native structure and may be poorly drained, excessively mixed with subsoils or with building materials. Roots may be damaged or soils compacted by vehicles and other equipment. Trunks are wounded by mowers and yard tools. Levels of pollutants may be high along busy streets. If you add to all of these abuses, the common environmental factors which affect plants, it is not surprising that there are a variety of tree declines in urban and suburban areas.

Many diseases such as wilts caused by *Verticillium*, leaf scorches and declines caused by *Xylella*, and various virus diseases are declines with known causes. However, many secondary organisms and weak pathogens can cause declines of stressed trees (78). Wounds on trunks or large limbs allow entry of wood-rotting fungi. These rots weaken trees which then collapse during storms. In most cases, it is difficult or impossible to identify the cause(s) of the tree decline. In some cases, trees may recover if properly watered and fertilized. In others, the damage by weak pathogens may be to the point where it is no longer reversible.

WALDSTERBEN

Waldsterben or "forest death" is listed by Agrios (1) as one of the major diseases of unknown etiology. It was first recognized in the early 80s as a large scale decline of the forests of central Europe (79). It was characterized originally by slow growth of the trees with some root loss, leaf or needle drop resulting in thin tree canopies. Many growth abnormalities such as altered leaf morphology, production of adventitious shoots and roots, and excessive seed production were noted. The disease seemed to affect both conifer and broadleaf trees and even resulted in the death of understory plants. It seemed to occur on all soil types and was independent of forest management practices or climatic factors. The possible causes were listed as–aluminum toxicity due to soil acidification, deficiency of magnesium, ozone pollution, general stress, and excess nitrogen or other nutrients.

However, this type of forest decline has not progressed in many areas and some investigators have questioned whether it is even an identifiable disease syndrome (9,58,80). These types of situations have occurred even in the 1920s and 30s when many of the current factors were not present. There does not seem to be any evidence that the disease has spread. Certainly, there are cases of air pollution damage to forest trees, but these seem to be localized rather than general. Magnesium deficiency may result in generalized tree dieback in some areas. Well-known forest tree diseases or insect problems appear to be the cause of the decline in some areas. Thus, the consensus seems to be that Waldsterben represents a heterogeneous collection of individual problems which periodically result in widespread forest decline. There at least does not appear to be cause for alarm.

Citrus Blight

With most diseases of unknown etiology, plant pathologists can at least provide an educated guess as to the nature of the causal agent. However, citrus blight is one of the few economically important diseases where the cause is truly unknown. Intense study has eliminated many possibilities as causes of the disease, but has failed to pinpoint the responsible factor.

Citrus blight is one of the most important decline diseases of citrus in the world. It is responsible for the loss of about 650,000 trees annually in Florida and perhaps as many as 10 million trees in Brazil every year (28). This disease occurs widely in many other countries in Central and South America as well as in South Africa, Australia, and other areas. Blight is rare in arid, winter-rainfall areas such as the Mediterranean, California, and inland areas of Australia.

One of the key factors in establishing the cause of any disease is to define and characterize that malady. As long as a single disease name encompasses a number of maladies, there will be confusion about the origin and nature of the disease. That is especially true of decline diseases which often have few characteristic symptoms. That certainly was true of blight. In Florida, this disease has been variously referred to as young tree decline, rough lemon decline, roadside decline, and sandhill decline in addition to blight.

A disease referred to as blight has been studied in Florida for over 100 years (75). Many of the early reports and studies involved were declines of trees on sour orange and sweet orange rootstocks. Those stocks are now known to be the most tolerant of citrus blight. Some of the early studies may have been of declines caused by tristeza virus, Phytophthora root rot, nematodes, or edaphic factors. Serious tree losses to blight were noted in the 1960s and early 70s when large acreages of trees on the highly susceptible rough lemon rootstock were planted in the eastern and southeastern coastal areas of Florida (82,90).

Only in the 1970s and 80s were studies conducted that led to clear differentiation of blight from other decline diseases. Attempts to inject control chemicals into the trunks of affected trees led to the finding that water uptake in the trunk was blocked (22). That discovery led to the development of a syringe injection test which is used as a quick diagnostic technique in the field (66). As a result of subsequent anatomical studies, amorphous plugs were found in the xylem vessels of affected trees (14). This type of plug is unique to blight-affected trees and does not occur in trees affected by other decline diseases. Investigation of nutritional status as a factor in the disease led to the finding that zinc accumulated to high levels in the bark and wood of the trees affected by blight (81). The elevated zinc levels are also useful as a diagnostic tool (91).

Thus, by the mid-1980s, blight was reasonably well-characterized. Fundamentally, blight is a vascular wilt disease (12,14,87). Trees at first have off-color foliage which may wilt in the heat of the day. Such symptoms gradually become more general and trees often show zinc deficiency symptoms. Severely affected trees may produce trunk sprouts. If pruned severely, blight-affected trees will produce vigorous new growth. However, once the tree begins to bear fruit again, it goes back into decline. Young, non-bearing trees are never affected by citrus blight. Affected trees usually remain in a weak unproductive state and never recover from the disease. Trees on some rootstocks may die from blight especially in humid, tropical areas.

Once blight was well-defined, it was possible to conduct more meaningful studies of its cause. When the disease first appears in a citrus grove, its distribution is random. With time, the distribution may be more clustered, suggesting that affected trees may be a source of inoculum. However, affected trees are not so tightly clustered that a soil-borne pathogen would be indicated. Disease progress in Florida groves is often linear which would suggest an abiotic disease (19,94). However, growers in Florida remove affected trees quickly which may slow disease progress. In Brazil, where declining trees are not removed, disease progress is often exponential (6,63).

Microscopic studies have failed to reveal the presence of any obvious pathogen (14,73). Early studies suggested that *Physoderma* was present in blighted trees, but these were actually fibrous plugs in xylem vessels which are present in blight-affected trees as well as in trees affected by other diseases (20,21). Some unusual filamentous structures have been found in xylem extracts of blighted trees, but the nature of these has never been elucidated. Various viruses (13) and *Xylella fastidiosa* (53) cells have been found in blighted trees, but none has been consistently associated with the disease.

Soil-borne organisms have also been suggested as the cause of blight (68,70). *Fusarium solani* has been extensively studied in relation to the disease. However, it has never been conclusively demonstrated that this fungus is capable of causing the disease in the field (44). Transmission tests using large volumes of soil from beneath blighted trees failed to transmit the disease to healthy trees (85).

Uncertainty about the biotic or abiotic nature of the disease has led to many studies on the effect of soil pH (92) and other edaphic factors (69), liming and fertilization, and other management practices (8) as factors in the disease. Blight has been attributed to clay layers in the soil, to liming of groves, and to "modern agricultural practices." However, blight occurs on virtually every soil type where citrus is grown in Florida and under a wide variety of cultural practices (83). Blight, known as declinio in Brazil, declinamiento in Argentina, and marchitamiento repentino in Uruguay occurs on an even wider range of soils and cultural practices in those countries. The disease has never been reproduced in the field or its incidence reduced by changing cultural practices.

Early work on graft-transmission was largely unsuccessful (93). Buds from blight-affected trees produced healthy trees whether grafted onto healthy seedlings or onto sprouted roots from blighted trees. Trees propagated from such materials were no more likely to decline than those from clean material when grown in the grove for many years. Nevertheless, subsequent attempts at graft transmission were successful when bearing trees were graft-inoculated with root pieces from blighted trees or grafted directly to blighted trees (84,88). A high percentage of trees inoculated in this manner succumbed to the disease, but symptoms did not appear for 1½ to 3 years. Inoculated trees had all of the characteristic symptoms of blighted trees–typical symptoms, elevated zinc in trunk wood, poor water uptake, and amorphous plugs in the xylem. Similar experiments with above-ground portions of the tree have failed to transmit blight (3).

Thus, blight appears to be caused by a systemic, infectious agent that is limited to the root system (28,87). Several systemic agents have been suggested as causes of blight. Initially it was proposed that blight was caused by a variant of tristeza virus that affected trees on rough lemon rootstock (81). An isometric virus has been reported to be associated with blight (13). No further evidence has been published to support these hypotheses.

The possibility that blight is caused by *Xylella fastidiosa* has been extensively investigated (49,50,52,53,54,86). This bacterium has been detected in blight-affected citrus trees. Symptoms somewhat resemble those diseases caused by *X. fastidiosa* and the bacterium is widespread in other plants in Florida. Symptoms resembling blight have been produced in young trees inoculated with *X. fastidiosa* (50). However, the quantities of bacteria usually associated with other diseases caused by *X. fastidiosa* are not present in blighted citrus. Despite some circumstantial evidence for *X. fastidiosa* as the causal agent, no conclusive results have been forthcoming. The presence of a new disease of citrus in Brazil, citrus variegated chlorosis (CVC), caused by *X. fastidiosa* and the lack of association of blight and CVC argues against *X. fastidiosa* as a cause of blight (5).

Much of the recent research on blight has centered on proteins in plant tissues which are specifically associated with the disease (4,27). Two proteins, p12 and p35, have been the most extensively investigated. p35 is produced even in healthy plants but reaches much higher levels in the xylem of blighted trees, especially in roots. p12 is produced only in blight-affected trees. Antisera produced to both proteins are useful for disease diagnosis (25). Since p12 is produced in leaves which are easily collected and assayed, serological diagnosis is now the most widely used method of disease diagnosis, especially for large numbers of samples.

Neither the p12 or p35 proteins appear to be associated with a pathogen in diseased trees. p35 was found to be similar to a β-1,3-glucanase and has not been further investigated. The p12 protein is related to expansin genes in *Arabidopsis* (17), but is much smaller and soluble rather than being cell-wall bound. The nucleotide sequence of the p12 gene is very close to that of another hypothetical protein in *Arabidopsis* (28). Sense and antisense p12 genes have recently been transformed into citrus in an attempt to elucidate the role of this gene in disease development (59).

The causal agent for blight remains undetermined. The only conclusion that can be drawn is that it is a systemic infectious agent that is limited to the root system. If blight were produced by some known agent, the cause would probably have been determined some time ago. When the cause is finally known, it will probably be truly novel.

Concluding Remarks

Superficially it might appear to some that once the causal agents for all the diseases have been determined and described that task should be complete. However, etiology is a dynamic science. First, there are serious, well-studied problems like citrus blight whose cause remains unknown. Then, there are large numbers of diseases caused by pathogens which are already known but remain to be elucidated. Add to those the many diseases of complex etiology which are not well-understood and scientists have a significant amount of work remaining.

We do not appear to be dealing with a finite number of diseases of a finite number of plants as the APS lists of diseases of crop plants might imply. Rather, parasitic micro-organisms are often moved into new plants by man, insects, or by other avenues and suddenly we have new disease problems. Just to cite a few examples, cachexia viroid is a member of the hop stunt viroid genus. At some point, this pathogen was probably moved mechanically into citrus. This viroid produces no symptoms in many citrus species, and thus was propagated vegetatively. No one noticed until the viroid was introduced into a new sensitive cultivar or propagated on a sensitive rootstock. Voilá, we now have a new disease to sort out. In the case of citrus variegated chlorosis in Brazil, *Xylella fastidiosa* was probably introduced into citrus by sharpshooter vectors, perhaps from coffee. It was accidently propagated by man and then spread further by sharpshooters. A similar situation probably occurred with citrus chlorotic dwarf and the bayberry whitefly in Turkey. Neither citrus variegated chlorosis nor citrus chlorotic dwarf are known in areas of Asia to which citrus is native.

Similar situations occur with fungi. Sweet orange scab, caused by *Elsinoe australis* Bitancourt & Jenk. is known only in South America. If it was not transported there from the native home of citrus, how did it get there? *Alternaria alternata*, the cause of brown spot of citrus, may have come originally from another host plant. It is also possible that *Alternaria* is capable of acquiring additional toxin genes and expanding its host range. Postbloom fruit drop, caused by *Colletotrichum acutatum*, is known only in the Americas. Did it move to citrus from some other host?

At some time, we may reach a point where all of the groups of causal agents of disease in plants are known. But, given the kinds of situations described above, we will be studying the causes of diseases for a long time to come.

References

1. Agrios, G N (1997) Plant Pathology, 4th Edition Academic Press, San Diego
2. Ainsworth, G C (1969) The history of plant pathology in Great Britain. Annu. Rev. Phytopath. 7:13-30
3. Albrigo, L G, Timmer, L W, Derrick, K S, Tucker, D P H, Graham, J H (1993) Failure to transmit citrus blight by continuous limb grafts Pages 127-130 in: Proc. 12th Conf. Int. Organ Citrus Virologists P Moreno, L W Timmer, J V da Graça, eds. IOCV, Riverside, CA
4. Bausher, M G, Sweeney, M J (1991) Field detection of citrus blight using immunological techniques. Plant Dis. 75:447-450
5. Beretta, M J G, Barthe, G A, Ceccardi, T L, Lee, R F, Derrick, K S (1997) A survey for strains of *Xylella fastidiosa* in citrus affected by citrus variegated chlorosis and citrus blight in Brazil. Plant Dis. 81:1196-1198
6. Beretta, M J G, Derrick, K S, Lee, R F, Barthe, G, Rossetti, V (1993) Citrus declinio in Brazil: rate of spread and serological comparison with other declines Pages 113-115 in: Proc. 12th Conf. Int. Organ Citrus Virologists P Moreno, L W Timmer, J V da Graça, eds IOCV, Riverside, CA
7. Beretta, M J G, Leite, R P, Jr (2000) Variegated chlorosis Pages 50-51 in: Compendium of Citrus Diseases, 2nd edition L W Timmer, S M Garnsey, J H Graham, eds APS Press, St Paul, MN
8. Berger, R D 1998 A causa e o controlle do declinio dos citros Laranja 19:91-104
9. Blank, L W, Roberts, T M, Skeffington, R A (1988) New perspectives on forest decline. Nature (London) 336:27-30
10. Bove, J M, Garnier, M (2000) Stubborn Pages 48-50 in: Compendium of Citrus Diseases, 2nd edition L W Timmer, S M Garnsey, J H Graham, eds. APS Press, St Paul, MN

11. Bove, J M, Garnier, M (2000) Witches' Broom Page 51 in: Compendium of Citrus Diseases, 2nd edition L W Timmer, S M Garnsey, J H Graham, eds APS Press, St Paul, MN
12. Brlansky, R (2000) Blight Pages 65-66 in: Compendium of Citrus Diseases, 2nd edition L W Timmer, S M Garnsey, J H Graham, eds. APS Press, St Paul, MN
13. Brlansky, R H, Davis, C L, Howd, D S (1993) Purification partial characterization of a virus isolated from trees affected by citrus blight. Phytopathology 83:1372 (abstr)
14. Brlansky, R H, Lee, R F, Timmer L W (1987)Cytology of citrus blight: microscopic search for causal agents characterization of xylem occlusions water blockage. Pages 383-394 in: Proc Int Symp Citrus Canker, Declinio/Blight Similar Diseases, Sao Paulo, Brazil
15. Broadbent, P (2000) Dry root rot or sudden death Page 71 in: Compendium of Citrus Diseases, 2nd edition L W Timmer, S M Garnsey, J H Graham, eds. APS Press, St Paul, MN
16. Cavalier-Smith, T (1987) The origin of fungi pseudofungi Pages 339-353 in: Evolutionary Biology of the Fungi A D M Rayner, C M Brasier, D Moore, eds.. Cambridge University Press, Cambridge, UK
17. Ceccardi, T L, Barthe, G A, Derrick, K S (1998) A novel protein associated with citrus blight has sequence similarities to expansin. Plant Mol. Biol. 38:775-783
18. Chang, C J, Garnier, M, Zreik, L, Rossetti, V, Bove, J M (1993) Culture and serological detection of the xylem-limited bacteria causing citrus variegated chlorosis and its identification as *Xylella fastidiosa* Curr. Microbiol. 27:137-142
19. Chellemi, D O, Sonoda, R M, Pelosi, R R, Cohen, M (1991) Temporal and spatial comparisons between epidemics of citrus blight and citrus tristeza. Pages 289-296 in: Proc. 12th Conf. Int. Organ Citrus Virologists P Moreno, L W Timmer, J V da Graça, eds. IOCV, Riverside, CA
20. Childs, J F L (1979) Florida citrus blight Part I Some causal relations of citrus blight. Plant Dis. Rep. 63:560-564
21. Childs, J F L, Kopp, L E, Johnson, R E (1965) A species of *Physoderma* present in citrus and related species. Phytopathology 55:681-687
22. Cohen, M (1974) Diagnosis of young tree decline, blight and sand hill decline of citrus by measurement of water uptake using gravity injection. Plant Dis. Rep. 58:801-805
23. Davis, M J, Purcell, A H, Thomson, S V (1978) Pierce's disease of grapevines: isolation of the causal bacterium. Science 199:75-77

24. Derrick, K S, Barthe, G A (2000) Psorosis. Pages 58-59 in: Compendium of Citrus Diseases, 2nd edition L W Timmer, S M Garnsey, J H Graham, eds. APS Press, St Paul, MN

25. Derrick, K S, Barthe, G A, Hewitt, B G, Lee, R F, Albrigo, L G (1992) Detection of citrus blight by serological assays. Proc. Fla. State Hortic. Soc. 105:26-28

26. Derrick, K S, Brlansky, R H, Lee, R F, da Graca J V, Timmer, L W, Nguyen, T K (1988) Partial characterization of a virus associated with citrus ringspot. Phytopathology 78:1298-1301

27. Derrick, K S, Lee, R F, Brlansky, R H, Timmer, L W, Hewitt, B G, Barthe, G A (1990) Proteins associated with citrus blight. Plant Dis. 74:168-170

28. Derrick, K S, Timmer, L W (2000) Citrus blight other diseases of recalcitrant etiology. Annu. Rev. Phytopathol. 38:181-205

29. Diener, T O (1971) Potato spindle tuber "virus" IV A replicating, low molecular weight RNA. Virology 45:411-428

30. Diener, T O (1973) Potato spindle tuber viroid: A novel type of pathogen. Perspectives in Virology 8:7-30

31. Doi, Y, Teranaka, M, Yora, K, Asuyama, H (1967) Mycoplasma or PLT group-like micro-organisms found in the phloem elements of plants infected with mulberry dwarf, potato witches' broom, aster yellows, or paulownia witches' broom. Ann. Phytopathol. Soc. Jpn. 33:259-266

32. Dollet, M (1984) Plant diseases caused by flagellate protozoa (Phytomonas). Annu. Rev. Phytopathol. 22:115-132

33. Duran-Vila, N, Semancik, J S, Broadbent, P (2000) Cachexia Pages 52-53 in: Compendium of Citrus Diseases, 2nd edition L W Timmer, S M Garnsey, J H Graham, eds. APS Press, St Paul, MN

34. Duran-Vila, N, Semancik, J S, Broadbent, P (2000) Exocortis Pages 53-54 in: Compendium of Citrus Diseases, 2nd edition L W Timmer, S M Garnsey, J H Graham, eds. APS Press, St Paul, MN

35. Fudl-Allah, A E-S A, Calavan, E C, Igwebe, E C K (972) Culture of a mycoplasma-like organism associated with stubborn of citrus. Phytopathology 63:403-408

36. Garnier, M, Bove, J M (2000) Huanglongbing (Greening) Pages 46-48 in: Compendium of Citrus Diseases, 2nd edition L W Timmer, S M Garnsey, J H Graham, eds. APS Press, St Paul, MN

37. Garnsey, S M (2000) Other virus and viruslike agents. Pages 66-68 in: Compendium of Citrus Diseases, 2nd edition L W Timmer, S M Garnsey, J H Graham, eds. APS Press, St Paul, MN

38. Garnsey, S M (2000) Budunion creases and incompatibilities. Pages 79-81 in: Compendium of Citrus Diseases, 2nd edition L W Timmer, S M Garnsey, J H Graham, eds. APS Press, St Paul, MN

39. Garnsey, S M, Gonsalves, D, Purcifull, D E (1977) Mechanical transmission of citrus tristeza virus. Phytopathology 67:695-698

40. Garnsey, S M, Jones, J W (1967) Mechanical transmission of exocortis virus with contaminated budding tools. Plant Dis. Rep. 51:410-413
41. Garnsey, S M, Timmer, L W (1980) Mechanical transmissibility of citrus ringspot isolates from Florida, Texas, California Pages 174-179 in: Proc 8th Conf Int Organ Citrus Virologists E C Calavan, S M Garnsey, L W Timmer, eds. IOCV, Riverside, CA
42. Goheen, A C, Nyland, G, Lowe, S K (1973) Association of a rickettsia-like organism with Pierce's disease of grapevines and alfalfa dwarf and heat therapy of the disease in grapevines. Phytopathology 63:341-345
43. Gonsalves, D, Purcifull, D E, Garnsey, S M (1978) Purification serology of citrus tristeza virus. Phytopathology 68:553-559
44. Graham, J H, Brlansky, R H, Timmer, L W, Lee, R F, Marais, L J, Bender, G S (1985) Comparison of citrus tree declines of major roots and their association with *Fusarium solan.i* Plant Dis. 69:1055-1058
45. Graham, J H, Menge, J A (2000) Tree collapse and branch and twig diebacks Pages 70-71 in: Compendium of Citrus Diseases, 2nd edition L W Timmer, S M Garnsey, J H Graham, eds. APS Press, St Paul, MN
46. Hewitt, W B (1942) Pierce's disease of grapevines. Calif. Agric. Expt. Sta. Circ. 353:1-32
47. Hewitt, W B, Houston, B R, Frazier, N W, Freitag, J H (1946) Leafhopper transmission of the virus causing Pierce's disease of grape and dwarf of alfalfa. Phytopathology 36:117-128
48. Hocquellet, A, Toorawa, P, Bove, J M, Garnier, M (1999) Detection and identification of the two *Candidatus* Liberobacter species associated with citrus huanglongbing by PCR multiplication of ribosomal protein genes of the beta operon. Mol. Cell. Probes 13:373-379
49. Hopkins, D L (1982) Relation of Pierce's disease bacterium to a wilt-type disease in citrus in the greenhouse. Phytopathology 72:1090-1092
50. Hopkins, D L (1988) Production of diagnostic symptoms of blight in citrus inoculated with *Xylella fastidiosa.* Plant Dis. 72:432-435
51. Hopkins, D L, Mollenhauer, H H (1973) Rickettsia-like bacterium associated with Pierce's disease of grapes. Science 179:298-300
52. Hopkins, D L, Mortensen, J A (1971) Suppression of Pierce's disease symptoms by tetracycline antibiotics. Plant Dis. Rep. 55:610-612
53. Hopkins, D L, Thompson, C M, Bistline, F W, Russo, L W (1989) Relationship between xylem-limited bacteria and citrus blight. Proc. Fla. State Hortic. Soc. 102:21-23

54. Hopkins, D L, Thompson, C M, Wichman, R L, Bistline, F W, Russo, L W (1995) Effect of inoculation of mature citrus trees in the grove with *Xylella fastidiosa* on citrus blight incidence. Proc. Fla. State Hortic. Soc. 108:103-106
55. Huettel, R N, Golden, A M (1991) Nathan Augustus Cobb: The father of nematology in the US. Annu. Rev. Phytopathol. 29:15-26
56. Igwebe, E C K, Calavan, E C (1970) Occurrence of mycoplasma-like bodies in phloem of stubborn-infected citrus seedlings. Phytopathology 60:1525-1526
57. Ishie, T, Doi, Y, Yora, K, Asuyama, H (1967) Suppressive effects of antibiotics of tetracycline group on symptom development of mulberry dwarf disease. Ann. Phytopathol. Soc. Jpn. 33:267-275
58. Kandler, D (1990) Epidemiological evaluation of the development of Waldsterben in Germany. Plant Dis. 74:4-12
59. Kayim, M, Ceccardi, T L, Beretta, M J G, Barthe, G A, Derrick, K S (2001) Introduction of a citrus blight associated gene into Carrizo citrange (*C sinensis* x *Poncirus trifoliata* [L] by *Agrobacterium tumefaciens.* Phytopathology 91:547
60. Keitt, G W (1959) History of plant pathology. Pages 61-97 in: Plant Pathology J G Horsfall A E Dimond, eds., Vol 1, Academic Press, New York
61. Kitajima, E W, Costa, A S (1968) Electron microscopy of tristeza virus in citrus leaf tissues. Pages 59-64 in: Proc 4th Conf Int Organ Citrus Virologists JFL Childs, ed. Univ Florida Press, Gainesville
62. Korkmaz, S, Çinar, A, Kersting, A, Garnsey, S M (1995) Citrus chlorotic dwarf: A new whitefly-transmitted viruslike disease of citrus in Turkey. Plant Dis. 79:1074
63. Laranjeira, F F, Guirado, N, Beretta, M J G, Derrick, K S, Lee, R F (1996) Temporal spatial dynamics of citrus blight in Brazil Page 414 in: Proc 13th Conf. Int. Organ Citrus Virologists J V da Graça, P Moreno, R K Yokomi, eds. IOCV, Riverside, CA
64. Lee, I-M, Davis, R E (1984) New media for rapid growth of *Spiroplasma citri* and corn stunt spiroplasma Phytopathology 74:84-89
65. Lee, R F, Garnsey, S M (1996) Citrus virus and virus-like pathogens, a continuing evolution of progress and problems. Pages 1-11 in: Proc 13th Conf Int Organ Citrus Virologists J V da Graça, P Moreno, R K Yokomi, eds. IOCV, Riverside, CA
66. Lee, R F, Marais, L J, Timmer, L W, Graham, J H (1984) Syringe injection of water into the trunk: a rapid diagnostic test for citrus blight. Plant Dis. 68:511 513
67. Moreno, P (2000) Young leaf flecking diseases. Pages 64-65 in: Compendium of Citrus Diseases, 2nd edition L W Timmer, S M Garnsey, J H Graham, eds. APS Press, St Paul, MN

68. Nemec, S, Baker, R, Burnett, H (1980) Pathogenicity of *Fusarium solani* to citrus roots and its possible role in blight etiology. Proc. Fla. State Hortic. Soc. 93:36-40
69. Nemec, S, Fox, A N, Horvath, G (1977) The relationship of subsurface hardpan to blight and development of root systems. Proc. Soil & Crop Sci. Soc., Florida 36:141-144
70. Nemec, S, Myhre, D L (1992) Citrus blight Pages 209-276 in: Plant Diseases of International Importance:Volume III, Diseases of Fruit Crops J Kumar, H S Chaube, U S Singh, A N Mukhopadhyay, eds. Prentice Hall, NJ
71. Parthasarathy, M V, van Slobbe, W G, Soudant, C (1976) Trypanosomatid flagellate in the phloem of diseased coconut palm. Science 192:1346-48
72. Ploetz, R C, Benscher, D, Vásquez, A, Colls, A, Nagel, J Schaffer, B (1996) A reexamination of mango decline in Florida. Plant Dis. 80:664-668
73. Purcifull, D E, Garnsey, S M, Story, G E, Christie, R G (1973) Electron microscope examination of citrus trees affected with young tree decline (YTD). Proc. Fla. State Hortic. Soc. 86:91-94
74. Ramos, L J, Davenport, T L, McMillan, R T, Jr, Lara, S P (1997) The resistance of mango (*Mangifera indica*) cultivars to tip dieback in Florida. Plant Dis. 81:509-514
75. Rhoads, A S (1936) Blight -a non-parasitic disease of citrus trees. Florida Agric. Expt. Sta. Bull. 296, 64 pages
76. Roistacher, C N, Calavan, E C, Blue, R L (1969) Citrus exocortis virus-chemical inactivation on tools, tolerance to heat and separation of isolates. Plant Dis. Rep. 53:333-336
77. Schafer, B (1994) Decline. Page 43 in: Compendium of Tropical Fruit Diseases R C Ploetz, G A Zentmyer, W T Nishijima, K G Rohrback, H D Ohr, eds. APS Press, St Paul, MN
78. Schoenweiss, D F (1981) The role of environmental stress in diseases of woody plants. Plant Dis. 65:308-314
79. Schutt, P, Cowling, E B (1985(Waldsterben, a general decline of forests in Central Europe: Symptoms, development, and possible causes. Plant Dis. 69:548-558
80. Skelly, J M, Innes, J L (1994) Waldsterben in the forests of Central Europe and Eastern North America: Fantasy or reality? Plant Dis. 78:1021-1032
81. Smith, P F (1974) Zinc accumulation in the wood of citrus trees affected with blight. Proc. Fla. State Hortic. Soc. 87:91-95
82. Smith, P F (1974) History of citrus blight in Florida. Citrus Ind. 55(9):13-18
83. Timmer, L W (1990) Blight-uma doença infecciosa dos citrus. Pages 195-209 in: Proc 1st Int Seminar on Citrus Rootstocks Bebedouro, Sao Paulo, Brazil

84. Timmer, L W, Brlansky, R H, Derrick, K S, Lee, R F (1991) Transmission of citrus blight by root graft inoculation. Pages 244-249 in: Proc 12th Conf Int Organ Citrus Virologists P Moreno, L W Timmer, J V da Graça, eds. IOCV, Riverside, CA
85. Timmer, L W, Graham, J H (1992) Nontransmission of citrus blight by soil. Plant Dis. 76:323
86. Timmer, L W, Lee, R F (1985) Survey of blight-affected citrus groves for sharpshooter-borne, xylem-limited bacteria. Plant Dis. 69:497-498
87. Timmer, L W, Lee, R F, Brlansky, R H, Graham, J H, Albrigo, L G, Derrick, K S, Tucker, D P H (1992) The infectious nature of citrus blight. Proc. Fla. State Hortic. Soc. 105:21-26
88. Tucker, D P H, Lee, R F, Timmer, L W, Albrigo, L G, Brlansky, R H (1984) Experimental transmission of citrus blight. Plant Dis. 68:979-980
89. Vermeulen, H (1963) A wilt of *Coffea liberica* in Surinam and its association with a flagellate *Phytomonas leptovasorum* Stahel J. Protozool. 10:216-222
90. Wheaton, T A (1985) Citrus blight: One hundred years of research in Florida. Citrus Ind. 66(2):25-27, 30-32
91. Wutscher, H K, Cohen, M, Young, R H (1977) Zinc and water-soluble phenolic levels in the wood for the diagnosis of citrus blight. Plant Dis. Rep. 6:572-576
92. Wutscher, H K, Lee, O N (1988) Soil pH and extractable mineral elements in and around an isolated blight site. Proc. Fla. State Hortic. Soc. 101:70-72
93. Wutscher, H K, Youtsey, C O, Smith, P F, Cohen, M (1983) Negative results in citrus blight transmission tests. Proc. Fla. State Hortic. Soc. 96:48-50
94. Yokomi, R K, Garnsey, S M, Young, R H, Grimm, G R (1984) Spatial and temporal analysis of citrus blight incidence in Valencia orange groves in Central Florida. See Ref 55, pages 260-269 in: Proc 9th Conf. Int. Organ Citrus Virologists S M Garnsey, L W Timmer, J V Dodds, eds. IOCV, Riverside, CA
95. Zreik, L, Carle, P, Bove, J M, Garnier, M (1995) Characterization of the mycoplasma like organism associated with witches' broom disease of lime and proposition of a Candidatus taxon for the organism "*Candidatus* Phytoplasma aurantifolia". Int. J. Syst. Bacteriol. 45:449-453

Ion Fluxes in Nod factor Signal Transduction

Hubert H. Felle

Introduction

Soil bacteria belonging to the genera *Azorhizobium, Bradyrhizobium* and *Rhizobium* are able to induce nitrogen-fixing nodules on the roots of leguminous plants. This close plant-microbe interaction is initiated after the excretion of flavonoids by the legume root into the immediate rhizosphere to serve as primary signal for the expression of rhizobial nodulation genes. As a direct consequence thereof the rhizobia synthesize lipochito-oligosaccharides (Nod factors), which interact with the legume root (hairs) in a host-specific manner. Of these responses, plasma membrane depolarization (9, 13, 22) and ion fluxes (1, 5, 6, 16, 23) are the most well known events that occur within seconds or minutes of encounter of the root (hair) with the appropriate Nod factor.

Early responses of root hairs to Nod factors

To access the root symplast, rhizobial bacteria penetrate the cell wall and overcome the membrane barrier at the just emerging cell wall of a growing root hair tip. The consequence of the encounter between rhizobia and root hair is a disturbance of the root hair growth pattern, which culminates in the typical curling forming a pocket around the area where the rhizobia attempt to penetrate.

Before the root hairs visually start to curl or deform, characteristic ion activity changes can be picked up within the root hair space of alfalfa (Fig. 1). So far, the very first measurable event that can be measured 2 to 5 s after Nod factor addition, is a Ca^{2+} influx which results in an increase in cytosolic Ca^{2+} activity (17). A few seconds thereafter, anions begin to leave the cells, the plasma membrane transiently depolarizes and external pH transiently alkalizes, from which it was concluded that depolarization was the result of rapid Cl^--efflux and alkalization was due to organic acid anions leaving the cells through the same channel as Cl^- did.

K^+-fluxes are the last in line. This is because K^+ as the so-called dominating ion is distributed across the plasma membrane close to its electrochemical equilibrium.

$$E_K = -RT/F \ln ([K^+]_o/[K^+]_i) \qquad (1)$$

R is the gas constant, T the temperature (K), and F is the Faraday constant. When the membrane potential, while depolarizing, becomes positive of E_K, the driving force for K^+ is inverted (too much K^+ is in the cell) and K^+ must leave the cell. In the signal transduction described here, K^+ acts as "membrane potential buffer" in that it compensates the anion efflux, stops depolarization and initiates repolarization, fueled by the H^+ pump (16).

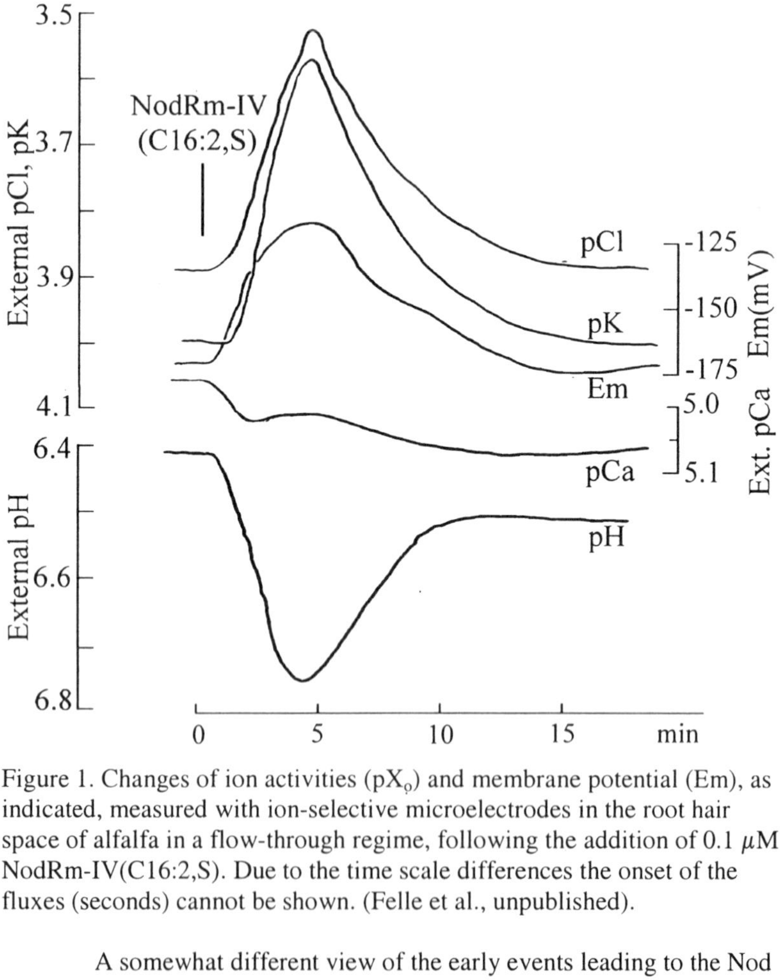

Figure 1. Changes of ion activities (pX_o) and membrane potential (Em), as indicated, measured with ion-selective microelectrodes in the root hair space of alfalfa in a flow-through regime, following the addition of 0.1 μM NodRm-IV(C16:2,S). Due to the time scale differences the onset of the fluxes (seconds) cannot be shown. (Felle et al., unpublished).

A somewhat different view of the early events leading to the Nod factor-induced membrane depolarization has been brought forward by Kurkdjian et al. (23). Using the discontinuous single-electrode voltage clamp technique Nod factor-induced electric membrane currents (consisting of different ion fluxes across the membrane) were measured and their identity analyzed using transport inhibitors. The authors argue that the depolarization was caused by an increase of the inwardly directed positive current (= outwardly directed negative current) as well as by inhibition of the H^+ pump. Whereas some decrease in pump activity was also allowed for by Felle et al. (16), but its impact on depolarization thought less drastic, the interpretation of the inwardly directed current raises some problems. Although Kurkdjian et al. (23), in accordance with the results of Felle et al. (16), also report the activation of anion efflux, the view that K^+ influx was a considerable factor of the process leading to depolarization appears to be a misinterpretation. As the dominating ion K^+ balances charge by responding immediately to any change in membrane potential. Thus, once the membrane potential has started to depolarize, be it through pump deactivation or anion efflux, the inwardly directed driving force for K^+ decreases, which rules out an increase in net K^+ influx large enough to depolarize the root hair. Since it takes time until the membrane potential has passed E_K, K^+ efflux must occur <u>after</u> anion (Cl^-) efflux has started, as demonstrated (16). As the voltage clamp technique cannot resolve the occurrence of the different ion currents in a chronological order, this important detail is missing in the analysis of Kurkdjian et al. (23) and thus has led to some misinterpretation.

Role of the Ion fluxes

It should be emphasized that the Nod factor-induced depolarization is very likely not a signal, but is just the sum of the electrical charges, *viz.* ions that cross the plasma membrane in a certain order. On the other hand, ion fluxes themselves may function as signals, either specifically in their identity as ions or more general as net electrical current or as local charge dislocation.

Ion fluxes across a membrane will *nota bene* result in altered ion activities on either side of the membrane. While the ion activities of the bulk are not relevant for further responses, the activities adjacent to the plasma membrane itself are. These changed conditions will affect the transport behavior of the root hair as well as that of the rhizobia. As symbiotic responses are thought to have emerged from defense strategies, the ion fluxes triggered by the Nod factors and their suspected role must be discussed from this point of view as well.

CALCIUM

To our current knowledge, Ca^{2+} influx is the first measurable event that occurs following the external application of Nod factors and their perception (28). This has been measured directly by using Ca^{2+}-selective microelectrodes placed within the responsive root hair zone (16). The external Ca^{2+} activity drops, while the cytosolic Ca^{2+} activity increases simultaneously. Although it has not been proven unequivocally that the internal increase in Ca^{2+} activity is a quantitative measure of the Ca^{2+} leaving the root hair zone, channel inhibitor tests and external ion exchange tests strongly support that notion. The Ca^{2+} response to Nod factors on both sides of the plasma membrane is specific, showing that nonsulfated Nod factors have no effects (17). Using the extracellular ion-specific vibrating electrode, Allen et al. (1) first noted small Nod factor-induced Ca^{2+} net current changes at root hair tips of alfalfa with unclear direction (influx or efflux), however. Cárdenas et al. (5), in a more quantitative analysis clearly demonstrated in *Phaseolus vulgaris* root hairs that Nod factors induced a substantial inwardly directed Ca^{2+} net current which, in its essential parts, was confined to the tip, thus underscoring the idea that the Nod factor-induced increase in cytosolic Ca^{2+} activity originates from extracellular stores. Although the vibrating probe (21) may detect smaller currents than stationary electrodes placed within the root hair space, the self-referencing vibrating electrode suffers a detection time lag after changing conditions, i.e. no information is available for minutes after adding the Nod factor. This means that neither lag-phases, nor onsets of the early ion fluxes are detected. The stationary ion probe picks up any change in ion activity that occurs at the sensitive tip from the moment of occurrence, which is essential with events like Nod factor responses that start seconds after changing the experimental conditions.

Nod factor induced elevations of cytosolic Ca^{2+} activity in root hairs have also been reported by de Ruijter et al. (7), where the importance of both tip Ca^{2+} and of Ca^{2+} influx across the plasma membrane for growth is demonstrated. About 1 h after adding the Nod factor to non-growing root hairs, i.e. to root hairs with no internal Ca^{2+} gradient, these cells regain such a gradient together with the ability of tip growth. The response time of an hour appears long for a typical Nod factor response, and it is doubtful whether non-growing root hairs are in fact a target of the rhizobia *in natura* (see rationale below). Nevertheless, the study clearly shows that Nod factors activate Ca^{2+} channels with the result of a resumption in tip growth, a direct indication that root hair deformation and internal changes in Ca^{2+} activity are causally interrelated. This is in line with observations of Cárdenas et al. (4), who demonstrated that the Ca^{2+} influx at the root hair tips lead to elevated cytosolic Ca^{2+} activity and caused dramatic changes of the root hair cytoskeleton. Since the cytoskeleton determines the form of the root hair (27) and very likely also the direction of its growth, the typical curling of root hairs appears a direct consequence of this local Ca^{2+} influx.

Yokoyama et al. (37) report Nod factor induced Ca^{2+} elevations in protoplasts of soybean-cultured cells. The changes observed are rather small, indicating that possibly not all protoplasts were actually importing Ca^{2+}. This result is not surprising, since only protoplasts isolated from root hair cells would be expected to respond in a specific manner to Nod factors. Moreover, the cell-wall degrading enzymes used to prepare the protoplasts very likely will mask any Nod factor response, a suspicion verified recently in patch-clamp tests on alfalfa protoplasts, where Carden and Felle (unpublished) found that the responses to Nod factors were either absent or minor.

Root hair curling vs. root hair deformation. As all tip growing cells, root hairs also build up a cytosolic tip-to-base Ca^{2+} gradient (3, 5, 15). This gradient is dynamic in that it is maintained by net Ca^{2+} influx (31), and obviously plays a pivotal role in Nod factor-induced root hair curling. In fact, Bibikova et al. (3) have demonstrated that tip growth of root hairs follows the direction of externally elevated Ca^{2+}. Similarly, the relevance of Ca^{2+} net influx at the tip can also be demonstrated by applying locally the ionophore A23187, which likewise causes Ca^{2+} to enter the cell at the tip and forces growth into the direction of A23187. Since it has been demonstrated that Nod factors stimulate Ca^{2+} influx (5, 16), the root hair will bend to the side where rhizobia dock and release the factors. Whereas directional curling is observed when the root hair comes into contact with the rhizobia in the soil, non-directional root hair deformation occurs when the entire root or root hair is flooded with Nod factors as usually occurs under laboratory conditions. Since the Nod factor/root hair interaction is not confined to a small surface area behind the root hair tip, the Nod factor exerts its effect across the entire cell surface. the root hairs deform at random.

Calcium spiking. Observed 8 to 10 minutes following Nod factor addition, Ca^{2+} spiking (8, 9, 35, 36) is not likely to be connected directly with the early ion fluxes and obviously follows a different line of signaling. This notion is underscored by the observation that calcium spiking is a process located near the nucleus, not influenced by Ca^{2+} from exogenous sources. It is thought that Ca^{2+} spiking should be interpreted with respect to gene activation, but could also play a role in transducing signals to the cortex (8, 35).

ANION FLUXES

Due to their electrical charge, anions (especially Cl^-) have a steep outwardly directed gradient, built up or maintained by the proton pump. Cl^-, unlike K^+, is not distributed across the plasma membrane close to its equilibrium, which is given by equation 2, where the electrochemical gradient of Cl^- ($\Delta\mu_{Cl}/F$) across the plasma membrane is expressed in terms of

$$\Delta\mu_{Cl}/F = E_m + RT/F \ln[Cl^-]_i/[Cl^-]_o \qquad (2)$$

where E_m is the membrane potential and R,T and F have the meanings denoted for equation 1. Since the anion channels have a low opening probability under resting conditions, Cl^- does not contribute considerably to membrane permeability and hence also not to the resting membrane potential. Thus, activation of these channels always means a rapid efflux of negative charge, puts a load on the proton pump and thus depolarizes the membrane.

Following Nod factor treatment, anion channels are activated when cytosolic Ca^{2+} activity increases, as a consequence of which Cl^- along its steep outwardly directed electrochemical gradient rapidly leaves the cells and depolarizes the plasma membrane. Anion channels to a variable extent also permit the transport of organic acid anions, which causes the alkalization of the weakly buffered medium (see below).

Since the Cl^- fluxes follow a transient kinetics, Cl^- must be taken up again. This Cl^- influx is mediated by a H^+/Cl^- symporter which is fueled by the sum of the membrane potential and the transmembrane proton gradient, better known as the proton motive force. As long as the anion channels are activated the anion efflux exceeds anion influx. This changes when the anion channels inactivate and the negative charges are compensated for.

Interestingly, Nod factors are fundamentally not required for anion channel activation; any increase in cytosolic Ca^{2+} activity, regardless of its origin (intra- or extracellular), will activate these channels. This has been shown by the application of the Ca^{2+} ionophore A23187 which translocates Ca^{2+} into the cell, and mimics the Nod factor response with respect to external alkalization, Cl^- efflux and depolarization (16). Likewise, internal release of Ca^{2+} using 2,5-di(t-butyl)-1,4-benzohydroquinone (BHQ, an agent which releases Ca^{2+} from IP_3-sensitive stores) increased cytosolic Ca^{2+} activity, caused Cl^- efflux and membrane depolarization (17). Similar responses are observed when oligochitin elicitors (18) were brought into contact with the root hairs, thus underscoring the conclusion that the Ca^{2+}-triggered activation of anion channels and possibly subsequent processes may be a general principle of cellular signaling.

POTASSIUM FLUXES

K^+ fluxes are obviously not an integral part of the Nod factor signal chain. K^+, according to its transmembrane distribution, responds rapidly to changes in membrane voltage flowing in one or the other direction. In doing so it balances charges and initiates repolarization. It must be emphasized, however, that K^+ is by no means unimportant in the signaling process. Due to its fast response to voltage changes it guarantees undisturbed charge translocation and serves turgor regulation.

ION FLUXES, SIGNALS FOR NODULATION?

In alfalfa the specificity of the Nod factor effects (depolarization, ion fluxes, extracellular alkalization, cytosolic elevation of Ca^{2+} activity) closely correlates with the grade of nodulation. For all responses the hierarchy, starting with the strongest response is: NodRm-IV(C16:2,S) ≈ NodRm-IV(C16:2,S,Ac) > NodRm-IV(C16:0,S) >>NodRm-IV(C16:2) (13, 14). Such a finding is striking, considering that nodule formation occurs days after the root hairs had first contact with the Nod factors. It is also noteworthy that in alfalfa the Nod factor signal alone (without the presence of the rhizobia) causes formation of nodules (which of course have no function with respect to nitrogen fixation). This is a strong indication that the early events are required for nodulation, that a signal from the root hair tip to the cortex must be transduced, but that the infection thread is not the primary transducer of this signal.

Other systems. As shown in Figure 2, preliminary tests carried out on *Medicago truncatula* cv. R108 yield as clear responses to Nod factors as *M. sativa* and, with the exception of Ca^{2+}, essentially follows the pattern measured on *M. sativa*.

On the other hand, as shown in Figure 3, *M. truncatula* cv. Jemalong shows less pronounced responses to external addition of Nod factors and so far has resisted a rigorous analysis (Felle et al., unpublished). The low response of *M. truncatula* cv. Jemalong indicates that neither membrane potential nor ion fluxes directly (with a possible exception of Ca^{2+}) may be part of the signal propagation. On the other hand, an electrical membrane current, locally induced, could carry information to the cortex. Since no action potential is induced by Nod factors which would propagate along the root hair, all information will suffer a decrement. This means that any current induced at the tip will decrease while propagating along the root hair according to the existing space constant (λ):

$$\lambda = \sqrt{Rm/Ri} \quad (3)$$

where Rm is the membrane resistance and Ri is the internal resistance of the root hair cell. Since λ is the distance after which a signal will have dropped to 1/e (≈ 37%) and λ is around 0.3 to 0.5 mm for thereupon investigated cells , this means that only a fraction of a signal, triggered at the tip of a root hair, will reach the basis or even cortex cells, provided the root hair is short. Thus, only young root hairs 1 mm or less in length would be able to transfer information to the cortex. So far, this has not been tested and no information is available whether Ca^{2+} is carried by cytoplasmic streaming. In this context the

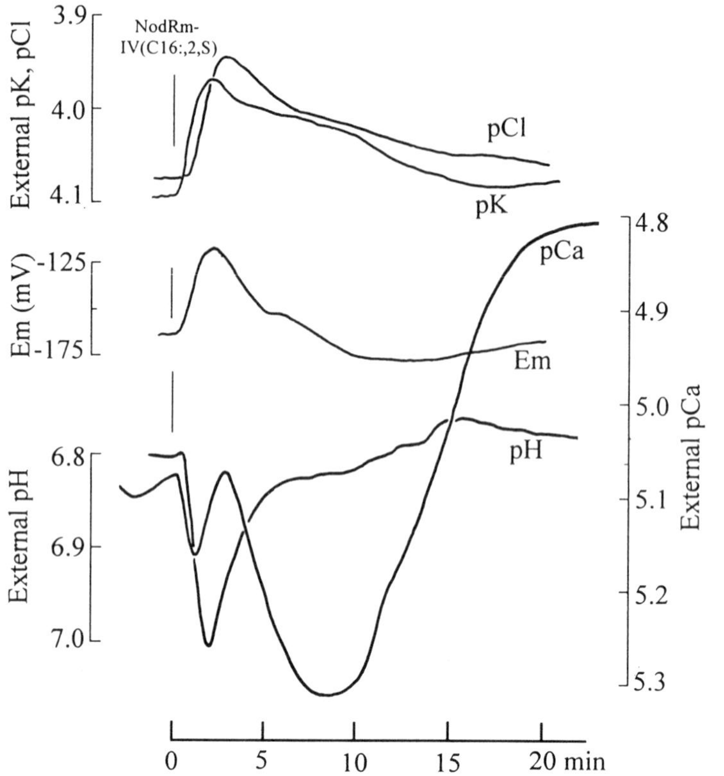

Figure 2. Changes of ion activities (pX_o) and membrane potential (Em), as indicated, measured with ion-selective microelectrodes placed in the root hair space of *Medicago truncatula* cv. R108 in a flow-through regime, following the addition of 0.1 μM NodRm-IV(C16:2,S). (Felle et al., unpublished)

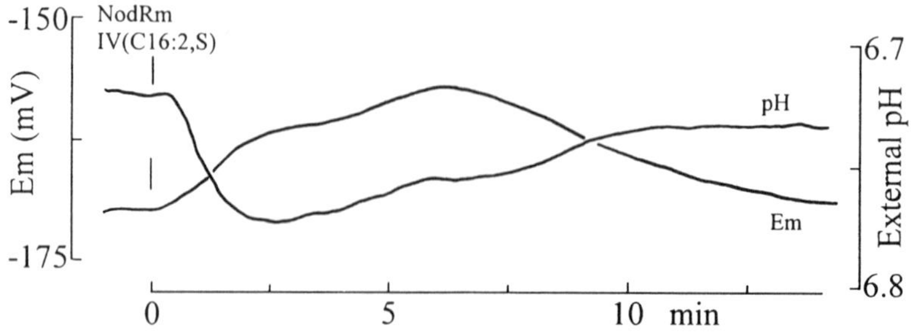

Figure 3. Changes in pH (pH) and membrane potential (Em), as indicated, measured with a pH-sensitive microelectrode placed in the root hair space of *Medicago truncatula* cv. Jemalong in a flow-through regime, following the addition of 0.1 μM NodRm-IV(C16:2,S). (Felle et al., unpublished).

increase in Ca^{2+} activity at the tip could trigger Ca^{2+} spiking. However,cytosolic Ca^{2+} alone is not sufficient to induce Ca^{2+} spiking or nodulation, as shown with the Ca^{2+} -ionophore A23187. Very likely, a variety of other factors - one of them could be pH - must accumulate to trigger the necessary information transfer.

Proton fluxes and pH changes

THEIR ORIGIN

The plasma membrane H^+ ATPase, widely called the "proton pump", provides the electrochemical "driving belt" by which all electrophoretic and proton-driven transport is fueled and by which transmembrane gradients of membrane permeable matter are maintained. Therefore, any change in pump activity will have an immediate impact on transport and on transmembrane gradients.

Extracellular alkalization is not only inherent to the legume/rhizobial symbiosis, but seems common following defense-related encounters of plant cells or organs with elicitors and physiologically related compounds (2, 11, 29). This alkalization has been subject to speculation both with respect to its physiological role and also to its nature. Extracellular alkalization can have a variety of causes: (i) deactivation of the primary plasma membrane proton pump which may indeed lead to external alkalization and this has been shown (16). Since the proton pump is the motor that hyperpolarizes the plasma membrane, deactivation of the pump would cause a massive depolarization, which was not observed, as Nod factors induce a relatively slow and moderate transient depolarization only. Still, in the light of the elevated cytosolic Ca^{2+} activity, a partial impact of Nod factors on the pump is not ruled out. It should be kept in mind, however, that an external alkalization arising from a pump deactivation alone would not recover, i.e. the pH change could not be transient, as observed. (ii) Influx of H^+ either through channels or cotransport-mediated. Although often favored, of all possibilities passive H^+ influx is the least likely case. H^+ influx through H^+ channels can be ruled out for the plasma membrane, as this would flatly violate chemiosmotic principles and waste energy. The influx of H^+ mediated by cotransporters is a possibility; it is not effective, however, because Cl^-, the only possible ion involved therein, leaves the cells and the membrane depolarizes which decreases the driving force for any symport. (iii) Ion-exchange within the cell wall. Pectic cell wall constituents like glucuronic acid carry negative charges, to which cations and protons bind and exchange for each other, depending on the concentrations present in the adjacent fluid. This means that ion fluxes from and into cells could cause cell wall pH shifts, which in fact has been shown in roots: addition of K^+ or Ca^{2+} to the medium caused acidification at the root surface and in the root apoplast (12). The situation here is different, because the pH changes occur prior to the K^+ efflux. Still, to some extent ion exchange within the cell wall will contribute to the form of the pH kinetics at a later stage. (iv) Strong ion effects, which are an important factor in any pH change that occurs within compartments separated by a membrane. In this context it should be kept in mind that pH changes do not have to be the direct result of immediate transmembrane H^+ fluxes, but may arise simply from transport of strong ions (e.g. K^+, Ca^{2+}, Cl^-) from one compartment into another. According to the strong-ion concept Cl^- efflux should acidify the extracellular space, K^+ on the other hand would alkalize it. Since in the case discussed here both K^+ and Cl^- move into the same compartment, their effects on pH largely compensate each other. Thus, strong ion effects may not be effective here. To appreciate fully the importance of the widely ignored principle of pH development, the reader is referred to Stewart (33). (v) Export of organic acid anions. As the onsets of Cl^- (anion) fluxes and pH changes in the root hair space are inseparable and their kinetics are similar, their origins may be identical. Since Cl^- can be ruled out as the cause, organic acid anions which pass through the same anion channel as Cl^- are the most likely candidates. Organic acid anions, due to their weak acid dissociation properties, will protonate after moving from the neutral cytoplasm to the acidic extracellular space, protonate and thus alkalize the root hair space. As soon as the anion channel inactivates, the efflux of organic acid anion ceases, anions are symported and both Cl^-- as well as the pH kinetics become transient. Mathieu et al. (25) explain the transient ion fluxes induced by oligogalacturonides differently: they propose that the responses result from a temporary desensitisation of the plant cells to the bioactive compounds.

EXTRACELLULAR AND INTRACELLULAR pH

There is a widespread (but erroneous) opinion that an extracellular alkalization (like the Nod factor-induced one) should accompany a simultaneous intracellular acidification. This notion arises from the idea that an ion that vanishes from a compartment on one side of a membrane must appear almost simultaneously on the other side. This may be true for membranes of a closed system that separate two compartments only. A cellular system, however, is different in that on one side of the membrane the cytoplasm contains many other compartments into which protons can be transported, whereas on the other side the pectic cell wall components may bind protons. Protons can temporarily "vanish" from a certain compartment through buffering, binding to molecules, by translocation into another compartment, and through H^+-consuming metabolism, more so than most other ions. Moreover, it should also be kept in mind that proton buffering is usually considerably stronger in the cytoplasm than in the apoplast and thus, even in those cases where one would expect a pH response, it may not be detected. Therefore, the observation that Nod factors cause alkalization on both sides of the plasma membrane is no paradox, but reflects the complexity of a cell with respect to pH regulation and indicates that both alkalizations arise from processes of different origin following separate lines of signal transduction.

THE MEANING OF THE pH CHANGES

Since extracellular alkalization obviously is quite common following the encounter of plant cells with defense related compounds (2, 29, 32), it is feasible that these pH changes are directed against pathogens. Since pathogenic bacteria or fungi frequently attempt to intrude by cell wall digesting enzymes, a first and effective measure would be to shift the existing pH from an optimal to a suboptimal value which slows down the digesting process. An increase in pH also means less driving force for H^+ mediated cotransporters, the main source of energy for saprophytic organisms, a measure which likewise slows down the activity of any pathogen. Alkalizations, due to elicitor action, may exceed 1 pH unit, but are only about 0.3 pH in alfalfa and less than 0.1 pH unit in *Medicago truncatula* cv. Jemalong following Nod factor treatment *in vivo*. This indicates that the proposed function of external alkalization has markedly declined in symbiosis and may reflect only a remnant of a defense reaction. As a matter of fact, alfalfa suspension cultured cells hardly yield a pH change to Nod factors at all (2). Thus, a specific function of the Nod factor induced pH changes for symbiotic interaction and signal transduction is not evident.

Internal pH changes are of a different quality. These apparently signal a change in metabolism and may provide one basic condition for gene activation/deactivation. For instance, the cytosolic acidification following the encounter with defense-related compounds is thought to be essential for the activation of defense genes, whereas an alkalization would prevent such an activation, as observed with Nod factors. Thus, it is well documented that defense related compounds acidify the cytosol by 0.3 to 0.5 pH units (20, 24). The Nod factor induced alkalization is around 0.2 to 0.3 pH units. For the well regulated cytosolic pH a difference of 0.7 to 0.8 pH means 'worlds'. In the plant kingdom there is no physiological event known so far that would shift the pH by such a margin. The largest shift known is the anoxic acidification by 0.6 pH units, which occurs during flooding. We do not know whether the Nod factor induced alkalization has another function than to prevent defense gene activation, as we also do not know where the pH shift comes from. It definitely does not arise from membrane transport, but may be indicative of a shift in metabolism. It was suggested that G-proteins may be involved in Nod factor signaling (30), and recently it was discovered that activation by mastoparan to some extent mimicked the action of Nod factors with respect to external alkalization (Fellé et al., unpublished). Experiments will have to establish, whether the alkalization occurs already at that stage of the signal transduction.

OTHER FLUXES

Apart from the ion fluxes mediated by constitutive membrane transporters, *Rhizobium leguminosarium* bv. viciae possesses a nodulation gene (*nodO*) that encodes a secreted protein (NodO) in pea and vetch nodulation. Although there is no evidence that mutation of *nodO* would block nodulation, *nodO* is required for nodulation. Studies on planar lipid bilayers show that NodO forms cation selective channels (34) and it was suggested that it may enhance the nodulation process by forming pores. As such, ion fluxes occurring this way would have to be discriminated from the early fluxes occurring shortly after the encounter of the roots with the rhizobia.

Conclusions

It is tempting to compare Nod factor- and pathogen-induced ion fluxes and speculate on their function within the interrelationship between the various partners. Since symbiosis very likely developed from situations where plants were attacked by potential pathogens, and to some extent may reflect a dynamic equilibrium of forces, some of the early responses may have been conserved, whereas others may have undergone adequate modifications. It is possible that the primary signal (Nod factor, elicitor) is perceived by different receptors and hence may be transduced differently. There are strong indications, however, that a common path exists for most bioactive compounds (Fig. 4): receptor(s), activation of Ca^{2+} channel, increase of cytosolic Ca^{2+} activity, activation of anion channel, depolarization and external pH changes, K^+-efflux, stimulation of H^+-ATPase. In the course of events parts of the signal chain may be modified, damped or enhanced, depending on what kind of relationship the host and the microorganism represent to each other.

Acknowledgements

Thanks goes to Dr. David Carden who considerably improved the English of this article.

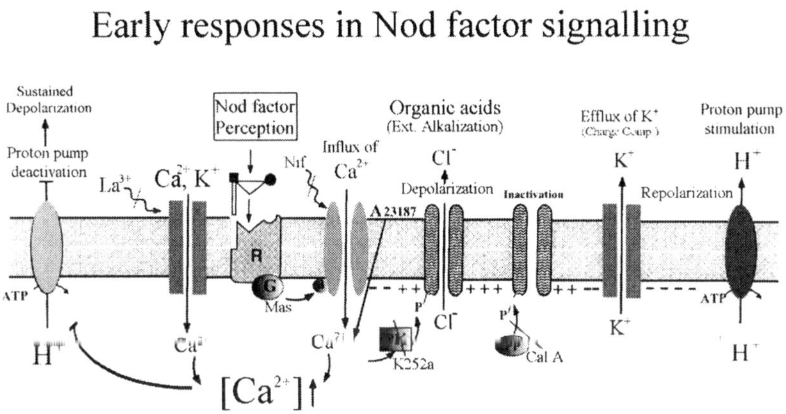

Figure 4. Model of ion fluxes, as measured in the root hair space of alfalfa, following the external addition of 0.1 μM NodRm IV(C16:2,S). Also incorporated in the model is the effect of the broad band protein kinase inhibitor K252a and the protein phosphatase inhibitor Calculin A (Cal A), the latter of which prevents inactivation of the anion channel. Early responses of alfalfa root hairs to Nod factor addition are numbered in temporal order. (1) Nod factor specific perception is (2) followed by G-protein activation (to be mimicked by mastoparan). (3) Activation of Ca^{2+} channel(s) (inhibited by nifedipine) is followed by (4) an increase in cytosolic Ca^{2+} activity. Increased Ca^{2+} activity to some extent deactivates the proton pump (5a) and (5) activates anion channels through which either Cl^- rapidly leaves the cell and causes membrane depolarization (6). Simultaneously, organic acid anions leave the cell causing extracellular alkalization. Anion efflux is stopped by efflux of K^+, which compensates the anion charge (7) and initiates repolarization, supported by the pump (8). Ion fluxes can be mimicked by the Ca^{2+} ionophore A23187, but prevented by the protein kinase inhibitor K252a.

References

1. Allen N S, Bennet M N, Cox D N, Shipley A, Ehrhardt D W, Long S, R (1994) Effects of Nod factors on alfalfa root hair Ca^{2+} and H^+ currents and cytoskeleton behaviour. Pages 107-114 in: Advances in Molecular Genetics of Plant-Microbe-Interactions. Kluwer Academic Publishers, Dordrecht, The Netherlands.
2. Baier R, Schiene K, Kohring B, Flaschel E, Niehaus K

(1999) Alfalfa and tobacco cells react differntly to chitin oligosaccharides and *Sinorhizobium meliloti* nodulation factors. Planta 210:157-164.

3. Bibikova T N, Zhigilei A; Gilroy S (1977) Root hair growth is directed by calcium and endogenous polarity. Planta 203:495-505.
4. Cárdenas L, Vidali L, Domíngues J, Pérez H, Sánches F, Hepler P K, Quinto C. (1998) Rearrangement of actin microfilaments in plant root hairs responding to *Rhizobium etli* nodulation signals. Plant Physiol. 116:871-877.
5. Cárdenas L, Feijó J A, Kunkel J G, Sánchez F, Holdaway-Clarke T, Hepler P K, Quinto C (1999) *Rhizobium* Nod factors induce increases in intracellular free calcium and extracellular calcium influxes in bean root hairs. Plant J. 19:347-352.
6. Cárdenas L, Holdaway-Clarke T, Sánchez F, Quinto C, Feijó J A, Kunkel J G, Hepler P K, (2000) Ion changes in legume root hairs responding to Nod factors. Plant Physiol. 123:443-451.
7. De Ruijter N C A, Rook M B, Bisseling T, Emons A M C (1998) Lipochito-oligosaccharides re-initiate root hair tip growth in *Vicia sativa* with high calcium and spectrin-like antigen at the tip. Plant J. 13:341-350.
8. Downie J A, Walker S A (1999) Plant responses to nodulation factors. Curr. Op. Plant Biol. 2:483-489.
9. Ehrhardt D W, Atkinson E M, Long S R (1992) Depolarization of alfalfa root hair membrane potential by *Rhizobium meliloti* Nod factors. Science 256:998-1000.
10. Ehrhardt D W, Wais R, Long S R (1996) Calcium spiking in plant root hairs responding to *Rhizobium* nodulation signals. Cell 85:7-20.
11. Felix G, Regenass M, Boller T (1993) Specific perception of subnanomolar concentrations of chitin fragments by tomato cells: induction of extracellular alkalinization, changes in protein phosphorylation, and establishment of a refractory state. Plant J. 4:307-316.
12. Felle H H (1998) The apoplastic pH of the *Zea mays* root cortex as measured with pH-sensitive microelectrodes: aspects of regulation. J. Exp. Bot. 49:987-995.
13. Felle H H, Kondorosi É, Kondorosi Á, Schultze M (1995) Nod signal-induced plasma membrane potential changes in alfalfa root hairs are differentially sensitive to structural modifications of the lipochito-oligosaccharide. Plant J. 7:939-947.
14. Felle H H, Kondorosi É, Kondorosi Á, Schultze M (1996) Rapid alkalinization in alfalfa root hairs in response to rhizobial lipochito-oligosaccharides. Plant J. 10:295-301.
15. Felle H H, Hepler P K (1997) The cytosolic Ca^{2+} concentration gradient of *Sinapis alba* root hairs as revealed by Ca^{2+}-selective

microelectrode tests and fura-dextran ratio imaging. Plant Physiol. 91:1239-1242.

16. Felle H H, Kondorosi É, Kondorosi Á, Schultze M (1998) The role of ion fluxes in Nod factor signalling in *Medicago sativa*. Plant J. 13:455-463.

17. Felle H H, Kondorosi É, Kondorosi Á, Schultze M (1999) Elevation of the cytosolic free [Ca^{2+}] is indispensible for the transduction of the Nod factor signal in alfalfa. Plant Physiol. 12:273-279.

18. Felle H H, Kondorosi É, Kondorosi Á, Schultze M (2000) How alfalfa oot hairs discriminate between Nod factors and oligochitin elicitors. Plant Physiol. 124:1373-1380.

19. Irving H I, Boukli N M, Kelly M N, Broughton W J (2000) Nod-factors in symbiotic development of root hairs. Pages 241-265 in: Root hair Cells and Molecular Biology. Ridge R W, Emons A M, eds. Springer-Verlag, Tokyo.

20. Kuchitsu K, Yazaki Y, Sakano K, Shibuya N (1997) Transient cytoplasmic pH change and ion fluxes through the plasma membrane in suspension-cultured rice cells triggered by N-acetylchito-oligosaccaride elicitor. Plant Cell Physiol. 38:1012-1018.

21. Kühtreiber W, Jaffe L F (1990) Detection of extracellular calcium gradients with a calcium-specific vibrating probe. J. Cell Biol. 110:1565-1573.

22. Kurkdjian A C (1995) Role of the differentiation of root epidermal cells in Nod factor (from *Rhizobium meliloti)*-induced root hair depolarization of *Medicago sativa*. Plant Physiol. 107:783-790.

23. Kurkdjian A, Bouteau F, Pennarun A-M, Convert M, Cornel D, Rona J-P, Bousquet U (2000) Ion currents involved in early Nod factor response in *Medicago sativa* root hairs: a discontinous single-electrode voltage-clamp study. Plant J. 22:9-17.

24. Mathieu Y, Kurkdjian A, Xia H, Guern J, Koller A, Spiro M D, O'Neill M M, Albersheim P, Darvill A (1991) Membrane responses induced by oligogalacturonides in suspension-cultured cells. Plant J. 1:333-343.

25. Mathieu Y, Guern J, Spiro M D, O'Neill M A, Kates K, Darvill A G, Albersheim P (1998) The transient nature of the oligogalacturonide-induced ion fluxes of tobacco cells is not correlated with fragmentation of the oligogalactoronides. Plant J. 16:305-311.

26. Miklashevichs E, Röhrig H, Schell J, Schmidt J (2001) Perception and signal transduction of rhizobial NOD factors. Crit. Rev. Plant Sci. 20:373-394.

27. Miller D D, de Ruijter N C, Bisseling T, Emons A M (1999) The role of actin in root hair morphogenesis: studies with lipochito-oligosaccharides as a growth stimulator and cytochalasin as an actin perturbing drug. Plant J. 17:141-154.
28. Niebel A, Gressent F, Bono J-J, Ranjeva R, Cullimore J (1999) Recent advances in the study of Nod factor perception and signal transduction. Biochimie 81: 669-674.
29. Nürnberger T, Nennstiel D, Jabs T, Sacks W R, Hahlbrock K, Scheel D (1994) High affinity binding of a fungal oligopeptide elicitor to parsley plasma membranes triggers multiple defense responses. Cell 78: 449-460.
30. Pingret J-L, Journet E-P, Barker D G (1998) *Rhizobium* Nod factor signalling: evidence for a G protein-mediated transduction mechanism. Plant Cell 10:659-671.
31. Schiefelbein J W, Shipley A, Rowse P (1992) Calcium influx at the tip of growing root hair cells of *Arabidopsis thaliana*. Planta 187:455-459.
32. Staehelin C, Granado J, Müller J, Wiemken A, Mellor R B, Felix G, Regenass M, Broughton W J, Boller T (1994) Perception of *Rhizobium* nodulation factors by tomato cells and inactivation by root chitinases. Proc. Natl. Acad. Sci., USA 91: 2196-2200.
33. Stewart P A (1983) Modern quantitative acid-base chemistry. Can. J. Physiol. Pharmacol. 62:1444-1461.
34. Sutton J M, Lea E J A, Downie J A (1994) The nodulation-signalling protein NodO from *Rhizobium leguminosarium* biovar viciae forms ion channels in membranes. Proc. Natl. Acad. Sci., USA 91:9990-9994.
35. Wais R J, Galera C, Oldroyd G, Catoira R, Penmetsa R V, Cook, D., Gough M, Denarié J, Long S R (2000) Genetic analysis of calcium spiking responses in nodulation mutants of *Medicago truncatula*. Proc. Natl. Acad. Sci., USA. 97: 13407-13412.
36. Walker S A Viprey V, Downie J A (2000) Dissection of nodulation signaling using pea mutants defective for calcium spiking induced by Nod factors and chitin oligomers. Proc. Natl. Acad. Sci., USA 97:13413-13418.
37. Yokoyama T, Kobayashi N, Kouchi H, Minamisawa K, Kaku H, Tsuchiya (2000) A lipochito-oligosaccharide, Nod factor, induces transient calcium influx in soybean suspension-cultured cells. Plant J. 22:71-78.

Index